CHINESE
HOUSES
of Southeast Asia

The Eclectic Architecture of Sojourners and Settlers

Ronald G. Knapp

Photographs by **A. Chester Ong**

Foreword by **Wang Gungwu**

TUTTLE PUBLISHING
Tokyo • Rutland, Vermont • Singapore

Published by Tuttle Publishing, an imprint
of Periplus Editions (HK) Ltd., with editorial
offices at 364 Innovation Drive, North
Clarendon, Vermont 05759, USA and 61 Tai
Seng Avenue, #02-12, Singapore 534167

Text © 2010 Ronald G. Knapp

Photographs © 2010 A. Chester Ong and
Periplus Editions (HK) Ltd

Photographs pages 34 (bottom left and right)
and 232–9 © 2010 Luca Invernezzi Tettoni

LCC No: 2009939293
ISBN: 978-0-8048-3956-3

Distributed by
North America, Latin America & Europe
Tuttle Publishing
364 Innovation Drive
North Clarendon, VT 05759-9436, USA
Tel: 1 (802) 773-8930; Fax: 1 (802) 773-6993
info@tuttlepublishing.com
www.tuttlepublishing.com

Japan
Tuttle Publishing
Yaekari Building, 3rd Floor, 5-4-12 Osaki
Shinagawa-ku, Tokyo 141 0032
Tel: (81) 03 5437-0171; Fax: (81) 03 5437-0755
tuttle-sales@gol.com

Asia Pacific
Berkeley Books Pte Ltd
61 Tai Seng Avenue, #02-12
Singapore 534167
Tel: (65) 6280-1330; Fax: (65) 6280-6290
inquiries@periplus.com.sg
www.periplus.com

12 11 10
8 7 6 5 4 3 2 1

Printed in Singapore

Front endpapers A detail of the upper register of
a carved cabinet in Emerald Hill, Singapore (page 88).

Back endpapers A close-up of the pressed glass
window panes in an upstairs bedroom of the Chee
Jin Siew home, Malacca, Malaysia (page 69).

Page 1 A view through the moon gate in the Loke
Yew mansion, Kuala Lumpur, Malaysia (page 162).

Page 2 The side entrance of the Chung Keng Quee
mansion, Penang, Malaysia (page 102).

Right A wedding chamber with an alcove bridal bed
and a separate bed for the groom, Wee residence,
Singapore (page 100).

Page 8 The Siek family home, Parakan, Indonesia
(page 190).

Tan Boon Chia residence, Rasa, Malaysia

Tan Yeok Nee manor, Singapore

Cheong Fatt Tze blue mansion, Penang, Malaysia

Tjong A Fie mansion, Medan, Indonesia

A FEAST OF COLORS AND DESIGNS

I do not know when professional architects of Chinese descent first began to design residences in Southeast Asia, or when their work began to change the built environment away from what was indigenous or traditionally Chinese. The buildings described in this book predate the rise of their profession and reflect the times when sojourners were beginning to transform themselves into settlers and could still exercise their personal choices.

The illuminating text and beautiful photographs also bring back memories of the numerous homes in the region that I have lived in. The first home I remember was a standard public works residence built for junior civil servants in the Malay state of Perak, a state that the British claimed to "protect" on the Malay Peninsula. This was in Ipoh, the capital of Kinta, one of the richest tin mining valleys in the world and where many wealthy Chinese built their mansions. Unlike their fine homes, our small house was inspired mainly by Malay designs and was built on short stilts not more than four feet above the ground. The most striking feature was the covered corridor that connected it to the kitchen and servants' quarters at the back of the house, some 20 yards away.

My family went on to live in houses built by the Chinese themselves. In Ipoh, the Chinese who moved up the social scale from unskilled mining and plantation laborers preferred to live in rows of shophouses beside the main streets. We had our share of living in several of these. Away from towns, there were those who followed Malay practice and built their houses on stilts. But, when they were ready to build their family homes, mostly on the edge of town, they turned to models of the traditional homes they admired in China. They also noted the work of European architects and adapted their newer homes to the need to appear fashionable.

We had the chance to live with one such upwardly mobile family and saw them transform a large Malay-type house into a new mansion. What struck me most was, the richer our host became, the more the Malay features about his house were replaced by things and shapes that were markedly Chinese or European. The overlap of Chinese ethnicity and Western modernity quickly edged out much of what was indigenous to the tropical environment.

Later, when I began to meet Southeast Asian Chinese trained in Britain and elsewhere in the West to be professional architects, I became conscious of how instinctively eclectic my host in Ipoh had been in the choices he made for his extended home. Whether in its external structure, the use of interior space, the adornments on the roof, the plan of the garden, or the selection of furniture for the public and private rooms, there was dissonance in the midst of elegance accompanied by several corners of splendid harmony. By that time, I realized that many other newly rich Chinese also displayed varying degrees of eccentric individuality that made their residences unforgettable.

Today, cautious public planners and venturesome private architects vie for the attention of new rich Chinese in every urban center. There is better appreciation of indigenous artistry, and the mixtures they offer are less whimsical and contrived. There is also brilliance surrounded by mediocrity. But overall the effect is one of confusion that the competing styles do little to minimize. It would appear that we need time to weed out the unmemorable so that, decades from now, the best of them that survive will be lovingly studied by someone like Ronald Knapp.

The houses described in this book represent some of the finest and best preserved or restored in Southeast Asia. I have visited most of those in Malaysia and Singapore and a few others in Jakarta, Semarang, Bangkok, and Manila. But Ronald Knapp has examined all of them closely. His sensitive and meticulous descriptions have opened my eyes to points of transmission and adaptation that I had missed. Altogether, the book provides a feast of colors and designs that appeals both to my interest in their histories and to my suppressed desire to have a family home of my own.

In particular, how he has described the mix of convention, sacral loyalty, and keeping up with the times captures the many layers of emotions that most sojourning Chinese experienced when they decided to settle down. By doing that, the author has opened new doors to all of us who are fascinated with the plurality of Southeast Asia. He has also enabled new generations of Chinese overseas to savor some of the delights in the lives of their transplanted ancestors.

Wang Gungwu
National University of Singapore

PART ONE

THE ARCHITECTURE OF SOJOURNERS AND SETTLERS

THE ARCHITECTURE OF
SOJOURNERS AND SETTLERS

Migration has been a recurring theme throughout Chinese history, continuing to the present at significant levels. The dynamic relationship among push and pull factors has long motivated both the destitute as well as the adventurous in China's villages and towns to uproot themselves in order to move to locations within China and throughout the world in search of opportunities. Settling on a new place to live by building a home, which Chinese called *dingju*, has always resulted from a complex combination of individual resolve, cultural awareness, and financial resources. *Chinese Houses of Southeast Asia* examines the products of these decisions and actions, the surviving eclectic residences of Chinese immigrant pioneers *and* many of their descendents who, for the most part, flourished in their new homelands while living in dwellings reminiscent of those in China. This book presents the eclectic nature of their residences in terms of style, space, and materials. A companion volume will focus on the full range of objects enjoyed by Peranakan families within their architectural spaces or settings—the rooms—of their terrace houses, bungalows, and mansions as well as the layers of ornamentation around and about these residences. It is clear that these families were proud of their Chinese heritage.

The maintenance of that which is familiar while adapting to new circumstances is a recurring theme in Chinese history. The pushing out from core areas into frontier zones, indeed the sinicization of both landscapes and indigenous peoples, is a dominant part of China's historical narrative. While complete families and whole villages in China sometimes migrated without ever going back to their home villages, there also was a tradition of sojourning in which fathers and/ or sons left with the expectation of only a temporary stay away before returning home. In Chinese history, merchants and financiers from the Huizhou and Shanxi areas, especially, epitomize the concept of sojourning. The resigned sentiments of this concept for a sojourning merchant and dutiful household head from Huizhou can be sensed in the note: "Those like us leave our villages and towns, leave our wives and blood relations, to travel thousands of miles. And for what? For no other purpose but to support our families" (Berliner, 2003: 5). Like those from Huizhou and Shanxi, traders, peasants, and coolies from

the southeast coastal provinces of Fujian and Guangdong sojourned and settled in far-flung places, including Southeast Asia.

Reified by scholars as "mobility strategies," sojourning, whether in metropolitan regions of China itself or to a distant outpost in Southeast Asia, was for most traditional families a well thought out and logical traditional practice that heightened aspirations, providing enterprising families with opportunities for diversifying sources of income and acquiring wealth. Sojourning took many forms. In the fifty years from the late nineteenth century to the middle of the twentieth century, for example, some 25 million peasants from the densely populated North China plain provinces of Hebei and Shandong traveled seasonally to the relatively sparsely populated areas of Manchuria in order to open up for cultivation what were essentially virgin lands. They were called "swallows" or *yan* by their kinfolk because of the seasonal rhythm of their sojourn (Gottschang and Lary, 2000: 1). G. William Skinner, in his presentation of mobility strategies in late imperial China, provides a contemporaneous description of the Hu family's approach to sojourning that involved not only trade in salt and porcelain but also finance and foreign trade (1976: 345):

When a family in our region has two or more sons, only one stays home to till the fields. The others are sent out to some relative or friend doing business in some distant city. Equipped with straw sandals, an umbrella and a bag with some food, the boy sets out on the journey to a place in Chekiang [Zhejiang] or Kiangsi [Jiangxi], where a kind relative or friend of the family will take him into his shop as an apprentice. He is about 14 years old at this time. He has to serve an apprenticeship of three years without pay, but with free board and lodging. Then he is given a vacation of three months to visit his family, who in the meantime have arranged his marriage for him. When he returns to his master he leaves his wife in his old home. Every three years he is allowed a three months' vacation with pay which he spends at home.

This strategy to acquire wealth, which was pursued by territorially based lineage systems in inland China, operated as well in the coastal villages and towns of southern Fujian, and later in Guangdong. In this coastal region, embayed river ports and their hinterlands were the principal homelands for peasants, laborers, and traders who set sail in junks along the coasts and across the seas into what was for some *terra incognita*, but for many others parts of well-known trading networks.

Beyond the borders of imperial China, no area of the world experienced more sustained contact with Chinese or in-migration of Chinese over a longer period of time than the region referred to today as Southeast Asia, and which the Chinese have historically called the Nanyang or Southern Seas. Characterized by landmasses, peninsulas, and islands of many sizes, this is a region of great complexity and vast expanses, yet significant interdependence. Most of the maps of Southeast Asia show the region as a pendulous outlier of mainland Asia at a substantial distance from both China and India. Yet, from a Chinese

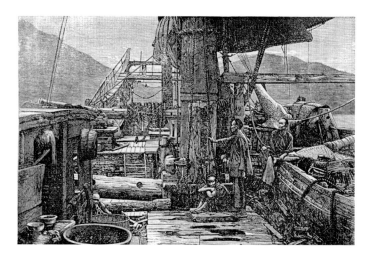

perspective, the Nanyang was a sea-based region where even the most distant islands could be reached by sailing along well-known and charted routes. The maritime system within which Chinese coastal traders operated actually spanned an area greater than that of the Mediterranean Sea. Including both the East China Sea and the South China Sea, the immense maritime region stretched 5000 kilometers from Korea and Japan in the north to the Malay Archipelago in the south, and 1800 kilometers from coastal China eastward, beyond Taiwan, to the Philippines. Perhaps as many as 80 percent of the 35 million who trace Chinese ancestry and live beyond the political boundaries of China reside today in the crossroads of Southeast Asia.

Arab, Indian, Japanese, and Chinese merchants arrived in the regional trading ports of Southeast Asia more than a thousand years before the appearance of the Portuguese, Spanish, Dutch, French, and English. Raw and processed silk was carried from China along the Maritime Silk Road westward through the Indian Ocean where it was exchanged for exotic items from Europe. Among the earliest concrete evidence of the direct trade between China and the western Indian Ocean was a ninth-century Arab or Indian shipwreck filled with Chinese ceramics that was excavated in 1998–9 off Beitung Island between Sumatra and Borneo (Flecker, 2001: 335ff). Moreover, beginning in the eighth century, residential quarters called *fanfang* for foreign traders from Western Asia were located in Chinese port cities, including Guangzhou (Canton) in Guangdong and Quanzhou (Zaytun) in Fujian as well as farther north in Ningbo (Mingzhou) and Hangzhou in Zhejiang. Exotic commodities such as ivory tusks, gold, silver, pearls, sandalwood, kingfishers' feathers, pepper, cinnabar, amber, and ambergris, among many other precious goods, found their way to China from the distant lands via the southern sea trade.

In time, the polities within the Southeast Asia region increasingly were brought within the Chinese tribute system that peaked during the Ming dynasty in the fifteenth century. Zheng He, the Muslim

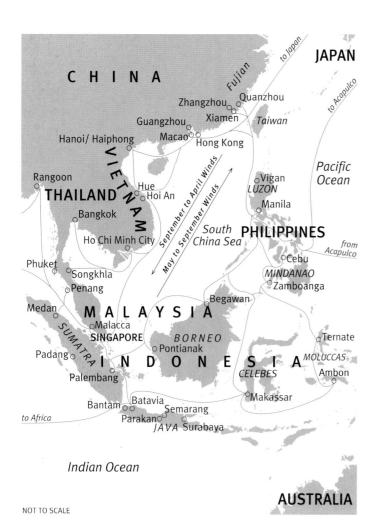

NOT TO SCALE

Chinese mariner who carried out seven fabled expeditions between 1405 and 1433, traversed the region, reaching some forty destinations that stretched from the Horn of Africa eastward along the southern, southeastern, and eastern shores of Asia. Over the following centuries, many of the ports visited by Zheng He became hubs for Chinese trading networks as well as sites for Chinese settlement and development. Even today, many of these places recall in their historical narratives the visits by Zheng He six centuries earlier.

Sometimes sojourning resulted simply because Chinese traders were forced to stay for many months at a time at distant emporia waiting for the seasonal shifting of the monsoon winds. Indeed, over the centuries, the seasonal reversal of monsoonal winds was critical in establishing the trade patterns of Chinese traders. From September to April, the winds blew from the northeast to southwest carrying sailing ships from China southward. From May to September, the flow was reversed with the arrival of the southwest monsoon. Following these same routes, Arab traders took as long as two years for a round trip to China. From the fifth to the twelfth century, "the skippers trusted—when venturing out of the sight of land, to the regularity of the monsoons and steered solely by the sun, moon and stars, taking presumably soundings as frequently as possible. From other sources we learn that it was customary on ships which sailed out of sight of land to keep pigeons on board, by which they used to send messages to land" (Hirth and Rockhill, 1911: 28). By the twelfth century, maritime navigation improved with the introduction of a "wet compass" or *yeti luojing*, a magnetic piece of metal floating in a shallow bowl of water. Zhao Rukua, also known as Chau Ju-kua, a customs inspector in Quanzhou during the Song dynasty, chronicled in his book *Zhufan Zhi* (Records of the Various Barbarous Peoples) the places and

commodities known to peripatetic Chinese during the twelfth and thirteenth centuries. It was in this way that Chinese sojourners and settlers populated distant lands in increasing numbers as both sojourners and settlers. Their tales of prospects and opportunities no doubt infiltrated the outlooks and hopes of others in their home village.

The greatest flow of Chinese migrants by sea occurred from the mid-eighteenth century through the early twentieth century. While Wang Gungwu describes four overlapping out-migration patterns from southern China to Southeast Asia, only two will be discussed (1991: 4–12). *Huashang*, Chinese traders/merchants/artisans, comprised the dominant and longest lasting pattern. *Huashang* during the early periods generally settled down and married local women even when they had a wife in China. As their businesses became more profitable, other family members might leave China and join them. Some *Huashang* returned to China, according to the rhythm of trade, chose a spouse, and then maintained separate households for their different families. The *Huashang* type of migration pattern was employed especially by Hokkien migrants from southern Fujian to the Philippines, Java, and Japan; the Hakka on the island of Borneo; and those originating in the Chaozhou region of northeastern Guangdong province. It is both a fact and a curiosity that the *Huashang* pattern of migration had been practiced for many centuries *within* China.

Huagong were Chinese contract workers who arrived between the 1850s and the 1920s, usually as sojourners who intended to earn money and then return to their home villages to live out their remaining days. Unskilled contract workers were usually referred to as coolies, an English loanword whose roots reside in many Asian languages, including the Hindi word for laborer, *qūlī*, and the Chinese term *kuli*, meaning "bitter work." *Huagong* especially played important roles in the opening up of rubber and palm plantations in Sumatra as well as tin mines and plantations along the Malay Peninsula. Substantial numbers of Chinese contract workers/coolies or *Huagong* also migrated to North America and Australia where they worked as laborers in mining enterprises and in railway construction. As opportunities arose, some of those who arrived as coolies or traders eventually became storekeepers or artisans, while others became farmers or fishermen. Patterns of settlement and return, living and working, varied from period to period. Indeed, as described by Anthony Reid, "It is the curious reversals of the flow southward, periodically running evenly, occasionally gushing, sometimes tightly shut, more often dripping like a leaking tap, that provide the rhythm behind the historical interaction of China and Southeast Asia" (2001: 15). While many other broad and complex topics—the history of migration, reputed business acumen and entrepreneurship, acculturation and assimilation, as well as tortuous issues relating to loyalty and nationality—are important and worthy of study, they will not be explored in this book.

Descendants of both *Huashang* and *Huagong* are found today throughout the countries of Southeast Asia where popular lore as well as the memories of descendant families trumpet tales of once penniless males who came to "settle down and bring up local families" (Wang Gungwu, 1991: 5). Through what is called chain or serial migration, pioneers arrived first, then sent information about new opportunities to those back home, which then spurred additional migration from their home villages. The ongoing arrival of related individuals helped maintain connections between the original homeland and new locations. Indeed, for many, their hearts remained back in China, and they saw themselves as Chinese in a foreign land. Yet, circumstances often meant that dreams of returning home were thwarted, and sojourners became settlers, forced to "bear hardship and endure hard work," *chiku nailao*, as the common phrase ruefully states it, dashing their prospects of "a glorious homecoming in splendid robes," *yijin huanxiang*, also *yijin ronggui*, as someone who had made off well and could have a proud homecoming. To do otherwise, according to Ta Chen, "his unrecognized distinctions might be compared with a gorgeous costume worn by its proud owner through the streets on a dark night" (1940: 109).

While this book highlights the homes of Chinese who had done reasonably well in the places they ventured to, it is important to keep in mind that most Chinese and their descendants lived and continue to live in much more modest homes in these places. Significant numbers of arrivals and their descendants, of course, never broke the debilitating chains of poverty, living on as an underprivileged underclass, the hard-working but powerless who dreamed of a better future that was never realized. Coolies, peasant laborers, rickshaw pullers, trishaw pedalers, pirates, fisherfolk, even prostitutes and slaves, lived in the back alleys, on the upper floors of commercial establishments, and on sampans along the banks of streams without ever "settling down" or *dingju* (cf Warren, 1981, 1986, 1993, 2008). Voiceless in life, they left illegible traces of their subsistence lives.

Homelands in China

While it is common for outsiders to describe migrants from China in terms of the province of their origin, most migrants, in fact, traditionally identified home as a smaller subdivision, as a county or village. In southeastern China, river basins and coastal lowlands, circumscribed by surrounding hills, mountains, and the ocean, formed well-understood units of local culture and identity, shared cultural traits that were affirmed with the population speaking a common dialect. For Chinese, the awareness of origins in terms of a native place has traditionally been as significant as consciousness of the connections to forebears via their surname and lineage. Indeed, old gravestones and ancestral tablets memorialize place-based identity even when the deceased was many generations removed from the family's homeland. Children and grandchildren born in an adopted homeland, moreover, inherit the native place of their immigrant parents and grandparents. Native-place associations, called *tongxiang hui*, and lineage or clan associations, *tongxing hui*, traditionally served as ready reminders of the two most meaningful relationships Chinese individuals had with their broader world. The place-name origins of migrants thus signify more than a link to an administrative division, more than a reference to a mere location. Rather, native places connote a shared cultural context that clearly separates one migrant group from another.

Until the end of the eighteenth century, a majority of the emigrants from China originated from Fujian, a province with a rugged coastline and a tradition of building boats for fishing and seafaring. The encyclopedic *Shan Hai jing* (Classic of Mountains and Seas), an eclectic two-millennia-old compendium of the known world, states: "Fujian exists in the sea with mountains to the north and west", *Min zai haizhong, qi xibei you shan*. With limited arable land to support a growing population, the Fujianese turned to the neighboring sea, using small boats for fishing and seagoing junks for distant trade to the Nanyang where they exchanged manufactured wares for food staples. "The fields are few but the sea is vast; so men have made fields from the sea" is how an 1839 gazetteer from Fujian's port city of Xiamen viewed the maritime opportunities afforded its struggling population during the last century of the Qing dynasty (Cushman, 1993: iii).

Referred to collectively as Hokkien, the local pronunciation of the place-name Fujian, the homelands of migrants can be readily subdivided in terms of at least three main dialects found in areas to the south of the Min River in this complex and fragmented province. Called Minnan or "south of the Min River" dialects, each is a variant of the others and is centered on one of the area's three major ports: Quanzhou, Xiamen, and Zhangzhou. Although the three dialects are mutually intelligible to some degree, and are spoken in geographic locations that are relatively near to one another, the speakers of these dialects traditionally have

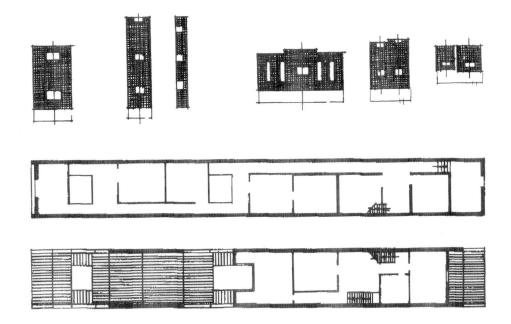

Above right These simple plans reveal the characteristic forms of residences found throughout Fujian. The white areas indicate the variety of *tianjing*, skywells that open up the buildings to air, light, and water.

Center and bottom right Elongated two-storey urban residences in Guangdong include multiple skywells, narrow corridors, steep stairs, and stacked rooms.

seen themselves as belonging to distinct local cultures with dissimilar mores. In neighboring Guangdong province, another source region for significant numbers of migrants to the Nanyang, are other dialect-based communities: Chaozhou (Teochew, also Teochiu) and Hainan hua (Hainanese), which are also in the family of Minnan dialects, as well as Kejia (Hakka) and, farther west, those who speak Guangdong hua (Cantonese). One characteristic shared by all of these groups is that they occupy areas either adjacent to or connected by short rivers reaching the Taiwan Strait that connects the East China Sea and the South China Sea.

Along the Fujian–Guangdong coast, there are countless areas that are known in the vernacular as *qiaoxiang*, literally "home township of persons living abroad." The term *qiaoxiang* was used in the nineteenth century to apply not only to sojourners, temporary residents who were abroad, but also to those who had been away for generations. Those Chinese who left China were referred to as *Huaqiao*, a capacious term often translated as "overseas Chinese," but essentially meaning "Chinese living abroad." "Overseas Chinese" itself historically has been a descriptor of considerable elasticity, applying not only to those temporarily abroad but also to those who are Chinese by ethnicity but have no actual connection with China. *Guiqiao*, indicating those Chinese who returned from abroad, and *qiaojuan*, indicating the dependants of Chinese who are abroad, are expressions still heard today. *Qiaoxiang*, as "emigrant communities," traditionally were bound by social, economic, and psychological bonds in which emigration became a fundamental and ongoing aspect of country life. While poverty and strife may have induced earlier out-migration, over time migration chains create a tradition of going abroad that propels outward movement. In some ways, overseas sites arose as outposts of the *qiaoxiang* itself, linked to it by back and forth movements of people and remittances of funds to sustain those left behind. Indeed, as Lynn Pan reminds us, "emigrant communities are not moribund. The men might be gone, but, collectively and cumulatively, they send plenty of money back. Many home societies have a look of prosperity about them, with opulent modern houses paid for with remittances by emigrants who have made good abroad" (2006: 30).

As later chapters will reveal, individual *qiaoxiang* are linked with specific locations in Southeast Asia, indeed throughout the world. Emigrants from the Siyi or Four Districts of Guangdong province on the west side of the Pearl River, for example, favored migrating to the goldfields and railroad construction opportunities in California. Farther east and clustered around the port of Shantou, once known in English as Swatow, those who spoke the Chaozhou dialect sailed to Siam and elsewhere in Southeast Asia. Kejia or Hakka from the uplands beyond Shantou, and accessible to it via the Han River, spread themselves widely. The area between Xiamen and Quanzhou, more than other areas in Fujian, fed the migrant streams throughout Southeast Asia. Jinjiang, once a county-level administrative area just to the south of the port of Quanzhou, not only looms large as the homeland of countless migrants throughout Asia, it is the ancestral home of over 90 percent of those of Chinese descent in the Philippines. Each of these distinct *qiaoxiang* areas is noted for its own variant forms of vernacular architecture, which explains in at least a limited sense many of the differences in the residences built by migrants in their adopted places of residence. The section below highlights some of the common features among these vernacular traditions, while later chapters will reveal some of the differences.

Old Homes Along China's Coast

Chinese dwellings throughout the country share a range of common elements even as it is clear that there are striking regional, even sub-regional, architectural styles. Given China's vast extent, approximately the size of the United States and twice that of Europe, it should not be surprising that there are variations to basic patterns that have arisen as practical responses to climatic, cultural, and other factors. While there is no single building form that can be called "a Chinese house," there are shared elements in both the spatial composition and building structure of both small and grand homes throughout the country. In addition, Chinese builders have a long history of environmental awareness in selecting sites to maximize or evade sunlight, capture prevailing winds, avoid cold winds, facilitate drainage, and collect rainwater. Details of these similarities and differences are considered at length in some of my other books (Knapp, 2000; 2005).

Adjacent open and enclosed spaces are axiomatic features in Chinese architecture, whether the structure is a palace, temple, or residence. Usually referred to in English as "courtyards" and in Chinese as *yuanzi*, open spaces vary in form and dimension throughout China and have a history that goes back at least 3,000 years. Courtyards emerged first in northern China and then diffused in variant forms as Chinese migrants moved from region to region over the centuries. The complementarity

of voids, apparent emptiness, and enclosed solids is metaphorically expressed in the *Dao De Jing*, the fourth-century BCE work attributed to Laozi: "We put thirty spokes together and call it a wheel: But it is on the space where there is nothing that the usefulness of the wheel depends. We turn clay to make a vessel; But it is on the space where there is nothing that the usefulness of the vessel depends. We pierce doors and windows to make a house; And it is on these spaces where there is nothing that the usefulness of the house depends. Therefore just as we take advantage of what is, we should recognize the usefulness of what is not" (Waley, 1958: 155).

While sometimes what is considered a courtyard is simply an outdoor space, a yard, at the front of a dwelling, a fully formed courtyard must be embraced by at least two buildings. Two, three, or four structures along the side of a courtyard create an L-shaped, inverted U-shaped, or quadrangular-shaped building type. Nelson Wu called such a composition a "house–yard" complex, with the encircling walls creating an "implicit paradox of a rigid boundary versus an open sky" (1963: 32). The framing of exterior space by inward-facing structures arranged at right angles to and parallel with the fronts of other buildings creates configurations that are strikingly similar to the character 井, a well or open vertical passage sunk into the confining earth. The proportion of open space to enclosed space is generally greater in northern China than in southern China, fostered by the desire to welcome sunlight in the north but to avoid its intensity in the south. As a result, courtyards found in southern homes are usually much smaller than elsewhere in the country.

Chinese in southern China use the term *tianjing* to describe open spaces within their dwellings, whether they are fairly large or indeed even mere shafts that punctuate the building. The term *tianjing* is usually translated into English as "skywell" or "airwell," terms that are especially appropriate in multistoried structures where the verticality of the cavity exceeds the horizontal dimension. Atrium-like *tianjing* are found in Ming and Qing dynasty residences throughout central and southern China, including along the coastal areas. *Tianjing* evacuate interior heat, catch passing breezes, shade adjacent spaces as the sun moves, and lead rainwater into the dwelling where it can be collected. Adjacent to skywells, which are relatively bright compared to enclosed darker rooms, "gray" transitional spaces such as shaded verandas are common in Fujian and Guangdong. In order to reduce humidity levels that effectively lower the apparent temperature felt by the body, architectural devices such as open-faced lattice door panels, half-doors, and high-wall ventilation ports are employed in southern houses to enhance ventilation. Throughout Southeast Asia, where the sun is elevated in the sky year round and ambient temperatures are high, it is not surprising that immigrants from southern China continued to use *tianjing* in their new homes. Many examples will be shown in the chapters that follow.

Where building lots were restrictive and space was at a premium, Chinese builders traditionally adjusted the dimensions and shapes of their structures. In urban areas, narrow residences adjacent to each other along a street were constructed as long structures with small skywells punctuating the corridor-like receding building. Where it was possible to construct a more extensive residence, either narrow or broad parallel structures were constructed alongside a wider central unit. Over time, if wealth and family circumstances allowed, additional side-to-side wing units were added. Examples of this modularity and replication of enclosed and open spaces can still be seen throughout Fujian and Guangdong, indeed throughout China.

The Tan Tek Kee Residence, Jinjiang

Migrants who departed Fujian and Guangdong were generally poor, leaving behind family homes that were simple and unremarkable. In some cases, however, where the family already had a home and migration by a son was part of a family's strategy to further increase its wealth, there was usually hope that improvements in the residence would take place as remittances came from abroad. In the early twentieth century, travelers in the region noted the presence of emigrant communities because of the superior quality of the dwellings. Ta Chen states that these fine homes, traditional and modern, were "the most effective way to express one's vanity." Moreover, "an effective display of pride does not mean only a large house, but it has to have evidences of taste and culture. This may be supplied either by modernity or, on the contrary, by an ostensible show of liking for those things which traditionally stand for refinement.... The ideal of 'complete happiness' ... is not in fact anything new the emigrants bring back with them from abroad, but embodied in the folkways of the countryside. What they do contribute is financial ability to gratify these tastes and, sometimes, innovations which produce curious contrasts between old and new in the homes and the furnishing of homes" (1940: 110–11).

While there is no "typical" home of a migrant, the residence discussed below illustrates the dynamic nature of space in a fully formed residence of a family who sent their son to the Philippines. The dwelling expresses what Chinese broadly considered a fine home for harmonious family life during the late imperial period. It exhibits well the layout and materials of a traditional Fujian dwelling, as well as reflecting aspects of family organization, ways of living, and ritual requirements in one of China's preeminent *qiaoxiang* in Jinjiang county to the south of Quanzhou. Because of deterioration over the past half-century and lack of documentation, however, it is not possible to ascertain with certainty the specific changes brought about by the remittances from their successful son.

This expansive residence was built sometime during the latter half of the nineteenth century either by the father or grandfather of Tan Tek Kee,

who was born in the family home in 1900. Family lore recalls that Tan Tek Kee's forebears themselves had migrated southward from Henan province in northern China, perhaps an explanation for the fact that descendants have been tall compared to their neighbors. Tan Tek Kee's father is said to have gained fame and perhaps some modest wealth from his fishball business. Fishballs, made from minced fish mixed with other ingredients, are still a distinctive component of cuisine in Fujian, whether served in noodle soups or deep-fried, skewered, and served with various sauces. Raised by his elder brother and sister-in-law, Tan Tek Kee married at the age of thirteen or fourteen before being sent to the Philippines in 1914 or 1915 with family friends surnamed Cheng, who served as his surrogate parents. Working first as a cook, then a courier, and then later a manager, he branched out on his own in the 1930s, even as he made many return trips to his family's Jinjiang home and his birthplace. According to family custom, he retained some rights to the residence, which was sufficiently roomy so that the multigenerational families of his surviving siblings lived comfortably. The father of ten children, two of whom were adopted, Tan Tek Kee over time amassed sufficient resources to bring his wife to Manila where he died and was buried in 1966.

At one time, the home was a solitary structure surrounded by rice paddies, but as can be seen in the bird's-eye view photograph, new-style multistoried structures have encroached upon it, diminishing to some degree not only its tranquility but also heightening its sense of being forlorn. Like other residences of this type, it was built with an overall rectangular shape, which could be considered square if one includes the walled open space in front. While its overall form remains today intact, renovation and dilapidation have altered its original appearance. In terms of the composition of its spatial elements, the three-bay central structure, with a generous square *tianjing* between the entry hall and the ancestral hall, has a pair of perpendicular structures that complete the quadrangular core. A second pair of parallel, perpendicular two-storied buildings was added to complete the layout. Each of the outer wings, called *hucuo*, is separated from the core building by a narrow longitudinal *tianjing* running from front to back, which could be entered directly from the outside via a doorway. Indeed, it would have been these two side entries that would have been used on a daily basis in the past, rather than the recessed central entryway, with its elegant didactic ornamentation.

Cut granite slabs, some of which are carved, were used throughout the residence for the foundation, steps, sills, and columns. Granite or *huagangshi*, a coarse-grained igneous rock known for being more durable than marble, was used in the core building. Readily available in the nearby mountains of the province, yet considered an expensive building material, granite has traditionally been employed as a building material in temples and fine residences throughout central and southern Fujian. (Today, parenthetically speaking, Fujian is a major source for polished granite countertops used in modern kitchens and bathrooms throughout the world.) The sunken entryway was created using interlocking vertical and horizontal pieces of granite of different dimensions. At the base of the entry portico, as well as inside the core structure, granite was used as flooring. After crossing the raised granite threshold, a visitor will note that the middle bay, including the full *tianjing*, is covered completely with granite dimension stone. Along the sides, granite slabs were used only to frame areas that were covered with kiln-fired red tile flooring. As the view from the entry hall through the *tianjing* to the main hall reveals, the *tianjing* was sunken, with drains to lead rainwater out of the home. Just beyond the *tianjing* and in front of the main hall, the level of the flooring was elevated to express the hierarchical importance of the hall.

Set upon carved granite bases, square granite columns with auspicious couplets carved into them, were placed around the *tianjing*. Atop each of these stone columns was fitted a short wooden column, linked together by mortise-and-tenon joinery, to lift the wooden framework supporting the roof. The horizontal and vertical wooden members as well as the elaborate wooden bracket sets still comprise an important ornamental aspect of the house that complements the hard stone beneath the feet. No room was designed to have more richness than the main hall, which was surrounded with solid wooden walls and sturdy hardwood columns. Sadly and tragically in recent years, the ridge beam that supported the roof rotted and fell to the floor, bringing down with it the wooden purlins, rafters, and roof tiles, and leaving the room open to the elements. What once must have been an imposing family altar with ancestral tablets atop it, has been replaced by a low table with a small collection of old photographs and votive pieces with a triple mirror above.

Throughout this region of Fujian, the exterior walls of many dwellings are constructed of either slabs of cut granite or composed only of red bricks, *hongzhuan*, made of local lateritic soils and fired in nearby kilns. The ancestral home of Tan Tek Ke, on the other hand, was constructed using both granite and red brick as structural and ornamental building materials. From a distance, the red brick of the façade and sidewalls appears to be laid with common bonds, yet on closer inspection it is clear that all of the red brick in the façade was used to serve ornamental purposes, with a number of different motifs. Adjacent to the entryway, the thin red bricks were decorated with a zigzag pattern of dark lines,

which appear to have been painted on the bricks before they were fired. Surrounding each of the four granite windows are thin red bricks in a modified herringbone pattern with a box bond. Unlike Western bricklaying patterns, where stretchers vary to create named bonds, this Chinese pattern utilizes the wider top or face of the brick and the narrow header, which is darkened, to create the pattern. Carved bricks and tiles in geometric and floral patterns were also arrayed as a frame around the block of herringbone patterned bricks. Carved human figures were inset in five locations on each of two walls, but most are still obscured by a coating of white plaster. During the Great Proletarian Cultural Revolution, these carvings were plastered over as a precaution in order to prevent their destruction, but only several have been restored.

The gaze of a visitor approaching a residence of this type is drawn to the upswept ridgeline above the entry hall at the center of the complex, which is matched by a more impressive, and slightly higher, one on the main hall behind. This type of graceful ridgeline is called the *yanwei* or "swallowtail" style partly because it is upswept and tapered, but mainly because it is deeply forked at its tip. Each of the adjacent perpendicular buildings was constructed with a lower upswept ridgeline, with shed roofs that framed the sides of the central *tianjing*. These created a pair of flat rooftop terraces, which were accessible from below using stairs, outdoor spaces that once provided a place for quietude to enjoy the breeze in the evening or the moon at night. The relatively gentle pitch of the roofs was governed by the spacing ratio between the beams and struts that supported the roof purlins. Arcuate roof tiles, which appear like sections of bamboo, were used to cover the roofs. Today, the roof of one of the outer wing structures is undergoing renovation and currently only has a tar paper surface, which is held in place by bricks. What once was its symmetrical double on the other end of the house has been altered significantly with the removal of the original second floor and its replacement by a "modern" higher structure with a flat roof.

Traditional residences such as this have significantly declined in number over the past half-century, not only because of the disinterest of descendants and lack of maintenance but also because of deterioration due to age, dilapidation, and abuse. After 1949, especially during the class struggles associated with Land Reform, both land and housing were confiscated from landlords and merchants before they were redistributed to poor peasants. As a result, many grand residences, which represented the patrimony of Chinese living abroad, came to be occupied by destitute local families whose interest was more in shelter than preservation. While the 1950 Land Reform Law stated that ancestral shrines, temples, and landlords' residences "should not be damaged," and together with the "surplus houses of landlords ... not suitable for the use of peasants" be transformed into facilities for "public use" by local governments, most began a process of corrosive decline that was accelerated during the transition to communes, which began in 1958. During this period, in which there was a craze for collectivized living, stately structures representative of China's glorious architectural traditions—residences, ancestral halls, and temples—were transformed into dining halls, workshops, administrative headquarters, and dormitories, among other group-centered uses for the masses (Knapp and Shen, 1992: 47–55). Moreover, during the Great Proletarian Cultural Revolution a decade later, there was frenzied activity throughout the country that brought about the smashing and burning of ancestral altars and tablets, including substantial amounts of applied ornamentation handed down from the past. Ornamental and ritual elements made of wood, clay, and porcelain suffered the greatest loss, while those made of stone and brick managed to survive in significant numbers.

During what is known as the Reform and Opening-up Period in the decade after 1979, Overseas Chinese as well as local families, whose property in China had been confiscated during "the high tide of socialism" after 1949, were invited to apply for its return. Descendants

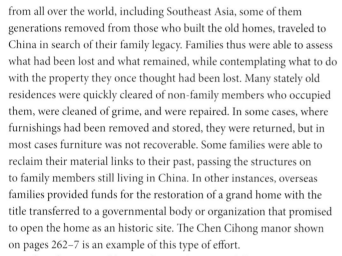

Right It is likely that the Tan Cheng Lock residence on the right and the narrower residence on the left, which share an architectural style, were built at the same time in Malacca, Malaysia. Perhaps they were originally owned by a single family who later sold the units to different families.

Opposite above As will be seen with later examples, the entryway of many Chinese homes differs little from temples in terms of form and ornamentation, such as Malacca's Cheng Hoon Teng Temple, whose origins go back to the 1640s and is Malaysia's oldest Chinese temple.

Opposite center The expansive three-bay structure of the Cheng Hoon Teng Temple is made possible because of an elaborate wooden structural framework. This is a view towards the main and side altars.

from all over the world, including Southeast Asia, some of them generations removed from those who built the old homes, traveled to China in search of their family legacy. Families thus were able to assess what had been lost and what remained, while contemplating what to do with the property they once thought had been lost. Many stately old residences were quickly cleared of non-family members who occupied them, were cleaned of grime, and were repaired. In some cases, where furnishings had been removed and stored, they were returned, but in most cases furniture was not recoverable. Some families were able to reclaim their material links to their past, passing the structures on to family members still living in China. In other instances, overseas families provided funds for the restoration of a grand home with the title transferred to a governmental body or organization that promised to open the home as an historic site. The Chen Cihong manor shown on pages 262–7 is an example of this type of effort.

When the ancestral home of Tan Tek Kee was fully returned to the family, it had been stripped of all of its furniture and had suffered badly from lack of maintenance. The ritual heart of the residence in the main hall was derelict, with all of the tangible material elements long gone, and only faded memories remain. What once had been exquisite compositions of fine furnishings, ritual paraphernalia, paintings, and other art works, all had been lost. In recent years, the collapse of the central ridgepole above the altar opened the heart of the dwelling to water damage, which has accelerated its deterioration since resources have not been expended to make necessary repairs. The residence today is owned by descendants of Tan Tek Kee, who now must struggle with decisions about its preservation. While most of them today live comfortably beyond Fujian in the Philippines and Hong Kong, they have put forth substantial funds in an effort to both maintain and restore the patrimony of their forebear. Making decisions within an extended family about allocating resources and how the burden should be shared is not easy. Without the daily life and periodic ritual of the family that once occupied this fine home, and who gave it life, the structure today is a melancholy shell of its former splendor. Today, only a caretaker and his family now occupy the rambling old dwelling in order to keep it clean and protect it from vandalism while distant family members ponder its future.

New Homelands in Southeast Asia

Southeast Asia, like other major realms of the world, as discussed above, is diverse and fragmented in terms of its physical and cultural geographies. The region can be divided fundamentally into two contrasting subdivisions: an Asian mainland that extends south from China, and an array of large and small islands that includes the world's most extensive archipelago. Volcanic peaks, mountain spines, rugged coastlines, long rivers, short rivers, deltas, mangrove swamps, rich soils,

and virgin forests are but some of the line-up of physical features that indigenous people and immigrants have adapted to.

Much of what we know of Chinese migration in Southeast Asia is fragmentary, with ebbs and flows guided both by imperial policy and individual decisions made by resourceful seaborne traders. During the Song dynasty in the twelfth century, the Ming dynasty in the fifteenth and sixteenth centuries, and throughout the Qing dynasty, which began in 1644, Chinese trading communities of various sizes and compositions emerged at scattered port locations throughout the islands and peninsulas in the Nanyang. Over time, what once were scattered and isolated became tied into commercial networks. The arrival of Europeans, first as traders and then as colonialists, as well as Japanese, brought about competition and rivalries even as Chinese traders flourished and arriving Chinese settlers increased in number. Enterprising Chinese immigrants, as later chapters of this book will reveal, commercially exploited the profuse variety of flora and fauna as well as minerals and metals, resources providing work and a modest livelihood for countless contract laborers and bountiful wealth to a smaller number of migrants from China. The plantation cultivation of rubber, coffee, sugar, and spices, in addition to the collection of birds' nests from caves in the wild and exotic flora and fauna from the biodiversity-rich ecosystems, played key roles in these transformations. The sections that follow will examine the dispersal of Chinese migrants, emphasizing the disparate character of history and geography of various settlement sites, as a prelude to the featured residences in Part Two.

Malacca

In the area clutched between the Malacca River and the Strait of Malacca, a casual visitor sees old buildings lining the narrow streets that appear on the exterior to be quintessentially Chinese. Indeed, Chinese characters arrayed above the lintels and windows and on the door and shutter panels, as well as the bulbous red lanterns hanging beneath the eaves, all seem to proclaim that this neighborhood has deep roots as a place of settlement by Chinese immigrants and their descendants, perhaps even to the earliest days of Malacca. Looking more closely at the exteriors, however, one also observes Dutch-period architectural features, Victorian glazed tiles, eclectic façades of uncertain age and origin, Chinese protective amulets, rooflines that span East and West, among other elements that confound the observer's judgment. Glimpses through the doorways of hotels, restaurants, shops, even residences, seem to affirm that the occupants are principally Chinese in origin.

Those fortunate to be invited into homes along the lanes see that many are quite similar to the shophouses and terrace homes found in towns in southern China in that they have prominent skywells—small courtyards—that open up the interiors to light and air. In many of these residences, moreover, there is an abundance of antique Chinese and

Western furniture, a proliferation of symbolic Chinese ornamentation, a mélange of curios, art works, and bric-a-brac from China as well as Europe, and an occasional architectural detail that appears odd in a Chinese home. It is a fair to ask: what can old residences like these tell us of the lives, aspirations, and tastes of the Chinese, and others, who have occupied them?

These buildings and these streets in Malacca indeed are more than they seem at first glance. On closer examination, one is able to see a multifaceted and layered history of successive occupancy by different groups, with the Chinese being but one prominent part, over five centuries from the 1500s to the present. Historical geographers call the succeeding stages of human inhabitation of a location over intervals of historic time "sequent occupance." The coming and going of a group, which entails using and abandoning areas and buildings, is a dynamic process of creating and modifying to meet different cultural norms. Indeed, any of the residences that appear to be Chinese are, in fact, transformed artifacts representing both added *and* deleted elements when compared to what was inherited from others. To help understand similarities and differences, Malacca needs to be looked at in terms of different temporal and spatial scales.

At one scale, there is a sequence represented by the successive arrival in Malacca of different nationalities, some more powerful than others, but each leaving significant imprints on the landscape. Once a small and remote fishing village inhabited by indigenous Malays, Malacca began to develop as a port in the fourteenth century under the leadership of Parameswara, a Srivijayan prince from Sumatra. The Portuguese arrived in 1511, surrendering control to the Dutch in 1641 for a century and a half of development, before passing the region to the British in 1795, with a Dutch interlude again from 1818 to 1824, at the end of which the Dutch returned Malacca to the British in exchange for territory in Sumatra. Each of these occupancies was overlain by the arrival, presence, and activity of Muslim Arabs, Hindus from the Gujarat and Tamil regions of today's India, and, of course, Chinese from Fujian and Guangdong provinces. All of these interacted with indigenous Malays. Moreover, the rise of Penang in 1786 and Singapore from 1819 onwards was accompanied by Malacca's slipping in importance as a trading center

Left Built early in the twentieth century on the northern out-skirts of Malacca, in Tranquerah, this narrow terrace residence houses a multigenerational family. The façade is richly deco-rated with stucco patterns and calligraphic ornamentation. Just inside the entryway is a round table with a formal grouping of furniture with mother-of-pearl inlay. Beyond this area is a sky-well framed with fluted columns, which are painted to match the façade.

with its relegation to a relative backwater. One result of this new status was that the layout of the town and its solid buildings, which passed from one group to another, were for the most part not destroyed but survived to be occupied and were then transformed by different residents.

When the Portuguese arrived, they constructed a pentagonal fort on the south side of the Malacca River, while some joined Gujaratis and Tamils on the north bank where they lived in simple dwellings built from easily available materials such as timbers, mud, and thatched nipa palm called *attap*. Towards the end of the sixteenth century, successful merchants began to build more substantial houses in an area that was favored by cool breezes from the sea and came to be called Kampung Belanda or "Dutch Village."

After disastrous fires that accompanied the Dutch siege in 1641, in addition to constructing residences and other buildings in Malacca's administrative and commercial center, the Dutch laid out along the north side of the river a somewhat rectangular street plan with two major roads running parallel to the coast, which were intersected by minor ones. In this area, increasingly wealthy Dutch and other settlers constructed brick and stone homes with their backs aligned along the sea and their fronts along a road called Heerenstraat or "Gentlemen's Street," which was later renamed Heeren Street by the British. In time, multistoried residences, which were narrow in the front and elongated as they receded towards the water, were built, then no doubt modified from time to time to meet changing needs. Similar, but generally less grand homes were built along Jonkerstraat, an inland road parallel to Heerenstrat. While some of the elements of these evolving houses drew upon experiences the Dutch had in colonies elsewhere in the tropics, the residences also reflected the designs known to Chinese masons and carpenters who did much of the actual construction using common building practices in use in China. The intersecting of Dutch and Chinese patterns in the organization of space, building structure, fenestration and roofing of many residences along these narrow old roads is indisputable yet still, to some degree, remains a puzzle.

The successive arrival of Portuguese, Dutch, and British colonialists and the roles played by Indian and Chinese mercantile immigrants brought about Malacca's transformation into one of the region's most important entrepôt by virtue of its strategic location on the Strait of Malacca. The multicultural heritage of Malacca has bequeathed not only a remarkable vitality to an arguably significant historic city but also a mixed assemblage of heritage buildings. The destruction of old buildings, unbridled land reclamation, construction of high-rise buildings, and inattention to traffic management, all in pursuit of short-term commercial gains, have contributed to diminishing Malacca's frayed multicultural past. While the preservation of Malacca's exceptional material heritage remains imperiled, significant elements of the city's Chinese heritage remain.

The recently restored Cheng Hoon Teng Temple, whose origins go back to the 1640s, and Bukit Cina (Chinese Hill), an expansive cemetery that dates to the mid-fifteenth century, both exemplify the rich links between China and the Malay Peninsula. Marriage and concubinage involving males from China and local women gradually brought about a distinct community known as Peranakan Chinese, whose porcelain, cuisine, clothing, architecture, language, and literature are prominent aspects of their culture. Peranakan Chinese residences in Malacca as well as in Singapore and Penang, the original three Straits Settlements, include not only eclectic terrace homes, which are also called townhouses, but also ornate villas and mansions.

Four Malacca residences are featured in Part Two, which together provide insights into the historical, geographical, architectural, and social aspects of life in Malacca from the eighteenth into the early parts of the twentieth century. The restored shophouse at No. 8 Heeren Street (pages 42–5), which once served as a *kuli keng*, literally "the quarters where coolies live," provides a simple spatial template for the succession of larger homes built later. No Peranakan Chinese Malaysian is better known than Tan Cheng Lock, whose ancestral home, also on Heeren Street (pages 46–57), reveals Dutch features plus multiple layers of Chinese and Western influences. Two buildings associated with the Chee family are discussed: one was built in 1906 to memorialize Chee Yam Chuan, the notable forebear of the lineage (pages 58–63), and another the late nineteenth-century residence of Chee Jin Siew (pages 64–9) that provides a glimpse of a substantial home that has undergone only limited restoration. While each of the townhouses, shophouses, and villas in Malacca is unique, they share common aspects that can be gleaned from looking at their façades, floor plans, and ornamentation.

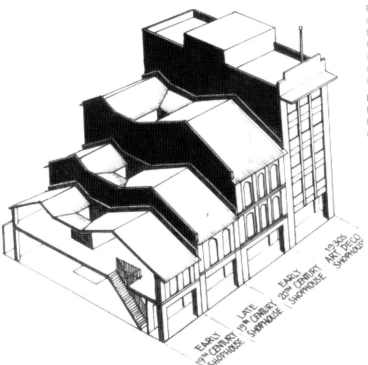

EARLY 19TH CENTURY SHOPHOUSE · LATE 19TH CENTURY SHOPHOUSE · EARLY 20TH CENTURY SHOPHOUSE · 1930s ART DECO SHOPHOUSE

Singapore

Cities like London, Rome, Paris, and Beijing, and even younger cities such as New York and Singapore, are veritable museums of changing architectural styles in which old residences and other structures encapsulate in their physical forms the dynamic nature of individuals, families, and communities. Scattered homes and buildings together tell the story of each city's evolution and, to some degree, national history in microcosm, from humble beginnings to their flourishing as commercial or governmental centers. Old residences, in particular, help tell the story of once prominent families, even the whole era in which they lived, giving contemporary visitors an opportunity to experience, within the confines of four walls, how life was lived in times past. Through the massing of architectural form and structure as well as building style, including external features and interior spaces, the tempo and character of daily life of times past can be made understandable for the curious visitor. Furnishings and ornamentation point toward what a family valued, providing windows into understanding what their hopes and aspirations for themselves and sometimes even their descendants. This is as true of the homes of the wealthy as it is for those struggling to find a place of modest comfort for their families.

Established by the British East India Company in 1819 on the site of a fishing village on an island at the tip of the Malay Peninsula, the trading post that became Singapore emerged in the nineteenth century as a strategic hub of British commercial and military power in Asia. Sir Stamford Raffles, acknowledged as the founder of Singapore, outlined early on a town plan some three kilometers wide along the sea and two kilometers inland, with priority on creating efficient docking and unloading facilities along the Singapore River. In order to forestall the emergence of disorderly settlements, a plan was proposed that created a segregated layout defined by ethnic subdivisions: a European Town, a Chinese Campong, Chulia Campong for ethnic Indians, Campong Glam for Malays, and an Arab Campong. "Campong" is the Anglicized form for the Malay word "kampong," which means a hamlet or village. As an entrepôt that welcomed traders, planters, and coolies, Singapore subsequently thrived with the arrival of immigrants from China, India, Malaya, and elsewhere, in addition to a significant number of enterprising Peranakan Chinese from Malacca and Penang.

In the early years, in addition to Chinese merchants and artisans, Chinese peasants arrived in increasing numbers to open areas to the north and west of the port city for the production of gambier and pepper, which, as we will see, contributed to the wealth of Chinese businessmen resident in Singapore. An 1879 survey of the manners and customs of Chinese in the Straits Settlements tallied some 200 different occupations pursued by immigrant Chinese. While the intent of many Chinese newcomers was to return to China, many settled in the new homelands. "Many did not go back to China," according to Victor Purcell, "because ... they were too poor, but some did not return because they were too rich and dared to leave their property and their interests" (1965: 254).

Many of the early dwellings inhabited by Fujian and Guangdong immigrants in the Chinese Campong were flimsy Malay-type structures raised on stilts above the marshy ground. In time, this area expanded over four phases from the 1820s into the 1920s into what today is known as Chinatown, a robust commercial and residential district of eclectic shophouses of various designs. Paradoxically, Singapore's "Chinatown" is but a single neighborhood in a country that is predominantly populated by the descendants of immigrants from China.

The elongated Singapore shophouse, which has been called an Anglo-Chinese vernacular form by Lee Ho Yin, provided working and living space for merchants, artisans, and service-oriented firms (2003: 115). Over the years, shophouses evolved in terms of relative scale while

maintaining features such as the linear covered veranda known as the "five-foot way" and the presence of at least one interior skywell. Built contiguously in blocks separated by party walls, there is a lively rhythm to the columns, pilasters, shutters, and ornamentation of the façades of adjacent Singapore shophouses, with elements that are Chinese, European, and Malay.

The eclectic style of the multifunctional Singapore shophouses in Telok Ayer, the heart of Chinatown, was in time carried over to their cousin, the purely residential structures called terrace houses or townhouses. By the later decades of the nineteenth century, as increasing numbers of new migrants arrived from China, Chinatown became overcrowded and unhealthy. Some Chinese merchants began to consider moving beyond their place of livelihood to more residential neighborhoods that were being developed, first in areas adjacent to Chinatown and before long elsewhere across the island. Nearby areas along Neil Road, Blair Road, Spottiswoode Park, and River Valley Road, then in the Emerald Hill area, once a nutmeg plantation, and later in the Joo Chiat and Katong areas in the eastern part of Singapore, all became new centers of Chinese residential life. In these areas, a mélange of building types, predominantly shophouses and terrace houses, took root in varieties that defy easy summary (pages 80–9). As other Chinese families moved to the eastern section of the island early in the twentieth century, some built raised bungalows that evoke the Malay-style *rumah panggung* along the seacoast. Constructed on piles with a broad veranda and abundant fenestration, the design of these bungalows allowed air to move under and through them, thus increasing comfort for those living within. In addition, the possible flooding during high tides was mitigated by elevating the residence.

Several terrace houses are presented in detail in Part Two. Among the most interesting is the multistoried Wee family residence on Neil Road (pages 90–101), which was initially built as a two-storey structure between 1896 and 1897 that was subsequently raised to three storeys. More than a century old, this residence provides not only entry into the lives of an old Singapore family but also provides a template for understanding the layout and use of a typical terrace house. In 2008, after a successful restoration, the residence was opened as the Baba House Museum. Other terrace residences in the Emerald Hill, Blair Flat, and River Valley Road areas are also featured in Part Two.

During the nineteenth century, a coterie of tycoons, merchants with extraordinary wealth and power, emerged in Singapore. One of the most celebrated was Hoo Ah Kay, usually referred to as Whampoa (Huangpu) after his place of origin in Guangdong and the name of his father's firm, Whampoa & Co. Whampoa was described as the "most liked Chinaman in the Straits," "a fine specimen of his countrymen; his generosity and honesty had long made him a favorite," and "a very upright, kind-hearted, modest, and simple man, a friend to everyone," who was known for his "sumptuous entertainments" (Buckley, 1902: 658–9). He acquired a neglected garden on Serangoon Road about four kilometers outside town, where he built a "bungalow," a magnificent country house, as well as an aviary and "a Chinese garden laid out by horticulturalists from Canton," which became a "place of resort for Chinese, young and old, at the Chinese New Year" where "the democratic instincts of the Chinese would be seen, for all classes without distinction would mix freely and show mutual respect and courtesy" (Song, 1923: 53–5). Whampoa gained fame also for the dinners he hosted that included Westerners and Chinese at the estate he called

"Bendemeer," the name of a river in Persia mentioned in a poem written in 1817 by Thomas Moore that was popular at the time. There appears to be no record of how Whampoa referred to the garden in Chinese.

Tan Seng Poh, Seah Eu Chin, Wee Ah Hood, and Tan Yeok Nee, among other wealthy nineteenth-century Chinese businessmen built between 1869 and 1885 what Singaporeans once called the Four Mansions. Tied to one another to homelands in the Chaozhou area of eastern Guangdong province, they built Chinese-style mansions that survived well into the twentieth century. Today, only the residence of Tan Yeok Nee, the subject of a chapter in Part Two (pages 70–9), remains.

In the 1980s during urban redevelopment in the Kampong Bugis area, the last grand courtyard residence in Singapore in the architectural style of southern Fujian was demolished along Sin Koh Street, which itself was obliterated. This expansive red brick residence, with its swallowtail roofline, which is reminiscent of the home of Tan Tek Kee in Jinjiang discussed above, had been built in 1896 by Goh Sin Koh, a timber merchant who also was in the shipping business. Although records are incomplete, Goh's grand home at some point was transformed into an ancestral hall for his family and others from their home village in Fujian. The only surviving images of this sprawling and derelict residence were taken in the late 1970s when the building was being used to store lumber.

Penang, Medan–Deli, and Phuket

Penang and Medan–Deli, one on the Malay Peninsula and the other on the island of Sumatra on opposite sides of the funnel-shaped Strait of Malacca, as well as Phuket along the Andaman Sea farther north, have a history of economic and social interdependence. Hokkien traders and settlers reached all three areas in the distant past, well before the late nineteenth century when the numbers of Chinese arrivals increased substantially. In 1786, after the British naval officer Francis Light negotiated with the Sultan of Kedah to cede Pulau Penang, the island of Penang, to the East India Company as a dependency of India for the annual payment of £1,500, Penang began its transformation from being a mere maritime roadstead to a thriving commercial center. Penang began to thrive first, serving as a kind of "mother settlement" that helped spawn and then sustain distant satellites commercial towns like Phuket and Medan–Deli and inland areas on the mainland, such as Sungai Bakap, and in the northern portions of the island of Sumatra where plantation economies thrived.

Legions of Chinese, especially from Fujian but also other areas of China's southeast coast, as well as Indians, Malays, and Europeans quickly transformed the developing townscape of George Town, named in honor of King George III, and, once it was ceded in 1798, the fertile plains of Province Wellesley, named in honor of the Governor-General of India, across the harbor on the mainland. Indeed, within

months of Light's initial transaction, he was already remarking that "Our inhabitants increase very fast—Chooliahs (Tamils), Chinese, and Christians; they are already disputing about the ground, everyone building as fast as he can." Eight years later, he boasted ("Notices of Pinang," 1858: 9; quoted in Purcell, 1965: 244):

The Chinese constitute the most valuable part of our inhabitants; they are men, women, and children, about 3,000, they possess the different trades of carpenters, masons, and smiths, are traders, shopkeepers and planters, they employ small vessels and prows and send adventures [sic] to the surrounding countries. They are the only people of the east from whom revenue may be raised without expense and extraordinary efforts of government.... They are indefatigable in

the pursuit of money, and like the Europeans, they spend it in purchasing those articles which gratify their appetites. They don't wait until they have acquired a large fortune to return to their native country, but send annually a part of their profits to their families. This is so general that a poor labourer will work with double labour to acquire two or three dollars to remit to China. As soon as they acquire a little money they obtain a wife and go on in regular domestic mode to the end of their existence.

Late in the eighteenth century, well before Chinese began to arrive in significant numbers, Light had already seen the potential value of Phuket in Siam, today's Thailand. Using Phuket's common name at the time, he commented that "Junk Salong 45 miles long and 15 broad, is a good healthy island, has several harbours where ships may careen, wood and water safe in all seasons, but it will be six or seven years before it is sufficiently cleared and cultivated to supply a fleet with provisions, it is exceedingly rich in tin ore and may be fortified at a small expense; it belongs to Siam. The inhabitants tired of their slavery are desirous of a new master" ("Notices of Pinang," 1858: 185). Through-out the nineteenth and early twentieth century, shophouses in the style of those built in Penang as well as mansions in what is called Sino-Colonial style were constructed in large numbers in Phuket.

The northeastern coast of Sumatra, which lay across the Strait of Malacca opposite Penang, had received only limited visits by Chinese traders who previously only focused on the potentiality of sites along the east coasts of the strait. Some had come to Laboehan (Labuan) at the mouth of the Deli River, which had been the seat of the Sultan's power; but there is little evidence of early Chinese settlement there. However,

once the Dutch proclaimed their territorial claims to northern Sumatra in 1862, setting in train the opening of the area to large-scale plantation agriculture organized by a variety of European and American firms based upon export crops such as tobacco, rubber, coffee, and oil palm, there was an extraordinary demand for coolie labor that could only be satisfied by immigrants. At first coolies were brought from Penang and Singapore before hundreds of thousands were recruited directly from China and Java using intermediaries who resided in Penang. Because of the insalubrious environment at Laboehan, a decision was made to build a modern planned town at a site called Medan, some 10 kilometers inland, which was connected by rail to the port at Laboehan. By 1917 Medan was described as the "queen city of the island of Sumatra," "a charming city, brisk and bustling in its business quarters, surrounded by pretty suburbs, with a sanitary system equal to that of any English town. It has two fine hotels, a railway station of handsome architecture, a racecourse, a palatial club, sports ground for football and land tennis, a cinema theatre, and all the modern attributes of an up-to-date centre" (quoted in Buiskool, 2004: 6). Even the Sultan of Deli built an imposing *istana* or palace, which was designed by a European architect, in Medan.

While Penang began to lose some of its prominence after Raffles founded Singapore in 1819, its role as a regional center continued to expand, especially after it was joined with Malacca and Singapore in 1826 to form the Straits Settlements. Initially, Penang was the capital of this far-flung network governed by the East India Company, but in 1832 the rapidly developing Singapore eclipsed Penang as the seat of government. In 1867 the tripartite Straits Settlements commercial entity became a Crown Colony under direct British colonial administration. Through strategic alliances, which were often based on Chinese dialect relationships, business increasingly was transnational, going beyond the British Straits Settlements to the Netherlands Indies, Siam, Burma, as well as ports in eastern India and southern China. Interestingly, not all of the linkages were by sea. Transpeninsular overland trade routes from Pattani, Nakhon, and Songkhla on the east coast of southern Siam linked Penang on the west coast to Bangkok's thriving commerce. Merchandise was carried by caravans of elephants in five days along easy pathways that formed a kind of land bridge, a "vein of commerce" of enormous utility, the length of which came to be known as the "Kedah Road" (King, 2002: 96–7).

By the last quarter of the nineteenth century, there were as many as 200 Chinese merchants "plying the seas and accumulating wealth" in the region straddling the Strait of Malacca and beyond, with Penang as the hub (Wong, 2007: 107). The so-called "Penang's Five Major Hokkien Clans," *Bincheng Fujian wu da xing*—Tan, Yeoh, Lim, Cheah, and Khoo—especially, were major players in developing the regional, indeed

with the peripatetic efforts of the revered Chinese leader Sun Yat-sen, is presented as typical of a building typology of great significance (pages 114–19). Chung Keng Quee, one of the principal tin magnates of the Straits Settlements (pages 102–13), and Cheong Fatt Tze, an extraordinary multinational entrepreneur who amassed fortunes from mining, plantation agriculture, banking and shipping (pages 128–39), built in Penang a contrasting pair of mansions that share many underlying themes. One special feature of Chung Keng Quee's home, as will be discussed later, is that he had a spacious private ancestral hall built adjacent to his home. Constructed as the nineteenth century came to a close, these grand residences evoke the styles of the late Victorian era during a period of increasing global interdependence when eclectic decorative arts styles were in fashion throughout the world. Significantly, in the case of homes discussed in this book, there was a concomitant resurgence of pride by well-to-do Chinese in the culture of their ancestors. For many, it was essential that craftsmen from China were "imported" to design and fabricate multifarious forms of applied ornamentation and furnishings in order to assure authenticity, even as they sought fixtures and art works from Europe to express modernity.

In spite of material success, international fame in his adopted homeland, and the building of an opulent Chinese-style residence in Penang, Cheong Fatt Tze also constructed a grand manor in his hometown in Dabu, Guangdong province (pages 274–7), but sadly died before he could retire there. Chung Keng Quee did not follow that route, leaving behind children in Malaya who were more comfortable with life in a British colony. Kee Lai Huat, a pioneering planter of sugarcane and manufacturer of brown sugar, founded Sungai Bakap, a town in Province Wellesley. Here, in a rambling compound of residences and an ancestral hall, which he hoped would become the permanent abode of his descendants who would live together harmoniously, he declared his Chineseness (pages 120–7).

Sumptuous eclectic residences were built as well in Phuket and Medan during this period, which reveal clearly their economic and social linkages with Penang. With wealth acquired first from tin mining and smelting and later from rubber plantations, Tan Ma Hsiang, whose Thai name was Prapitak Chyn Pracha, built in 1904 what is called in Thailand a Sino-Portuguese villa with obvious elements blending generic Western architectural forms *and* Chinese elements (pages 140–5). Between 1895 and 1900, Tjong A Fie constructed an opulent mansion in the thriving town of Medan on Sumatra in the Netherlands Indies (pages 146–55). A fine example of architectural eclecticism, Tjong's mansion mixes fashionable European-style furnishings and fine arts with centuries-old styles of Chinese furniture, altars, and ornamentation in a striking brew of material modernity.

even transnational enterprises involving tin mining, revenue farming, coolie recruitment, and shipping. Diversifying into the wholesaling and retailing of staple foodstuffs, daily needs, and furnishings made in China and Europe not only met but also stimulated demand by consumers and brought wealth to merchant families. The prosperity generated from these economic activities altered expectations about housing, hygiene, comfort, and education, among other aspects of modernization, in areas where immigrants from Europe, China, India, and elsewhere mixed.

As the population swelled in Penang, Phuket, and Medan, shophouses of various types were built and rebuilt to meet the evolving commercial and service needs of residents along newly planned streets that spread beyond the town core. Sumptuous residences and government buildings, some of which were quite grand, as well as Christian churches, also increased in number. As affluent merchants gained wealth from plantation agriculture, mining, and shipping in the mid- to late nineteenth century, bungalows and mansions of substantial proportions and eclectic styles were also built in each of these regions. In addition to the broad range of residential structures, Chinese settlers also continued to renovate existing or build new Daoist and Buddhist temples, which universally were modeled after those in their hometowns in China. Buildings to meet the needs of their thriving clan associations, usually called *kongsi*, also increased in number. Bricklayers and carpenters from China arrived to erect many of these structures, some of which were constructed using fired bricks and roof tiles carried as ballast on trading ships outbound from China. Because of the richness of the hardwood forests in Southeast Asia, timber was usually sourced locally.

In the sections that follow, examples of each of these housing types are presented. In Penang, a late nineteenth-century shophouse associated

Selangor

While Malacca and Penang trace their roots to early Chinese seaborne trading, the prosperity of areas in between, today's Perak, Selangor, and Negeri Sembilan, came only in the mid-nineteenth century with the boom in tin mining that was spurred by global demand. Up to that time, fluctuating economic conditions in the agricultural, commercial, and even the tin mining sectors, which had absorbed Chinese immigrants and who had worked side by side with Malays since the eighteenth century, frustrated the region's development. Indeed, contemporary records underscore periodic impoverishment and hardship. For example, "In 1829, ... Sultan Abdullah asked the Resident Councillor of Penang to induce Chinese ships to visit Perak annually to buy elephants, for this would provide a great relief to the distressed inhabitants." What had been a "trickle of Chinese labourers into the mining areas was beginning to develop into a flood" by the middle of the nineteenth century, with resourceful Chinese entrepreneurs breaking the tin mining monopoly once held by Malay ruling chiefs (Khoo, 1972: 33, 51). The subsequent development of the Larut and Kinta tin deposits in Perak and then those in the Klang Valley of Selangor brought great wealth to the region. The overlapping interests and intraregional financing of tin mining, like other commercial endeavors, operated within networks of Chinese entrepreneurs spread rather widely but linked by dialect and native place associations. In Selangor, tin mining expanded quickly between 1874 and 1905, first with investment by Chinese from Singapore and Penang, and then by locals such as Yap Ah Loy, Loke Yew, and Yap Kwang Seng, each with an idiosyncratic rags-to-riches story, who became wealthy from tin mining as well as diverse other interests, built grand mansions, and were community leaders noted for their philanthropic endeavors.

Until 1980, when textbooks in Malaysia anointed Raja Abdu'llah of Klang as the reputed founder of Kuala Lumpur in 1857, Yap Ah Loy, who had arrived a few years later, had generally been recognized as the founder of the town that was eventually to become the national capital (Carstens, 2005: 38–9). In the mid-nineteenth century, Kuala Lumpur was merely a tin miners' camp, a frontier outpost of squatters, a "great Chinese village," according to Isabella Bird (1883: 117), and "consisted almost wholly of wooden, attap or mud houses, arranged in the haphazard manner which had resulted from its rapid and unplanned growth" (Jackson, 1963: 117). After a fire in 1881, which is said to have been started by an overturned oil-lamp in an opium den and consumed the prevalent *attap* and timber homes, as well as civil unrest that decimated Kuala Lumpur, Yap Ah Loy, a major property owner, financed the rebuilding of the town. Bricks and tile from kilns amidst the clay pits of what now is known as Brickfields, which were owned by both Yap

Ah Loy and Yap Kwan Seng, helped transform the town into a level of permanence not seen previously. Yap Ah Loy lived in a splendid mansion amidst gardens with his family in Kuala Lumpur before he died at the age of forty-eight. During the last decade of his life, Yap Kwan Seng and his family occupied an interconnected set of three-storey terrace houses on Pudu Street in the heart of Kuala Lumpur's Chinatown. When Yap Kwan Seng died in 1901, he left "a family of fifteen sons and ten daughters, and estates valued at several million daughters" (Wright and Cartwright, 1908: 898).

While neither of the residences of Yap Ah Loy or Yap Kwan Seng is still standing, the residence of Loke Yew, which was begun in 1892 and finished in 1904, survives and is featured in Part Two (pages 156–63). Constructed on the site of an earlier home built in the1860s by Cheow Ah Yeok, Loke Yew's mansion is an eclectic structure that mixes European and Chinese elements in addition to modern conveniences. Loke Yew's new home was the first private residence in Kuala Lumpur with electricity for interior lighting. East of Kuala Lumpur and not too far from the tailings of old tin mines and amidst groves of coconut palms, is the recently restored home of Tan Boon Chia. Constructed in the early 20th century (1918), it was amongst the earliest mansions built by an overseas Chinese. Tan Boon Chia, who was born in 1868, arrived at the tender age of 18 from China, landing first in Singapore before settling down in Kuala Selangor. The patriach arrived penniless, but rose through diligence and sacrifice to become a successful tin miner and planter.

The tin industry has since lost its grandeur but the house built by Tan Boon Chia has been diligently restored by his descendants. Tan Boon Chia's grand residence is celebrated in Part Two (pages 164–71).

Indonesia

While those of Chinese descent have been a highly visible minority in Indonesia, it is not easy to weave a comprehensive narrative that captures the dynamic nature of their in-migration and settlement in terms of temporal scope *and* spatial extent. This is compounded by the incompleteness of the written record and material remains concerning the presence of Chinese traders and settlers in Srivijaya and Majapahit, the two great kingdoms that spanned the period from the seventh through the end of the fifteenth century, and later throughout the region during the age of commerce with the arrival of the Dutch East India Company (Vereenigde Oost-Indische Compagnie or VOC).

In terms of spatial extent, Indonesia is the largest archipelago in the world, comprising 17,500 islands spanning 5000 kilometers from west to east, one-eighth the circumference of the Earth, and nearly 2000 kilometers from north to south. Both large and small islands dotted

with estuaries and riverine hinterlands straddling the equator attracted Chinese traders, sojourners, and immigrant settlers, providing them with limitless opportunities. It was not only in growing urban centers throughout the archipelago, such as Batavia, Surabaya, Bandung, Medan, Semarang, and Palembang, among many others, that Chinese sojourned or settled but also in small towns along the coasts and inland, like Banten, Tangerang, Cheribon, Gresik, Jepara, Rembang, Lasem, Parakan, Malang, Salatiga, Lawang, Solo, and Pasuruan on Java; Padang and Labuan Deli on Sumatra; Makassar on Celebes; Pontianak on Borneo; and Pangkal Pinang and Muntok on Banka. Some were visited and settled by Chinese well before the Dutch arrived, while others only flourished from the nineteenth century onwards. An intriguing and representative variety of old Chinese homes, both grand and common ones, in these locations are shown in the pages that follow in Part One and Part Two.

Chinese, Indian, and Arab seaborne merchants used two long-distance routes early on to transit through this intricately vast archipelago between the Indian Ocean and the South China Sea. Passage through the narrow Sunda Strait, some 24 kilometers wide, between the islands of Sumatra and Java, was regarded as difficult to navigate but more direct. The alternate route through the Strait of Malacca between the Malay Peninsula and Sumatra provided a protected, yet restricted, channel some 800 kilometers long. Long-distance trade in large ships through these straits was accompanied by fleets of smaller vessels that hugged the coastline from China southward, braving the sometimes violent seas to sail not only to the Philippines but also south to more distant locations on the large island of Borneo, the oddly shaped Celebes, the Spice Islands of the Moluccas, and beyond to the Banda, Flores, and Java Seas. The far-flung, seemingly random scattering of Chinese settlements along the fringes of the South China Sea and its connecting water bodies attests to the navigational prowess and daring of Chinese seamen over long periods.

Gradually, pockets of Chinese small-scale traders, merchants, craftsmen, and peasants established themselves at the mouths of short coastal rivers or inland for security and the convenience of petty commerce. Many married local Javanese women and became Muslims; others formed local family units while retaining the full spectrum of their Chinese folk beliefs and rituals. Still others, who were of Han ethnicity but Muslim in belief in China, married local Muslim women, thus comfortably choosing their religion over the broader aspects of Chinese culture. Over time, descendants sometimes lost even awareness of their Chinese ethnicity as they assimilated. For many Chinese, they remained a very small minority in host communities, while in others their presence, even if absolute numbers were low, was prominent. For example, in Makassar in the Celebes in the eighteenth century, as many as a third of

the Chinese community was Muslim, and a Peranakan Chinese mosque stood there well into the twentieth century (Sutherland, 2003a: 6).

The equatorial climate across the archipelago fostered an abundant array of flora, fauna, and marine products that had substantial markets in coastal China. What the Chinese found and preferred was a cornucopia of raw and processed items: aromatic and preservative spices like nutmeg, cloves, and pepper; medicinal herbs and animal parts; *agar-agar* (a gelatinous substance derived from seaweed); animal and vegetable waxes; avian and marine delicacies such as birds' nests and sea cucumber (also called trepan and *bêche-de-mer*); tortoiseshells; rattan; resins; hardwood timber; among other commodities, which were gathered or harvested in the wild. In return, Chinese monsoon traders brought back from China manufactured and processed goods such as fired earthenware, silk thread, cotton textiles, umbrellas, paper, tea, and tobacco. The gathering of natural products involved both local and immigrant labor. Feeder networks using vessels of various types and sizes brought communities of indigenous peoples into an evolving network of globalizing trade that involved not only Chinese junks but also Dutch ships.

When Dutch seafaring traders first reached the coast of northern Java in 1596, they found Chinese settlement along the lower courses of many of the streams. Unlike in the Americas where the Dutch encountered and interacted only with aboriginal or native American populations, the Dutch in Asia benefited from the additional presence of mercantile networks already set in place by countless Chinese sojourners and settlers. In the early part of the twentieth century, a French traveler offered this effusive judgment: "What would become of the European and the Dutch Government without the presence of the Chinaman in Java? A hard worker, meditative, mindful of his responsibilities, he is the linch-pin of all great public or private enterprises; to the native the necessary intermediary, the obscure but necessary cog-wheel, the middleman, the go-between, whom the European would not and Javanese could not as yet replace. One finds him everywhere; one needs him everywhere; one must therefore accept him, while limiting as far as possible, the bad effects of his role." He preceded this with an explanation: "One finds them wherever there is money to be made; and their presence anywhere is enough to denote some known or possible source of gain" (Cabaton, 1911: 158–9).

Some of the oldest Chinese residences in Indonesia are found in the small coastal towns of the north, while nineteenth- and twentieth-century structures are best found in the major cities. Ten of Indonesia's fine Chinese residences are presented in Part Two. Nine are spread across the island of Java, from Tangerang in the west to Pasuruan in the east: the Oey Djie San plantation home in Tangerang (pages 180–5); the Khouw family manor (pages 172–9), the Tjioe family residence,

Right The residence of Souw Tian Pie, whose forefathers had migrated from Fujian in 1696, was built in Batavia in the early nineteenth century. Originally it was composed of three parallel buildings and a pair of perpendicular side wings, but its overall scale has been diminished over time, first by the destruction of the tall rear building at some time in the past, second by the demolition of a wing unit in the 1980s so that a multistoried block could be built, and third by modernization of the opposite wing.

Below Many portions of the wooden framework within the Souw Tian Pie dwelling survive and suggest its past grandeur.

which is now the St Maria de Fatima Catholic Church (pages 186–7), in Jakarta; the Tan Tjion Ie home in Semarang (pages 188–9); Kwik Djoen Eng's mansion, now the Institut Roncalli, in Salatiga (pages 198–201); the Siek family home, now the Prasada Mandala Dharma, in Parakan (pages 190–7); the Liem compound in Lasem (pages 202–3); the Han Bwee Kio ancestral hall in Surabaya (pages 204–9); and the Han and Thalib residence in Pasuruan (pages 210–13). The magnificent Tjong A Fie mansion in Medan in northeastern Sumatra is also included (pages 146–55).

Batavia/Jakarta

In late 1596, when the Dutch arrived on the northwest coast of Java, they entered the Ciliwung River where they encountered a small village of Chinese peasants who planted rice and vegetables and made arrack, a beverage distilled from fermented sugarcane and rice. This Chinese settlement, about which very little is known, was adjacent to a trading center called in succession Sunda Kelapa and Jayakarta. Portuguese traders had visited as early as 1513 and Arab, Indian, and Chinese traders, who had come even earlier, continued to arrive seasonally. It was not until 1619 that the Dutch destroyed Jayakarta, which had a population of about 10,000, on the west bank. In its place, they created both a fortification on the right bank at the mouth of the river and began to lay out a colonial town surrounded by a wall and moat.

By 1650 the planned settlement of Batavia, with more canals than streets, became a commercial emporium for regional and global trade. Its ordered ground plan was filled in with administrative buildings, offices, churches, residences, bridges, wharfs, and godowns, collectively a cosmopolitan center for a thriving Asian commercial enterprise, with separate quarters for Javanese, Chinese, and others from islands near and far. Chinese traders, shopkeepers, craftsmen, and laborers who dredged the canals and constructed buildings, arrived in increasing numbers in search of opportunity. They had been permitted to live within the walled city, where their shops sold silks, lacquerware, porcelain, tea, and other products from China. Outside the walls, they engaged in market gardening for the residents of the town and built ships. Their numbers varied from year to year. In 1699 the number of Chinese reached 3,679, followed by 2,407 freed slaves called Mardijkers, 1,783 Europeans, 670 mixed race people, and 867 classified as others. Between 1680 and 1740, the population of Chinese doubled in Batavia (Blussé, 1986: 84).

Tensions that arose with the increased numbers of Chinese immigrants led to stringent Dutch regulations to control them and plans to remove them en masse to Ceylon. Following on the heels of an uprising by Chinese, whose passions were fueled by rumors, a senseless massacre of perhaps 5,000 Chinese in 1740, the survivors either fled to other locations in Java or returned to China. The massacre is well documented and memorialized in a visually striking mid-eighteenth century engraving of their residences being burned to the ground. A census after the riot revealed that the total Chinese population had dropped to just 3,431: 1442 traders and merchants, 935 peasant farmers, 728 working in sugar mills and as woodcutters, and 326 as artisans (Lohanda, 1996: 16). Chinese eventually returned to Batavia but settled in an area outside the southern wall known as Glodok, which is today at the heart of Jakarta's Chinatown. Yet, from early on, the Chinese, many of whom were Peranakan, dominated the commercial life of

Batavia, even surpassing other groups in population. Leonard Blussé indeed describes Batavia as a "Chinese colonial town under Dutch rule" (1981: 159ff).

There is little evidence that remains in Jakarta of the presence of Chinese in the seventeenth and eighteenth centuries. Of significance is the grave, the *yin zhai* or "residence of the dead" in contrast to the *yang zhai* or "residence of the living," of Souw Beng Kong, also known as Souw Bwee Kong, the first Kapitan China of Batavia, who was selected by the Dutch to settle disputes, carry out an annual census, collect various taxes, manage benevolent associations such as cemeteries and hospitals, and participate in Dutch civil entities. All the while, he gained wealth and experience as a building contractor, shipbuilder, leaseholder, and proprietor of a gambling house. Appointed in 1619, Souw had previously served as Kapitan of the Chinese community at Bantam, which had been a thriving port on the Sunda Strait to the west of Batavia for the spice trade with Europe from the sixteenth century through the eighteenth century when its harbor silted up.

Souw Beng Kong's career reveals the expansive nature of life for some Chinese as they moved easily throughout the broader region in pursuit of opportunities. In addition to his move from Bantam to Batavia, Souw Beng Kong, who the Dutch called Bencon, left Batavia in 1635 for Zeelandia in Taiwan, a Dutch colony since 1624, where he recruited peasants from Fujian to fulfill the Dutch desire for agricultural development there. Perhaps as many as 50,000 Hokkien peasants, traders, and craftsmen made the sea journey to Taiwan by the end of Dutch rule there in 1662 (Hsu, 1980: 16–17). When Souw Beng Kong died in 1640, he was buried in the countryside outside Batavia, an area that today has been swallowed up by the city. His grave was lost until 1909 and restored in 1929, then at some point, strangely, the gravestone was incorporated into the interior of a slum dwelling. In 2008 the Souw Beng Kong Foundation removed the structure and restored the gravesite to both acknowledge and memorialize his role in supporting early Chinese migrants to Java.

No Chinese residences from the eighteenth century remain in the city, but there are some from the nineteenth century, a period when many fine Chinese-style homes were built in Glodok. Late nineteenth-century photographs provide us with glimpses of the façades of the large residences as well as shophouses that may have been built in the later part of the eighteenth century. Three mansions were built near each other along the fashionable Molenvliet West, alongside older Dutch mansions and hotels, by members of the Khouw family. Of these three, only one, which was constructed in either 1807 or 1867, survived well into the twentieth century. Its tortuous journey from being threatened with destruction multiple times to miraculous survival in a fragmented condition is detailed in Part Two (pages 172–9).

Semarang

Now the largest city in Central Java, Semarang not only once was a natural harbor like other small ports along the northern coast that vied with each other for Chinese traders, it is a location that claims to have a storied past linked to visits by Zheng He in 1406 and 1416. The often told tale is that Ong King Hong, Zheng He's second in command, was so ill aboard ship during one of the visits that the fleet dropped anchor in the harbor. After coming ashore and locating what has since become a fabled cave, Ong King Hong was left behind with a squad of men and sufficient provisions to support them. Zheng He then sailed on while Ong and his men settled down with local women, cleared land and raised crops, in what eventually became a small Chinese village along the narrow plain. After building some small craft, the community increased its prosperity with active trading along the coast. Ong, like Zheng He, was a Muslim who committed efforts at spreading Islam while at the same time revering Zheng He, who was enshrined as Sam Po by Ong by his followers. In time, according to the well-known tale, Ong placed a small statue of Sam Po (Zheng He) in the cave to be venerated for his greatness. The isolated cave evolved into a shrine known to locals as Gedong Batu or "Stone Building." Those of Chinese descent revere the Sam Po Kong Temple, which has expanded in recent years far beyond the cliff face, and is the focus for an annual festival that links those of Chinese descent with their illustrious forebear.

Wang Ta-Hai (Ong Tae-Hae), a Hokkien who had lived a decade in Batavia, Pekalongan, and Semarang, published a book in 1791 of his experiences in and impressions of Java that was reprinted several times in the mid-nineteenth century: "Semarang is a district subject to Batavia, but superior to it in appearance. Its territory is more extensive, and its productions more abundant. Merchant vessels are there collected and its commerce is superior ... the fields are fertile and well-watered, and the people rich and affluent; whence it may be considered the crown of all those lands. With respect to climate, the air is clear and cool, and thus superior to Batavia; the inhabitants are seldom troubled with sickness, provisions are reasonable and easily obtained ... the manners of the people are so inoffensive that they do not pick up things dropped in the roads; and the laws are so strictly enforced, that men have no occasion to shut their doors at night' (1850: 7–8).

While Semarang had a Chinatown, the boundaries of life were said to have been more fluid than in other towns and cities across Java. After several centuries of immigration and intermarriage, the Peranakan Chinese community generally divided into two groups, one of which preserved its Chinese identity and used the Sam Po Kong Temple as its anchor, while the other, who had adopted Islam, became Javanese in culture. Still others blended the two approaches. These divisions can be seen in several residences lived in by successive generations of those of Chinese descent.

None of the nineteenth-century grand manors remain in Semarang. Preserved only in several photographs are the residence of Tan Tiang Tjhing, called Gedung Goelo or "Sugar Mansion," built in 1815, and the home of Be Ing Tjioe and his son Be Biauw Tjoan, which was built around 1840 along the Semarang River. Each had a tripartite layout, with a set of three parallel buildings with a pair of perpendicular wing structures. Since it was not common for the front building of a residence to be two storeys tall, it is possible that the front building actually served commercial purposes as offices for the enterprises in which the Tan and Be families were involved. This type of dual use can be observed in structures throughout southern China. The addition of a freestanding rectangular open building with a broad eaves overhang is an unusual feature, perhaps serving as a kind of Javanese *pendopo*, the pavilion-like structure used to receive guests and provide sheltered space for work and relaxation.

Semarang today has wide, tree-lined boulevards with modern commercial and administrative buildings, narrow lanes with old shophouses, areas with large mansions for the wealthy, and smaller, yet comfortable homes in eclectic styles that were built in the nineteenth century. Along Besen Lane, in what once was the Chinese quarter, is an old shophouse that is now undergoing renovation as a gallery of Chinese art. Constructed late in the nineteenth century as a shophouse selling the well-known Frog brand of floor tile, the spacious brick building has Chinese brackets that extend the roof in the front. In addition to the wooden door, hinged into three leaves and divided horizontally into two sections so that the bottom could be kept shut while the upper left open, the shop has a rectangular panel on swivel hinges that once served as a display counter as well as a covering to secure the window at night. In addition to ventilation ports set high on the walls, there is a skywell in the back half of the building, which together with the front and rear windows kept the building quite airy. Chinese characters are still found above the doorways leading from room to room, but other of the applied ornamentation that once was found there is long gone. The upstairs area probably was used for sleeping space for employees. Across the lane is a similar two-storey shophouse. Elsewhere in Semarang, Peranakan Chinese sometimes live in nineteenth-century homes that evoke more Dutch Indische than Chinese styles. The eclectic residence of Tan Tiong Ie, which was built in 1850 a century after his ancestors arrived in Java, is featured in Part Two (pages 188–9).

Thonburi, Bangkok, and Songkhla

Siam, today's Thailand, has a long history of overland migration and trade with southwest China. Maritime trade and migration, on the other hand, is of more recent origin, beginning before the Yuan dynasty (1279–1368), and flourishing for more than five centuries spanning the

Ming and Qing dynasties (1368–1911). During most of this time, trade was carried out not only as part of a tributary system but also through the efforts of countless private traders who plied the waters in seagoing and coastal junks. The volume of trade was so great that many of these Chinese-style junks were actually built in Siam using locally available and superior teak timbers. Reciprocal trade between Siam and China— except for Siam's export of necessities such as rice, sugar, pepper, and woods—historically was in high-value luxury commodities: elephants' teeth, sapanwood (a medical plant and source of a reddish dye), deer hides, rhinoceros horns, sticklac resin, decorative birds' feathers, and birds' nests from Siam, in exchange for a range of chinaware and textiles, especially porcelain and silk, as well as other manufactured goods and foodstuffs from China.

By the end of the eighteenth century, an additional "commodity"— immigrant Chinese—from areas along the coasts of Fujian and Guang- dong began to scout, trade, and then settle in increasing numbers at various ports along the Gulf of Siam as well as spread into the interior. Irregularly shaped and approximately half the size of the Gulf of Mexico, the Gulf of Siam, which is a relatively shallow body of water that bleeds on its southern edge into the vast South China Sea, is bounded on three sides by land: the southern cape of Vietnam, coastal Cambodia, and the continental and peninsular portions of Siam/Thailand. An increasingly close relationship grew between Chinese merchants and Siamese aristocracy, who appointed some of the immigrants as tax farmers with monopoly rights in collecting birds' nests, tobacco, and other commodities in exchange for a payment of silver.

At the apex of the gulf, along the banks of the lower Chao Phraya River, Chinese merchants established trading posts and residences not only at the old imperial capital at Ayutthaya but also at its successor site downstream at Thonburi on the west bank, followed by Bangkok on

the east bank. The Siamese kingdom of Ayutthaya, which thrived from 1351 until it was destroyed by the Burmese in 1767, had a cosmopolitan capital city with a substantial Chinese immigrant population. After a lengthy siege, the grand city was burned to the ground, leaving no evidence of the residences, temples, markets, or shops of the Chinese who once lived there. Today, only magnificent stone and brick ruins remain to suggest its past splendor, much like Angkor to which it is often compared. In 1991 the Ayutthaya Historical Park was inscribed as a UNESCO World Heritage site. Muang Boran, an open-air museum some 33 kilometers east of Bangkok, which includes both reconstructed buildings and replicas, features many structures that display Chinese influences in their construction and ornamentation.

After the destruction of Ayutthaya, the new monarch, Taksin, shifted the capital 80 kilometers downstream to Thonburi, a move that brought in its wake the increasing in-migration of Chinese merchants to the new capital. Taksin, called Zheng Xin and Zheng Zhao in Chinese, was born in 1734 of a Chinese father and a Siamese mother. Taksin's father, who in Siam used the name Zheng Yong and Hai-Hong, had migrated to Ayutthaya from Chenghai in eastern Guangdong province. Conversant in the Chaozhou dialect as well as the Siamese language, Taksin served as monarch for fourteen years (1767–82). He is not only revered today in Thailand for his role in unifying Siam after the Burmese invasion, but is also celebrated in Chenghai, which takes great pride in being the ancestral home of a king of Siam. In 1782 some of Taksin's clothing was brought back to his father's ancestral village, Huafu, where the garments were buried in a tomb that is the focus of tourism today.

King Taksin built his Thonburi palace in 1768 on the west bank of the Chao Phraya River. The largest structure in the palace complex incorporates both a Siamese-style throne hall and a residence with many Chinese features. After King Rama I ascended the throne in 1782 and moved the capital across the river, Taksin's Thonburi palace became known as Phra Racha Wang Derm, and was used as a residence by royal family members. The Chinese-style residences that were built there between 1824 and 1851, while having undergone considerable renovation to become modern exhibition spaces, still have gables and roofs that evoke styles reminiscent of the Chaozhou region. In 2004 the complex won a UNESCO Asia-Pacific Heritage Award of Merit for its restoration. This royal site today serves also as the headquarters for the Royal Thai Navy.

Well into the twentieth century, Thonburi remained much less developed than Bangkok across the river, with which it merged as a metropolitan area only in 1972. Along both sides of the river, Chinese-style residences as well as those in more eclectic styles were sited adjacent to riverside rice mills, warehouses, and berths. Thonburi and Bangkok indeed were Chinese towns in a Siamese kingdom. The home

of Koh Hong Lee, the oldest rice milling Chinese family, is shown in an adjacent photograph. While this residence is no longer standing, there are a handful of nineteenth-century mansions that have, perhaps somewhat surprisingly, survived even as newer homes and commercial structures were built adjacent to them. Part Two focuses on two of these Chinese-style residences. One, which is known today as the Wanglee Mansion (pages 228–31), was identified in 1908 by Arnold Wright as the residence of Tan Lip Buoy, whose father had returned to Shantou, the port city for the Chaozhou region.

Not too far from the Wanglee mansion is the ancestral home of another Chaozhou immigrant family known today by the surname Poshyanonda, whose progenitor was Kim Lo Chair. Arriving in Siam from a village on the outskirts of Shantou sometime between 1824 and 1851, he initially lived on a wooden boat on the Chao Phraya River while supervising other Chinese workers. His home, which was constructed sometime during the last half of the nineteenth century, is a three-bay, single storey structure and a pair of flanking buildings. Known for its elaborately ornamented wooden components and friezes around its entry and two courtyards, the ornately carved and richly gilded triple altar is but one one of its most outstanding features.

A second featured home, which is located across the river in what is today Bangkok's Chinatown, was build in the late nineteenth century by Soa Hengtai, an immigrant from Fujian. Today, it is the home of Soa's descendants who have the Thai name Posayachinda (pages 222–7).

The narrow sea-flanked region known as peninsular Siam, which is washed on the east by the Gulf of Siam and on the west by the Andaman Sea, traditionally was a crossroads area in which Indian and Chinese traditions came into contact with each other. On the west coast of the peninsula is the coastal town of Ranong, which is said to have "looked and felt like a transplanted Fukkien village, with houses, shophouses, and temples" in the nineteenth century (Aasen, 1998: 169). Here, Khaw Soo Cheang, born in Zhangzhou, Fujian, in 1797, migrated first to Penang in the 1820s with only a carrying pole to start life as a coolie, before moving to Ranong farther up the peninsular where marriage and alliances set a foundation for economic success.

During the reign of King Rama III, in 1844, he was granted tin-mining rights and opium concessions, setting in train a veritable family dynasty that thrived until 1932. In 1854, under the patronage of a Siamese family, he became governor, as did his eldest son. All four sons prospered as able administrators. Khaw Sim Bee, who became one of Phuket's leading shipping and insurance magnates and was well known in Penang, is said to have traveled to the capital in 1901 where he "formally changed his nationality by going through the ceremony of having his queue cut off in the presence of a large gathering of princes and officials" (Campbell, 1902: 100). Although he married a Chinese

Enterprising merchants from China set up shops and warehouses that not only looked to the seas but also traded up and down the coast and rivers within a mercantile network of increasing complexity. Along a series of narrow streets lining the Thu Bon riverbank, which were intersected at right angles by slender lanes, a Chinese quarter soon emerged in Hoi An, complete with shophouses, merchant residences, temples, ancestral halls, guild halls, native place associations, pagodas, and tombs. By the end of the 1700s, however, as the estuary of the river silted up and as the port of Da Nang 30 kilometers to the north overtook it as the new center of overseas trade, Hoi An became a rather languid backwater. Yet, while entrepôt trade diminished at Hoi An, Chinese merchants from the Zhangzhou and Quanzhou areas of southern Fujian nonetheless continued to grow, diversify, and to some degree flourish. Intermarriage with local women was common (Wheeler 2001: 34, 168).

For the past 200 years, unlike so many other Vietnamese towns and cities that suffered the destruction of warfare, Hoi An remained relatively untouched. The overall street plan seen today is much as it was when the port developed centuries ago. One, one-and-a-half, and two storey shophouses as well as merchant terrace houses constructed of wood survive from the seventeenth and eighteenth centuries although many were reconstructed during the nineteenth century using brick as well as wood. Pastel-colored façades and rooflines are little changed from the past, and there is only limited evidence of modern materials like concrete and corrugated metal added to the old structures of wood and tile. At the end of September 2009, Typhoon Ketsana brought three-meter-deep flooding of filthy brown water to the historic areas of Hoi An, causing levels of destruction not experienced for decades.

woman from Penang, his family adopted the name Na Ranong, which today is known throughout Thailand. Khaw Sim Bee's introduction of rubber into southern Thailand helped transform the economy, just as it had earlier in British Malaya and in Sumatra. Only the pillars of the Khaw family residence are still standing in Ranong, and thus there is no full sense of its scale and style. On the other hand, the cemetery Khaw Soo Cheang established for his family, was laid out according to strict Chinese *fengshui* principals. After he died at the age of 86 in 1882, stone guardian figures and ornamented stelae were set in place to grace his gravesite. On the east side of the peninsula in Songkhla, another Fujian immigrant from Zhangzhou prospered under similar circumstances. Wu Rang, also known as Wu Yang, migrated in 1750. His descendants built a magisterial residence in 1878, which is featured in Part Two (pages 214–21), that surpasses any other Chinese-style structure in peninsular Siam. Their family, with the adopted surname Na Songkhla, is also well known throughout Thailand.

Vietnam

From the seventh to the tenth century, the Kingdom of Champa controlled not only what is known today as central and southern Vietnam but also the seaborne trade in spices, incense, silk, and ivory between China, India, Java, and as far west as the sprawling Abbasid Caliphate with its capital at Baghdad. Hoi An, the most important Champa entrepôt along the sea lanes of the South China Sea that stretched from coastal China to the Strait of Malacca, became during the seventeenth and eighteen centuries a cosmopolitan town for Chinese, Japanese, Indian, Portuguese, and Dutch merchants. Each of these nationalities left traces of their cross-cultural presence, including the well-known Japanese covered bridge, which was built in 1593.

Philippines

When the explorer Ferdinand Magellan, a Portuguese by birth sailing under the flag of Spain, anchored in the harbor at Cebu in 1521, his intent was to claim the land for the Spanish Crown and convert the people to the Roman Catholic faith. Magellan was killed in Cebu that same year and it was decades before other Spanish conquistadors vanquished native tribes, set up defensive settlements, initiated a flourishing trade network, and began the proselytizing of Catholicism across the sprawling archipelago. Magellan's initial discovery led to results that at the time could not easily have been foretold: East Asia's only Christian nation and one in which the blood of immigrants from China mixed with that of natives to create a vibrant and syncretic mestizo culture. In 1543 another explorer reached the islands, naming them Felipinas, the Philippines, to honor Crown Prince Don Felipe who later was to become Felipe II de España, the Spanish monarch Philip II.

During the more than three and a half centuries that the Philippines were a colony of Spain, the Spanish only found limited riches, unlike the riches they obtained in Mexico and Peru or the spices they had sought as they journeyed towards the East Indies. However, once the Spanish had established their capital at Manila, they recognized the profits that could be made from transshipping China's luxuries to Europe and from encouraging the immigration of Chinese laborers, traders, and artisans to the Philippines. From 1565 into the early decades of the nineteenth century, a far-flung and lucrative trading network using large sailing ships called galleons, sailed in convoys once or twice a year from Manila in Nueva España or New Spain and back. Chinese luxury goods such as porcelain, ivory, silk, precious stones, copper cash, mercury, and lacquerware, as well as spices from the Moluccas and elsewhere in the Nanyang, were amassed at Manila and then carried in galleons across the Pacific to Acapulco on Mexico's west coast. The sailing routes depended upon favorable winds for voyages that spanned a three or four month period. From Mexico the goods were carried overland to Vera Cruz for transshipment by sea, first to Cuba and then across the Atlantic Ocean to Spain in annual treasure ships. In exchange, vast quantities of Mexican and Peruvian silver were transported via the Philippines to China. The route across the Pacific Ocean made it possible for the Spanish to avoid a much longer and more dangerous voyage across the Indian Ocean and around Africa's Cape of Good Hope.

To facilitate this trade, the number of Chinese living in the Philippines, not counting transient merchants and traders, increased to more than 15,000 by the beginning of the seventeenth century (Schurz, 1939: 27). Until the 1750s, Chinese junks and Chinese traders were necessary to acquire, move, and dispose of cargo from China destined for Manila. Within the century afterwards, not only was Manila thriving but regional centers like Vigan and Cebu were also drawn into profitable trading system involving not only China but also the United States and England. Export commodities included items in great demand in China, such as mother-of-pearl, birds' nests, tortoiseshells, salted fish, ebony, rice, and black pepper, as well as those destined for markets beyond Asia: sugar, tobacco, coffee, and the newly popular fiber plant abaca. Well before Westerners took an interest in it, Chinese traders had sought out abaca, a light, strong, and durable plantain fiber used to make rope, string, fishing nets, and textiles. Grown only in the southern region of the Philippines, abaca, one of only a few economically important native plants in the islands, became the most important export product of the Philippines in the early twentieth century.

For much of the Spanish colonial period, Chinese immigrants were thought to be immune to conversion to Catholicism and other aspects of Hispanic culture, unlike the more receptive indigenous people. This led initially to cultural pluralism as an element of colonial policy in which there were distinct communities of Spaniards, Chinese immigrants, native *indios*, and mestizos of varied compositions. Over time, however, the differences became less distinct. During the Spanish colonial period, this tiered system of legal classification of different "races" was used for purposes of administration and taxation. Those of pure Chinese ancestry were called *sangley*, derived from the Chinese term *changlai* meaning "frequent visitor," or other terms. "Within a few years after the Spanish conquest, the relations between the Chinese and the Spaniards fell into a pattern of distrust and latent hostility" (Wickberg, 1965: 8). *Mestizo de sangley* was used to refer to persons of mixed Chinese and indigenous ancestry. Throughout the eighteenth and nineteenth centuries, the boundaries separating Spaniards, some of whom were actually of Mexican descent, Chinese *sangleys*, and native *indios* increasingly became blurred because of intermarriage and conversion. Accompanying these transformations was the rise of both pure Chinese and hispanized Chinese mestizos to economic and social prominence. The Spanish viewed the *sangleys* and Chinese *mestizo* as cultural minorities, yet the actual number of Chinese always exceeded the number of Europeans in the Philippines. Today, the word Tsinoy, also Chinoy, is the general term used to describe Filipinos with a Chinese heritage.

Discrimination, uprisings, and massacres of Chinese populate the historical narrative of the Philippines during the colonial period. In Manila, Chinese were controlled with the establishment of a distinct quarter called Parian, which was an enclave outside the walls of Intramuros, close enough for the Spanish to benefit from their labor yet sufficiently distant for the purposes of security. Non-Christian Chinese were forced to live in the Parian ghetto, and were only permitted through the Puarta del Parian, one of the seven gates into Intramuros. Although Parian also were created in other towns, Chinese traders and settlers were able to skirt the colonial efforts at controlling them by seeking

Below Cebu City's Calle Colon, which is named after the navigator Christopher Columbus, is said to date to 1565. In this photograph, taken in 1910, it is lined with wooden shophouses.

Right This late sixteenth-century painting indicates that the word *Sangley* comes from the Chinese word *changlai*, meaning "frequent visitor" in Hokkien.

opportunities throughout the archipelago, a dispersal that contributed to the emergence of the widespread *mestizo* culture that characterizes the Philippines.

Religious conversion of all those living in the Philippines to Catholicism was clearly an overall objective, a consequence of the close association of State and Church in the colonial enterprise. While some Chinese were receptive to the incorporation of elements of Catholicism into their own fundamental syncretic beliefs, others saw baptism as a "shrewd business move." "Besides reduced taxes, land grants, and freedom to reside almost anywhere, one acquired a Spanish godparent, who could be counted upon as a bondsman, creditor, patron, and protector in legal matters" (Wickberg, 1965: 16). The absence of Chinese women contributed to marriage with *indio* women and the

bearing of *mestizo* children. Raised by their *indio* mothers, children accepted Catholicism and perhaps even the Spanish language but without identifying themselves as "Spanish." Depending on the interest and efforts of their Chinese father, some of whom also maintained a family in China, attitudes and practices that were Chinese were consciously or subconsciously adapted by their children.

Unlike in the Dutch and English colonies farther south, Chinese in the Philippines did not establish the type of independent associations of kinsmen called *kongsi* that spurred the opening of tin mines and rubber plantations. Some Chinese gained wealth as recruiters of coolie laborers and as contractors for government monopolies, such as that controlling the importation and distribution of opium. Most, of course, merely maintained their families with modest incomes from small shops that retailed whatever was needed, or used their hands and simple tools to work tin, wood, leather, iron, among other materials, into useful and marketable objects Rather, Chinese in the Philippines principally acquired wealth through wholesale and retail trade.

A *bahay na bato* residence, which dates to 1830, is described on pages 240–7. Located in Vigan in the Ilocos region along the northwestern coast of Luzon, the Syquia mansion has a distinguished lineage and is maintained as a heritage residence in a town in which some Chinese immigrants who married local women from élite families established an upper-class lifestyle. A much smaller, simpler, and earlier residence, the Yap–Sandiego residence in Cebu, in the Visayan region of the central Philippines, is illustrated on pages 248–53. Resemblances among the eighteenth- and nineteenth-century *bahay na bato* as both residences and commercial establishments throughout the Philippines are well noted by Fernando N. Zialcita and Martin L. Tinio (1980: 29ff, 212ff).

Below Tjong A Fie, a worldly entrepreneur whose eclectic mansion for one of his families in Medan on Sumatra is featured in Part Two, constructed this manor near that of his brother for the family he maintained in China.

Bottom The fabled Nanyang Mandarin-capitalist Zhang Bishi/Cheong Fatt Tze, whose Blue Mansion is also featured in Part Two, built this expansive manor as his retirement home in his remote home-town village in eastern Guangdong. Sadly, he died while still abroad and never lived in the house.

Residences from the eighteenth and nineteenth centuries are not common in the Philippines, and many of those surviving from earlier times are deteriorating because of indifference and neglect. Those still standing have somewhat miraculously endured earthquakes and war, while now suffering the abuse of poor residents who know nothing of their historical significance. Wandering the crowded streets and side lanes of Binondo, it is easy to spot buildings with obvious historical character that have fallen into decay through lack of maintenance with only hasty repairs that are unsympathetic with the original character of the structures. Interest in preservation in the Philippines emphasizes monuments, landmarks, and historically important sites, including a wealth of ecclesiastical architecture of great significance. Interest in the preservation of common dwellings is only now emerging.

Overseas Chinese Houses in China

In villages throughout Fujian and Guangdong today, it is possible to see countless structures that affirm that Chinese who once emigrated from their home villages indeed were able to realize their dream of one day returning to build a grand residence, "a glorious homecoming in splendid clothes." While it is not possible to know with full assurance how many Chinese succeeded in returning, port records of departures and arrivals reveal that two-way traffic was often substantial. Today, websites in the *qiaoxiang*, "hometowns of Overseas Chinese," in Fujian and Guangdong, highlight many of the *Huaqiao guju*, "ancestral homes of Overseas Chinese," most of which were built in the hundred years between the middle of the nineteenth and twentieth centuries. Many are notable because they were built as *yanglou*, "foreign" in style, while most retained traditional characteristics.

Even prior to a majestic home being built by a returnee, remittances usually flowed back over decades to spouses and families that led to alterations and oftentimes expansion of the original homestead. Return visits, which were surprisingly frequent for some, provided opportunities to inject new ideas about domestic architecture and life in general that already were in flux. The multigenerational aspect of these changing circumstances is shown in the pages that follow. Virtually all of these emphasize the oft-repeated family narrative of a penniless migrant who labored abroad while accumulating meager savings, but who was able to return home and live in a sufficiently commodious grand residence that accommodated many generations, all hopefully living in harmony.

Below These are three of nine *diaolou* in Zili village, which sent migrants to the United States, Canada, Singapore, Malaysia, and Indonesia.

Right Among the most outstanding *dialou* is Ruishi Lou in Jinjiang village.

Opposite left Built between 1945 and 1949 as a retirement home by Gao Jingsheng, who had become wealthy in the Philippines, the residence was abandoned as the Communists came to power.

Bottom This expansive manor was constructed outside Shantou by Tan Yeok Nee, whose grand home still stands in Singapore and is shown in Part Two.

Opposite right The Yang family manor was built in Jinjiang, Fujin, to accommodate the families of six brothers who had become wealthy in the Philippines tobacco business.

For Overseas Chinese, nothing stated success and wealth more clearly than the construction of a grandiose residence that combined traditional elements with whatever ornamentation and furnishings were *au courant* and that spoke the language of modernity. From the first Opium War (1839–42) for more than a century, China endured an ongoing series of convulsions, some of which were cataclysmic, that impacted the ability of the wealthy to prosper and build fine homes: domestic upheaval during the Taiping Rebellion (1850–64), the disintegrating Qing imperial system and its failed efforts to save itself, the actual end of the imperial system in 1911, rampant warlordism in the 1920s, the global economic crisis in the decade after 1929, the Japanese invasion from 1937 to 1945, the establishment of the People's Republic in 1949, together with widespread unsettled conditions in the country, especially banditry.

During some short intervals and in isolated pockets, there sometimes was hope and optimism that the tide had changed that led to building boomlets. Partially completed homes from these periods still dot the countryside, which attest to dashed hopes and frustrated confidence. Sometimes hopefulness and optimism were accompanied by patriotic fervor on the part of Chinese who lived abroad, some of whom had the financial means to invest in railroads, real estate, factories, mines, schools,

banks, and other infrastructure projects that they believed would improve their homelands.

Four homes, which were built in China by Returned Overseas Chinese from Indonesia, the Philippines, and Thailand, are featured in Part Two. Chen Zihong built a mansion in Bangkok, Thailand (pages 228–31), and a retirement residence in Chaozhou, Guangdong (pages 262–7). The Qiu family, who prospered in Indonesia early in the twentieth century without building fine residences there, decided to take their wealth back to China where they built two adjacent, but very different, homes in the Meixian, Guangdong countryside over a prolonged period between 1914 and 1934 (pages 254–61). Dee C. Chuan (Li Qingquan) had palatial homes in the Philippines, where his business was centered, but they no longer exist. However, his grand home on Gulangyu Island, adjacent to Xiamen, which was completed in 1926, still stands and is discussed in Part Two (pages 268–73). Dee's interest in majestic architecture is also reflected in the towering three-storey mausoleum in Manila Chinese Cemetery that he had erected as his final home. Built in Art Deco style, with a double-tiered Chinese roof as well as interior and exterior Chinese ornamentation, his resting place has adjacent to it a residence for a full-time caretaker.

Two other prosperous merchants, Tan Yeok Nee in Singapore, and Cheong Fatt Tze in Penang, whose homes are featured in Part Two, built grand Chinese-style manors back in their home villages. Tan Yeok Nee, who was born in the Chaozhou region of Guangdong province, began in 1870 to build a manor and ancestral hall in his ancestral village in China as a place to which he hoped someday to retire. Construction there took until 1884 to be completed, just as his new Singapore home was finished. It is not clear when Tan returned to China, but he died there in 1902. He was saddened by the fact that his sons had predeceased him, although he had surviving grandsons. Cheong Fatt Tze, also known as Zhang Bishi, whose grand residence in Penang is described on pages 128–39, built a manor in his home village in Dabu county, Guangdong (pages 274–7), as well as a handful of other grand homes throughout his trading empire, including in Batavia and Hong Kong. He was an inveterate traveler as he visited his eight wives and families. In 1916, after his death in Batavia in the Netherlands Indies, his body was returned to his native village in China for burial.

Perhaps the most extravagant and exceptional collection of the residences of Returned Overseas Chinese are those found just four hours by boat from Hong Kong. Here, in the Pearl River Delta of western Guangdong province, in the Siyi (*sze yap* in Cantonese) area—Four Districts of Kaiping, Taishan, Xinhui and Enping—was a major center of Chinese emigration across the Pacific to the United States and Canada as well as Southeast Asia. Nearly 2,000 multistoried residence towers, known as *diaolou*, survive in this area from the 1920s and 1930s, a time of great disorder, including banditry, abductions, murders, and kidnappings. Constructed of reinforced concrete, with walls some 40 centimeters thick and iron bars and shutters on windows, the towers provided a level of security that exceeded that of other traditional defensive structures. Several of the finest and most fanciful examples

of *dialou*, built by returnees from the United States, reveal similarities and differences with those constructed in other *qiaoxiang* by returnees from Southeast Asia.

Two examples of the many villas built in the area south of Quanzhou in Fujian province by Returned Overseas Chinese from the Philippines are Yangjia dalou, the Yang family manor, and Jingsheng bieshu, the Jingsheng villa. Little is known of the families that built these expansive homes except they both made their fortunes in the tobacco business in Luzon, the Philippines. The Yang family manor includes a late nineteenth-century building that faces the more dramatic twentieth-century structure called Liuye ting, "The Pavilion for Six," which is said to have been built with more than 170 rooms to house the families of six brothers. Gao Jingsheng built Jingsheng villa between 1946 and 1949 during a period of transition in China. With the defeat of the Japanese in 1945, a civil war raged between the Nationalists and the Communists from 1945 to 1949. When the Communists gained control of Fujian in 1949, defeating the retreating Nationalists, Gao Jingsheng abandoned his new home and returned to the Philippines. For much of the following half century, the residence remained empty, suffering little damage except for Great Proletarian Cultural Revolution slogans.

Those homes built in China by Returned Overseas Chinese in the twentieth century underscore the fervor of their attachment to the native soil of their ancestral homeland and the enduring dream of multigenerational residency, a large family living together. Most of their residences incorporate Chinese as well as Western elements and thus are more than mere *yanglou*. While there are clearly conservative building elements and practices, it is easy also to see innovative and foreign aspects. The willingness to use modern construction materials, even when they needed to be imported, was accompanied by a willingness to adapt to changing fashions and evolving aesthetic preferences.

PART TWO

CHINESE HERITAGE HOUSES
of Southeast Asia

HEEREN STREET SHOPHOUSE

MALACCA, MALAYSIA

Late 1700s

Not all of the homes built and/or lived in by Chinese are grand structures that epitomize economic success or celebrate prosperity. Most Chinese migrants and their descendants lived modestly in common dwellings, types which have not been presented in this book either because of their ubiquity or rarity. Indeed, even those whose family narrative is one of rags-to-riches over several generations most likely lived once in a simple dwelling, sometimes no more than a cot in the back of a shop or in simple quarters for coolies and laborers. Surviving examples of such common structures from the distant past are exceedingly rare, not only because of their relatively ephemeral nature but also because little attention was ever paid to their preservation. It is clear that the demise of old shophouses and their replacement with more modern forms diminishes the historical record of life in the past. Fortunately, for those who value a comprehensive view of a community's

heritage, great efforts were expended in recent years in restoring a common shophouse in Malacca that dates to the late 1700s.

Somehow surviving through many periods of cataclysmic change, this early shophouse has undoubtedly served many purposes—shop, residence, storehouse, dormitory, stable, among other possibilities—and may have been occupied at various times by members of any of Malacca's multinational residents—indigenous Malays as well as immigrants who arrived over the centuries from China, Portugal, the Netherlands, and Britain. In terms of its layout and construction, the building indeed reveals cultural mixing that is consistent with Malacca's multicultural heritage. It embodies a layering of form and function from an earlier time while representing one stage in the evolutionary process of a streetscape from earlier structures of timber and thatch to more permanent buildings of brick and tile. Much of the attention given to

Left The horizontal wooden shutters not only could secure the building at night, the lower one could be propped up and used as a display shelf for the sale of goods. The woven screen blocked passersby from viewing life inside the building.

Below Divided door panels, usually called "Dutch doors" in the West, are also forms found locally in southern China.

Opposite Dwarfed by the adjacent later styles, this pair of historically significant two-storey eighteenth-century shophouses is owned by the Cheng Hoon Teng Temple in Malacca.

Previous pages A detail of the upper façade of the Cheong Fatt Tze blue mansion in Penang (page 128).

this modest shophouse underscores the presence of purported Dutch aspects, yet most of these same elements would have been familiar to Chinese craftsmen because they were also present in their home villages and towns in southern China. Thus, it is likely—but by no means knowable with certainty—that Chinese masons and carpenters, who probably built the structure, even if under contract to a Dutch owner, would have felt quite comfortable with the forms that emerged.

Known today simply by its address—No. 8 Heeren Street—the restored shophouse is located not too far from the quays where boats of various sizes were loaded and unloaded in times past. What type of uses the small building was put to over the years is not known, but for fifty years in the twentieth century, from 1938 through 1989, it served as a *kuli keng*, which in Hokkien literally means "the quarters where coolies live." The materials used in its construction were wood for the doors and windows, including the shutters, the staircase, the balustrades for the balcony, and the upstairs flooring, in addition to the battens supporting the roof tiles; clay for bricks and tiles, laterite blocks for the foundations, and lime-based plaster for the walls. There is essentially no applied ornamentation and no way to determine how families in the past might have decorated their humble home.

This modest two-storey building has a narrow façade similar to that of its neighbor, approximately 4 meters wide, and a depth of 26 meters. Both buildings are set back from the street and have an overhanging

tile-faced shed roof covering what, under other circumstances, might be a called a front porch. Here, however, the sheltered space is actually an extension of what would have been a shop inside. The wooden entryway is a door divided into two parts so that the bottom half could be shut while the top half was left open. Doors of this type in America are called "Dutch doors" since they are said to have been "invented" in the Netherlands in the 1600s and then introduced by the Dutch in their American colonies. Yet, divided doors have a long history of use in common homes throughout southern China in both urban and rural areas. The wooden shutters covering the large horizontal window that runs across the front wall open in two sections, the larger of which, when secured, provides a broad shelf that could be used to display goods for sale. One sees today a woven screen that blocks passersby from viewing the inside, a utilitarian addition when the building was used as a residence but not particularly useful when it served as a shop. This type of shutter-shelf can still be seen in front of shops in small towns and villages in southern China. The upper portion of the wooden shutter is held in place with two hooks to completely open the front. If desired, the larger bottom shutter can be latched closed, leaving the narrower upper portion open for ventilation and privacy. A single two-shutter wooden window provides light and air for the bedroom on the second floor.

The layout of the interior includes a front room, which could serve as shop or residential space, with a smaller room behind it. Beyond is an area that Chinese call a *tianjing* or skywell, sometimes also called an airwell or lightwell, which is a roofless void form that rises through both storeys to ventilate and bring light into the interior. While rainwater falling into the void could be collected as needed, the building also included a well, which was shared through the party wall of the neighboring structure. Although the Dutch did not have skywells as part of their own architectural tradition, they adapted the form in

various parts of their empire, carrying it with them as they spread their sphere of influence. Set off to the side is a wooden staircase that leads to a balustraded balcony. A small kitchen and even smaller *tianjing* are found in the rear of the building. The second floor provides ample space for bedrooms.

Held in trust by the Cheng Hoon Teng Temple, Malaysia's oldest Chinese temple, which acquired No. 8 Heeren Street as a donation from Tjan Tian Quee sometime before the Second World War, the restoration of this Dutch-era shophouse was initiated in 2001 by Badan Warisan Malaysia (Heritage of Malaysia Trust). In addition to restoring a unique building representative of Malacca's early built heritage, which had become essentially a derelict structure at the end of the twentieth century, the project was designed to demonstrate the value of "how early shophouses can be restored to high levels of authenticity yet also be adapted successfully to new uses" (Badan Warisan Malaysia, 2005). Substantial funding was provided by the US Ambassador's Fund for Cultural Preservation and the Ford Foundation ("Historical Discovery").

Opposite above A small storage area beneath the plain stairway that leads to the second level.

Opposite below left The semicircular half of a well that was located as part of the skywell so that it could be shared through the party wall of the neighboring shophouse.

Opposite below right This view across the skywell reveals the gallery-like passageways on the second level.

Top The upstairs room, which was once perhaps a bedroom, enjoys wooden shutters, latticed panels, and the adjacent skywell that together underscore the attention paid to ventilation.

Above left A view of the height of the original low roofline. At some point, the roof was raised.

Above center This cut-away section through the lime-based plaster exposes the original brick bonding pattern of the original wall.

Above right One of the iron nails and two bricks uncovered during restoration work.

TAN CHENG LOCK RESIDENCE

MALACCA, MALAYSIA

Late 1700s with subsequent changes

One residence along Malacca's Heeren Street, today renamed Jalan Tun Tan Cheng Lock, provides an opportunity to unravel on a different scale some of the many layers of history and culture that have enlivened Malacca over the past three centuries. Tan Cheng Lock, a fifth-generation descendant of an eighteenth-century immigrant from China and a distinguished twentieth-century statesman whose leadership led to the establishment of an independent Malaysia upon the departure of the British, was born in 1883 at No. 59 Heeren Street. This residence had been acquired in 1875 by his grandfather, Tan Choon Bock, who willed it on his death in 1880 to Tan Keong Ann, his son and Tan Cheng Lock's father. No reason is given in the grandfather's will as to why the house was granted to the third son rather than his elder brother. In the preceding eight decades, the residence had passed through numerous hands before coming into the ownership of the Tan family, who have continued to maintain it for nearly a century and a half since then as their "ancestral" home. Today, the residence, renumbered No. 111, is important not only for its age and layered provenance but also for its historic association with an important man and his family.

Surviving probate records show that there was already a residence on this site in 1797, and extant title deeds, which are remarkable in their detail, trace each of the transfers during the nineteenth century. In 1801 the widow of Daniel Roetenbeek, Silviana de Graca, inherited the property upon his death, and then in 1804 gave the property to her son-in-law, Johann Anton Neubronner, a German, whose widow then inherited the property in 1815. It was owned by the Neubronner family until 1849 when the home was bought at auction by a Chinese named Yeo Hood In, a Malacca-born property owner then living in Singapore. The house was then resold in 1864 to Tan Loh Seng. In 1875, as mentioned above, the property was purchased by Tan Choon Bock, who had become quite wealthy as a pioneer in the tapioca and gambier business as well as being the founder of a major steamship company.

This date, 1875, is fully a hundred years after the arrival of Tan Hay Kwan, an immigrant from Nanjing county in Zhangzhou prefecture near the port of Xiamen in Fujian province, who is the progenitor of the

Previous pages The Tan Cheng Lock residence shares an architectural style with a building on its left. Both were built at the same time and were likely originally owned by a single family, who later sold the units to different families.

Left A close-up of the painting above the altar showing General Guan Gong, who is said to personify many virtues—courage, honor, integrity, justice, loyalty, and strength—and Zhang Fei, another loyal warrior and his comrade of the Three Kingdoms period.

Below Dominating the entrance hall is an altar table with images of various deities as well as a painting of Guan Gong and Zhang Fei. The characters *yiqi* above the altar translate as "righteousness."

lineage that was to produce Tan Cheng Lock. As a trader with his own junk who followed the alternating seasonal winds of the monsoon from his base in Malacca, Tan Hay Kwan's commercial activity ranged widely, to Makassar in the Celebes, Bandjarmasin in Borneo, Rhio at the tip of the Malay Peninsula, nearby Penang and distant Australia, as well as the southeast coast of China (Agnes Tan Kim Lwi, 2006: 2; Tan Siok Choo, 1981: 20). Nothing is known of Tan Hay Kwan's residence in Malacca or elsewhere, nor that of his son, nor even the home or homes that Tan Choon Bock lived in before 1875 when he purchased the late eighteenth-century property we now regard as the family's ancestral home. Indeed, throughout the nineteenth century, affluent Peranakans, the offspring of Chinese and indigenous marriages, as well as recent arrivals from China who had the financial wherewithal, purchased many of the old Dutch merchant residences in Kampung Belanda (Dutch Village), thus transforming the area into a veritable Chinatown that has endured to the present day. There are no formal records of what renovation or rebuilding took place over these decades along the streets of the old Dutch town. Physical evidence, however, provides proof that some houses were merged and expanded. Others were modified in one way or other to accommodate family and commercial needs as well as carriages and horses.

Those writing about the old residences in Malacca sometimes point to purported Dutch architectural influences, perhaps to provide incontrovertible "proof" of Dutch origins and dates for buildings. These include the use of iron wall-anchors, archways, stone corbels,

Above The spacious vestibule-like sitting room is just beyond the entrance hall. While the tables and chairs in this room are Western in style, the wall decorations are all Chinese. The embroidered wall hanging with figures representing the Three Stellar Gods, Fu, Lu, and Shou—Good Fortune, Emolument, and Longevity—was given to Tan Cheng Lock's son, Tan Siew Sin, on the occasion of a birthday.

Right On the right is one of a pair of lattice windows that act as a screen filtering the view through the doors from the entrance hall into the interior. Circular stairs to the second floor rise within the alcove.

Far right An assemblage of deities on the altar table.

fired bricks and roof tiles, recessed cupboards, even steep staircases (De Witt, 2007: 145–9). While Dutch building traditions very well may have employed them, most of these architectural elements also have been a part of the repertoire of building practices in southern China, not only with residences but also with temples and palaces. Traditional masons and carpenters in China and those who migrated, as with vernacular builders elsewhere in the world, were fundamentally pragmatists who would alter their materials and methods to meet local conditions. In Malacca, it is certain that the inherited building conventions brought from the varied homelands of immigrants, including Dutch and Chinese, were adapted to local conditions, factors that were facilitated by the overlap of common ways of doing things. Moreover, as wealthy Chinese acquired older homes once occupied by the Dutch and other Europeans, they frequently employed craftsmen from China to make modifications that expressed not only the practical needs of the Chinese occupants but also to embellish them with the types of calligraphic and pictographic ornamentation found in finer homes in China. In addition, Peranakan culture thrived in the fine residences along Heeren Street as the Victorian era came to an end, a time when new layers began to be added to the homes that not long before had been dressed in Chinese adornment. Now, floor and wall tiles imported from England, mirrors and glass from Italy, prints and objets d'art from throughout Europe, and furniture of many styles, including the increasingly popular Peranakan brown-and-gold carved teak furniture gilded in gold leaf, which was made locally rather than imported, were added. Even as these changes in the material culture of the residences were taking place, the observance

of Chinese rituals continued during annual celebrations such as the New Year and the festivals related to rituals for the dead, such as Qingming (Clear and Bright) on the fifteenth day after the vernal equinox, and Zhongyuan (Hungry Ghost Festival) on the fifteenth day of the seventh lunar month.

Isabella Bird, the noted Victorian globetrotter who visited Malacca in the late 1870s, caught glimpses of the rising prominence of Chinese families, a milieu that Tan Cheng Lock was born into (1883: 133):

And it is not, as elsewhere, that they come, make money, and then return to settle in China, but they come here with their wives and families, buy or build these handsome houses, as well as large bungalows in the neighbouring coco-groves, own most of the plantations up the country, and have obtained the finest site on the hill behind the town for their stately tombs. Every afternoon their carriages roll out into the country, conveying them to their substantial bungalows to smoke and gamble. They have fabulous riches in diamonds, pearls, sapphires, rubies, and emeralds. They love Malacca, and take a pride in beautifying it. They have fashioned their dwellings upon the model of those in Canton, but whereas cogent reasons compel the rich Chinaman at home to conceal the evidences of his wealth, he glories in displaying it under the security of British rule. The upper class of the Chinese merchants live in immense houses within walled gardens. The wives of all are secluded, and inhabit the back regions and have no share in the remarkably "good time" which the men seem to have.

"Many of the women who lived there vied with each other for the distinction of having the finest set of jewellery, the most exquisite clothes, the best *nyonya* ware, and the most magnificent furniture. They also tried to out-do each other in culinary skills and beadwork—both attributes for every *nyonya* girl" (Tan Siok Choo, 1983: 51). Today, visitors to Malacca can experience this culture by visiting the private Baba-Nyonya Heritage Museum outfitted in an adjacent pair of nineteenth-century terrace houses. Once homes of prominent families, some properties have been refashioned as boutique hotels—Hotel Puri and Baba House Hotel—where visitors can experience the richness of Peranakan culture. Along the street is a smaller but well-restored old terrace house that has been elegantly transformed into a bed-and-breakfast called The Snail House.

Tan Cheng Lock, the Man

Tan Cheng Lock is best known in Malaysia as a statesman because of the prominent role he played with other political leaders such as Tunku Abdul Rahman and V. T. Sambanthan in negotiating independence from the British, his promotion of Malaysia as a multiethnic state, and as the founder and first president of the Malayan Chinese Association. The Tan ancestral home was the venue for much discussion about issues relating to obtaining independence from the British.

A true son of Malacca, Tan attended Malacca High School, an English-medium institution established in 1826 after the Dutch ceded the city to the British, before furthering his education at the Raffles Institution Singapore. After graduating, even before turning twenty, he was invited to

Above Tan Cheng Lock's study is aligned along a wall adjacent to the skywell, with a plaque proclaiming "Honor Results from Actual Achievements."

Left An elaborate ornamental lattice screen runs from wall to wall between the skywell and the ancestral hall.

Opposite above Punctured by a rectangular skywell, a shaft that reaches up through the second storey, this bright space is filled with pots of ornamental palms of various sizes. The elongated wall is covered with historic photographs and horizontal commendation plaques.

stay on and teach young boys at the Raffles Institution. As one of the few Chinese in the Straits Settlements with a Cambridge School Certificate, he was a voracious reader of European literature, philosophy, and history, as well as translations into English of books about Chinese culture. Although he taught at Raffles Institution from 1902 to 1908, "he was out of his depth teaching unruly schoolboys," according to his daughter Agnes, and was urged by his mother to look for a future in rubber, a crop and industry that in time was to flourish in British Malaya (Agnes Tan Kim Lwi, 2006: 2). With the help of his cousin as well as close friend and businessman, Chan Kang Swi, Tan Cheng Lock created several firms that ran labor-intensive plantations of the *Hevea brasiliensis* or rubber tree, which produced the seemingly magical elastic latex called "rubber." Commercial planting of rubber trees had only begun in the Malay States

in 1895, with soaring expansion of acreage between 1905 and 1911 to meet increasingly robust world markets, just when Tan Cheng Lock was seeking a new challenge. The United Malacca Rubber Estates, which was established in 1910, brought him some prominence, and he was appointed in 1912 as a member of the Malacca Municipal Council by the British authorities. In time, his involvement in social issues ranged from condemning the use of opium, a major source of revenue for the British in Asia, and countering the common Chinese practice of polygamy by encouraging monogamous marriages.

In 1913, at the age of thirty, Tan Cheng Lock married Yeo Yeok Neo, an heiress whose father had arranged the union. Tan Cheng Lock and his wife had five children, a son and four daughters. Tan Siew Sin, Tan Cheng Lock's only son, who was born in the Heeren Street family home

Top left Lee Seck Bin, Tan Cheng Lock's mother, who recognized her son's un-happiness as a teacher and urged him to consider venturing into the rubber business where he thrived.

Top right Late nineteenth-century photograph of Tan Keong Ann, Tan Cheng Lock's father, who is shown here wearing a mixture of clothing, including a Chinese-style jacket, a Western-style fedora and leather shoes.

Left Wearing Malay attire, Tan Cheng Lock is standing with his only son and three daughters.

Right With a three-character board above it proclaiming "Hall of Filiality," the Tan family ancestral altar holds the ancestral tablets of three genera-tions, including Tan Cheng Lock and his wife, Tan's parents and their son, Tan Siew Sin. Above the altar is the ancestral portrait of Lee Chye Neo, the wife of the progenitor Tan Hay Kwan. On the left wall are images of Tan Cheng Lock's grandparents. The furni-ture, brought from Hong Kong on the occasion of daughter Lily's wedding in 1935, is a mixture of traditional Chinese forms with Western elements.

Tan Tan Cheng Lock with his son, Tan Tan Siew Sin and daughters, Lily, Alice and Agnes

in 1916, also became a distinguished public servant, serving as Malaya's first Minister of Commerce and Industry before becoming Malaysia's first Minister of Finance from 1959 to 1974. Four daughters, Lily (Tan Kim Tin), Nellie (Wee Geok Kim), Alice (Tan Kim Yoke), and Agnes (Tan Kim Lwi), were born into the household. Tan Cheng Lock's attention to the teachings of Confucius is well known, especially the emphasis on the filial duty of remembering ancestors through periodic ritual. Even with Tan Cheng Lock's business and political careers underway, according to his granddaughter, he was "relieved of the necessity of having to earn money in less salubrious ways, … [and] set about increasing his wife's inheritance" (Tan Siok Choo, 1981: 24). Because of his civic activity, he was appointed an unofficial member of the Legislative Council of the Straits Settlements in 1926, and in 1933 a member of the Executive Council of that body.

Tan Cheng Lock, the Residence

The Tan Cheng Lock ancestral residence is a notable structure replete with furnishings, ornamentation, and memorabilia that declare his appreciation and understanding of the several cultures within which he lived. Although Tan Cheng Lock could neither speak nor read the Chinese language, his home celebrates the power of the written word in Chinese culture and gives evidence of the high regard in which the Chinese community in pre- and post-independence Malaysia held him. The ground plan of his residence, approximately 10 meters by 68 meters, is similar to those of other larger houses along the seaside section of Heeren Street. Set back from the street, the two-storey façade is separated by a shed-like roof that creates a streetside veranda paved with large

terracotta tiles, a passageway known as a five-foot way and a requirement imposed by British planners. This type of setback with a veranda is not common in China. Just inside the double-paneled entryway is an entrance hall dominated by a high rectangular altar table accompanied by a square offerings table. Both of these are set in the central portion of a wall that has doorways on both sides. Formal sets of chairs and tables line the walls. Couplets and auspicious four-character phrases adorn the room. The two-character phrase *yiqi*, meaning "Righteousness," is hung just below the ceiling and above an old painting of the Daoist deity General Guan Gong, also known as Guan Yu, who is said to personify many virtues—courage, honor, integrity, justice, loyalty, and strength— and Zhang Fei, another loyal warrior and his comrade of the Three Kingdoms period. A wooden panel on a stand has images of all Three Brothers of the Peach Orchard, Guan Gong, Zhang Fei, and Liu Bei, who were celebrated in the *Romance of the Three Kingdoms* as individuals who shared a desire to serve their country in difficult times. Two large paintings and calligraphic hangings, which face each other across the room, add both formality and brightness to the space.

Just beyond the doors is a spacious vestibule-like sitting room with a round marble-topped table. While the furniture in this room is Western in style, the wall decorations are all Chinese. Of particular note is a large celebratory piece of embroidery that was given to Tan Cheng Lock's only son, Tan Siew Sin, on the occasion of one of his birthdays. At the center of the piece and along the top are figures representing the Three Stellar Gods, Fu, Lu, and Shou—Good Fortune, Emolument, and Longevity— together with an unidentified woman, perhaps an attendant. Arrayed along the sides are the Eight Immortals.

A pair of beautiful lattice windows acts as a screen filtering the view through the doors from the entrance hall into the interior areas. A central door then leads from the sitting room into an elongated room punctured by a rectangular skywell, a shaft that reaches up through the second storey. This bright space is today filled with pots of ornamental

palms of various sizes. An informal setting of a table with four light chairs contrasts with the rows of formal hardwood chairs that stand along the walls. Throughout this area the walls are covered with historic photographs and horizontal commendation plaques. On the right, tucked into an alcove and reached through an archway, is a spiral stair-case leading to the second level. A study with a desk and bookcases filled with classic texts is aligned along a wall adjacent to the skywell. Above the desk is a commendation plaque presented to Tan Cheng Lock proclaiming "Honor Results from Actual Achievements." A fine example of a Milners Patented Fire Resisting safe stands beside the desk. On top of the safe is a signed photograph presented by Chiang Kai-shek to Tan Cheng Lock in 1940, which is propped up by a bust of Robert Baden-Powell, the founder of the Boy Scout movement in 1907.

Just beyond the first skywell is an ornamental lattice screen running from wall to wall that frames a sitting room dominated by the Tan family ancestral altar with three characters, *xiaosi tang*, meaning Hall of Filiality, on a horizontal board above it. The three ancestral tablets, also called ancestral soul tablets, within the receptacle are those of Tan Keong Ann and his wife Lee Sek Bin; the ancestral soul tablet of Tan Cheng Lock and his wife Yeo Yeok Neo, and at the lowest level, the ancestral soul tablet of Tan Siew Sin. Above the altar is the ancestral portrait of Lee Chye Neo, the wife of the progenitor Tan Hay Kwan. On the left wall are images of Tan Cheng Lock's grandparents, Tan Choon Bock and Thung Soon Neo, in frames with oval mounts, while on the right wall are pastel portraits of Tan Cheng Lock's parents, Tan Keong Ann and Lee Seck Bin. The furniture in this room, which mixes traditional Chinese forms with Western elements, includes low-back armchairs and settees made of *hongmu* with marble inserts. The furniture was brought from Hong Kong on the occasion of daughter Lily's wedding in 1935. Each of the settees has three marble inserts in the shape of a peach, a symbol of longevity. On the side walls, each with an elaborate framed mirror and among the photographs of family members are paintings and four

Below The master bedroom facing the street has circular ventilation ports along the top register of the wall. The Art Deco furniture was purchased in London for the marriage of Tan Cheng Lock's daughter Lily in 1935.

Above right The second floor sitting room showing a doorway into the bedroom. Above each window is a painting of a fruit with symbolic associations: on the left is an odd fruit called *foshou* or "Buddha's Hand," whose names is homophonous with good fortune and longevity; on the right is a pomegranate with its red seeds exposed that expresses the meaning of abundant posterity.

horizontal commendation plaques presented to Tan Siew Sin with celebratory phrases: "Benefit the Country and Workers," "Carrying a Heavy Responsibility Over a Long Period," "Pillar of the Nation," and "Merit is in Educating the Young."

Prior to the Second World War, the formal space housing the ancestral soul tablets marked the boundary between the public and private areas of the residence. Non-family members rarely were permitted to go beyond the formal halls and single skywell in the residence. The doorway on the left side of the altar leads to a small bedroom, which was created by adding a wall to a wider open area, which then became a narrower passageway. Within this small room is a cupboard that is identical to one along the wall of the passageway on the right. Beyond this passageway are the two remaining skywells, spaces for family dining and informality. In these areas, as with the other skywell in the front, it was possible also to capture and store rainwater. While most houses on Heeren Street in the past had two wells, the Tan household only had one and that was located in a bathroom. Both of the skywells today are landscaped with abundant greenery. Looking up, one sees the louvered windows that can be opened on the second level. Just below the louvered panels is a geometric ornamental panel with duplicated representations of the running *wan* character, an inverted swastika meaning "longevity." Two bathrooms, a pantry, and a kitchen

are also found in this area in addition to a steep staircase leading upstairs. In a circular masonry planter in the third skywell is a tall *jambu* tree with evergreen leaves that produces a red bell-shaped edible fruit called *lianwu* in Chinese and wax apple in English. Family lore recalls that this thriving and productive tree was planted when Tan Cheng Lock was born. At the far rear end of the house is a second dining area and a terrace, which early on had been the place where children ate. In recent years, this space was renovated as a two-level apartment for a housekeeper and her children. When the residence was built early in the nineteenth century, this rear area extended out over the sea below and was supported by pilings. A trapdoor in the wooden floorboards could be lifted for reaching a small boat moored below. In the nineteenth century, the area began to be silted up and in recent decades infilling was accelerated that pushed the shoreline some 200 meters away from the old houses.

The upstairs area covers fully two-thirds of the ground floor, with two of the skywells opening up the rooms on that level as well. This private area has two large bedrooms with adjacent sitting rooms. Until Tan Cheng Lock's daughter Lily was married in April 1935, the front bedroom had been the bedroom of his younger brother, Cheng Juay and his wife. In preparation for the marriage, fashionable new furniture for the bridal chamber was brought from London via Singapore.

Unlike Chinese custom where the daughter-in-law generally married in to the home of her husband, Tan Cheng Lock and his wife Yeo Teok Neo chose to follow local Baba custom of matrilocal residence and live with *her* mother, Yeo Tin Hye, in Tranquerah. This continued even after the birth of their eldest daughter Lily. Their son Siew Sin and daughters Alice and Agnes, however, lived at the ancestral residence on Heeren Street with their grandparents, Tan Keong Ann and Lee Seck Bin, as well as with Cheng Juay, Tan Cheng Lock's younger brother and his wife. Nellie, the second daughter, was adopted at birth by Tan Cheng Lock's sister, who was childless. Living arrangements such as this met practical considerations and revealed the strength and flexibility of an extended family. Meanwhile, Lee Seck Bin, the matriarch, urged her husband to find a larger house that all could live in. Such a house was found six kilometers north of Heeren Street in Klebang Besar facing the Strait of Malacca. After 1947, when Tan Siew Sin married Catherine Lim Cheng Neo, this became the home in which he raised his three daughters. Today, along Jalan Klebang bordering the sea one can still see some of the large mansions built by prominent Peranakan families at the turn of the twentieth century.

Left Portrait of Tan Choon Bock, Tan Cheng Lock's grandfather.

CHEE MANSION

MALACCA, MALAYSIA

1906

The façades of old buildings along Heeren Street in Malacca generally share a number of common features: white lime-washed two- or three-storey structures, each with a gently sloping shed-like roof over a passageway forming either a private veranda or a five-foot passageway. The ancestral home of Tan Cheng Lock (pages 46–57) is a fine example of such a terrace house. Punctuating this harmonious succession of townhouses is a fanciful three-storey building that is set back from the street with a watchtower-like pinnacle atop it. While often called the Chee Mansion, the four characters across the doorway today proclaim that it is the Chee Family Ancestral Hall, commemorating a lineage whose ancestor, Chee Soo Sum, arrived in Malacca in the second half of the eighteenth century from Zhangzhou in China's Fujian province. Ancestral halls of this type are called by Peranakan *rumah abu*, a loan word from Malay. On the front gate there is a four-letter monogram, CYCT, set within concentric circles, standing for "Chee Yam Chuan Temple." These initials highlight the fact that the shrine does not reach back to the *kaijizu* or focal (founding) ancestor of the Chee lineage, Chee Soo Sum, but instead to his great-grandson, Chee Yam Chuan, the most notable forebear in the lineage.

Chee Yam Chuan (Xu Yanquan) was born in Malacca in 1819 and died tragically in 1862 from an assassin's bullet at a wedding dinner in Malacca (Hamidah, 2000). During his short life, he became, at twenty-one, the head of the Hokkien *huiguan* in Malacca and amassed a substantial fortune from investments in the economic development of Malaya. Since the Hokkien *huiguan* was a veritable Chamber of Commerce of Malacca's business interests, Chee Yam Chuan was, in effect, the leader of the community of all immigrants and their descendants from Fujian. His rise to such a position may have come about because of the death of his father the year before, in 1839, who himself was an important merchant and civic leader in Malacca. Known as a planter of nutmeg in both Malacca and Singapore, Chee Yam Chuan amassed sufficient resources to advance capital for investment in the tin mining industry in the Lukut district of southern Selangor. He was noted for the partnership he had with two Malay princes, Raja Juma'at and his brother Raja Abdullah, loaning them substantial sums in return for shares of profits in their tin mining ventures. A further indication of

Previous pages Set back from the street with a row of trees lining its approach, the tiered and ornate Chee Mansion serves as a memorial hall for the family.

Left The entry hall reaches from front to back with rooms opening along both sides.

Top The arched front doorway is emblazoned with four characters indicating the Chee (Xu) Family Ancestral Hall.

Above The rear doorway is even more elaborate in style than the front entry.

Right Looking up through the atrium-like stairwell.

their mutual trust was that Raja Juma'at's son moved to Malacca to live with Chee Yam Chuan in order to facilitate contact with other Malays eager to solicit capital from Chinese merchants. His success at amassing investment capital contributed, some historians believe, to quickening the clearing of the jungle and the development of Kuala Lumpur as a prosperous town (Andaya and Andaya, 1982: 139). In 1848 Chee Yam Chuan and several other prominent businessmen figured prominently in the restoration of the Cheng Hoon Teng Temple, the oldest Chinese temple in Malaysia, which dates from 1645.

Chee Yam Chuan had ten sons and an unknown number of daughters, whose families have flourished, increasing significantly over the next six generations to the present. His grandson Chee Swee Cheng, together with Chee Yam Chuan's sons Chee Lim Bong and Chee Quee Bong, all of whom were successful businessmen in Singapore, conceived the idea of building an ancestral home in 1906 to venerate Chee Yam Chuan. This was a time, as is discussed in other chapters of the book, of a resurgence of Chinese culturalism, a renaissance of an awareness of Chinese values such as filial piety, especially among those educated in Western schools who considered themselves worldly and cosmopolitan. It was in this context that an extravagantly Western-style building was built to venerate a Chinese forebear, creating a place for an ancestral altar for the tablets of successive generations of Chees. Furnished with chairs, tables, cabinets, screens, and ornaments imported from China, this grand building declared that the Chee family gained strength from a fusion of their Chinese and European heritages. From time to time

over the years, Chee family members have lived in the house, most recently during the renovation of a neighboring terrace house, but the expressed function of this opulent structure was to acknowledge their ancestors with regular offerings and to assert their broader familial ties by gathering at Chinese New Year and at other significant occasions.

Set back from the street with a garden and parking area in front as well as behind, the building sits on a 1022-square meter plot of land with traditional, but modernized, terrace houses abutting it. Whether viewed from the outside or the inside, the lines, textures, and scales articulate the refined hands of a skilled architect and the craftsmanship of many trades. The building, a neoclassic blend of Dutch, Portuguese, Chinese, and English styles, was designed by a Malacca Dutch-Eurasian architect from the Westerhout family, who trace their roots in Malacca to the eighteenth century. It is said that the floor tiles and colored glass for the doors and windows were imported from France and Italy. Highly qualified artisans were employed for the construction and finish work.

Just inside the arch-shaped front doorway, which opens from a covered porch, is an entry hall with marble floors. Ahead through an arch is a well-proportioned colored glass window that bathes the entryway with bright light. Two large rooms are off to the left and right, one with a long dining table with seating capacity for at least a dozen people and the other a sitting room with Chinese furnishings. In addition to a framed diagram listing all the male descendants for the five generations after Chee Yam Chuan, as well as his father, grandfather, and great-grandfather, are many family photographs on the walls. In the

Below center A blackwood settee with mother-of-pearl and marble inserts rests alongside the stairwell leading to the floors above.

Below right A view from the entry hall into one of the side rooms showing the elaborate composition of shapes and colored glass.

back portion of the entry hall, tucked in a corner and set on a pedestal is a large iron safe made by a Chinese firm with offices in Penang and Singapore to safely store the family's treasures. The kitchen and quarters for servants are located in the back of the building. After exiting a rear door and passing parked cars, it is impressive to see that the rear elevation is also characterized by elaborate architectural and ornamental details.

A prominent element of the house is the intricate and complex set of stairs with rosewood treads that reaches from the ground floor upwards to the domed cupola soaring above. In effect, the staircase and landings create an open central atrium that extends the full height of the building. Several large, but now vacant, rooms are found on both the second and third floors.

The Chee family ancestral altar is located on the mezzanine floor between the ground and second floor, with tablets arrayed on tiers representing at least four generations.

The Chee family created the Chee Yam Chuan Temple Trust to fund and manage the maintenance of this historic structure as well as the burial sites of family members. According to a news report quoting Chee Swee Hoon, the Executive Chairman of the Trust, "the Trustees are also planning to set up a company with the aim of sharing the benefits with the Chee descendants, by way of offering them shares and dividends" (Wee, 1999). The public, while viewing the magnificence of its expansive outer courtyard, ornate façade, and towering spire, must come to realize that this imposing structure embodies more than what merely appears on the outside. The building is an expression of the Chee family's identity, which straddles both the Chinese and Western worlds, transforming what some might see as only an abstract concept of intergenerational relationships into a material form.

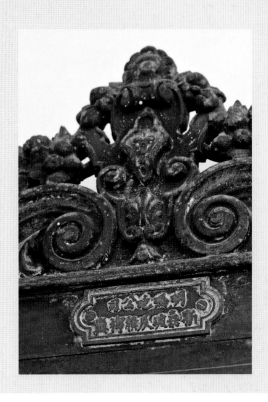

CHEE JIN SIEW HOME

MALACCA, MALAYSIA

Mid-19th Century

The façades of townhouses lining both sides of Heeren Street remain a gallery of Malacca's early twentieth-century élite. Parallel Jonker Street, on the other hand, once known for its mixed uses—gilded clan halls, a school and a theater, and an array of shophouses selling traditional as well as more modern goods—has undergone a metamorphosis. Today, many of the old structures are gone and replaced by venues such as cafés, pubs, and souvenir shops catering to the mass of tourists who flock to Jonker Walk, a rebranded nighttime bazaar launched by the city government. "Since 2000 Jonker Street has reeled under repeated assault: the depletion of a traditional resident community, in which the Straits Chinese are now reduced to a single family; the eviction of established traders and the demolition of their premises; the decay of heritage structures amid new campaigns designed to lure the indiscriminate tourist; the encouragement of more outlets peddling kitsch that already bristles along the road; and the sanctioning of yet more projects that misrepresent the street's historic fabric. All have cost Jonker Street its soul" (Lim and Jorge, 2005: 80). Indeed, many who are concerned with the authentic representation of Malacca's heritage have been saddened by this makeover. It is somewhat ironic that the English translation for Jonkerstraat, the original Dutch name for Jonker Street, is Nobleman's Street.

Yet, even with these coarse transformations, some residents have been able to maintain their old homes in a fashion that would be recognizable to a returning visitor from the early twentieth century. One home that is especially notable is the Chee residence at No. 9 Jonker Street, not too far from the river, which is one of a cluster of traditional residences whose skywell voids and rooflines are clearly seen today in satellite images. The residence is owned by a branch of the family whose patriarch, Chee Yam Chuan, is highlighted in the previous chapter (pages 58–63). While it is not possible to date the initial construction of this residence, it is certain that Chee Jin Siew, a son of Chee Yam Chuan, lived there until his death in 1881. Over the span of the following five generations, including the young children living there today, the family made a variety of renovations to accom-modate the changing expecta-tions of modern life, but the residence still preserves significant aspects of its original plan, furnishings, and ornamentation. Today, the home is occupied by the small nuclear family of Chee Gim Chye, the great-grandson of Chee Jin Siew.

To passersby who take only a quick look, the late nineteenth-century façade appears somewhat unremarkable and pedestrian, combining a traditional lower portion with an updated set of rectangular windows

Opposite and left With a standard placement of doorway and windows that open on to the covered five-foot way, a through-the-wall arched opening connects this residence with that of the adjacent home.

Above Details of the painted scrolls above the façade windows that include not only paintings of birds and flowers but also two pairs of charac-ters meaning "Bright Mountains, Beautiful Waters," a phrase com-monly used in *fengshui* to indicate a favorable site.

Top left Placed before the portrait of Chee Eng Cheng, this simple yet elegant censer is used to hold the aromatic incense sticks that are lighted daily.

Center left With characters indicating "Chee Family" on the right and the family's emblem *ruixing* on the right, this lantern also includes images of four of the Eight Immortals.

Bottom left Along a side wall of the family room, an antique brown-and-gold tiered Peranakan cabinet serves as a surrogate ancestral altar with the portrait of Chee Eng Cheng at the central position. The photographs of other deceased family members are arrayed on the wall nearby.

Opposite above A view of the main hall with the traditional positioning of blackwood furniture centering on the deity altar featuring Guan Gong and his cohort. Behind is a rectangular transitional room that leads then to the more private family quarters.

Opposite below left Along one side of the main family room, a blackwood settee with inlaid mother-of-pearl and marble sits beneath an elaborately ornamented framed mirror.

Opposite below right The stairway leading to the second floor. Wooden parts are set upon a granite base.

above. Closer inspection reveals the through-the-wall arch of the original five-foot way, a classic set of doors and windows, and a booklet of Chinese phrases ornamenting the surfaces. Above the door are the two characters *ruixing*, an invocation meaning "May That Which Is Propitious Flourish." This idea is amplified by appearing in a set of two-character phrases, *ruiqi* and *xinglong*, on the door panels with the combined meaning of "May the Propitious Vapors Flourish." Similar auspicious phrases appear on the folding panels of the window shutters. Paintings of birds and flowers within lobate forms above the windows proclaim *mingshan* and *xiushu*, "Bright Mountains, Beautiful Waters," a common phrase used in *fengshui* to indicate not only beautiful scenery but also a favorable site. Since the theft of antique furnishings continues to be a perennial problem in Malacca, the presence of a folding iron gate and secure locks are prudent additions to old homes like this one.

The main hall, as is the case with others illustrated in this book, is furnished with handsome blackwood furniture with marble inserts, carved in styles common in the waning years of the Qing dynasty. Featured prominently above the altar is a painting of the venerated deity and folk hero Guan Gong, esteemed as a symbol of righteousness and loyalty. Above the doorways leading to the next room are the four characters *nanzhou donghai*, with obscure metaphorical meanings. The traditional paper lamps seen in this hall, which normally would be hung outside, are out of place since they reference the goddess Mazu and her Tianhou temple rather than the Chee family. A small sitting room is located behind the main hall with a central passageway into yet another large room. A notable feature of this small room are the molded glass window panels with a design that includes a flowering *prunus*, indicating "happiness," among pineapples, which in Hokkien are called *onglai*, said to be roughly homophonous with characters meaning "the arrival of good luck" (Welch, 2008: 57).

The next room, which continues the old glazed tile flooring of the front hall, is also furnished with sumptuous furnishings, some of which are inlaid with mother-of-pearl. Other pieces, including hanging mirrors and multitiered cabinets, are typical of Peranakan furniture of the late nineteenth and early twentieth centuries. Known as "brown-and-gold" furniture and made in Malaysia and Singapore, each is characterized by ornately carved designs and ornamentations that are not only clearly Western in inspiration but also detailed flourishes that are Chinese. One of these tiered cabinets, with its elaborate crown, is set as if it were an ancestral altar. A photograph of the grandfather of the current owner, Chee Eng Cheng, who died in 1916, has before it a single ancestral tablet as well as incense and candles in addition to fresh fruit and small cups that tell us that the family still venerates this ancestor on a regular basis. Pictures of other Chee family members are arrayed on the walls flanking this "altar." Some of the old photographs of weddings in the 1930s, with the bride and groom dressed in Peranakan finery, were taken in front of this multitiered cabinet at a different location in the room. A pair of glass-faced cupboards with a carved arched top is recessed into the facing walls. The hanging lanterns in this room are elegant, painted not only with characters indicating this is the Chee home but also their expressive symbolic name *ruixing*, which was seen above the entryway to the residence.

In the kitchen towards the back of the house, adjacent to a skywell, is a shelf with a tablet representing the Stove God with the four characters *dingfu Zao Jun*, "Zao Jun, Determiner of Good Fortune." Just off the kitchen area is a curious configuration in which a narrow passageway

juts off perpendicular to the main axis of the house, leading to a gated back entryway on First Cross Street. The rear of the Chee dwelling abuts up against the restored eighteenth-century shophouse at No. 8 Heeren Street described on pages 42–5 of this book.

An elegant curved stairway sweeps up to the second level where the age of the building becomes more apparent because of weathering of the wooden flooring and painted walls. Here are found bedrooms and passageways, some of which are currently used by family members and others used to store old furniture. The walls and tables are replete with family memorabilia. Two features of the wooden floor are especially noteworthy. Under the carpets in some rooms, floorboards can be removed to open up storage space beneath, said to have been a place to store family valuables during the Japanese occupation of Malaya. In the front bedroom, which is directly above the front hall below, a square block of wood can be removed to open up a peephole for women to see who is being received below. From the upstairs verandas it is possible to catch glimpses of the distinctively Chinese ridgelines and gables of nearby residences and some of the physical linkages between them.

While this nineteenth-century Chee residence retains the essential character of the times when it was built, there also is evidence of the corrosive effects of Malaysia's hot and humid climate on old buildings. Mildewed walls, flaking plaster, rotting wood, deteriorating paper, and fading photographs all present intrusive challenges to owners of old homes. The maintaining and maintenance of an ancestral home involves not only a sense of history and determination but also the necessity to expend substantial amounts of money and time in the endeavor. Private owners of historic homes bequeathed to them, such as Chee Gim Chye, work quietly and usually alone without governmental assistance. They deserve not only acknowledgment for their heroic efforts but also the support of the broader community.

Far left The seating area in a back corridor showing the corroded nature of the wall surface.

Top left A shelf in a corner of the kitchen serves as the location to make offerings to the Kitchen God Zao Jun, who is represented by the plaque on the wall. Incense, tea, and fresh bananas are shown as offerings.

Center left One of several panels found on the walls in the rear of the house. It is conjectured that these represent Chinese characters but they are indecipherable.

Bottom left On the second level of the residence, floorboards can be removed to open secure space beneath which can be used to store valuables. Once the boards are in place, the area is covered with a rug.

Below The upstairs front bedroom overlooking Jonker Street. Full-length wooden louvers and half-length pressed glass window panes make it possible to regulate both airflow and privacy.

Above left An undated Peranakan wedding photo taken in the residence. The groom is wearing a Western double-breasted suit while the bride is dressed in an ornate Chinese gown.

Above right A traditional Peranakan wedding was a twelve-day affair with many changes of clothing. Here, in a photograph dated October 24, 1939, the Peranakan bride and groom plus two young attendants are attired in elaborate costumes appropriate for the first of the twelve days.

TAN YEOK NEE MANOR

SINGAPORE

1880s

In highly urbanized Singapore today, it is difficult to recall a time when it would have been possible for a wealthy businessman to build both an urban residence and a rural mansion and, at the same time, live in a fabulous European-style home within several kilometers of each other. Such was one of the accomplishments of Tan Yeok Nee, also spelled Tan Hiok Nee, Tan Hock Nee, Tan Heok Nee, Ch'en Hsu-nien, and Chen Xunian, an enterprising immigrant from Caitang township in the Chaozhou region of Guangdong province. Tan prospered first as a young trader in textiles, then pepper and gambier, before amassing great wealth as a participant in the burgeoning development of an international opium syndicate centered on the southern tip of the Malay Peninsula. He capped his career with investments in lucrative properties in Singapore as the city became the commercial and military hub of British power in Southeast Asia after it became a British Crown Colony in 1867.

The planting, processing, and exporting of gambier, a chemical used in Europe in the dyeing and tanning industries to make leather soft to the touch, burgeoned first on the island of Singapore and then spread northward during the period 1840–60 to Johor on the Malay Peninsula, where the jungles were cleared by Chinese immigrant laborers. Allied with gambier was the production, trade, and use of opium, which became critical elements in a colonial "economy … characterized by a combination of monopolies and free enterprise in an atmosphere of unrestricted expansion" in which "Thomas A. Raffles, who established the East India settlement on Singapore Island in 1819, actually had a great deal to do with creating the system that led to the addiction of millions of Chinese laborers" (Trocki, 1990: 4).

Immigrant entrepreneurs like Tan Yeok Nee, using Chinese economic and social institutions, were involved in the development of both the prospering gambier plantations and the flourishing opium farms, which brought "colonial governors, Straits Chinese merchants, Teochew pepper and gambier traders, secret society chiefs, and masses of Chinese labor into the same arena" (Trocki, 1990: 5). By the middle of the nineteenth

century, more than a third of the region's Chinese population was employed in the production of gambier and pepper, with about two-thirds of Chinese in Singapore addicted to opium. It is no surprise then that throughout the nineteenth century prosperity, indeed extraordinary wealth, was generated from locally consumed opium in addition to more far-flung commodities trade.

In celebrating the centennial of Singapore's founding by the "great Empire-builder, Sir Stamford Raffles," Song Ong Siang prepared a book entitled *One Hundred Years' History of the Chinese in Singapore*. Comprising nearly 600 pages, the book is a decade-by-decade catalog of countless Chinese immigrants who fulfilled their dreams of rags-to-riches, arriving penniless but within their lifetimes acquiring great wealth. While some of these nineteenth- and early twentieth-century luminaries continue to be well known, memorialized in the names of roads, bridges, hospitals, and other buildings that jostle with the more numerous residual names of British colonial origin, many Chinese who were once wealthy and well known a century ago have faded from contemporary memory.

Four tycoons from the latter half of the nineteenth century, on the other hand, continue to stand out. This is not only because they were

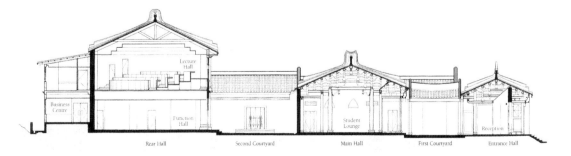

Opposite above Featured on a postcard mailed in 1910, Tan Yeok Nee's residence clearly was situated in a pastoral setting at that time.

Above Once isolated in the quietude of Oxley Rise, today the Tan Yeok Nee manor shares the area with the luxurious high-rise Visioncrest Residence behind it, the landmark Istana Park opposite, and the Orchard Road commercial area nearby.

Left and below Both the elevation and section views reveal the hierarchical sequence of spatial organization as one moves from the entryway deep into the residence.

bound by affinities of dialect and kinship ties in being of Chaozhou, also called Teochew, origin but also because each built an ornate Chinese-style mansion that together are still recalled as a significant part of Singapore's architectural heritage. Collectively called the Four Mansions or *Si da cuo*, these were the residences of Tan Seng Poh, built in 1869; Seah Eu Chin, built in 1872; Wee Ah Hood, built in 1878; and Tan Yeok Nee, built in 1885. Older residents of Singapore recollect all of these stately nineteenth-century homes, but only the mansion of Tan Yeok Nee survives at the beginning of the twenty-first century. According to Yen Ching-Hwang, affluent Chinese as a group "not only enjoyed their wealth and expressed it, but also enjoyed their leisure in a way that many ordinary Chinese could not afford to do" (1987: 424). Measured by any scale, the fortunes and lives of these four men, of course, were not typical of the greater population of Chinese immigrants, most of whom struggled and remained, by contrast, relatively poor.

With Tan Yeok Nee, as with successful Chinese businessmen in general, prosperity was expressed publicly in the building and furnishing of opulent residences for themselves and their families. Some residences built by others, as can be seen elsewhere in this book, were eclectic in style, marrying architectural and ornamental idioms from around the world. Over a period of less than a decade, three residences in Singapore were associated with Tan Yeok Nee. The oldest was a two-storey structure called Lianyi xuan ("Ripples Pavilion") built among the shophouses and godowns along the bank of the busy Singapore River. Second was a European-style home built by George Drumgoole Coleman, the first architect in Singapore and a Superintendent of Public Works, which Tan lived in temporarily while his third home, a Chaozhou-style mansion, was being built on Tank Road. It is interesting to note that even while Tan was living comfortably in a series of homes

in Singapore, he had already begun, in 1870, to build a grand ancestral hall and manor in Jinsha, his ancestral village in China, as a place to retire (see pages 38–9). Construction there took until 1884 to be completed, just as his new Singapore home also was being finished. Although it is not clear when Tan returned to China, it was in the familiarity of his boyhood village and in his ancestral hall called Congxi gongsi that Tan Yeok Nee passed his days in old age until his death in 1902.

Tan Teok Nee's stately two-storey Lianyi xuan home was situated at Clarke Quay along the east bank of the Singapore River, a flourishing area of rows of shophouses and warehouses for the busy river port, which made it easy to mix his gambier and pepper business with his domestic life. At the time, many Chinese believed that this winding location resembled the underbelly of a carp, a fortuitous shape believed to presage prosperity and good luck for those who resided there. Facing the water, where countless bumboats ferried provisions and goods to and from larger vessels at Boat Quay and beyond, the imposing residence declared to all that Tan Yeok Nee was a key businessman. With open verandas on both the ground and upper floors, the building was covered with a distinctive tiled roof and an upturned ridgeline. Across the façade were four rectangular lattice windows and a pair of circular moon-shaped openings in addition to prolific multicolored ornamentation. While this residence was comfortable, commodious, and convenient, Tan Yeok Nee, however, soon set his mind to building a larger country estate in Chaozhou style not too far away. His Lianyi xuan home, meanwhile, was to continue to be used as a residence as well as a clan hall and facility for business and storage. After nearly a century of deterioration and lack of attention, Lianyi xuan was restored in 1993 when other buildings along the river were being rejuvenated as part of the proposed Clarke Quay entertainment district of restaurants

and shops. In 1995, renamed River House, the structure received an Architectural Heritage Award from Singapore's Urban Redevelopment Authority. This historic residence was reborn in 2004 as a sumptuous concept destination complex called IndoChine The Forbidden City, with a facility called Restaurant Madame Butterfly on the top floor and Bar CoCoon on the ground floor. Imposing terracotta warriors line the entrance and the building is bathed with colored lights at night.

Tan Yeok Nee's decision to build a detached country home gave him an opportunity to construct the type of sprawling residence enjoyed by landlords and rich merchants in southern China. He chose an undulating area that had once been a part of an expansive and luxuriant plantation owned by Thomas Oxley, whose nutmeg trees had begun to succumb to blight in the 1860s, forcing him to sell off building lots. In the succeeding decades, prosperous European and Chinese owners acquired parcels in what was referred to as "country situations" in order to live beyond the bustling urban core of the city. Tan Yeok Nee's parcel was nestled along the eastern side of a hillock called Oxley Rise and looked towards the Serangoon harbor in the distance, all in all an auspicious site for a Chinese residence. Moreover, facing north and east, with the extensive hill occupied by Fort Canning to its right, which also contributed to its positive *fengshui*, the siting of Tan's new home metaphorically connected him to his ancestral roots in southern China.

Although little is known of the composition of Tan Yeok Nee's family, it is clear that he built the Oxley Rose residence large enough to provide space for his children and their children. However, by the time he died in 1902 in China, at the age of seventy-five, his sons had all predeceased him, leaving eight grandsons to inherit his estate. Because of the laying of a nearby meter-gauge railway line between 1900 and 1902 that reached the Johor Straits, the Tan family reluctantly decided to vacate the house, selling it to the colonial government, some say, to be used as the residence for the stationmaster of the Tank Road Station. The thought of steam locomotives passing near their country home, which would have brought dust as well commotion to a once tranquil location, clearly must have factored into their decision. A 1910 postcard of the façade of a solitary residence (see page 70) reveals a fine old structure with the grasses and roadway of the countryside adjacent to it, a view that would have been typical in rural areas of China at the time. Of course, by then the railway was not too far away.

The stately Tan mansion passed through many hands over the next century, each one changing its use and its identity. With shifting needs of the railway system, the British colonial government transferred the building, in 1912, within a trust agreement to the Anglican Bishop of Singapore, Charles James Ferguson-Davis. For about two decades this Chinese-style residence was administered by British churchmen as St Mary's Home and School for Eurasian Girls. As need decreased for such a social institution, St Mary's was closed and the old mansion then served for a time as a boarding house. In the meantime, the Salvation Army, which had arrived in Singapore in 1935 to minister to the underprivileged and had originally occupied another smaller Chinese residence on Killiney Road, acquired the venerable Tan Yeok Nee mansion in 1938 in order to expand their programming. After Singapore fell to the Japanese in 1942, Japanese military forces occupied the residence and interned the Salvation Army staff. Records tell of bombing and later looting of the building to the degree that much time, effort, and money had to be expended in order to reopen it again in 1951, six years after the end of the war. As public and official consciousness of the

Opposite below As a result of road work that cut away the earth in front of the residence, a series of steps must be mounted to reach the main entry.

Right Each of the wooden braces supporting beams just inside the main door-way includes a carving of one of the Eight Immortals.

Top right Along the wall under the eaves at the entry is a complex plaster relief composition that includes a stylized bracket set with a *guatong* (see close-up on page 78) as well as a mythical *feiyu* or "flying fish" and a lion.

Center right A carved stone lion and "flying fish" and an incised seal above the entryway.

Below right Tilting one's head upwards provides a glimpse of the three characters *zi zheng di*, which mean "Mansion of Administration," carved into the granite lintel.

historical significance of the Tan Yeok Nee residence became apparent, the building was gazetted by the Singapore Preservation of Monuments Board in 1974 as the only dwelling in the first group of a dozen structures, which included mostly churches, temples, mosques, and shrines. The Salvation Army continued to function in the building until 1991 when it was sold to the owner of the nearby twelve-storey Cockpit Hotel, which sold it five years later to a consortium headed by Wing Tai Holdings. When Cheng Wai Keung, the Chairman of Wing Tai Holdings, learned that the University of Chicago Booth School of Business, from which he had earned an MBA, was scouting for a site for an Asian campus, he suggested that a restored Tan Yeok Nee mansion would provide a fitting site for the school. After many years of restoration, whose purpose was to recover the "cultural significance" of this unique building and respect its age, the residence was adaptively transformed to meet the needs of a twenty-first century global educational enterprise. Formal instruction for the University of Chicago Booth School of Business began in the restored and renewed Tan Yeok Nee mansion in the fall of 2000.

The Tan Yeok Nee Mansion

When one encounters the Tan Yeok Nee residence today, it appears to sit on a raised podium, accessed by climbing stone steps. This raised condition was brought about by the removal of earth and thus the elimination of surrounding open land resulting from the cut-and-fill required by the alignment and widening of Penang Road and

Clemenceau Avenue. Early twentieth-century photographs reveal that the building was once at grade level with the surrounding area, just as such a residence would have been in China's countryside. Even when the building was occupied by the Salvation Army in the 1930s, the driveway leading to the entryway was nearly at the same grade as the nearby road so that only a few steps had to be climbed to reach the front portico.

With a ground plan of approximately 2000 square meters, the rectangular building that Tan Yeok Nee created looked inward and was arranged along a central axis from front to back. This axis passes through two large courtyards fitted within three buildings, the first two of which are single storey while the rear building is two storied. A pair of linear, slender courtyards flanks the core building, which is made up of open and enclosed spaces. While the five bays of the central building complex are placed symmetrically, the three front-to-back buildings and the adjoining outer side buildings are asymmetrical in that they vary in height. As can be seen in both the front elevation and the longitudinal section views, the entry hall building is lower than the middle building, which served as the main hall, while in the rear is a tall two-storey structure that likely served as the principal living space for the Tan family. A hierarchical disposition of space is underscored by this step-like increase in height of the rooflines as well as the fact that each of the three buildings from front to back is on a slightly higher foundation. The flanking side buildings also differ in height, the northern one being single storied while the opposite one is two stories high.

The entry veranda is a richly ornamented space that is characteristic of similar large residences in southern China. At eye level in the middle

Opposite above From the rear of the courtyard, the view towards the entry hall is dominated by an impressive ridgeline.

Above A view across the courtyard from the entryway to the grand middle hall, which today serves as a commons for students and professors at the University of Chicago Booth School of Business in Asia.

Right At the end of a subsidiary ridge is a richly ornamented assemblage of colorful porcelain pieces arrayed into dramatic patterns.

Below A close-up of a *qianci* porcelain cut-and-paste ensemble of horses along a side ridgeline.

Far left This side doorway, which is to the right of the main entryway, was commonly used in the past for everyday use by family members.

Center left This elongated skywell separates the main body of the manor from the side wing.

Near left This *huisu* tree includes carved swallows, whose presence is as symbols of good fortune.

Opposite below The broad sweep of the main hall is made possible because of a

multitiered gilded timber framework that rises above the squared granite columns.

Right This view from the rear quadrant of the residence along a skywell shows the two-storey rear structure on the left, a gate into the back courtyard, and another open doorway leading to the front section of the residence.

Below Adjacent to the main hall, the eaves are extended towards the courtyard and ornamented with a profusion of carved and gilded timber members.

the *huisu* panels here had been covered over by multiple layers of white paint, which had obscured both the details and the coloring.

Stepping through the entryway of the stately Tan Yeok Nee manor, one sees to the left and right similar, but larger, *faux* bracket arms fashioned out of *huisu*, each with several open-mouthed *feiyu* and a drooping *guatong*, which looks like a carved melon, and serves as an ornamented and tiered short post. The rolled ceiling of the entry hall is supported by heavy timber beams, gilded with gold, which lift a complicated assemblage of carved wooden members. Just beyond the entrance hall is the first courtyard and beyond that the main hall. Because the courtyard has been enclosed with glass panels, one sees a reflection of the upturned eaves of the front entrance hall when one looks towards the broader main hall. The central section of the granite slab courtyard today has as its focal point a submerged impluvium, with a pair of well-worn boulders resting in the water.

Standing in the center of the first courtyard, it is possible to see a variety of rooflines as well as an assortment of *jiantie* ornamentation. *Jiantie*, which can be literally translated as cut-and-paste, involves the use of carefully cut porcelain pieces set in mastic to form shapes. In addition to linear and curved *jiantie*, as on the upturned ends of the roof, the method is used also to create floral and animal patterns, including birds, dragons, and an abundance of horses arrayed along a frieze. In each of the four corners of the front courtyard, white and red carp-shaped porcelain figures overlaid with *jiantie* chips function as waterspouts to throw rainwater away from the adjacent halls. At the front of each of the flanking narrow courtyards are pockets of greenery. On two walls are exceptionally colorful *huisu* trees, one of which is visited by

register of the front wall, the granite panels are elegantly simple, with two vertical diamond motifs on panels adjacent to the door itself and on the end walls, and two horizontal panels between them. When a visitor looks up, however, the ornamentation is extraordinarily vivid. First, above the doorway are three characters, *zi zheng di*, meaning "Mansion of Administration," carved into a granite panel. A couple of three-dimensional lions resting on the lintel are wedged beneath this horizontal panel in order to support it, much as they would lift a heavy wooden ornamental board. Beneath each of the lions is a square medallion with stylized auspicious Chinese characters and a *feiyu*, which translates literally as "flying fish," but is a mythical dragon-like creature with wings and the tail of a fish.

One literally has to bend one's neck, however, to see clearly the four fine decorative plaster relief panels called *huisu*, which are tucked in the upper register of the wall. *Huisu*, also called *nisu*, sometimes are in relatively high relief supported by iron rods, but those here are in low relief and made more vivid by being finished in polychrome painting. *Huisu*, as a form of ornamentation, is much more susceptible to deterioration than is either stone or wood, thus its placement in a protected location has preserved it. Unfortunately, it is not possible yet to recall with any certainty the tales narrated in these four panels except to say that they tell historical stories. Separating the *huisu* panels are two elaborate carved wooden eaves brackets that extend out to the chamfered granite columns. A pair of three-dimensional *shizuo*, lion-shaped timber blocks, is inserted above each beam. At the end of the veranda, a cantilevered stone beam, which extends beyond the end columns, has an intricate *faux* bracket arm fashioned out of *huisu* applied to a mortar base. This architectural sculpture is highlighted in black. Over the years,

swallows, symbols of the arrival of good fortune, while the other is laden with split open pomegranates, which because of the abundance of seeds is a symbol of fecundity. In the courtyard, it is also easy to see the nature of the roof tiles, which include a base tile, a cylindrical tile, a triangular dripping tile, and a circular end tile.

What was once the main hall of the house is now an expansive student lounge, whose width was made possible by the use of an extensive roof truss system composed of large beams raised by eight granite pillars, four of which are square and four octagonal in shape. The beams and other structural members here all have a finish in a format known as subdued-gilding in which the patina emerges gradually because of the natural oxidation of the tung oil sealant that is applied in several layers (Chan, 2003: 57). Five large *guatong* rise from each set of multitiered beams to support the roof purlins. Each shimmering *guatong* and associated beams is covered with calligraphic and pictorial ornamentation. Two pairs of *feiyu* "flying fish" are suspended from the wooden framework on each end of the hall. It was against the back wall of this main hall that the Tan ancestral altar must have originally been located. Looking up towards the ceiling one sees not only the gilded main beam with esoteric and auspicious writing on it but also the underside of the roof tiles.

The second courtyard, which is located behind the main hall, is today a place of quiet contemplation with limited seating and abundant vegetation. The two-storey structure, which once contained bedrooms and perhaps even the altar for family deities, faced this back courtyard. Today, this building includes a function room on the ground floor and a large amphitheatre-like lecture hall on the second level.

Opposite above and below Carved like a drooping melon, one *guatong* serves as a gilded block between two beams within the wooden framework of the main hall, while the other is a *faux* block formed out of plaster.

Above This three-dimensional carved wooden lion is used as a strut within the wooden framework.

Below The back courtyard, which is adjacent to the two-storey rear building, once was the most private area of the residence.

SHOPHOUSES AND TERRACE HOUSES

SINGAPORE

1870s–1930s

No architectural form is more characteristic of Singapore's past than the shophouse, "an Anglo-Chinese urban vernacular" that emerged "in the wake of the rise of one mighty empire—Britain—and the fall of another—China" (Lee Ho Yin, 2003: 115). With commercial space on the ground floor opening on to the street as well as living spaces behind and upstairs, rows of contiguous shophouses met the needs of generations of Chinese immigrant merchants, craftsmen, and workers in what Sir Stamford Raffles called the island's "Chinese campong," a China Town on the southwest side of the Singapore River. The earliest shophouses in Singapore, as can still be seen in small towns in Indonesia, were unembellished timber buildings with *attap* or thatched roofs, utilitarian structures that over time were covered with more substantial roofing materials before being replaced by buildings constructed of brick. John Cameron described the "native part of town" in the middle of the nineteenth century as having "buildings … closely packed together and of uniform height and character. The style is a compromise between English and Chinese. The walls are of brick, plastered over, and the roofs are covered with tiles. The windows are of lattice woodwork—there being no glazing in this part of the world. Under the windows of many houses occupied by the Chinese are very chaste designs of flowers

Above A Peranakan couple pose for a studio portrait.

Left Crowded with pedestrians and rickshaws, "China Street" in Singapore in the early 1900s was lined with an assortment of two-storey shophouses whose wares spilled sometimes on to the street itself.

Opposite above With generous forecourts and similar façades, the varying colors and details create an appealing rhythm for this row of 1920s terrace houses along Koon Seng Road.

or birds in porcelain. The ridges of the roofs, too, and the eaves, are frequently similarly ornamented, and it is no unusual thing to see a perfect little garden of flowers and vegetables in boxes and pots exposed on the tops of houses. Underneath run, for the entire length of the streets, the enclosed verandahs of which I spoke before" (1865: 60).

Throughout the nineteenth and well into the twentieth century, the prototypical shophouse structure evolved from its original form, which was introduced from southeastern China, to meet the requirements of life in the hot and humid equatorial region. British colonial ordinances helped to standardize shophouses by mandating the use of fireproof materials, introducing the continuous veranda-like covered walkway known as the five-foot way, and eventually requiring service lanes in the rear that ended the need to carry human waste and other refuse through the front doors. Interior floor plans changed little over the years, even as widths grew longer as reinforced concrete beams replaced timbers. Until the late nineteenth century, shophouses were constructed usually by Chinese craftsmen under the supervision of local Chinese and Indian contractors who replicated existing buildings with the assistance of pattern books, which were readily available. By the turn of the twentieth century, the façades of Singapore shophouses underwent a metamorphosis involving a lively eclecticism. Architectural design elements based upon European Classicism—"freely plagiarising Western architectural motifs," according to Gretchen Liu—but also Malay-style floral ornamentation and symbolic embellishment derived from traditional Chinese motifs (1984: 21).

The juxtaposition of these changing elements not only marks the Singapore shophouse as a truly eclectic structure with an international patrimony but also one of considerable versatility as many structures came to be designed to serve exclusively as townhouse-type residences without any commercial purpose. Curiously, the working drawings of architects in Singapore well into the early decades of the twentieth century continued to include the generic designation "shophouse" to describe them, even when such buildings no longer incorporated a "shop." Even today, any narrow and long structure aligned along an urban street is considered a "shophouse" by some observers, but this lingering category is all too often inexact and anachronistic. It is now common in Singapore to call side-by-side structures whose roots are in the shophouse tradition, but that serve purely residential functions, "terrace (or terraced) houses." This nomenclature conforms to long-standing usage in the United Kingdom and is the convention employed in this book.

With heightened immigration from China as the nineteenth century ended, the core of Singapore's Chinatown became overcrowded, congested, and unsanitary. Some prosperous Chinese merchants and entrepreneurs, swapping convenience for improved quality of life, began to move to newly developing residential neighborhoods along Neil Road and Blair Road to the west, as well as River Valley Road to the north of the core of the original Chinatown. The fabulously wealthy Tan Yeok Nee, as discussed on pages 70–9, built a freestanding Chinese-style estate in 1885 in an area along Clemenceau Road that was then quite rural and near the Colonial Secretary's residence, while the Wee family's terrace house, discussed on pages 90–101, was constructed along Neil Road in 1895 as one of a sequence of attached terrace dwellings. By the early years of the twentieth century, the once remote Emerald Hill, which had been a nutmeg plantation, was subdivided into building plots. Although most of the developers and builders of fashionable terrace houses in Emerald Hill were Straits-born Chinese whose ancestors came from Chaozhou, wealthy Peranakan Chinese families came to outnumber other Straits-born Chinese owners there (Lee Kip Lin, 1984: 5–6). Richly ornamented terrace houses and shophouses proliferated also in the eastern portions of the island, principally in Joo Chiat and Katong in the 1920s and 1930s, which up to that time had been dominated by coconut plantations. While many of the new terrace houses included a linked five-foot way, some incorporated a forecourt or yard with gateposts rather than opening directly on a roadway. Available building plots varied in depth and width to meet the needs of families with differing economic circumstances, yet there was a consistency in the traditional floor plan to suit varying family circumstances. The earliest structures rarely exceeded two storeys because of the limitations of building materials and the constraints of construction techniques, but increased to three and even four storeys as cement became the preferred building material. Greater affluence led to wider and deeper structures,

with increasing floor-to-floor heights. External ornamentation varied considerably over time, especially as patterns reflected whatever styles were currently in vogue.

The public face of any terrace house or shophouse is its façade, which can be viewed in isolation or as part of a continuous sequence of rhythmic elevations that incorporate mixed sets of architectural elements. By the early 1900s, as can be seen in the images here, European-style stucco ornamentation, which included draping swags, complemented Peranakan Chinese glazed tile motifs of colorful birds and flowers. Added to these were Chinese symbolic motifs, such

as deer, dragons, and *qilin*, as well as pithy four-character Chinese aphorisms and signboards declaring a Chinese ancestral hometown. The mixing of European aesthetic traditions with Chinese and Malay patterns sometimes led to a pastiche, the incongruous combining of patterns, materials, and motifs that is sometimes dissonant rather than harmonious. Fluted pilasters and columns, Palladian-style fanlights, arched French windows, ornate Corinthian and austere Doric columns, intricate Malay fretwork and ventilation grilles, egg and dart molding, Chinese friezes, extravagant cornices, tropical timber louvers, glazed English tiles, among many other elements, created sometimes fanciful and flamboyant compositions that jostled with hoped-for utilitarianism. Overall, until the end of the First World War, there continued to be a profusion of repeating handcrafted details in a variety of building media on both shophouses and terrace houses. After the war, the buildings "shed their Chinese elements and decorations" and "assumed a more 'Western' appearance" (Lee Kip Lin, 1953: 127).

The ground floor exteriors of many, if not most, terrace houses express a Chinese personality: a paneled entry door with inscribed Chinese characters, a *pintu pagar* half-door with carved panels, and a pair of windows also with Chinese characters. The placement of several registers of colored glazed tiles on the walls below the ground floor windows was an adaptation of a pattern employed by Peranakan Chinese families in Malacca. Unlike in China, moreover, where exterior colors traditionally were either mottled white or muted earth tones, terrace houses and shophouses in Singapore began to be painted with a palette of pastel hues across the full color spectrum that varied from neighborhood to neighborhood. The subdued, even somewhat restrained, aesthetic of Emerald Hill terrace residences, which were designed by architects, contrasts strikingly with the extravagancy of the façades found in Joo Chiat, along Blair Road and Neil Road, as well as along Serangoon Road in Singapore's Little India.

Such eclectic borrowings created a distinct vernacular aesthetic that has worn well over time in spite of having fallen out of fashion for nearly a half century. In residential as well as commercial buildings in the late 1920s and 1930s, interest turned to Art Deco designs, followed by a wave of post-war functionalism. These architectural trends not only affected new construction but also were applied in the "modernization" and general updating of some old terrace houses and shophouses throughout the island, while many others became dilapidated and effectively abandoned. In the 1970s, extensive areas of old buildings were summarily demolished as Singapore carried out urban renewal that included the construction of high-density public housing estates, which were emerging to meet a critical shortage of adequate domiciles

for the country's population. Beginning in 1986, the prior overemphasis on urban development was altered as Singapore planners began to look seriously at conserving the island's dwindling multicultural built heritage. Successful projects in gazetted conservation areas included the concentration of terrace houses in Emerald Hill, Joo Chait/Katong, River Valley Road, and Blair Plain, where many historic structures have been sensitively renovated as residences that meet the needs of discriminating owners who value the Peranakan Chinese legacy.

Top Vibrant colors and a variety of plaster bas relief patterns provide a strikingly individualistic appearance to Singapore's shophouses and terrace houses. From left: Blair Road; Emerald Hill; Emerald Hill; Emerald Hill; Koon Seng Road; Koon Seng Road; Emerald Hill.

Opposite below Katong Antique House, which was established in 1979 by Baba collector Peter Wee, is a shop-cum-museum of Peranakan material culture.

Below left The doorway, including a gilded *pintu pagar* half-door of a handsome terrace house in River Valley Road.

Below right, clockwise from left An elaborate window, Emerald Hill; painted glass depicting three of the Eight Immortals, River Valley Road; the upper façade of a terrace house, Blair Road; cast-iron balusters, Emerald Hill.

Above left A mother-of-pearl inlaid bridal bed surrounded by other Peranakan antiques, River Valley Road.

Above right A collection of antique vases and stands, River Valley Road.

Opposite above In the rear area of this double-wide terrace house in Emerald Hill, an expansive dining room is at the foot of a double-rise staircase with access also to the rear courtyard on the right.

Below A heavily ornamented gatepost, Koon Seng Road.

Left Door panels with the calligraphic phrase *shili, chuanjia* "May the belles-lettres (Book of Songs and the Classic of Rites) be passed on through the generations," Emerald Hill.

Below Applied ornamentation, such as these floral swags and other relief features, were given shape using Madras *chunam*, a hard-wearing plaster compound made of lime, sand, and other ingredients, Koon Seng Road.

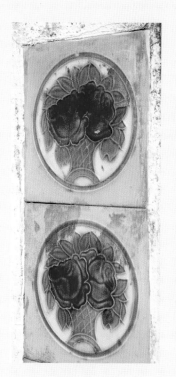

Above Glazed and patterned tiles, some in bas relief, are common features of Singapore terrace houses. From left: Koon Seng Road; Koon Seng Road; Koon Seng Road; Emerald Hill (top right); River Valley Road (bottom right).

Above A display of Peranakan photographs, Katong Antique House, East Coast Road.

Left The view from a corner of a dining room, one wall of which is dominated by a mirrored brown-and-gold sideboard, River Valley Road.

Left An ancestral altar and a display of antiques, River Valley Road.

Below One of a set of two swing half-doors with designs expressing the four seasons and glass panes along the top register. A recessed wall cabinet is on the right, Emerald Hill.

Bottom A sitting area just inside an entryway, Blair Road.

Left Ten-feet tall, this rare sideboard features a finely carved and gilded phoenix amidst peonies and foliage as well as a delicate openwork canopy, Emerald Hill.

Below With four swiveling doors and three drawers beneath, this solid cabinet has through-cut sculptured panels and shallow-cut carvings, Emerald Hill.

Above An antique day bed for sitting, Blair Road.

Far left A hardwood settee with marble panel inserts that express naturalistic scenes, Emerald Hill.

Left The intricately carved foot of the day bed shown above, Blair Road.

Below An inclined chair with carved legs, Emerald Hill.

Left A bat, which symbolically represents *fu* for good fortune, River Valley Road.

Below left Ying Chuan—the family's chop name or *zihao*—indicates the ancestral origin of a branch of the Tan lineage, River Valley Road.

Opposite below, left to right An ornamented doorway and stairs with cast-iron balusters, Emerald Hill; an antique Victor-brand phonograph— a Victrola—on a Chinese stand, River Valley Road; a recessed wall cabinet and side table, Emerald Hill; a monkey god statue in a shrine, River Valley Road.

WEE RESIDENCE (BABA HOUSE MUSEUM)

SINGAPORE

1895

The tale of the Wee family in the nineteenth century reveals the continuing linkages between settled immigrants in Singapore and communities in China as well as the interlocking connections between families and enterprises. Personal and familial connections arguably contributed to an ongoing infusion of Chinese cultural elements and expectations into daily life that sustained the vibrancy of traditional patterns. At the same time, the increasing cosmopolitan nature of the Straits Settlements provided a robust environment for learning about and adopting objects and ornamentation that altered the material texture of people's homes.

Little is known of the early life of Wee Bin, the patriarch of the Wee lineage in Singapore, except for the fact that he was born in 1823 in Fujian province. By the middle of the nineteenth century, he had become a prosperous merchant in Singapore and was founder of Wee Bin & Co., the largest Chinese shipping firm in the region. Already a tycoon and twice married, Wee Bin died in 1868 at the age of forty-five. At Wee Bin's death, Wee Bin & Co. passed to his only son, Wee Boon Teck, who also died young at the age of thirty-eight in 1888. In time, Wee Boon Teck's only son, Wee Siang Tat, and Lim Ho Puah, the husband of Wee Bin's only daughter, shepherded the family enterprise to further prosperity as the nineteenth century ended. Sadly, Wee Siang Tat, Wee Bin's grandson, who had been only thirteen when his own father died and who was an accomplished violinist, died at the age of twenty-six in 1901—even younger than his father and grandfather at their passing—leaving the business in the hands of his uncle, Lim Ho Puah.

Lim Ho Puah, also an immigrant from Fujian where he had been born in 1841, is a tale of a humble worker who impressed his employer with his energy and intelligence before marrying the boss's daughter (Song, 1923: 115). Just two years before Lim Ho Puah's own death, in 1913, at the age of seventy-three, the business was transferred to his son, Lim Peng Siang, who over the next three decades had a distinguished career as a businessman and community leader in Singapore. Lim Peng Siang, who himself also was born in Fujian in 1872 and received a Chinese education, was noted for his perseverance, limitless drive, and business acumen. He was schooled in English in Singapore and became a naturalized British subject. Besides being Wee Siang Tat's cousin, he was also his brother-in-law, having married Wee Siang Tat's sister, Wee Guat Choo. Wee Siang Tat's other sister, Wee Guat Kim, married well also, to Lee Choon Guan, thus linking the Wee family to another wealthy family in Singapore. The commercial enterprises Lim Peng Siang established under the umbrella of Ho Hong enterprises included a steamship company, rice mills, oil mills, the Portland cement works, and the Ho

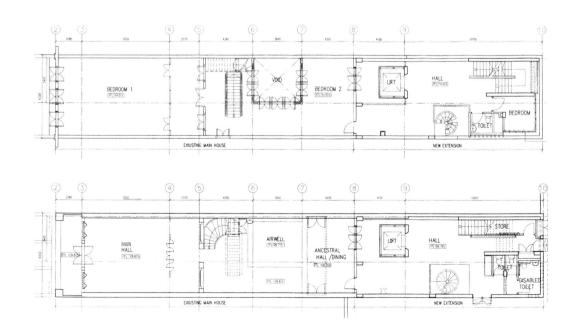

Above With restoration nearly complete, the triple-storey Wee residence expresses its originality alongside neighboring terrace houses.

Left These floor plans of the first and second stories show the disposition of rooms within a narrow configuration.

Opposite above With restoration complete, celebratory red colored cloth embellishes an already resplendent entryway that includes a richly ornamented *pintu pagar* (a double-panel swinging fence-door), a pair of lanterns, and prolific surface ornamentation.

Hong Bank, one of three Hokkien banks that flourished in Singapore in the 1920s. All three banks eventually merged, with the celebrated Malaccan Tan Cheng Lock on the founding board. A naturalized British subject, Lim Peng Siang played a key role in the establishment of the Singapore Chamber of Commerce. He was a director of public companies, and was viewed as a philanthropist because of his support of Raffles College and contributions to relief during the Second World War (Song, 1923: 331, 507, 518).

Over four generations, which were marred by early deaths, the Wee–Lim–Lee family enterprises expanded and prospered as family relations became more robust and interconnected. In the middle and latter parts of the nineteenth century, the twenty cargo and passenger ships of Wee Bin & Co. had plied the waters between Singapore and the fragmented ports of the Netherlands Indies. By the end of the century, they had linked into a network the far-flung trading outposts strung along the Java and Flores Seas, including those along the coasts of Borneo, Sulawesi, the Moluccas, Sumatra, and Java, ranging from Padang, Labuan, and Palembang in the west to Bali, Lombok, and Makassar in the east. In addition to tapping raw materials, the Wee Bin & Co. firm ran ships three or four times each week from Shantou and Xiamen in southeastern China via Hong Kong to Singapore and the riverine ports of British Malaya in order to deliver laborers to the burgeoning agricultural and mining enterprises that were developing in the region (Campo, 2002: 317–18). In contrast to the increasingly competitive European steam shipping firms at the beginning of the twentieth century, "the Chinese ships were known collectively as the 'mosquito fleet', a most appropriate nickname due to their large numbers, their tiny size, their buzzing activity and their swarming out to all corners of the archipelago" (Campo, 2002: 321). After Wee Siang Tat died intestate in 1901, leaving

behind only a young son and two widows, it took seven years to settle his estate, eventually dispersing wealth that had accumulated over many decades. Wee Bin & Co. was liquidated in 1911.

It was during this time of uncertainty in the family and their businesses that a terrace home was constructed and then occupied by the Wee family on Neil Road, not far from the already overcrowded area known as Chinatown. It is probable that the two-storey Wee residence was built by Wee Siang Tat in 1895, at a time when other terrace houses were being constructed in the neighborhood. They are now part of the Blair Plain Conservation Area. Sadly, Wee Siang Tat died in 1901 at the age of twenty-six when his only son, Wee Eng Cheng, was six years of age. In 1910, the property was put in the name of the young son whose mother and grandmother were still alive. As the Wee–Lim–Lee family grew through marriage, additional residences were acquired, and at one time it is said that the extended family owned fourteen houses, but the Neil Road home was viewed as the principal Wee homestead. Three homes were located nearby, on Everton Road, one of which was used as a garage for the family's automobiles while another one, which was elevated on pylons, provided dry space underneath for raising poultry to meet the family's needs for fresh meat.

Once Wee Eng Cheng married, he and his wife lived in the Wee residence on Neil Road with their only son. Alas, like his forebears, Wee Eng Cheng also died young, in 1928, at the age of thirty-three, while his widow lived to the grand age of ninety-five. Their son, Wee Seck Hock, who was likely born in the family residence in 1922, lived to the age of fifty. At some time in the 1920s or 1930s, it was felt that more space was needed and a third storey was added as the bedroom for the parents. Wee Seck Hock's two sons, Wee Lin and Wee Sun, the sixth generation of the Wee family in Singapore, inherited the Neil Road home, and it was these two gentlemen who consented to the sale of their family's terrace house to the National University of Singapore at the end of 2005. With a generous memorial gift from Agnes Tan, the daughter of the distinguished Peranakan Tan Cheng Lock (see pages 51–3), the Wee residence was extensively restored and carefully renovated to serve as an authentic site—a "living heritage home"—for showing how a Peranakan family lived in 1928 when the Wee family occupied the residence.

The Wee Residence

Like other old residences that once served well a growing family's needs, the 100-year-old Wee family home on Neil Road increasingly became emptied of family life with time, though certainly never abandoned, as descendants moved to newer, more modern dwellings elsewhere. Up until 1997, the old ancestral residence was inhabited by Wee An Keow, the widow of Wee Seck Hock who had passed away a quarter century earlier. She maintained the home for other family members who periodically arrived for visits as well as ancestral observances and family celebrations. Although the building was not allowed to deteriorate to the level of other nearby derelict terrace homes, the old structure suffered to some degree from a lack of ongoing attention that inevitably comes when rooms are not occupied every day. In time, especially after 1997, deferred maintenance inescapably led to damage from water, termites, and bats in the interior, and exterior weathering was accelerated because of Singapore's equatorial climate of intense sunlight and high humidity. Photos of the exterior taken by Lee Kip Lin in 1969 and Singapore's Urban Redevelopment Authority (URA) in 1986 clearly show the deterioration of features on the outside, which hinted at likely damage on the inside. Buildings do not survive in good condition on their own.

The decision to purchase the old building for a new purpose by the National University of Singapore went well beyond a desire to merely restore an artifact, a landmark building, to its past glory for some contemporary adaptive reuse. Rather than transform the residence into something it never was, the intent was to refit the home with original furnishings and other objects that were true to it at a point in its past history. Indeed, some 60 percent of the furniture now in place belonged to the Wee family, and other pieces necessary to complete the setting were acquired from Peranakan Chinese in Singapore and Malacca. As the discussion below will show, passing from room to room reveals the character of life in one of the Peranakan community's fine old residences, hence the name Baba House, which is being employed to spread the word about this exceptional piece of Singapore's Peranakan history.

Any Peranakan home, whether terrace house, bungalow, or mansion, encapsulates the accumulating and composite nature of immigrant life over periods of time that vary from a few generations to many generations. While each home is distinctive in time and place, there are sufficient similarities among residences to see the Wee family residence as a representative home, an amalgamation of various Chinese and

Left Between the first and second levels of the façade is an elongated mosaic fashioned out of shards of colored porcelain. The panels above include both auspicious Chinese characters and scenes.

Above The reception hall looking towards the entryway with its screen-like *pintu pagar*.

Western styles. Although the home has an eclectic mix of furnishings and ornamentation, it is clearly a Chinese residence in terms of the layout of its interior spaces, the formal arrangement of furniture, the abundance of meaningful ornamentation, and the presence of ritual objects. The concessions to modern life are those shared even with homes in China built at the same time.

While contemporaneous urban residences in China usually provided little evidence on the exterior of a residence of how sumptuous conditions might be once one crossed the threshold, the Wee family home, like other terrace homes in Singapore, presents a brightly decorated face. Centered between a pair of rectangular windows highlighted with gold colored trim is a *pintu pagar*, a reproduction of the original two-panel swinging three-quarter door whose surface is carved with ornate open fretwork. This external screen obstructs viewing the inside by passersby on the outside and provides a level of security while allowing the passage of air through its perforated surface. Oftentimes called a fence-door and said to be of Malay origin, screening features of this type are not without precedents in southern China where they are significantly less ostentatious but equally practical. Above the door is a black lacquered wooden board called a *jiho* in Hokkien, with two Chinese characters, *zhongsheng*, "The Glory of the Lineage," etched into it that were covered with gold leaf. Above the windows is a set of elongated pictorial screens, designed to look as if they fold, with two pairs of characters, *dangui* and *zijing*, referring to two flowers, the golden osmanthus and the purple bauhinia, which metaphorically symbolize wealth and prosperity as well as harmony within the household. These are complemented by a pair of hanging lanterns made of oiled paper

over a bamboo frame, each with the characters *Huang* (*Wee* in Hokkien) *fu*, meaning "Huang Residence," on one side and *fengzheng daifu*, indicating a Fifth Grade Qing dynasty title. While it is not certain who in the Wee family lineage actually had received the title, it was common in the waning decades of the Qing dynasty to obtain imperial titles of this type as a result of philanthropic acts. Attached to a sidewall is an elongated plaster vessel in which to place joss sticks in the shape of a citron fruit, called *foshou* or Buddha's Hand, which is homophonous with good fortune and longevity. Exquisite examples of *jiannian*, ornamental mosaics fashioned out of colorful porcelain shards, which are described in detail in the Cheong Fatt Tze chapter (pages 128–39), are arrayed above the overhanging entry roof.

Interior spaces on the ground floor include a reception hall followed by a narrow rectangular passage hall that leads to a combination space that includes both an open three-storey skywell and adjacent areas sufficiently large for family enjoyment and ritual purposes. Behind these two rooms are an expansive kitchen and a small back courtyard. While the original building was two storeys, the residual outline of which can be seen on one of the party walls, a third floor was added at some time in the past to meet the family's requirements. The upper floors are divided into bedrooms and storage rooms. Altogether, the floor space of the pre-restored three-storey Wee residence covered a spacious 437 square meters. Unlike the deeper Tan Cheng Lock terrace residence in Malacca, with its multiplicity of rooms with specific functions and two skywells and a rear courtyard that reaches some 70 meters from front to back, the Wee family's residence has fewer rooms with overlapping functions, a single skywell, and a rear courtyard, with a depth of 39 meters.

RECEPTION HALL

In the Wee residence, the reception hall, called *thia besar*, a Hokkien-Malay neologism, in Peranakan homes, essentially mirrors the main halls found in homes throughout China with some modern updating. With its conventional arrangement of furniture, guests were welcomed and entertained among the splendor of the family's prized possessions arrayed within an aesthetic shared widely by the Chinese community. Overall, the placement of furnishings is symmetrical and formal, with the focus on an imposing ornamental wooden screen called a *zhao*, which divides spaces without rigidly separating them, at the head of the room. Arranged along each side of the room are two sets of blackwood chairs and matching tables inlaid with mother-of-pearl and marble panels, a type of relatively mass-produced Chinese furniture readily available in import shops in Singapore early in the twentieth century. By contrast, in the middle of the room is a round wooden table in European style with a beveled edge marble top surrounded by six light beech wood

chairs said to have been copies of a design by the Austrian furniture maker Michael Thonet, who gained fame in the nineteenth century for the modernist simplicity of his bentwood style. Copies of mass-produced Thonet-style curvilinear chairs sold worldwide are said to have exceeded 50 million by the 1930s.

The Wee home, as with many others, had two altars, the one in this room revering Guan Gong and the one in the next room venerating the Wee ancestors. In front of the screen is a complementary set of tables, a high, heavy altar table with a variety of family objets d'art, and a lower square table with ritually important votive objects such as candlestick holders and a joss stick holder on it. Adjacent to these is a pair of jardinières, porcelain stands holding squat vases with floral arrangements, and a pair of tall candlestick holders. In many homes, this first altar recognizes a pantheon of gods, but here there is only a wooden statue of Guan Gong, literally Lord Guan, a Three Kingdom's period general said to exemplify righteousness, brotherhood, and loyalty. Guan

Gong is said to bless those who are upright and provide protection from those who are dishonest, thus serving here as an exemplary household deity. Perched on a miniature model of a low carved platform bed, Guan Gong is immediately recognizable because of his red face and lush beard. Wee Lin, the grandson of the first owner of the house, recalls that at one time there were other statues, such as Guanyin and the Buddha, on the altar as well as Tudi Gong, the Earth God, in a shrine beneath, and that joss sticks were lit daily and small cups of tea were offered during festivals such as at the New Year. It was here in the reception hall that funeral rituals, including those of Wee Lin's father, Wee Seck Hock, in 1972, were observed.

The upper walls of the reception hall are painted a soft aquamarine color, differing little from many other dwellings, in order not to overwhelm the traditional paintings and calligraphic scrolls hung on them. The lower dado walls, which for the most part are hidden behind the blackwood furniture, are noteworthy because of the variety of lime plaster ornamentation in low relief of geometric, floral, and fruit compositions with auspicious meanings. Restoration work of the dado walls was especially difficult because of harm done by dampness and the growth of salt crystals. Passageways on both sides of the altar lead to an elongated transitional space with an opening at its center that leads to the main family area. The disposition of these three openings insures that visitors to the reception hall cannot easily view the private family spaces beyond. The initial pair of openings is capped with a carved *feizhao*, a somewhat arcuate-shaped ornamental panel with pendant-like sides replete with auspicious ornamentation and an historical tale. Central to the carved *feizhao* on the left is a depiction of the tale of the Tang emperor Gaozong (r. 649–83) visiting the home of Zhang Gongyi, who lived together with the improbable number of nine generations of his family (*jiushi tongju*). When the emperor asked Zhang Gongyi for the reasons that such a larger family could live well together, Zhang Gongyi picked up a brush and wrote the character *ren*, meaning "forbearance,"

Top left The roofline as viewed from the third floor.

Center left The silhouette of the original two-storey structure was imprinted on the neighbor's party wall when the third floor was added.

Bottom left Along the upper wall of the skywell, one of a series of mosaic compositions was given shape using cut-and-paste porcelain shards.

Below Just beyond the transitional passageway and before the skywell is a curved wooden stairway, which rests on a stone plinth before climbing to the second level. A colorful nook filled with Chinese motifs is augmented with imported European tiles.

Opposite The view from a corner of the skywell looking towards the front reveals the seamless integration of interior and exterior space.

a combination of patience, tolerance, compassion, accommodation, and self-control, a hundred times. Behind each *feizhao* is an embroidered cloth with hanging tassels that are highlighted with images of the fabled Baxian or Eight Immortals.

The dado walls wrapping the reception room continue into the narrow transitional passageway, thus giving a sense that both spaces are interconnected. Moreover, a large vertical mirror is hung from the wall on each end of the rectangular passageway in order to visually open up the limited space as well as to splash reflected light into the area. Each of the pair of facing console tables beneath the mirrors holds a porcelain vase from China. The passageways, windows, and golden openwork of the screen wall admit varying degrees of diffused light to this area throughout the day.

FAMILY HALL

After passing through the reception hall and the transitional passageway, one enters the private family area of the home. As mentioned above, in some larger terrace homes the private areas are composed of many separate rooms, but here in the Wee residence there are only two spaces, one a multipurpose family hall and the other a kitchen, with both being commodious in order to serve a variety of domestic purposes, a level of flexibility that is characteristic of most Chinese residences. With an overall dimension of 12.4 x 6.3 meters, the first of the family spaces is essentially an inner hall, which has at its core a three-storey recessed skywell, a void that is surrounded on three sides by covered areas, each with an important function: a majestic staircase leading to the second floor, a rectangular walkway lined with photographs, and an area containing a long table with accompanying chairs and an imposing ancestral altar. The furnishings seen today in this commodious space are a mixture of Wee family heirlooms and sourced pieces intended to be representative of the times.

The curved wooden stairway, with its lacquered balusters, rests initially on a stone plinth before climbing to the second level. Under the ascending stairway is a colorful nook replete with Chinese motifs augmented by a variety of imported European tiles. On the left is a cracked ice lattice pattern overlaid with green vegetation while the underside of the rising stairs is accentuated with symmetrical golden shapes that evoke bats or butterflies, emblems of good fortune. The focal element of the corner is a square plaster central panel comprising a pair of mythological phoenixes, the male with five serrated tail filaments and the female with two smoother ones, and peonies, which together represent righteousness and prosperity. On the four corners of the central panels is a set of four bats or butterflies, emblems of good fortune. Surrounding these elements, beginning on the right side with a rat and continuing counterclockwise to end with the pig, are the twelve animals associated with the Chinese zodiac that collectively represent the cyclical nature of time. Underneath this feature and along the back wall of the skywell are ceramic tiles in a variety of designs, including Art Nouveau patterns. Preliminary research reveals that the ones showing a green sweet pea and blue tulips in the background were made in Staffordshire, England, by T. & R. Boote Ltd, a firm that was a creative manufacturer of Victorian colored tiles from the late nineteenth century until about 1910.

The wall opposite the skywell is filled with photographs of several generations of Wee family members as well as their prominent Lim and Lee relatives. Two large-format formal ancestral portraits, where

once there were three, hang among the black-and-white photographs of individual family members and others. The principal portrait is that of Wee Boon Teck, Wee Bin's son, while the adjacent one is of Tan Ah Keow, Wee Boon Teck's stepmother. At one time, a portrait of his wife, Ang Cheng An Neo, must also have hung adjacent to his, but it has been lost. Set back along the wall in front of the skywell and below the photographs and mirrors is a low sideboard with side chairs and tables along it. An upright piano, as seen in a photograph dated around 1972, once stood in this location.

Just beyond the skywell and the wall of family photographs is a pair of built-in cupboards, called *piaktu* in Hokkien, which face each other on opposing walls. Recessed cupboards of this type are not commonly found in China, but the nature of the carved ornamentation on the doors marks them as having been crafted by a Chinese carpenter. Along the edge of the frames are small carvings of the Baxian, the Eight Immortals, easily recognizable by their emblems. Below each cabinet is a wall panel with a repeated motif of running *wan* characters symbolizing longevity. The cupboard on the left holds a set of blue-and-white tableware suitable for daily use while that on the right contains a set of richly colored Nyonya ware bowls and plates for special occasions.

Ahead is a restored dining table or *tok panjang*, a neologism (*tok* is Hokkien for "table" and *panjang* is Malay for "long"), long enough to seat ten comfortably for meals, and the ancestral altar, a juxtaposition that underscores the centrality, unity, and continuity of the family. At the end of the table and just beyond the wall cabinets on each side is a blackwood settee inlaid with mother-of-pearl. Whether eating a regular meal together or assembling for a family celebration at this long table in front of the ancestral altar, generations of Wee family members were made aware of the importance of family and lineage. On the other hand, the placement of a family dining table in front of the ancestral altar is an odd juxtaposition, which would not have been found in a fully developed home. It is likely that the Wee family brought the dining table from a rear area that had been eliminated when the back of the long residence was reduced in length sometime before the Second World War in order to create a service alley to facilitate access for the fire brigade and make

it easier to remove human waste and other rubbish from the house.

In the Confucian tradition, these spaces together proclaim the pride of the family in its forebears and remind family members of obligations not only to the past but also to the future. The area behind the table and against the kitchen wall houses the ancestral altar for the Wee family atop a high wooden altar table that is especially notable because of the intricately carved frieze adjoining its upper surface and legs. The altar case serves as a didactic instrument with its intricately carved representations of the *Ershisi xiao*, "The Twenty-four Paragons of Filial Virtue." This important assemblage declares the family's devotion to Confucian filiality in a shrine encased within a hardwood shell, with doors that could swivel open to reveal the wooden tablets of the Wee progenitors arranged on shelves. The original Wee ancestral tablets, however, are now in a Buddhist temple since it is important to the family that offerings and prayers continue to their ancestors. Photographs of the ancestral tablets, which reveal names as well as birth and death dates, are now displayed on the adjacent wall.

Set beneath the altar table, as was the case in the reception room, is a square table used for food offerings during periodic rituals when the table would be covered with an embroidered cloth. On the two tables are found bronze and porcelain vases, candlesticks, as well as a bronze incense censer and covered tripod. On the back wall is a pair of couplets and a horizontal board with the characters *zhuiyuan* with the allusive meaning "To Honor One's Ancestors with Offerings," a cogent reminder to remember where one comes from. The ancestral portrait of Wee Bin, which was shown between the horizontal board and the shrine in a photograph taken in the early 1970s, is no longer there (Lee and Chen, 2006: 62–3). The original portrait of Wee Boon Teck, once above the piano, is now with the National University of Singapore Museum for restoration. All in all, the early 1970s photograph revealed a rather informal use of the space at that time: an aluminum-framed reclining chair facing a small television set on a blackwood table inlaid with mother-of-pearl, a modest square table beneath the altar set for daily use with two chairs facing it, and the recessed cupboard stuffed with old books rather than fine china dinnerware.

KITCHEN

Just beyond this room is a three-storey structure, which was originally constructed of reinforced concrete with a flat roof, providing a service block for a kitchen, bathrooms, and storage as well as a spiral staircase to the upper floors. As with other residences of this type, the household's kitchen was a rather bright and convenient space because it was adjacent to an open L-shaped courtyard with a back door leading to an outside lane. Sometime before the Second World War, the colonial government shaved off portions of abutting terrace residences in the rear in order to carve out service alleys, principally to facilitate the removal of night soil and provide access for the fire brigade. It is possible that the original kitchen may have been farther back and was moved forward when the back alley was completed. Consequently, the back entrance came to serve the family as a convenient way in and out as well as being handy for deliveries and casual visits by friends so that they neither had to navigate through the distant and more formal entryway at the front of the residence. Spiral staircases of either precast concrete or cast iron were innovations in Singapore in the early 1920s in order to provide a safe route of egress in multistoried buildings in case of fire.

As with Chinese generally and with Peranakans in particular, food is not only a necessity for life, it is a fundamental way to express social relationships within and outside the family. Peranakan homes enjoy a well-deserved reputation for their gastronomic eclecticism that blends Chinese culinary practices and ingredients with those characteristic of Malay cooking. The Wee kitchen is dominated by a brick stove along one wall in addition to low cabinets, one of which is faced with glass. Glazed earthenware containers, such as jugs, jars, and containers of many sizes, cake molds, baskets, and iron woks are displayed along them. Above the glass cabinet today is a meat safe, a wooden framed device with cage-like screened sides to keep flies and rodents away; the hook on top indicates the meat safe was usually suspended. Along the wall near the stove is a shelf with an inscribed plaque, rather than an effigy, above it a

Opposite above Looking from the skywell to the rear, one sees first the elongated dining table and the impressive ancestral altar. On both walls are recessed cabinets. The doorway leads into the kitchen.

Above Hung along the wall opposite the skywell are photographs of several generations of Wee family members as well as their prominent Lim and Lee relatives in addition to two large-format formal ancestral portraits. Below the photographs is a sideboard with chairs and tables alongside it.

Right What was once an area filled daily with activity today is merely a display space for objects used in the preparation and storage of food. The Kitchen God Zao Jun is represented by the red plaque on the wall while the shelf was used for offerings.

Far left and center Ornaments hung along the edges of the bridal bed.

Left Displayed on a table in the bridal chamber is this tall gift container said to have been sent by a Peranakan family living in Palembang on the island of Sumatra.

Below The wedding bed on the left and the single bed on the right are lavishly ornamented with beadwork and embroidered motifs that represent fertility.

Right The shuttered windows darken what could be a bright space with them thrown open. The furnishings complete the ensemble within the wedding bed chamber.

shrine to Zao Jun, the Kitchen God. Just before the twenty-fourth day of the twelfth lunar month, family members would make offerings to the Kitchen God before his annual ascent to Heaven to report on the family for the year just ending. Today, the rear skywell is occupied by a glass-enclosed elevator.

SECOND AND THIRD STOREYS

On the second floor are several bedrooms, storage areas, and hallways that were used flexibly over the years to meet the changing needs of the Wee family. The stairs from the first floor lead up to an L-shaped corridor space that functioned as a sitting room. Lined with chairs, tables, and cabinets, the space is ventilated and lighted via the adjacent wooden louvered windows that insured comfort deep in the interior areas of the residence. Wall space here today celebrates the life of Tan

Cheng Lock, whose ancestral home was discussed earlier (pages 46–57). There once was a small bedroom in the rear area that had been used by children in the family or by relatives who needed a place to sleep. Visitors to the second floor today see two bedrooms, a bridal chamber in the front and a second bedroom near the middle of the floor between the two skywells.

Set above the reception hall, a splendid wedding chamber, "the quintessential symbol of a family's wealth and status," occupies the largest and longest room on the second floor. This room receives light and air through a pair of symmetrical windows framing a larger door-like opening at the front. Peter Lee and Jennifer Chen declare that while "Peranakans did indeed spare no expense in the furnishings of their bedrooms ... the most lavish sets of furniture and ornaments were reserved for decorating a bridal chamber" (2006: 71). Peranakan bridal beds, like those used elsewhere by Chinese, usually came as part of a bride's dowry to be placed in a bedroom in the bridegroom's home. As a modular assemblage of wooden components held together by mortise-and-tenoned joinery, a bed of this type typically arrived at the home unassembled so that the pieces could be carried easily up narrow stairways to the room in which the bed was intended to be placed. In the bridal chamber, the wooden pieces, including an elaborately carved canopy, would be assembled at a spot adjacent to an interior wall. Beds of this type are lacquered with a red finish and emblazoned with gilded carved panels. What is especially noteworthy about this bridal chamber is that it includes two beds, one clearly for a couple and the other for a single person (see page 4).

An alcove bridal bed, which is open in the front and framed with low rails on three sides, is used for both nighttime sleeping and daytime sitting, a place for conjugal intimacy, to nurse a young child, and from time to time visit with friends. In many ways, an alcove bed within the larger room may itself be considered an intimate "room," which can be made even more private by dropping the surrounding curtains. Colors around and about the bridal bed are exuberant, replicating the hues of tropical flowers similarly found on Peranakan porcelain and women's clothing. Over a period of days after the assembling of a bridal bed, an extensive array of ornamented textiles would be spread or hung about the bed to enliven the mood for the bride and groom. Close inspection of the curtains and bolsters about any Peranakan bridal bed of this type reveals a plethora of embroidered and beaded auspicious motifs, especially dragons and phoenixes as well as magpies and mandarin ducks that express harmony between the marrying couple. Without exception, one finds always a *shuangxi* or doubled happiness character.

Unlike the classic Ming dynasty-style alcove beds, which are renowned for their elegant lines and relative simplicity, Peranakan bedsteads are more like those found during the Qing dynasty in southern China, where richly adorned styles vary to some degree from

region to region. The main bed on display in the Wee bridal chamber is said to be a variant form of Chinese bed in the style of those used by Peranakan in Palembang on the island of Sumatra, which was the hometown of Wee Boon Teck's young bride. This marital bed is accompanied by an adjacent single bed that functioned both as a settee and a place for the husband to sleep if he desired. On the floor of the bridal chamber are several colorful carpets imported from Scotland. Towards the front end of the room, which today is covered by a carpet, is a small block of wood that can be removed to reveal a peephole that could be used to see who entered the reception room below. Additional furniture includes two sewing chests, a wedding bench with baskets on top, several cabinets used to store clothing, and a Palembang-style tall gift basket. The typical trousseau of a Peranakan bride, including wedding garments, accessories, and jewelry, are displayed in the room.

Traditional Peranakan weddings, a topic that will not be discussed here, took place in the past over a twelve-day period, incorporating an elaborate, multifaceted, and prolonged ritual whose purpose was not only to unite the couple but also their families (Lee and Chen, 2006: 79–87). While weddings of this duration have long fallen out of fashion, news reports frequently tell of young Peranakan couples who have chosen an abbreviated version in an effort to have a memorable celebration echoing that of their forebears.

A second smaller bedroom on this floor has as its focal point a "modern" chrome-plated brass mother-of-pearl inlaid four-poster bed, which is enshrouded with gauze-like textiles. In the room also is a vanity with a triple-fold mirror, a chair, as well as a study area with a desk. Above the desk is a photograph of the SS *Hye Leong*, a ship owned by Wee Bin & Co. in the late nineteenth century, together with other family pictures. This room is especially airy because of the cross-ventilation through louvered windows on the two walls that are adjacent to the skywells.

Wee Seck Hock and his wife originally had their bedroom on the third floor, but because of illness as he got older, they moved to a lower floor. Quieter than the lower floors, the third floor bedroom had three

large windows, each with a fanlight, a half-circle opening with sash bars arranged like the ribs of a fan, above it. Today, the third floor space has been refashioned as a modern exhibition space that will be used to express the vitality of contemporary Peranakan culture. It is expected that this space will help facilitate and complement workshops that will teach Peranakan arts, crafts, and culinary skills within the old house in an effort to transform it into a "living" museum rather than merely a static one.

As one of the last surviving Peranakan-style terrace houses in Singapore with an intact interior from the late nineteenth century, the restored Wee family residence shines a spotlight on one significant element of the country's architectural past. Equally important is that the home highlights the material life of Peranakan in times past, especially the vitality and resilience of their Chinese heritage during a fluid period of great economic and social change. The emphasis on the importance of family over many generations, the power of calligraphic and pictorial symbolism, and the multicultural identity of the Peranakan are all represented well in this home. The fortuitous convergence of many who were willing to take risks with a complex landmark project underscores the potentialities of public–private collaborations in cultural heritage conservation: a generous and perceptive donor, a willing and sensitive owner, farsighted and well-connected members of the Peranakan Association, including Peter Lee who serves as the Honorary Curator, creative curators and administrators at the National University of Singapore (NUS) Museum, the extensive pre-restoration research conducted by Chan Yew Lih and her students from the NUS Department of Architecture, experienced professional architects and engineers at the government's Urban Redevelopment Authority (URA), as well as expert craftsmen from China contracted by LF Developments Pte Ltd, who were brought to Singapore to carry out restoration work.

CHUNG KENG QUEE MANSION (PINANG PERANAKAN MANSION)

PENANG, MALAYSIA

1890s

Chung Keng Quee, one of the most colorful, ambitious, and capable personages in nineteenth-century British Malaya, purchased two adjacent buildings in 1893 before replacing the headquarters of an organization with a modern residence and transforming the contiguous school into his own personal temple. A century later, after decades of neglect, the run-down residence was fully restored, then refitted and transformed into the Pinang Peranakan Mansion to house a portion of the extensive collection of artifacts owned by connoisseur Peter Soon. Chung Keng Quee, one of the great tin magnates of the Straits Settlements, was not a Peranakan himself, yet bequeathed a late Victorian mansion of substantial magnificence that serves well to showcase the traditions and lifestyles of Baba and Nyonya families in times past.

The third of five sons in a Hakka family, Chung Keng Quee was born in 1827 in Zheng New Village, Zengcheng county, just to the east of Guangzhou in Guangdong province. Unlike many penniless Chinese immigrants who came as a single family member to the Nanyang in search of a new life, Chung Keng Quee actually came in search of his father and elder brother who had earlier left China. Because his elderly mother was distressed about having no word from her husband or her second son, she consented for her third son to travel to Malaya around 1841 to search for them. Chung Keng Quee had many aliases, which depended on the romanization scheme and the dialect used: Chung Keng Kwee, Chung Ah Kwee, Chung Ah Kee, Cheang Ching-kuei, Cheang Keng Kwi, Teh Ah Quee, Cheng Ching-kuei, Cheng Ya-kuei, Cheng Ching Kui, Zheng Jinggui, and a host of others too numerous to list, all related in one way or other to the Chinese characters for his name.

Chung Keng Quee found his father and brother in Perak, running a well-established business. In time, the three of them set out to take

Opposite above and left Taken a century apart, these photographs show the traditional ancestral hall on the left and the residence on the right.

Opposite below Entered from a streetside gate is an expansive courtyard that offered a secondary entry to the residence. The imposing triple-bay ironworks of the protruding second floor balcony over this side entrance helped elevate its status to that of a handsome "main" entry.

Right Along the back of the side courtyard, which provides parking space for carriages and automobiles, are service buildings for the residence.

advantage of new opportunities that were arising in Perak, especially exploiting the alluvial deposits of tin ore. They played key roles in the profitable recruitment of Hakka coolie laborers from their home region who came in increasing numbers to participate in a "tin rush" and to escape the turmoil of the bloody Taiping Rebellion which flared up throughout south and central China between 1850 and 1864. Yet, peace was not found in the Perak region either, as a series of four episodes of social conflict, called the Larut Wars, raged on and off from 1861 through early 1874 over control of the tin mines by Chinese secret societies, whose organization was based fundamentally on the area of origin in China. One fighting faction, members of the Hai San Society led by Chung Keng Quee, fought against members of the Ghee Hin Society headed by Chin Ah Yam, as well as those loyal to Malay chieftains. Some 40,000 miners and followers were poised for battle during the protracted and intense conflict between 1872 and 1874, a period characterized by revenge, slaughter, and widespread bloodletting, principally because of competing economic interests. In the midst of the Larut Wars, the island of Penang became a Crown Colony in 1867 under the direct control of the British Colonial Office. Sadly, the eruption of large-scale conflict involving some 35,000 members of the fragmented Chinese secret societies, called triads, brought the conflict of Perak to

Penang itself. The Penang Riots lasted for more than a week, and fostered tensions that were to endure for decades, yet also set the stage for the transformation of social and economic life in the region.

During this period of intense struggle, Chung Keng Quee and other prescient Chinese leaders petitioned the British to intervene and mediate the deteriorating crisis. Although having lost one of the major battles, Chung Keng Quee, together with the leader of the opposition, Chin Ah Yam, were named by the British as Capitan China (Kapitan Cina in Malay). Through enterprise and innovation, Chung became the dominant force in the operation of tin mines in Larut by 1887. His wealth also increased by working with business associates to open opium and tobacco farms in addition to pawnshop and gambling facilities.

Besides making a fortune, Chung also was known for his generosity, much of which is noted on stone stele and wooden boards where both his name and amounts donated are recorded. In 1894 he hosted a magnificent garden dinner for Chinese Admiral Ting and his entourage with more than a hundred other Penang business luminaries in the name of the Chinese Vice-Consul Cheong Fatt Tze/Zhang Bishi. He was a benefactor of cemeteries and temples as well as schools in Penang, in addition to social associations there and in Perak. He and other prominent Overseas Chinese donated to relief efforts in China,

India, and South Africa. At a time when purchasing honors and titles was the official policy of the Qing court as it courted wealthy Overseas Chinese, Chung Keng Quee was granted the title Mandarin of Second Rank, an honor that was also bestowed posthumously on his father and grandfather. His generosity in Penang before he died in 1901 led to his being memorialized with the naming of two streets after him, Ah Quee Street and Keng Kwee Street, today called Lebuh Ah Quee and Lebuh Keng Kwee.

It is not known how many return visits Chung made to his ancestral village in Guangdong province, but it is certain he made several. Besides commemorating one of his mother's birthdays, he made generous contributions to improve education and transportation for villagers. He paid for the installation of a network of stone paths, stone bridges, and two roadside pavilions to ease travel for villagers in the mountainous region. After donating a substantial amount of money for flood relief in the Zhili region of northern China in honor of his mother, the Qing court sent a commemorative horizontal board with calligraphy proclaiming *jigong haoyi*, "Zealous for the Common Good." There are unverified reports that he also built a large manor in his home village, perhaps in anticipation of returning there one day or as a place for his progeny to return so that they would be reminded both of Chung's humble origins and his later prosperity.

In time, individuals such as Chung Keng Quee and even many lesser nouveau riche acquired land and built magnificent residences in Penang. At the age of sixty-six, in 1893, soon after secret societies were banned in Penang, Chung Keng Quee, by then quite prosperous and an established Chinese community leader who was well regarded by the British, purchased two properties on Church Street. The larger site

had once been the headquarters of his nemesis, the Ghee Hin Society, the secret society that he had battled during the Larut Wars. Here, he demolished the existing building and constructed a two-storey residence and office, calling it Hye Kee Chan or "Sea Remembrance Storehouse." The residence comprised a pair of equal sized buildings, a front structure and a rear structure, with a generous open space between them. Both buildings were covered with distinctive hipped roofs, each composed of a pair of triangular and polygonal-shaped sloping tiled roof surfaces. The opulent structure was fitted with an eclectic mix of Chinese and Western elements: intricately carved wooden panels and calligraphic boards from China, cast-iron columns and ornamentation by the venerable Scottish firm Macfarlane & Co., English floor tiles from the Stoke-on-Trent pottery works, and an astonishing assortment of furniture and decorative

Left With the skywell on the left and the doorway to the right, this space provides a welcoming area for the reception of casual visitors while giving them glimpses of the opulence of the Chung home.

Opposite and above These two views looking across the skywell reveal the extravagant use of cast-iron columns, brackets, and balustrades as well as the varying patterns within the adjacent semi-enclosed spaces around the atrium-like space.

styles from around the world. Unlike other Chinese mansions, which usually had a courtyard at the front, Chung's large townhouse fronted directly on the street, with an arcaded five-foot way tucked beneath the overhanging second floor. While the residence had a front entryway in the middle of the three-bay five-foot way, this doorway was used infrequently because of the presence of a convenient entryway from the large courtyard along the side of the residence. This side courtyard provided access to utility areas for the house staff in addition to generous parking space for carriages and, later, automobiles.

The imposing triple-bay ironworks of the protruding second-floor balcony over this side entrance nonetheless helped elevate its status to that of a handsome "main" entry. Above the entryway was placed a horizontal board with the characters *rongyang*, meaning "Glorious Sun/Yang," an especially auspicious invocation that is repeated elsewhere in calligraphy within the residence. Just inside the door is a sitting area with a table that opens to an extraordinary courtyard-like skywell with a granite impluvium, a slightly sunken area that drains rainwater falling into the building. A rich ensemble of cast-iron columns, brackets, and balusters helps elevate this space from being simply a traditional Chinese building element to one that proclaims "modernity." Patterned English tiles cover both the surrounding floor surfaces and the adjacent rooms. Inside to both the left and to the right of the side entryway are three rooms, a larger central one flanked by two smaller longitudinal rooms. Both of the central rooms are separated from the open space by elaborately carved wooden panels.

The carved wooden screen wall on the left leads to what would be the "front" parlor if entry had been made from the doorway from the street rather than from the side courtyard. The screen seen there today has six folding panels, the middle two left open, and a wider pair of side openings hung with curtains. The lower panels show bird and flower images in low relief, accented in gold, while the openwork upper panels are adorned with three-dimensional images carved in the round and set within a filigreed screen. It is likely that a similar screen was used in the original house as a means of separating public space from the private space beyond. Today, the room is furnished as a parlor with a mixture of European and Chinese furniture where visitors could sit and talk. The etched mirrors on the wall, made in Hong Kong, all evoke traditional auspicious themes. Doors lead to side rooms that today exhibit European furniture, Chinese wall hangings, and a large collection of curios from around the world.

To the right of the courtyard, one must mount a shallow step to enter the large room, which today is furnished as a formal dining room but that may have served at least temporarily as a location for the Chung family ancestral altar once the residence was completed. The elevation of an interior room in a Chinese home usually symbolizes that the space one is entering is a privileged area, which serves ritual purposes. However, it is unlikely that this room was used as an altar room for very long because Chung, unlike most of his contemporaries, had a dedicated building next to his residence as a private temple, which was to serve as the formal ancestral hall for his family. The placement of separate family ancestral halls adjacent to residences had begun during the Song dynasty and had been urged by the great neo-Confucianist scholar Zhu Xi. Symbolizing the continuity of the family as well as demonstrating wealth and power, freestanding ancestral halls, just like the altars found *within* individual homes, were central to rituals for honoring ancestors, for family celebrations such as at the New Year, and for birthdays and

Opposite above and below Viewed from two vantage points, the prominent stairway declares modernity with its imported components, such as cast-iron balusters from Scotland in a fleur-de-lis pattern, while the adjacent walls display traditional Chinese motifs.

Above A view across the skywell and through the carved wooden screen towards the front room of the residence. In the rear, the rarely used main entryway is visible.

Right Furnished as if it were a parlor, this "front room" with both Chinese and Western elements becomes a "side room" because of the altered access into the residence.

Left A detail of the lower register of the entry screens showing Chinese plum blossom and bird motifs.

Above Deity altars of this type are usually found in the front room facing the entryway, but this finely carved one with a porcelain statue of Guanyin is placed behind a screen and faces the back of the residence.

weddings. Chung Keng Quee's ancestral temple, a magnificent structure that celebrates him and his family, will be discussed below. The multi-tiered chandelier, carved furniture, and wall hangings seen today mark this space as an elegant room that reflects Peranakan aesthetic taste at the end of the nineteenth century. Framing the entry to the room is an immense and intricate inverted U-shaped panel replete with carved birds and flowering plants.

The grand staircase to the second floor has a polished wooden handrail and balusters of painted cast iron in a fleur-de-lis pattern. The plan of the second floor duplicates that of the first with two large rooms and four small rooms arranged around the balconied space of the courtyard below. Except for the wooden floors, solid doors with fanlights, and exterior shuttered windows with wrought- and caste-iron trim, the rooms visited today display Peranakan artifacts, clothing, and furniture from Peter Soon's extensive collection. One room shows a Nyonya bedroom from the 1930s–1950s, clearly well beyond the dates that Chung Keng Quee occupied the house. The room displaying a traditional Chinese bridal chamber shows the type of elaborate heavy furniture characteristic of the late Qing dynasty. The intricately carved bedstead, painted in the traditional red and gold and hung with embroidered panels and curtains, is a veritable room within a room. A chamber pot and washbasin, as well as a step, rest below the bed. On each side of the bed are elaborately carved stands, one with a mirror and basin for morning ablutions, the other used to apply makeup. Birds and butterflies, carved in pairs, remind the newly married couple to pursue marital harmony.

Adjacent to the two-storey mansion was one of Penang's earliest Chinese schools, the Goh Hock Tong or "Hall of Five Good Fortunes," often translated as "Five Luck Villa," which was founded in 1819. After finding a new location for the school on Chulia Street, Chung Keng Quee transformed an imposingly elaborate private temple, either by extensively renovating the old school or by building anew, that was to serve as his family's ancestral hall. Besides the requisite periodic ritual purposes relating to the veneration of ancestors, it is possible that the ancestral hall was viewed also as an appropriate place to tutor Chung's young children and grandchildren about traditional Confucian morality. The residence and the temple are directly connected with each other by a corridor. In front, a cast-iron fence and gate separate the busy street from an open yard with various plantings of bushes and flowers. Although the three-bay structure at ground level is rather plain, an elaborate roof system gives the gray brick structure a top-heavy yet imposing appearance. Granite columns, beams, brackets, and supporting ornaments were likely imported from China, either carved there or made by craftsmen who were brought in to do the carving on-site while the temple was being built. An intricately carved fascia board, which caps

and encloses the ends of the rafters, stretches just below the edge of the inclined roof tiles. An elaborate ensemble of colorful ornamentation that reaches nearly a meter above the roofline runs horizontally along the ridgeline and down the edge of both gable eaves. While some portions of the decoration are *jiannian* "cut-and-paste" porcelain mosaics, others are molded and fired porcelain pieces likely made in Foshan, Guangdong, which has a long history of producing fine ornamental pieces for temples and residences. Fired pieces of calligraphy invoking auspicious phrases such as *shoubi nanshan*, "May You Live as Long as the Southern Mountains," are mingled above the animal, floral, geometric, and human motifs. It is likely that craftsmen were brought from Foshan not only to install imported pieces but also to fabricate some on-site.

Above the entry are the four characters *Shenzhi jiashu* that may utilize Chung Keng Quee's *zi* or honorific name, meaning "Family School of Shenzhi" or possibly also "Family School of Prudence." A pair of magnificent door gods painted on the heavy wooden panels, each of which is set into a stone base from where they can pivot, protect the temple. Within the entry hall and the veranda that stretches to the altar hall, the beams and roof supports are all carved lavishly with tableaux of molded figurines telling traditional narrative tales along the wall. Many of these tableaux are situated within architectural models of homes and temples. In both the entry hall and the altar hall, late nineteenth-century chandeliers hang from the rafters.

The central bay of the darkened altar hall is entered through carved hardwood doors to reveal a magnificent tiered ancestral altar set within a carved and gilded wooden case. Just in front of the altar is a life-sized bronze statue of Chung Keng Quee dressed in the robe of a Chinese official of the Second Rank. Above the altar is a horizontal board with three characters, *jingzhen tang*, meaning "Hall for Celebrating Prudence." In front on the altar are three square tables used to hold candles and other ritual paraphernalia. Above the altar, within the stepped niche, is his ancestral tablet with the text that highlights his receipt of the Imperial honor *Zizheng dafu* or "High Counselor" (second rank), rewarded with the Peacock Feather and Expectant Daotai or "Magistrate" (fourth rank).

The China Mail in Hong Kong reported the death of Chung Keng Quee, calling him "Cheang Keng Kwi, Capitan of Perak, a millionaire," on December 12, 1901 at the age of seventy-four, leaving a wife, ten sons and five daughters, twenty grandchildren, and four great-grandchildren. (These numbers differ from what is noted on the ancestral altar in Penang: nine sons, six daughters, twelve grandsons, and six grand-daughters.) With fifteen children, one of whom was adopted and another by a woman he did not marry, the residences must have been once full of activity. Recognizing the importance of education in Western languages and culture, Chung Keng Quee made certain his children attended the finest schools in Penang and elsewhere. His adopted son is said to have

Left Decorated with ornate carvings of fertility symbols, intricate embroidery, and hanging tassels, a bridal bed dominates this space as a veritable room within a room, while other obligatory furnishings necessary for the outfitting of a Peranakan wedding chamber crowd the walls.

Below This modern bedroom, which is furnished in styles characteristic of the early decades of the twentieth century, suggests the fluidity of Peranakan life during that period.

been the first Chinese to play rugby. Three of his sons also were prominent sportsmen, especially horsemen with stables in Perak. Arnold Wright's 1908 compendium, *Twentieth Century Impressions of British Malaya*, devotes more attention to horse racing than to any other colonial pastime, such as polo, automobilism [*sic*], snipe and crocodile shooting, cricket, tennis, football, hockey, swimming, and rowing. Chung Ah Yong, an "enthusiastic sportsman," was also described as being "a member of the Society of Arts, London, a member of the Taiping Sanitary Board, and a Visiting Justice," whose sons were also learning English. After the death of Chung Keng Quee, his eighth son, Chung Thye Siong, who assisted in the management of his father's estate, resided in the mansion on Church Street while also maintaining a country residence called "Green Lodge" on Macalister Road.

None of his children, however, gained the prominence of Chung Thye Phin (Zheng Daping), his fourth son. Born in his family's home on Barrack Road in Taiping, Perak, in 1879, when his father was over fifty years of age, he was educated in Penang at St Xavier's Institution before beginning work at his father's side. Although Thye Phin was only twenty-two in 1901 when his father died, he increasingly assumed management of the tin mines and opium farms as well as expanding involvement in real estate in Penang and Ipoh. Under his management, modern methods of hydraulic mining were instituted that improved the quantity and quality of tin extracted. His level of civic engagement exceeded that

of his father, most likely because he moved easier in the world of the colonial masters because of his Western education and fluency in English. He was appointed as a member of the Perak State Council just as he turned twenty-one. In 1921, at the age of forty-two, he was bestowed the title Capitan China as head of the Chinese community in Perak. Like two of his brothers, he was an avid horseman, but also developed a passion for motoring in expensive automobiles and was known as a good billiard player. It is said that he made many overseas trips.

Chung Thye Phin is well known for the sumptuous homes he constructed. He built a stately mansion early in the twentieth century in European Art Deco style on North Beach, now Gurney Drive, among the coconut palms along the seashore. With a central dome, high ceilings, and balustrades, the residence was a veritable palace. Queeny Chang, the eldest daughter of Tjong A Fie in Medan, visited Chung Thye Phin's mansion with her aunt, recalling many fashionable European touches, but mentioning nothing of the kinds of Chinese motifs she highlighted in Cheong Fatt Tze's Penang home (Chang, 1981: 52–3):

When we entered the big hall, my eyes were arrested by a life size oil painting of an extremely handsome young man in a costume such as worn by English lords; white breeches, sapphire blue long-tailed cutaway coat, frilly white shirt and a high cravat. His head was covered with a white wig, his hand poised lightly on a small table and

on his little finger he wore a huge diamond ring, its unmistakable blue sparkle skillfully brought out by the artist. He held a white lace handkerchief in his left hand. He looked so elegant and grand that I could hardly take my eyes off him. "That's the owner of this castle," said Aunt Cheah number two, pointing to the picture.

Mrs. Chung ... led us through the house from one room to another, each laid out differently. Then she took us up stairs to their living quarters. Her bedroom was separated from that of her husband's by a cosy drawing room and a study. "We usually spend the evenings here because my husband likes the privacy of his study where he can read and write undisturbed while I do some embroidery," she told us. The bedroom was an absolute dream. The walls were paneled with *bois-de-rose* brocade which was also used for draperies for the windows over cream-coloured lace curtains. The soft sunlight shimmered through accompanied by a cool breeze from the sea. The bed was in the form of a big shell covered with a canopy decorated with silver cupids. The pillows and bedspread were of pink lace and satin. On the floor lay a fleecy coloured carpet and the high ceiling was painted with lilies-of-the-valley and forget-me-nots.

Adjoining the bedroom was the dressing room. In it stood a long three-sided looking-glass in which one could see oneself from three angles. Along the wall, near the window stood the dressing table arranged with big and small bottles of perfume, and in crystal containers—a variety of face powder! Noticing my curiosity, Mrs. Chung smiled sweetly and said: "I only use *bedak sejuk* (pure rice powder), it's best for the skin. A paneled closet contained her wardrobe of *sarongs*, *kebayas* and slippers embroidered with gold and silver threads, sequins and multi-coloured beads.

A connecting door opened to the bathroom laid with rose tiles. Even in this room, everything was luxurious: sets of towels in matching colours, soaps, bathcubes and other curiosities. Seeing this, Aunt Cheah remarked: "If I had to use all this, I'd rather go without a bath." It made us all laugh, but I felt for the first time like envy. To be surrounded by so much luxury and beautiful things all the time must be marvelous, I thought.

Finally Mrs. Chung took us downstairs to have tea in the dining room built under the sea. We sat at a long table laid with all sorts of delicacies. We really enjoyed the tea and I ate to my heart's content. When I happened to look up at the ceiling I saw it was not painted as I had at first thought. It was a glass dome through which I could see fishes swimming about! Seeing my astonishment, Mrs. Chung explained amiably: "Yes, they are real fishes. My husband designed

this room himself and had it built under the sea. He claims it will relieve our boredom if we have our meals in the company of fishes. It is a pity he's now in London buying racehorses and he will be back for the Gold Cup next month. Then, he can show you more of his eccentricities."

Chung Thye Phin made many trips to China with his wives, although there are few details. There is no record that he, or indeed any of his siblings, made any effort to search out their father's ancestral home in Guangdong province. At some point after his death in 1935, Chung Thye Phin's North Beach mansion was transformed into a hotel, which then ignominiously was demolished in 1964, erasing one of Penang's most elegant residences. Working with B. H. Ung, a Penang architect who pioneered the use of reinforced concrete buildings, in the 1930s Thye Phin designed a spacious holiday space called "Relau Villa," a veritable resort with the first swimming pool built on the island. In the Penang hills, among others constructed by wealthy British, he also built a retreat from the heat and called it "Highlands." In 2008, the Relau Villa stands as it has for many decades as a still grand but deserted derelict and deteriorating structure. When Chung Thye Phin died in 1935, he left behind three widows, ten sons, and seven daughters. In a span of a single generation, the fascination for things Chinese seems to have diminished substantially in the Chung family when his father's residence on Church Street is compared to the majestic homes of his sons.

Top The narrow skywell just inside the front entry leads to the ancestral altar, which is the dimly lighted area in the rear.

Above left Colorful ornamentation molded in plaster lines the walls of the ancestral hall.

Above right A life-sized bronze statue of Chung Keng Kwee attired in a Mandarin robe of the Second Rank and wearing a Mandarin's cap is positioned in front of the ancestral altar.

Right The main altar of the ancestral hall is a grand assemblage of interlocking wooden components, each carved and gilded, with porcelain and bronze votive articles on the tables.

SUN YAT-SEN SHOPHOUSE

PENANG, MALAYSIA

1880s

Among the many charms of Penang are the continuous rows of nineteenth-century shophouses that line its sprawling old streets. In most of Southeast Asia, the term "shophouse" is used only to describe buildings in which businesses are located on the ground floor and residential quarters are found upstairs or in the back, while in Penang a shophouse can be a purely residential structure, which elsewhere would be called a terrace house. Most shophouses in Penang, whether for business or residential use, principally have a history of interest to those who occupy them, but occasionally there is a structure that has international significance because of activities that took place within it. This is the case with the shophouse found at 120 Armenian Street because of its association with the indefatigable Dr Sun Yat-sen, often called the "Father of the Nation" or *Guofu*, an individual

venerated worldwide for more than a century by Chinese of all political persuasions. His efforts to engage Overseas Chinese living throughout the world at the beginning of the twentieth century led not only to anti-Qing uprisings but also eventually to the establishment of the Republic of China, on January 1, 1912. Moreover, the shophouse itself, which served as a significant base for Sun Yat-sen's activities in Penang, is a fine example of a late nineteenth-century architectural style whose significance has been enhanced by his personal association with it.

Born in Guangdong province in 1866, Sun sailed to Hawaii at the age of thirteen to be with his brother who had migrated there in 1871 as a laborer. In Honolulu, Sun studied in two schools before returning home in 1883, later studying English in Hong Kong before earning a medical degree there in 1892. Yet, rather than pursue a career as a physician or

some other profession where he could directly utilize his knowledge of English and Western science, Sun, who was a visionary, chose to devote himself as a nationalist to revolutionary change. Joining with other iconoclastic Chinese, Sun was instrumental in setting up the Xing Zhong Hui (Revive China Society) in 1894. His initial goal was to bring an end to the imperial monarchy, which had endured for nearly 2,000 years, in hopes of establishing in its place a constitutional monarchy form of government necessary for a modern nation. In a short period of time, his thinking further evolved to a more radical notion encapsulated in the slogan "Expel the Manchus, restore Chinese rule, and establish a federal republic." Sun's vocation to revive and strengthen China in order to set it on a course for economic and social development was to consume him for more than a decade and a half after 1895 as he continually strived to raise the consciousness of those who could help him. While living in Japan, he and others established the Tongmenghui, literally the United Allegiance Society, which came to serve as the vanguard political organization for building alliances of like-minded patriots throughout the world. He formulated the inspirational "Three Principles of the People" or *San Min Zhuyi*—Nationalism, Democracy, and Social Well-being—in 1905 as instrumental guidelines for transforming moribund China.

At critical junctures, Sun visited and lived in Penang, where the Southeast Asia branch of the Tongmenghui was headquartered, in order to solicit financial support from progressive Overseas Chinese as well as to plan a vortex of uprisings whose purpose was to topple China's imperial system. Between 1909 and 1911, the shophouse at

120 Armenian Street served as the headquarters for the Tongmenghui as well as for the *Kwong Wah Jit Poh* (Glorious China Daily), a Chinese language newspaper. In addition, it was the headquarters for the Penang Philomathic Union, an organization whose name in Chinese states its purpose clearly as a "reading club." Early in the twentieth century, its English name also would have been understood by educated people who loved learning, while today the name appears enigmatic. Between 1912 and 1913, all three organizations moved from 120 Armenian Street to other locations in Penang.

Opposite above The pair of ventilation ports above the exterior windows includes a stylized *shou* or longevity character in the center, which is surrounded by four bats (*fu*) that together symbolize the Five Good Fortunes.

Opposite below Painted in blue, the Sun Yat-sen shophouse is one of a sequence of adjacent shophouses linked by a five-foot way.

Right A detail of one of the colorful ceramic wall tiles found along the lower façade of the house.

Below What once would have been an altar for the worship of deities today holds several images of the venerated Sun Yat-sen.

In November 1910, after first holding a meeting with his associates at his formal office on Dato' Kramat Road, a two-storey bungalow within a walled compound, in Penang, Sun convened another emergency session around a table on the first floor of the shophouse at 120 Armenian Street. It was here that the Canton (Guangzhou) Uprising was planned and where the prospective Wuchang Uprising was broached, both events of great historical significance in the tumult that led to the demise of China's crumbling imperial system. Sun successfully pleaded at the Penang Conference for continuing financial assistance from faithful Overseas Chinese supporters living in Malaya, many of whom were disheartened because of the failure of nine earlier uprisings.

Even though the Canton Uprising failed—Sun's tenth disappointment—the event is still celebrated as a key link in a revolutionary chain with profound memories of seventy-two martyrs, including three young men from Penang, who sacrificed their lives. The Wuchang action that followed, moreover, takes pride of place in the canon of China's twentieth-century history because of its success. The date it erupted, October 10, 1911, generally known in Chinese as *shuangshi jie* or "Double Ten Day," the tenth day of the tenth month, is celebrated in the Republic of China as National Day, just as July 4th is in the United States, and July 14th, Bastille Day, is in France. Interestingly enough, Sun Yat-sen was traveling in the United States at the time of the Wuchang Uprising, only learning of the tumultuous event from a newspaper he was reading in Denver, Colorado; thus, Sun Yat-sen actually played no direct role in this decisive moment of upheaval. Nonetheless, after returning to China via London and Paris on a P&O steamship with stopovers in Penang and Singapore, Sun was elected provisional president and inaugurated on January 1, 1912, the founding day of the Republic of China. Puyi, the last emperor of China, then abdicated on February 12, 1912. Thus, it is in this scripting of the narrative of modern Chinese history that a common shophouse in Penang came to occupy a legendary position.

Constructed around 1880 by a Straits Chinese, the dwelling was owned by Cheah Joo Seang, a Straits Chinese and a prominent trustee of the Cheah Kongsi, an organization to serve the clansmen of one of Penang's five great Hokkien immigrant groups. At the time of Sun Yat-sen's use of the shophouse for his meetings, the residence was owned by Lim Boon Yeow, about whom little is known. Lim sold the house in 1913 to Madam Phuah Gek Thuan, who renovated the house to its current look in terms of installing a new kitchen and relocating the spiral staircase. In 1926 the property was acquired by Ch'ng Teong Swee, who had been born in Fujian but migrated to Penang in 1904 with his father. He lived in the house until 1932 when he moved his immediate family to a bungalow, leaving his stepmother and siblings behind. After Ch'ng died in 1972, the shophouse was administered by his estate until 1992 when the building was acquired by Khoo Salma Nasution, Ch'ng Teong Swee's maternal granddaughter, one of Penang's most fervent heritage conservationists. She and her colleagues view themselves as custodians of an internationally significant cultural property that is part of their family's legacy. The property has been restored as it must have looked early in the twentieth century and has been outfitted with displays of the residence's historic role in Sun Yat-sen's journey to create a modern China.

This brief chronology of family occupancy only partially sets out the dynamics of this residence over more than a century. At times, family business interests also intervened. For example, Teong Swee and his cousins set up a hardware shop not too far away, on Beach Street. While the business relationship broke up in 1919, Ch'ng Teong Swee continued to manage the hardware shop. During the depression around 1930, when a Penang firm selling arms and ammunitions was shutting down, Ch'ng Teong Swee was able to purchase its goods and folded them into his current business. He renamed the firm Ch'ng Eng Joo. The business thrived as he supplied British-made rifles and handguns to policemen, hunters, and planters. With the invasion of Malaysia by the Japanese in late 1941, the shop was bombed and the stock destroyed; it was not until after the war that business again was possible. For a short time thereafter, the shop operated in cramped quarters at 120 Armenian Street before moving to a larger nearby location. At that point, the historic structure at 120 Armenian Street was turned into a warehouse for the larger shop on Chulia Street.

The Armenian Street shophouse is a narrow double-storey structure with a covered walkway or five-foot way that was linked with the neighboring shophouses to facilitate pedestrian traffic. After a fire in 1814, the Municipal Commissioners of Penang mandated that new shophouses had to be built with bricks with a plaster coat and roofed with fired tiles rather than wood and *attap* thatch that had been common before. The full façade of the upper storey was sheathed with a series of wooden louvered shutters to regulate airflow and light. Today, there are two layers of glass windows; the wooden shutters have yet to be restored. Beneath the shutters is a series of ornamental ventilation ports made of thick ceramic tiles with carved openings in them. The façade is painted in a light blue hue.

The second storey of the building reaches to the street, with its overhang creating a veranda-like walkway beneath that provides protection against the intense sun and tropical downpours. Both the surface of the five-foot way and walls beneath the pair of windows of the veranda are covered with square and rectangular glazed tiles with floral and geometric patterns and colors commonly found at the time on Peranakan dwellings. Above each of the ground floor windows, in front of which is a series of protective iron bars, is a symmetrical ventilation port, a lobed opening in the shape of a butterfly or bat stretched laterally. Within each of these lobed openings is a painted wooden insert that is both ornamental and functional. The molded insert depicts a composition comprising four bats encircling a stylized *shou* or "longevity" character. Together, these five elements represent *wu fu*, the five essential elements of good fortune that can be traced to the fifth century BCE in the *Shujing* or "Book of History," and which were very popular during the Ming and Qing dynasties: longevity, wealth, health, love of virtue, and to die a natural death in old age. Above the door are three characters, *Zhuang Rong Yu*, on a horizontal signboard, indicating Ch'ng Eng Joo, the name of Ch'ng Teong Swee's firearms company. On the surface of the red doors are the characters *guorui jiaxiang*, "Prosperity for the Country, Auspiciousness for the Family."

With a width of approximately 5.5 meters and a depth of about 40 meters, an elongated building of this sort would have been quite dark in the inside without its characteristic spatial component called a skywell, sometimes also referred to as a lightwell or airwell. Skywells, called *tianjing* throughout southern China where they are common both in urban shophouses and country homes, provide a passive "mechanism" to facilitate internal ventilation and introduce light within the attenuated structure.

After passing through the front entry, one enters a room that is backlit by the skywell, with light radiating in through two doorways

Above Adjacent to the skywell, this sitting area is just behind screen wall.

Right Stacked painted baskets of this type were often used to hold gifts for weddings.

and openings in a carved wooden wall screen that separates this public area from the more cloistered family area behind. Fitted with both a rectangular altar table and a square table beneath it, this central space once probably served as a location for deities worshipped by members of the household, while a space deeper inside or upstairs would have been preferred as locations to place ancestral tablets. A table with stools in the center and heavy wooden chairs and side tables arranged symmetrically along the sides of the room provide a welcoming space for visitors who would not be invited beyond the screen.

The back of the carved wooden screen presents a richly ornamented "wall" of low relief carvings and lattice panels. Today, on this wall one finds the type of lithographed portrait of Sun Yat-sen commonly found in Chinese schools in the past. In addition to two flags, one of the Nationalist Party (Kuomingtang) and the other of the Republic of China, Sun's image is framed by a set of couplets with his admonition,

"The revolution is not yet over, comrades must continue their efforts." The table and chairs set in this area, which is adjacent to a rectangular skywell, provides a bright and airy place to drink tea and converse with guests. The skywell itself rises like an intimate atrium up through the second floor, allowing abundant space for a variety of vegetation that brings the outdoors inside the home. Large vats deployed in this area capture falling rainwater for domestic uses. Attached to the wall is an old wooden curio cabinet. Nearby is an iron safe, made in Birmingham, England, in 1900, that was used to keep account books and cash secure.

In one corner of the atrium-like indoor–outdoor room is a grand spiral staircase that leads to the family's rooms upstairs. Surrounding the second floor section of the skywell, wooden louvered panels make it possible to vary the receipt of light and air into the bedrooms and storerooms on that level. The master bedroom was at the front of the house since it had a full wall of shuttered and louvered windows. At

one point during the Second World War, as many as thirty-seven people lived in the house, including servants who watched over children, cooked, washed clothes, and kept the house clean.

The spaces surrounding the skywell at ground level—a veritable courtyard "room" partially inside and partially outside—are separated from the back of the house by tall glass windows resting on a brick masonry wall. In this rear area, which also has a smaller skywell lined with granite blocks, is a water tank, toilet, and areas for bathing and washing clothes. With a high ceiling rising two storeys in the space beyond the skywell, there is abundant space for a 1920s-style large brick stove that was fired using wood. This capacious space actually emerged because of a road-taking exercise at the back of the shophouse, which necessitated bringing a separate backyard kitchen inside the existing building in 1924. To do this required the removal of some rooms on the second floor, the construction of a clerestory with a jack roof, an

extension above the roofline with windows to enhance ventilation and light, as well as a storage loft. Today, one sees displayed throughout this spacious area a collection of cooking pots, hanging baskets, storage vessels, implements, and storage larder, which were characteristic of an early twentieth-century Nyonya kitchen, the type that was maintained by the last matriarch of the house, Tan Eng Siew, who died in 1953 and was the stepmother of Ch'ng Teong Swee.

An historical drama based on Sun Yat-sen's activities in Penang in 1910, called "Road to Dawn," literally "Night, Dawn" or *yeming* in Chinese, was filmed in 2006 on location at 120 Armenian Street and at other sites in the city of Penang. With an international cast and crew from China, Taiwan, Hong Kong, and Malaysia, the film won accolades from Chinese audiences and awards from festival bodies. The film premiered at Beijing's Great Hall of the People in June 2007 before it was released worldwide.

Left The large kitchen in the rear of the shophouse is used today to display all sorts of food storage containers and food preparation implements.

Above left This portable clay brazier can be used to burn either charcoal or coal and is used to simmer food being cooked in the covered clay pot.

Above center On the left is a stove for boiling water and on the right a stand to hold a wok for cooking.

Above right These stacked metal containers are used to transport a multicourse meal. Above them is a variety of hanging baskets.

KEE ANCESTRAL MANOR

SUNGAI BAKAP, MALAYSIA

1870s–1880s

Some enterprising Chinese immigrants opened farms or tin mines or started businesses. Kee Lai Huat, a pioneering planter of sugarcane and manufacturer of brown sugar, founded a town, Sungai Bakap, in Malaya, about 30 kilometers from Butterworth, which he hoped would become the permanent abode of his descendants. Today, more than 150 years later, the nineteenth-century Kee ancestral manor stands proudly, even somewhat ostentatiously, amidst rows of old single- and double-storey shophouses in Sungai Bakap that line the busy main road on the way to Ipoh. The establishment of this town and the building of a grand ancestral hall and associated dwellings in the late nineteenth century are a testament to the vision of this one man, Kee Lai Huat.

Here, on the mainland opposite the island of Penang in a hinterland once administered by the British as Province Wellesley, communities of Chaozhou-speaking immigrants transformed a swampy jungle into progressively prosperous farmland. Chaozhou, also spelled Teochew

and Teochiu, together with Cantonese and Hakka, represent the three principal dialect groups in Guangdong province. Originating in an area referred to in Chinese as Chaoshan, a composite term representing the neighboring Chaozhou and Shantou areas, Chaozhou-speaking people migrated throughout the eighteenth and nineteenth centuries in significant numbers, not only to Thailand and Cambodia but also to the peninsular and insular portions of the Nanyang. Proud of their distinctive culture, especially their cuisine and tea, opera and instrumental music, embroidery and woodcarvings, migrants from Chaozhou retained elements of their material and ritual cultures in the new communities they founded. For example, the preparation and drinking of Chaozhou tea, called *gongfu* tea, literally "tea brewed with great skill," is usually a concentrated brew with a strong taste that is prepared following a specific set of steps. It is said that Chaozhou people, wherever they are, "prefer to have no rice for three days than no tea for

a day." In Sungai Bakap, just as in the days of the early immigrants from eastern Guangdong province, there still are small restaurants serving tea that are noted also for their Chaozhou dishes such as *chai koay* (steamed vegetable dumplings), braised duck rice, yam paste cake, and steamed fish with sour plums and salted vegetables. Given Malaysia's multiethnic heritage, local folks in Sungai Bakap also eat Malay and Indian dishes such as *nasi lemak* (rice cooked in coconut cream with spices) and *cendol* (shaved ice, coconut milk, and palm sugar).

Born in 1834, Kee Lai Huat left his hometown in Chenghai county near Shantou in northeastern Guangdong province in 1853 at the age of nineteen. Unlike so many nineteenth-century Chinese immigrants who came as indentured laborers, often mere coolies who contracted to pay back their journey and living expenses in exchange for an opportunity to make a living, Kee Lai Huat is said to have had some basic education and indeed paid for his junk passage. He landed at Bukit Tambun, a small port at the mouth of a narrow stream that provided access into Province Wellesley. While much land was still available for development, by the middle of the nineteenth century this region had already begun to be transformed by Chaozhou immigrants into sugar-cane plantations. Kee Lai Huat's own drive, coupled with the good fortune to marry the daughter of the region's most successful sugarcane baron, Khaw Loh Hup, provided a foundation for his future financial and family success.

No one had become more prosperous in the burgeoning sugar business than Khaw Loh Hup, a native of Chao'an county, also near Shantou, who had arrived early in the nineteenth century. Serving first as a head laborer on a sugarcane plantation, Khaw Loh Hup eventually acquired his own sugarcane fields before gaining new lands for exploitation deeper into Perak. After marrying, he and his wife had

Opposite above A portrait of Kee Lai Huat wearing ceremonial robes of the Qing dynasty.

Opposite below Linked to adjacent shophouses via a five-foot way, the restored entry to the Kee ancestral manor marks it clearly as a Chinese building.

Above This early twentieth-century photograph of the area outside the Kee ancestral hall, portraying a time when many family members lived in the compound, may be compared with the current quieter view seen below.

Below The three-bay ancestral hall sits in front of the row of residences, which can be accessed through the gates.

three children in quick succession, a son, Khaw Boo Aun, born in 1825, who was to take over his father's extensive business holdings; a second son, and then, in 1828, a daughter, Bee Gek. In 1855 the marriage of Kee Lai Huat at the age of twenty-one to the twenty-seven year old Khaw Bee Gek, daughter of Khaw Loh Hup and younger sister of Khaw Boo Aun, joined the families in a personal relationship that went beyond business. Khaw Boo Aun became manager of his father's estates in 1866 when the old man retired and then subsequently left Malaya to spend his final days in his home village in China. Khaw Boo Aun himself prospered well beyond his father's level, cooperating with Kee Lai Huat, his brother-in-law. In addition, the two of them competed successfully with European speculators who were using science and advanced technology to develop the sugar industry. The Khaws and the Kees both succeeded in becoming sugar magnates and pillars of the community.

Unusually, after leaving the structure of her parents' home, the young bride Bee Gek faced a family situation quite unlike that of traditional brides in China—no mother-in-law to oversee her household work and no father-in-law for her to bow before. In addition, she did not have to contend with the inevitable maneuvering of sistersin-law or brothers-in-law, a common practice in traditional Chinese households. After the newlywed couple moved out of the Khaw family residence in Bukit Tambun, Bee Gek and her husband together became the sole authorities within their own home. Over time, their devotion to the six sons and two daughters who were born to them led to the construction of the Kee estate in Sungai Bakap to house them together in a fashion that expressed the unity of a family in the present as well as its hopes for the future.

Top A view from the skywell of the Kee ancestral hall looking through the *xiatang* or "lower hall" towards the front gate and the street.

Above The eight panels of the doorways leading to the skywell and altars of the ancestral hall have written on them more than 500 characters of the "Maxims for Managing the Home" by Zhu Bolu.

Above left Along the back wall of the *shangtang* or "upper hall" are three altars placed within elaborate cabinets with associated tables used for ritual. The inscribed horizontal board has the characters *Yong Si Tang* or "Hall of Eternal Remembrance." In front of the altar are miniature clay statues of Kee Choe Im and his wife, the parents of Lai Huat.

Above right Close-up of the central altar venerates Kee Lai Huat, the focal ancestor who established the lineage in Sungai Bakap, and his six sons.

Right One of the two side altar cabinets that commemorates succeeding generations of the Kee lineage.

As Kee Lai Huat began to plan for the construction of a family estate, he worked to clear jungle areas in cooperation with his brother-in-law, Khaw Boo Aun. Kee Lai Huat purchased an undeveloped area from a French businessman in Singapore and called it Val-d'Or (Valley of Gold) Estate, gradually transforming the land into sugarcane, rubber, and coconut plantations. Chaozhou, his home area in China, had gained fame as a major producer of cane sugar and it is possible that Kee Lai Huat and others from that area had already been aware of the growing, processing, and perhaps even trading of sugar as a commodity when they arrived in Malaya. Chenghai, Kee Lai Huat's home county, in fact, had a long-standing reputation as a producer of brown sugar. It was also well known as a center of advanced technology for processing the raw sugarcane juices and was a commercial center for the national distribution of the finished product (Needham et al., 1996, 1(3): 109–10, 116–17). Perhaps he understood implicitly the value of sugar as a commodity—food, drink, confectionary, condiments, medicine, preservative—because of the role it played as a cash crop in reclaimed land back in Guangdong province.

The Kee family compound took shape within an extensive walled compound. Alongside the roadway, an imposing three-bay gatehouse was built to open into a courtyard that led first to the ancestral hall and then beyond to the residences. As can be seen clearly today, the gatehouse is connected via a five-foot way to adjacent shophouses on both ends. Four square outer columns and a pair of round ones, each with a simple capital, lift the overhanging eaves and support the glazed tile roof of what was clearly meant to be an imposing entryway. At the center of this structure is a formal entry with a pair of long couplets

along both sides. The two characters, *Pingyang*, which appear above the doorway, indicate the name of the ancient ancestral home for this branch of the Kee lineage near Linfen in Shanxi province, which had been established first in Shandong province much earlier. Other Kee branches have their roots in Gansu, Hebei, and Liaoning provinces. Although records are incomplete, the ancestors of Kee Lai Huat only migrated from Shanxi in north China to the Chaozhou area of Guangdong some 700 years ago, perhaps passing through some intermediate locations. Kee Lai Huat's journey of more than 3000 kilometers from coastal southeastern China to the west coast of the Malaya peninsula is but a continuation of a long history of migration.

The Kee Ancestral Hall

The Kee Ancestral Manor consists of two sets of buildings: an ancestral hall just inside the gate and across an open courtyard, as well as a series of six connected terrace-like residences aligned together that face the back of the ancestral hall. Framed by high walls, the freestanding ancestral hall is a three-bay structure, which from the front elevation looks quite modest in size but from the side is clearly composed of two linked horizontal buildings of substantial dimensions with a courtyard between them. Organized much like a temple, the front building is lower and narrower than the much larger structure in the back, which houses the ancestral altars in three separate bays. The front structure, called a *xiatang* or "lower/entrance hall" to underscore its subsidiary position, has three doorways, one in the center and two flanking ones leading into side rooms. The central door, which is normally not open, has four gold

characters, *jiaguan jinlu*, a felicitous wish that "promotion and salary will be bestowed [on you]." This phrase usually accompanies a pair of door gods, but here there are only the calligraphic elements. One of the pair of hanging lanterns has a large character Kee for the family's surname on it while the other has *Pingyang*, the ancestral homeland. Panels below the windows have a plum blossom floral design while panels above have polychrome paintings with abundant incised and brushwork calligraphy fitted all across the façade. A horizontal granite panel above the doorway has five carved characters, *Jinzu Ji Gongshi*, "Collective Hall for the Golden Ancestors of the Kees." In Malaysia, as the horizontal panel indicates, clan halls of this sort are called *kongsi*, which should not be confused with *kongsi*, pronounced the same way and literally "public company," and sometimes a "secret society" that also maintained a temple or hall for its members.

After crossing the raised granite threshold and entering the *xiatang* or "lower hall," a visitor arrives in a rectangular room, a place to enjoy tea or a light meal on quiet days but also a space that comes alive on festival days when many family members are present. On the left and right of this room are smaller chambers used in the past as offices or places to tutor the children and grandchildren in the Kee family. Ahead is a magnificent screen set with eight panels, which can be pivoted open or closed. More than 500 Chinese characters written in gold on a vermilion background are in the upper register of the panels. When closed, the screen reveals the full text of the "Maxims for Managing the Home" by Zhu Bolu, a seventeenth-century moralist whose tracts have continued to be common staples in Chinese temples and almanacs ever since. At the end of the nineteenth century, Zhu Bolu's instructions were popularized throughout the Straits Settlements in Chinese as well as translations in romanized Malay and romanized Hokkien (Frost, 2005: 50). The fifty-three maxims, each written in literary style without punctuation, range from the practical to the obscure.

Above these eight vermilion panels is a carved and gilded horizontal board with four characters, *minzhisuohao*, the initial words in a phrase in *The Great Learning* or *Daxue*, quoting the even older *Book of Poetry* or *Shijing* linking familial ethics with political ethics: "When a prince loves what the people love, and hates what the people hate, then he is what is called the parent of the people."

Once the vermilion panels are pivoted open, three passageways lead to the central courtyard and two side areas before culminating in the taller and deeper building called *shangtang* or "upper hall," which contains three recessed areas holding three separate ancestral altars. While each of the three blackwood ancestral altars is magnificent, having been made back in Chaozhou by craftsmen whose woodworking skill is renowned, the central one not only is larger in terms of size and the elaborate nature of the ornamentation, but it rests within a separate wooden cabinet with carved and painted door panels. With pride of place, this central altar is the area for venerating Kee Lai Huat, the focal Kee ancestor who established the Kee lineage here in Sungai Bakap in the mid-nineteenth century, and his six sons—Kee Tek Thye, Kee Tek Kooi, Kee Tek Pang, Kee Tek Kow, Kee Teng Seng, and Kee Tek Leng—the first and second generations of Kees in Malaysia. As was customary, there are no tablets on this altar for his two daughters, Kee Siew Kee and Kee Siew Sin. Inside the tiered altar, Lai Huat's ancestral tablet rests on a step above the tablets of his six sons. Behind them is a wall with 100 representations of the character *fu*, which are invocations for good fortune. The side altars commemorate family members of the third, fourth, and fifth generations who have died. Directly in front of each altar is a carved and ornamented oblong high altar table. Above the bay holding the seven tablets of Kee Lai Huat and his sons is an inscribed horizontal board with the characters *Yong Si Tang* or "Hall of Eternal Remembrance," a common name used throughout southern China for ancestral halls. In front of the altar are miniature clay statues of Kee Choe Im and his wife, the parents of Lai Huat.

On the side walls of the *shangtang* adjacent to the altars are two pairs of ancestral portraits. Looking towards the altars, the pair hanging on the right is of Kee Lai Huat in an ornately carved European-style frame and his father, Kee Cheoe Im, in a simpler rectangular frame. On the opposite wall, in frames like those of their spouses, are Lai Huat's wife, Khaw Bee Gek, and his mother, whose name is not given, perhaps because in traditional China a woman was known as "the wife of a particular person" rather than having an identity of her own. Commemorative portraiture of this type, which has a long history in China, was often carried out posthumously, not only to memorialize parents and grandparents but also to create objects that go beyond ancestral tablets to facilitate the veneration of ancestors. While ancestral portraits usually were larger than life size in imperial households, here in the Kee ancestral hall the images are large but not life size.

Each human figure in ancestral portraits of this type is shown in an iconic forward-facing pose with a somewhat solemn yet majestic gaze. It was common in the past for family members to be shown a sketchbook of illustrative stereotypical faces by the artist commissioned to do a painting of deceased relatives in order to help summon up memories. It is reasonably certain that the portrayal of the faces of Kee Lai Huat's parents, while finely executed, was accomplished without reference to either existing images of them or corroboration by anyone who knew them because they may have died before the portraits were commissioned. On the other hand, it is likely that Kee family members were able to give guidance concerning the facial compositions of their parents. In fact, there are photographs of the aging parents that may have been used for reference, thus the pictures likely bear their likenesses. Seated on throne-like elevated chairs, each of the four figures is clothed in a colorful, elaborate, and formal costume. The carpets upon which the chairs of Kee Lai Huat and his wife Khaw Bee Gek rest help contribute to an illusion of three-dimensionality in the paintings.

The rectangular insignia, often called a mandarin square, on the front of the clothing signifies one of nine civil ranks represented by brilliant images of birds, which are unlike those of the imperial family who displayed dragons and phoenixes, or military officials who displayed animals. Since a husband's rank was extended to his wife as well, she too had a mandarin square attached to her clothing. It was the custom for the bird on a man's costume to look towards his right shoulder while that on the women faced left to create a kind of mirror symmetry, a convention seen with these paintings (Stuart and Rawski, 2001: 112–13).

Kee Cheoe Im's badge, which represents a first rank civil official, shows a white crane or *xianhe* with several black tipped feathers, poised in flight. A celebratory text on paper above the painting indicates an award date in 1879. Nothing is known of the circumstances of his life in China at that point. Kee Lai Huat's insignia in the portrait, which represents a fourth rank civil official, shows a wild goose with a light tan upper head, back, and wing covers. The wives show the same birds, and the celebratory Chinese text above Khaw Bee Gek's portrait clearly states that the badge she is wearing is a fourth rank one. Family records indicate that a "Bird of Paradise," which could be a paradise flycatcher or *lianqiao*, a white bird with a prominent crest and two long, sweeping tail plumes, was awarded to Kee Lai Huat as well as his six sons, two sons-in-law, and three grandsons. Later, before his death, according to family recollection, Kee Lai Huat himself received the first rank white crane insignia. Kee Lai Huat's son Teik Tye traveled to Suzhou on his behalf to collect the award. Along one wall is a beautifully carved and gilded vertical board with the large character *shou*, a felicitous wish for longevity, which was presented by the imperial court in the 34th year of the Guangxu emperor (1904–5).

In Kee Lai Huat's will, which was prepared in the months before he died, he detailed how certain properties were to generate an income to support a ritual that would be carried out in the ancestral hall by his sons in rotation, beginning with the eldest. His intention was that these annual rituals would be carried out by succeeding generations of descendants. Indeed, now more than a century after his death, the Kee family continues to assemble to commemorate their forebears. Details of these contemporary observances are given below.

The Residences

The Kee residential compound seen today evolved over the years. After marrying in 1855, Kee Lai Huat and his bride Khaw Bee Gek lived in a modest thatch-roofed house with a well. As he prospered, he built a two-storey brick house on the site of the current ancestral hall. Behind his house, in the area later to be the site of his first son Tek Tye's terrace residence, he proceeded to build an ancestral hall, but subsequently abandoned that plan. The rounded pillars seen today in the front room of the residence are relics of that earlier effort. With the conversion of this structure, he demolished his own home towards the front to build the ancestral hall complex seen today. In time, each of his sons was to have built for them a terrace residence adjacent to that of their elder brother. Although he did not believe it proper for his daughters to live within the Kee complex—or for that matter to be buried in the Kee cemetery—Kee Lai Huat built each of them a two-storey bungalow at opposite ends of Sungei Bakap as part of their dowry. A visitor arriving from George Town passes the elder daughter's residence, while the younger daughter's is passed as one travels from Sungei Bakap to Nibong Tebal heading towards Ipoh.

Rather than a ramified rectangular dwelling with multiple courtyards as was found all over southern China at the time, Kee Lai Huat created a linear two-storey structure to house the families of his six sons. The adjacent residences were built in phases, first a unit for Tek Thye, his eldest son, and then ones for Tek Seng and Tek Leng, the fifth and sixth sons, who married sisters. Tek Khoi and Tek Phang, the second and third sons, received the end units because they had larger families. After her husband died in 1892, Khaw Bee Gek, the mother of the sons and the matriarch of the family, lived with her No. 5 son, Tek Seng, so she could be cared for by her favorite daughter-in-law. Although details are not available, it seems likely the residential complex took the shape currently seen during the 1870s and 1880s. This elongated structure has the general appearance of a series of shophouses or terrace houses with a five-foot way running the full length of the long building.

Each of the sons and their families were allocated a three-bay-wide unit of equal dimensions, each of which was demarcated from its neighbor's by an open arch along the outside corridor. While the size of each residence is the same, the interior layouts varied principally in terms of the number of bedrooms required by the households of different sizes. Not only could family members visit each other along this external corridor, the units were joined together on the interior by passageways on both the ground and second levels. For the privacy of the families currently living in the complex, the doors were sealed during the recent renovation. The overhanging second level, which is supported by nineteen square masonry columns, is clad with three sets of eight wooden louvered shutters, which afford both shade and protection from downpours while admitting fresh air. On a wall along the outside corridor, each family has placed a red shrine to Tian Guan, the Deity of Heaven, with a shelf for incense and offerings of fruits. On these wooden shrines there are many propitious characters, including *Tianguan Cifu*, "May the Heavenly Official (Deity of Heaven) Bestow Blessings." Nearby is a red wooden stand with a concave metal pan with a lid that is used to burn offerings of paper money to the gods for protection, to beseech good fortune, and to give thanks for blessings. It is believed that the consumption of the paper offerings, rendered to ash, transforms them into a form accessible to the gods.

While each unit differs in layout, this section focuses on the patterns seen in the residence of the eldest son, Tek Tye, whose unit was second from the left end. In the middle bay of the unit is a doorway framed by a pair of windows with metal bars and wooden panels that can be closed. Above the two windows is a symmetrical set of ventilation ports, each also with five metal bars running vertically. Each of the adjacent bays also has a large window with a ventilation port above. The doorway comprises two pairs of wooden panels, the outer one with open lattice at the top, which permits air to pass through when the doors are closed, and an inner set of solid doors that can be secured from the inside. Each of the panels of inner doors has two characters, which together represent a felicitous wish. Passing through this door brings one to a

T-shaped room with smaller chambers adjacent on both sides. The upper register of each of the sidewalls is open to facilitate interior ventilation. On the surfaces of the walls, mirrors, paintings, and calligraphic panels are hung. Two hemispheric columns and a pair of rectangular columns dominate these spaces, while accentuating the square floor tiles. At the head of this room is a wall with a pair of doorways. As with most large Chinese residences, this wall provides a location for a high altar table with one or two square tables in front of it. On an altar of this sort in the front room is a semi-private location for worshipping gods of many types with incense and food offerings.

Passing through either of the doorways leads to a narrow, shallow intermediate space with stairs leading to the second floor. The wooden stairwell begins on a granite slab, said to provide stability but also to protect against termites, then leads to a landing before shifting direction upwards to the second floor. Under the wooden stairs is a motif of overlapping rhombuses or lozenges, known in Chinese as *fangshengwen*. While patterns of this sort are seen throughout China, their exact meaning is often described as being obscure and inexplicable. Since a lozenge is a pun for "victory," a series of them interlinked can mean "forever" or "everlasting."

After passing through the double set of doorways with the stairwell between them is a long room with a pair of utility chambers with slanted corrugated roofs flanking a portion before the space is opened up on both sides by adjacent skywells. These vertical shafts that rise up through the building allow light and air to enter this commodious area, which was used for eating and relaxing. One can look up on both sides to see the shuttered windows of the rooms on the second floor.

Beyond this airy area is yet another small transverse space with a stairway leading to the second level that then leads to an expansive T-shaped kitchen area with a loft for storage above one portion. With its high ceilings and adjacent skywell, this area for the preparation of food is both well ventilated and well lit. A large masonry stove, of the sort found commonly in southern China, and fired by wood or charcoal, is situated at a central location. Nearby are masonry counters and shelves to store cooking pots and other implements used on a daily basis. Wooden shelves hang from several of the walls and are accompanied by a variety of wooden cabinets to store dried and preserved ingredients as well as bowls, plates, and serving dishes of many types. Large urns were used in kitchens of this sort to hold the abundant amounts of water that were consumed daily within the household.

Looking upwards in any of the downstairs rooms, one sees a ceiling constructed of wooden planks, which in fact are the floorboards of the second floor. Massive masonry columns, some square and some partially circular, support granite brackets which lift perpendicular beams, functioning as floor joists, atop which the floorboards are laid. These stone brackets are often described in Malacca as being a feature of Dutch construction methods and thus used to differentiate whether a dwelling is in Dutch style or Chinese style. However, since stone brackets of this sort were employed widely in southern China from times that preceded the arrival of the Dutch, one can state confidently that those seen here in Sungai Bakap follow Chinese construction principals, since they were probably put in place by Chinese carpenters and masons working together in the construction of these residences.

Outside the compound, along the main road, Kee Lai Huat built a line of retail shops to generate income for the upkeep of the estate, while behind an expansive area was planted with coconut and durian

Top One of several low stoves used for cooking in a corner of the expansive kitchen. A small altar to Zao Jun, the Kitchen God, is on the left.

Above This view through the skywell provides a glimpse of the louvered fenestration on the second floor.

trees. Beyond these, he selected an auspicious area as a cemetery for his descendants. In his will, he revealed that he was a realist: "After the death of my wife, if my boys (the six sons) wish to continue to live together that would be a good consolation to my mind, but unluckily a large tree must branch off, and a great water course must divide into several streams." After completing the Sungei Bakap complex, he sent his eldest son, Tek Thye, back to his home village in Chenghai in Guangdong province to build a similar complex for his parents, his adopted brother, and other close relatives.

CHEONG FATT TZE BLUE MANSION

PENANG, MALAYSIA

1896–1904

Constructed between 1896 and 1904, the Blue Mansion in Penang was built by Southeast Asia's foremost Mandarin-capitalist at the time. Although celebrated throughout Southeast Asia today with the name Cheong Fatt Tze, he is better known in the international media and in scholarly and popular literature in English and Chinese by such a variety of names—Chang Pi-shih (Zhang Bishi), Cheung Pat Sze, Chang Chen Hsun (Zhang Zhenxun), and Thio Thiau Siat (Thio Thiaw Siat, Tio Tiauw-set, Thio Tiaw Siat)—that some observers doubt whether these multiple aliases are actually the same complex man. Indeed, they are. Here, he will be referred to as Cheong Fatt Tze since this is the name now associated with his reborn Blue Mansion. In whatever way his name is rendered, Cheong Fatt Tze stands out as an extraordinary multinational entrepreneur who amassed fortunes in the Nanyang region through investments in plantations (rubber, tea, coffee, and coconuts), commodity trading, land development, tin mining, banking, and shipping, and also for ventures within China itself in winemaking, glassmaking, brickmaking, textile mills, and railroads. As his success multiplied, he also burnished his reputation as a generous philanthropist. In his trips abroad, he showed himself to be an amiable, active, vigorous, and sophisticated gentleman, at home with Westerners and Chinese alike. In addition to his mansion in Penang, he built homes in Singapore, Hong Kong, and Batavia in Indonesia, and an expansive manor in his home village in China, which is discussed on pages 274–7.

Left The roadside entry-way through the wall surrounding the Cheong Fatt Tse's residential compound.

Below A view of the façade of the ornate triple-bay two-storey Blue Mansion.

Opposite below Photographed a century after the black-and-white image above, the façade shows little change over the years.

Opposite above On the right is Cheong Fatt Tze, also known as Thio Tiauw Siat, and on the left his manager, Thio Siauw Kong. His Penang home is depicted here in a photograph taken in the first decade of the twentieth century.

Cheong Fatt Tze was born in 1841 in a village in Xihe township, Dabu county, northeastern Guangdong province, a rugged area adjacent to the fabled Meixian Hakka stronghold. Little is known about his family, but it appears that his father was reasonably prosperous and was a village teacher. At the age of seventeen or eighteen, he traveled to Batavia in the Dutch East Indies where he got his first job as a water carrier for a small-scale shop owner who was quickly impressed by his determination and promise. Not only did Cheong marry his boss's daughter, his father-in-law provided him with sufficient funds to start a shop of his own at the age of nineteen. By 1860 he had become a contract supplier of foodstuffs and other goods to the Dutch army and navy, and was thus poised to take advantage of other profit-making prospects that would arise. As the Dutch gained control of the northern portions of the island of Sumatra after the Anglo-Dutch treaty of 1871, Cheong was enticed to reach for the opportunities emerging in this frontier area. Gaining lucrative rights to the revenue farms in Sumatra, his enterprises not only opened tobacco, rubber, coconut palm, and tea plantations but he gained rights as well in the lucrative production and distribution of opium. He was successful in sustaining cordial relations with Dutch colonial authorities, even to the point of gaining the contract to provision their ships. Before long, his efforts expanded across the narrow Strait of Malacca to the developing town of Penang, which was under British control, and his blossoming commercial empire came to include transport steamer

lines flying the Dutch flag. While opportunities and wealth certainly multiplied during this period in Southeast Asia, it was the circumstances that began to emerge in China itself that brought him new riches and international acclaim.

The decision by the Qing authorities in the imperial capital Beijing to allow Chinese who emigrated in the past to return home, and for there to be free movement for other Chinese in and out of China using passes issued by consulates, gratified Cheong as a harbinger of fresh opportunities. The September 13, 1893 edict also "marked another milestone in Ch'ing [Qing] policy and the beginning of a remarkable ... program to attract the active participation of overseas capitalists in the modernization of China" (Godley, 1975: 369). Utilizing the commercial network he had built up over several decades, Cheong's enterprising spirit made it possible for him to benefit from new possibilities by investing in China's modernization. Even as early as 1891, Cheong had received invitations to return to China to discuss a range of investment opportunities regarding railways, steam transport, textile mills, and even wine-making, but now he could move forward with assurance that his wealth and talent could be given full play.

In 1893 he was appointed the first Chinese Vice-Consul in Penang, a post which not only heightened his prestige but put him in a position as an official middleman and enabled him to court wealthy Overseas Chinese as part of a broader expansion of consular affairs. In 1894 he set out for Beijing where he was honored for his extraordinary efforts at convincing wealthy Overseas Chinese merchants in the Straits Settlements and in the Dutch Indies to invest in China. During his absence in Beijing, Cheong arranged for Tjong Yong Hian in Medan, Sumatra, to occupy the Chinese Vice-Consul position in Penang, thus strengthening commercial ties and personal loyalties.

One of Cheong's earliest and boldest efforts in China resulted in the establishment of the modern Chang Yü Pioneer Wine Company in Shandong province, an effort that revealed his willingness to invest in an imaginative enterprise that would take years to realize a payoff with a new product for Chinese consumers. Roots of grape plants were first imported from America and subsequently replaced with more suitable European stock. A glassworks factory was set up to produce quality bottles, and in 1914 good quality wine began to be marketed. Over the next half decade, his visits to China increased as did those of Chinese officials who came to Southeast Asia to meet and woo wealthy Chinese. Cheong was honored with an imperial title in 1894 in recognition of his efforts to enlist other Overseas Chinese in China's transformation, and in 1895 he was appointed as acting Consul-General of China in Singapore.

As a result of another visit to China in 1896, Cheong was named the Director-General of Southern Railroads, after which he drew investment, especially for railway lines, in those areas of eastern Guangdong province that had sent the majority of émigrés to Southeast Asia. In 1897, when the Imperial Bank of China was established in Shanghai, he became the largest private stockholder, and in the same year was granted the brevet title of *taotai*. By 1901 he had risen "from obscurity to considerable stature as one of the leading businessmen in late Ch'ing China," spending increasing amounts of time in China, even enjoying multiple audiences with Empress Cixi (Godley, 1975: 374).

The upsurge in interest in matters Chinese among the Overseas Chinese population in Southeast Asia was complemented by the promotion of modern Chinese schools in Penang and Singapore by Cheong and others, notably Lim Boon Keng. During this period, Cheong received imperial accolades, awards, and ranks one after another. In 1904 he was appointed Imperial Commissioner and Superintendent of Agriculture, Industry, Railroads and Mining for Fujian and Guangdong, a post that he financed. Traveling regularly to Singapore and Penang, he promoted the organization of Chambers of Commerce with an international outlook and with leaders who had also been granted Chinese imperial honors and ranks. He self-confidently spelled out a twelve-point program for the development of industry and commerce in China, which was of such a scope that it revealed clearly his perceptive understanding of China's deficiencies as well as his comprehension of how to transform the country by engaging successful Nanyang Overseas Chinese entrepreneurs—Mandarin-capitalists—in the effort.

Opposite below These three photographs show details along a portion of the façade, including a doorway and bracket set, a shed-like overhanging roof, and colorful cut-and-paste ornamentation at the peak of a gable.

Above left The front veranda provides an accessible and convenient place to park rickshaws, which had been invented in Japan in 1869 and were imported for use in the Straits Settlements in 1880.

Center left The profuse use of colorful shards of pottery arranged in a multiplicity of decorative mosaic patterns is evident in both of these additions to the overhanging eaves.

Below This bright and airy alcove room is one of a pair that juts off the entrance hall. Large Art Nouveau stained glass windows, which could be opened, and ventilation ports made it possible to control light and air. The lower wall surfaces are decorated with trompe d'oeil frescoes to resemble polished granite.

Bottom Upon entering the central doorway, a visitor sees a grand carved and gilded screen wall, which once probably had a deity altar before it. Today, a mother-of-pearl inlaid settee occupies the space and is accompanied by other blackwood chairs and tables.

Opposite This is one of a pair of hardwood stairways that lead to the second floor along each side of the atrium-like central skywell.

Right The architectural ironworks that define the edges of the skywell are especially noteworthy, having been custom-made by Walter Macfarlane & Co. Ltd in Glasgow, Scotland. Columns with dramatic capitals complement the ornately patterned balusters.

Below Like those found in other mansions of the wealthy in the nineteenth century, the fluted cast-iron columns, as well as the balusters, were fabricated in Scotland.

Even though Cheong spent less and less time in Penang, he and his associates there did not neglect the town that had provided them with so many business opportunities. Cheong, together with four other Hakka benefactors, contributed the core resources in the early 1890s for the expansion of the Kek Lok Si (Temple of Supreme Bliss), Penang's most renowned Buddhist temple. His patronage of the temple was acknowledged by the presentation of imperial plaques in the calligraphy of both the Guangxu emperor and Empress Dowager Cixi. In 1904 Cheong was the principal donor of funds to build the Chung Hwa School, a Chinese-language institution sanctioned by Qing imperial authorities. With a curriculum designed to produce graduates with high levels of Chinese as well as Western languages and modern subjects, the Chung Hwa School provided a significant alternative to the fine English-medium schools that had dominated Penang for nearly a century. In 1912, after the overthrow of the Qing dynasty and the establishment of the Republic of China, the school was renamed the Chung Hwa Confucian School to underscore its emphasis on traditional ethics and morality in addition to its modern curriculum.

Even with his extensive travels, Cheong began plans for two grand houses, one in Penang and the other in his home village in Dabu county, Guangdong province. Both residences were called *Guang Lu Di* or "Residence of Glorious Emolument," proclaimed on a horizontal board above the main entry. Both structures were built to be expansive and impressive. The one in Penang was commodious by virtue of its covering two floors and incorporating a series of service buildings across the road, while the Dabu residence was spacious because of its extensive ground plan that allowed for a seemingly endless multiplication of spaces in a traditional one-storey manor along an elevated riverbank (pages 274–7).

The Blue Mansion

The Penang mansion was begun in 1896 and essentially completed in 1904, serving not only as a family residence but also as an office for some of Cheong's far-flung enterprises. Tan Tay Po, his seventh and favorite "wife," occupied this stunning home together with at least six of his sons, born of several wives, who attended the English-medium progressive St Xavier Institution nearby because they were too old for the newly established Chung Hwa School he founded. It is said that wives three

Left to right A detail of the gilded carvings on the screen wall between the reception hall and the skywell; mother-of-pearl plum blossom detail on the back of a chair; encaustic floor tiles imported from Stroke-on-Trent, England; a circular lacquered box holding a set of porcelain containers; a lower door panel in the ornamented wooden screen between the entrance hall and the skywell.

and six also lived in the house from time to time. Cheong optimistically expressed the hope that nine generations of descendants would continue to occupy the home for decades to come. Other of his wealthy business friends also constructed their residences nearby, on Leith Street, to the extent that the area began to be called "Hakka Millionaires' Row" early in the twentieth century.

Given his international predilections, it is not surprising that Cheong's Penang mansion was built in an eclectic style that epitomized excellence in both Chinese and Western traditions. This was a choice that differed from that of his wealthy peers, such as the tin tycoon Leong Fee, whose mansion was just across the street, and the real estate magnate Tye Kee Yoon's residence nearby. Their mansions were essentially Western Anglo-Indian style structures with Victorian elements, but generally lacked any substantial Chinese ornamentation. It is not known whether Cheong engaged an architect or whether his house was "designed" by Chinese craftsmen who could have reasonably and easily adapted modern forms such as imported Victorian cast-iron columns and Art Nouveau stained glass windows for more traditional Chinese elements. Cheong certainly brought from China masons and carpenters as well as artisans for the finish work in order to guarantee structural and ornamental authenticity. Some elements of the house, such as the roof tiles, paints, and wooden lattice screens, were likely produced in Guangdong and then shipped to Penang. The prolific decorative porcelain mosaics demanded that a squad of Chinese artisans labored over a long period of time to complete the necessary tasks. The ornamental ironwork was fabricated in Glasgow, Scotland, by Walter Macfarlane & Co., a Victorian architectural iron foundry, while encaustic floor tiles were manufactured in one of the famous potteries at Stoke-on-Trent in England. The provenance of the nearly fifty stained glass

window panels is not clear, but is likely also to have been England, just as was the case with those found in Penang's Anglican churches. Common wooden floorboards and perhaps even fired bricks may have been sourced locally. Sets of wooden louvers shade exterior and interior windows. Although there is little evidence today of the original furnishings, wall hangings, chandeliers, mirrors, and objets d'art, these no doubt were gathered from many countries.

When viewed from the front and side, the two-storey residence is clearly a Chinese building with a grand sense of scale and proportion. While glazed tiles from China cover its roof and glistening porcelain mosaics are plentiful about the façade, it is the striking indigo blue exterior walls that dominate the colorful exterior of the residence. The three-bay central structure, with a covered porch at ground level and a covered balcony above, is complemented by a pair of wing structures placed perpendicular to it, all of which have conjoined open and closed spaces linked by covered hallways. Five commodious skywells—veritable courtyards—punctuate the interior of the residence in order to bring air and light into those rooms without exterior windows. These skywells, of course, are indispensable spatial elements in any large Chinese dwelling and are quite suitable for ameliorating the high humidity and temperatures of tropical Penang.

Overall, the house has twenty-six rooms, which are fully enclosed and entered through doors. In addition, for formal and ritual purposes, six sumptuous halls with a more fluid spatial structure were designed at the core of the central building. Lengthy corridors along the interior of the wings at ground and upper level provide covered, yet airy, passageways, while five stairwells and a single spiral stairway connect each section of the house to its complementary area on a different level. Six rooms, which principally served as bedrooms, are located in each wing, with a large sitting room at the front end of both floors of each wing. Stairs connect these sitting rooms so that family members could easily move throughout the house without entering the more formal central core. On the lower level of each wing, the rooms open out directly to the skywells, while on the second floor wooden louvers help shade the passageways from rain and sun. Along the back of the building, service corridors link the stairwell halls on both ends. In the rear of each wing, a large kitchen, the roof of which supported an open terrace above on the second floor, was built to meet the substantial food preparation requirements of the large family. No inside plumbing was installed in the original building so that the residents had to depend upon chamber pots and basins for their daily needs.

The functions and layout of rooms within the main building follow traditional patterns that are also common in other large homes of Overseas Chinese throughout Southeast Asia. Passing from the covered porch through a large double-paneled doorway emblazoned with a four-character metaphorically auspicious phrase, *longfei fengwu*, "Dragon Soars, Phoenix Dances," a visitor enters first an inverted T-shaped entrance hall. Ahead in the entrance hall is a magnificent Chinese-style gilded screen that reaches from wall to wall and floor to ceiling, which serves to separate public space from the more private family space beyond. This spacious entrance hall contains a mixture of Chinese and Western furniture, English encaustic floor tiles, and plaster dado wall decorations painted to look as if they were carved granite panels. Six rectangular stained glass windows, which are duplicated on the floor above, flood the room with light across a spectrum of colors. Solid wood panels can be shut on the inside of these windows in order to

Opposite One of two spiral staircases made of cast iron that are positioned in the back corridors.

Above A view across the skywell towards the front quadrant of the residence showing the upstairs iron-work and ascending stairs.

Above right A view of one of the spiral staircases as it rises from the first to the second floor of the mansion.

Centre right Small side rooms line the narrow skywells on both sides of the residence.

Below right One of the rectangular skywells that flank the main structure. The downstairs side rooms open to the skywell while those upstairs open on to a corridor that is shielded by wooden louvers.

Right Outside the ornamented wooden screen with movable door panels is a gallery that runs along the edge of the skywell.

Below Topped by carved filigree wooden panels, the cast-iron pillars and balusters surrounding the atrium on the second floor cast varying silhouetted shadows throughout the day.

Top This ornamented wooden screen separates the upstairs front room, which probably once was a formal room for entertaining since it is linked to the balcony along the front side of the house.

Above A close-up of the gilded door panels with carvings of animals on the wooden screen.

keep out heat and humidity. The two rooms adjacent to the entrance hall were likely used for Cheong's business.

After passing through the screen, one enters the heart of the home, a rectangular and cavernous skywell surrounded on both levels with an exceptional array of ornamental cast-iron assemblages, including custom-made fluted, rather slender columns with ornate capitals and intricately scrolled railings. These cast-iron decorative components, as with others throughout the house, such as oil-lamps and a spiral staircase, were all imported from Scotland. On both sides of the skywell are wooden staircases with wooden balusters that begin with a series of granite steps, said to prevent the movement of termites and to symbolize a firm foundation as one begins to move up. Beyond the skywell was an ancestral hall, which today only has a small altar table set between the two rear doors which at one time must have served as the location for the kind of grand wooden structure and tables commonly seen even today in some old manors of wealthy families in Southeast Asia. On the wall hangs a large seated portrait of Cheong Fatt Tse in Chinese clothing. On both sides are smaller photographs, one of him in Western top hat and formal dress and the other of his favorite wife, Tan Tay Po. One of the two large rooms adjacent to the ancestral hall most likely served as her bedroom. The bedrooms in the adjacent wings on both floors provided sleeping space for other family members.

The floor plan of the second floor duplicates that of the ground floor, with a pair of large rooms framing each of the upstairs halls. The arch-shaped cast-iron metalwork, combined with the carved wooden panels that rise above the cast-iron balustrade ringing the upstairs portion of the skywell, presents an appearance that is quite unusual for a traditional Chinese dwelling. Like the entrance hall below it, the T-shaped room above it is separated from the skywell by a richly carved wooden screen with gilded filigree panels and substantial carved ornamentation with traditional motifs. This large room, which must have been planned as a formal hall to be used for celebrations, leads to a balcony at the front of the house that is a veritable museum of Chinese narrative scenes composed using shards of colored porcelain.

One of the most common folk arts used to embellish temples in Guangdong, Fujian, and Taiwan provinces is the practice known as *jiannian*, literally "cutting and pasting." In areas of these three provinces where individuals have sufficient wealth, there was an inclination to use the *jiannian* technique to create ornamental mosaics not only on wall surfaces but also along the exterior ridge beam and edges of gables. From a distance, the effect sometimes looks like a painting, but closer inspection reveals that the art form is a kind of composite sculpture in which a nearly flat or slightly built-up area of limed clay is inlaid with colorful pieces of porcelain shards to form a dense mosaic of shapes and colors. Specially prepared porcelain bowls, which are glazed only on one side, serve as the raw material for *jiannian*. Using a pair of pliers, an artisan cuts pieces from the sides of the bowls before arranging the various shapes, sizes, and colors one by one in a predetermined yet flexible design. Not only are there lengthy panels of floral and geometric patterns in the mansion, there also are very elaborate mosaic panels showing tableaux of traditional narrative tales involving human and animal figures that serve a didactic purpose.

It is not clear how much time Cheong Fatt Tze spent in the mansion after it was completed in 1904, given his substantial travel over the next decade. He was already sixty-three years of age and would only live a little more than another decade. Cheong's Blue Mansion clearly reflects

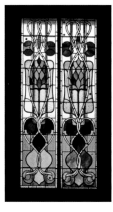

at least one aspect of his cosmopolitan character, eclectic interests, and complex family dynamics. No doubt his interests were broad and his family situation multifaceted, with family members living in far-flung places. His wealth made it possible for him to realize his dreams by engaging traditional artisans who were encouraged to explore new mediums, fashions, and styles in order to create a distinguished residence in Penang and another in Dabu, both of which are still standing a century later.

Even with the extraordinary efforts of Overseas Chinese, the collapse of the Qing imperial order could not be forestalled. Successful economic and social development occurred in pockets of southeastern China far from the heart of dynastic control in Beijing. Railroads and factories were built, businesses and factories were established, even as

administrative decay and bureaucratic collapse became increasingly endemic. While the imperial system collapsed in late 1911 and the young last emperor Puyi abdicated in February 1912, the birth of the Republic of China was fraught with difficulties. It was a fact that a great many of the wealthy businessmen in Southeast Asia were conservative and had worked more closely with the Qing imperial court than with the forces of revolutionary change represented by Dr Sun Yat-sen (see pages 114–19). Cheong Fatt Tze, as a septuagenarian, "moved with the fates of history and joined the Republic ... [and] promptly became a special advisor to President Yuan Shih-k'ai [Yuan Shikai], and gaining his ear as he had that of the empress dowager, he was formally appointed a first-class advisor to the government assigned the special task of developing inland ports" (Godley, 1981: 186).

Cheong was selected to head a delegation of the Chinese Commercial Commission to visit the United States for fifty days in 1915. The *New York Times* referred to him as "the most distinguished, eminent and richest of Chinese business men"—"the Morgan of China" and "China's Rockefeller"—stating that he was worth at least US$100,000,000 and "had $200,000 for pocket money" ("Chang," 1915: 10; Marshall, 1915: SM4). Cheong had become a "jet-set director of a multi-national conglomerate well before the invention of the airplane," making deals with foreign partners, flitting from one home to another, even enjoying the affections of different wives or woman friends, all the while experiencing the material innovations and angst of the fin de siècle (Godley 1981: 91).

Just months after his whirlwind tour of the United States, Cheong died, nearing the age of seventy-five, in 1916, in Batavia in one of his many homes spread across Asia. Cheong's vast business empire unfortunately slowly collapsed after he died in spite of the fact that some of his children, who had gained Western educations, were poised to increase the family's wealth. His body was returned to Dabu, Guangdong province, for burial near his ancestral home and the large manor he had built in hopes of living a quiet life in retirement.

Cheong's youngest son Kam Long was born to his seventh wife in 1914 when he was already seventy-four years of age. Successions of family members occupied the venerable family mansion but none had the resources to maintain it properly. Lynn Pan visited the Penang house in 1987, writing that by then "the house seems to have been allowed to go to seed, divided up among too many down-at-heel families. The ancestral hall, facing the central courtyard, feels dingy and derelict" (1994: 146). Thoong Siew Meee, the wife of Cheong Fatt Tze's last surviving son, "allowed rooms, corridor spaces, halls, stores, even outhouses, to be occupied by squatters, from whom she collected rental.... Washing lines were strung from gold-gilded timber carved panels and pigeon droppings filled ceiling spaces, while dozens of cats roamed the house, leaving leftover feathers and bones of the resident birds" (Lin, 2002: 15–16). Language similar to that used in these sentences has been uttered by many of us who have visited once grand but now dilapidated homes throughout East Asia. Sadly, most of such ramshackle structures continue to deteriorate until they reach a point of collapse when restoration is impossible. However, although on the brink of such a state, Cheong's Penang mansion stood on the cusp of ruin before it was reclaimed in order to undergo renewal.

When Kam Long, the last son of Cheong died in 1989, a small group of Penang conservationists purchased the neglected mansion and began to plan its restoration and its adaptive reuse as a heritage structure of significant value. The effort was spearheaded by Laurence Loh, a Penang-born and London-educated architect, and his wife Lin Lee Loh-Lim, who was emerging as a specialist in historic conservation. Together, their vision and commitment provided a blueprint for the salvaging and then rebirth of one of Southeast Asia's most extraordinary old mansions. The effort at the time, according to Lin, was made difficult by "lax conservation laws, development pressure on the land was tremendous and the level of conservation awareness was abysmal" (2002: 16). Since the completion of the restoration, the Blue Mansion has garnered many awards, including the Malaysian National Architectural Award for Conservation in 1995, and in 2000 the UNESCO's Asia-Pacific Heritage Award for Cultural Heritage Conservation.

Above A covered balcony with heavy ornamentation runs along the second floor of the main building.

Below With a geometrically organized painted ceiling and crowded surface ornamentation, the upstairs balcony presents many objects for discussion by visitors.

Bottom A close-up of one of the fan-shaped cut-and-paste porcelain mosaic vignettes that are found above each of the windows and doors along the balcony.

CHYN PRACHA RESIDENCE

PHUKET, THAILAND

1904–1907

Located along the shores of the Andaman Sea in southern peninsular Thailand, Phuket has gained international acclaim because of its magnificent beaches for swimming, sunbathing, windsurfing, and snorkeling in addition to its well-developed infrastructure of hotels, clubs, and restaurants. The devastating tsunami that struck the island on December 26, 2004 alerted the world to the island's fragility while heralding its beauty. Yet, well before the ascendancy of tourism as its principal industry and source of its contemporary prosperity, Phuket gained international prominence because of other natural resources, in a short period of time providing the wealth that made possible the building of large homes by Chinese immigrants and their descendants as emblems of modernity and declarations of their prosperity.

For more than a millennium, Phuket provided a safe harbor at a strategic crossroads location for Indian and Arab seafaring merchants, then later Portuguese, French, and British colonialists, before enterprising Chinese settlers—miners, traders, and farmers—arrived in increasing numbers to exploit the island's abundant deposits of high grade tin ore. The significance of tin arose principally from its use as the necessary alloy in producing bronze (tin and copper), which was easier to work and harder than copper alone, solder (tin and lead), or pewter (tin, copper, antimony, and lead). Although tin-plating sheet iron to

guard against rust was an old practice, it was only in the eighteenth and nineteenth centuries that tinsmiths developed the myriad utilitarian objects made of malleable tin that susequently became common items in homes throughout the world. With the patenting of the tin can as a vessel to preserve food in 1810 in England and the opening of a commercial canning factory three years later, a flurry of inventions led not only to improvements in the making of tin cans but also spurred the quest for productive tin ore mines around the world. "Tin mining in South Siam," according to G. William Skinner, "was almost a monopoly of the Chinese throughout the nineteenth century. Their knowledge of the country's mineral resources was supreme, and they kept it secret from both Thai and outsiders.... Every month brought new immigrants, and the Chinese population grew to 28,000 by 1870 and to over 40,000 in 1884, the great majority of whom labored in the mines" (1957: 109–11). Tin mining and smelting in Phuket, however, began to wane in the late 1880s as a result of changing global demand and political policies that led to a mass departure of Chinese workers, reducing the number to 12,000 by 1897. Yet, at the turn of the century, it was the legacy of riches from traditional tin mining practices as well as the modernization of mining practices with the introduction of dredgers and the expansion of rubber plantations that led to the dramatic transformation of Phuket.

Left Called Sino-Portuguese in style, the Chyn Pracha residence is a five-bay-wide structure with a double-sloped entryway. Except for the horizontal board above the front door with the Chinese characters *haoqi*, meaning "Nobility of Character," there is little to suggest that this is the home of a Chinese.

The expansion of rubber estates, beginning in 1903, was accompanied by the destruction of substantial amounts of the island's rainforests, just as the introduction of modern hydraulic dredgers also despoiled the coastline. This new commodity pumped great wealth into the town of Phuket as not only Chinese entrepreneurs but also Europeans and Thais were able to ride a wave of new prosperity based upon these marketable commodities. Increasing trade and cultural exchange between Phuket, Penang in Malaya, and Singapore during this period also contributed to each becoming a boomtown. Indeed, Phuket was coupled with Penang to a greater extent than it was to the Siamese capital Bangkok itself. Five preeminent Hokkien mercantile families in Penang—Tan, Yeoh, Lim, Cheah, and Ong—all played key roles in the expansion of diversified enterprises based in the hinterlands of coastal ports throughout the region, including Phuket in Siam, Medan in Sumatra, and Rangoon (Yangon) in Burma. Using strategic partnerships, they provided capital and know-how, ships to transport commodities, including opium, and even recruited coolies to meet the needs of labor-intensive mining and farming (Wong, 2007: 106–15).

The expansion of the urban fabric of Phuket was accompanied by the erection of grand buildings, not only for commercial and governmental purposes but also new mansions for prosperous citizenry. While a century later many of these mansions are derelict structures or have

Above This end of the two-storey residence has surfaces that are dominated by a series of louvered windows, each with an elegant fanlight set upon ornamented pilasters. The inclined bargeboard, which is carved in a replicating pattern, mirrors those found under the eaves around the house. The protected gable has a plastered motif.

been modified to serve non-residential purposes, several still stand as testaments to the wealth and taste, especially of Chinese residents, at the beginning of the twentieth century.

One type of residence that emerged is what today is referred to as Sino-Portuguese architecture, which is a misnomer since the form does not evoke specific Portuguese characteristics. While the Portuguese were among the first Western traders to have a presence in Phuket in the seventeenth century, it is a stretch to see any specific Portuguese influence in these twentieth-century mansions. The descriptors Sino-Western or Sino-Colonial perhaps are better terms since these large villa-type residences include obvious elements that blend both generic Western architectural forms *and* Chinese elements. Each of these homes generally includes a prominent portico, a second-floor terrace, interior courtyards, an inside water well, a prominent façade, and a disposition

of rooms that acknowledges homage to ancestors. The furnishings and ornamentation is invariably a mixture of Chinese and Western motifs, similar to what one would encounter in Penang. Indeed, Khoo Salma Nasution has called Penang and Phuket "Siamese Twins" (2006: 14). Using the Hokkien dialect, Chinese have referred to these buildings, just as they have done in Penang, as *ang moh lau*, "red hair houses," to underscore their European patrimony but, in fact, the owners mostly were Peranakan (Straits Chinese).

The Chyn Pracha Residence

Examples of *ang mor lau* are found along the roads that radiate out from the core of Phuket town into areas that a century ago provided expansive open spaces for extensive gardens and imposing homes. The broadening of roads and the infilling of commercial buildings has generally disrupted the bucolic ambience of times past, but it is still possible to glimpse the magnificence of the mansions in spite of these encroachments. Two of the best examples are found adjacent to each other along Krabi Road, which is an extension of Thalang Road that begins in the commercial center of the town. Both of these large residences were built by Tan Ma Siang (Phra Phitak Chyn Pracha), whose father, Tan Niaw Yee (Luang Bamroongjeenprated), had

migrated from Fujian to Phuket in 1854. Tan Niaw Yee made a fortune in tin mining in the nineteenth century, subsequently bequeathing substantial assets to his son, Tan Ma Siang, who then built two neighboring estates nearly forty years apart.

The first, which was begun in 1904 and completed in 1907, was a gift to Tan Ma Siang's new bride when he married at the age of twenty, soon after he returned from studying in Penang. Known as the Chyn Pracha residence after the Thai name for Tan Ma Siang, it is a fine example of Sino-European residential architecture, accentuated by the fact that the principal carpenter was recruited in Penang specifically to build a mansion that expressed the cosmopolitan times. Adjacent to it on an expansive corner plot is the larger Phra Phitak Chyn Pracha mansion, which was built in the 1940s (see page 27).

Tan Ma Siang, who was born in Phuket in 1883 and died in 1949, straddled the generations between his China-born father and those descendants who have come to regard themselves as Thai but of Chinese heritage. There are no detailed records of local women who married into the family, but there is no doubt that the Pracha family is Peranakan and that strategic marriages bolstered mercantile relationships among the élite of Penang and Phuket. One example is Tan Ma Siang's son, Tan Joo Ee, also known as Chyn Sathan Phithak, who studied at St Xavier's School in Penang and then married Lucy Goh Seok Choo, a Nyonya from Penang, in 1928 (Nasution, 2008: 64).

Set amongst what was once a magnificent garden, the two-storey, five-bay-wide symmetrical Chyn Pracha residence is raised off the ground on a stone and cement podium, which is accessed by three sets of steps. The sloping roof of the entryway, which is supported by fluted columns, frames a classical European surround for a Chinese-style doorway. Set above the door is a plaque with two Chinese characters, *haoqi*, meaning "Nobility of Spirit." In addition to this striking entry, the façade is ornamented with carved bargeboards, not only along the inclined jutting roof but also along the drip line of both the upper and lower storeys. Two-thirds of each wall is given over to windows on the first floor and shutters on the second. When viewed from the side, the elevations are no less dramatic in terms of architectural fanlights, shutters, bargeboards, and elaborate stucco ornamentation. While the front entryway was for formal use, a second side entry via a *porte-cochère*, literally a "coach door," provided protected access for visitors arriving by vehicle.

The spacious lower floor, with its high ceilings and encaustic tile flooring, comprises a series of rooms that encircle a large *tianjing*. While this *tianjing* functions much like those found traditionally in southern Chinese homes, this one appears more like a Roman atrium, not only because of its ornamented arches and fluted columns but also because of the water-filled impluvium with goldfish and flowers. The adjacent entry foyer, formal and informal eating areas, parlors, and a bedroom are crowded with an accumulation of the family's antique furniture. In addition to imported blackwood pieces inlaid with mother-of-pearl and marble, most all of the furniture lining the walls comprises "brown-and-gold" Peranakan items made of teak, which was popular in the late nineteenth and early twentieth century. From a distance, the over-sized Peranakan furniture does not look particularly Chinese, merely appearing heavily ornamented. Close inspection, however, reveals that much of the elaborate carved ornamentation, whether finials, crowns, or incised surfaces, consists of traditional Chinese symbolic designs juxtaposed with Western decorative flourishes. Cabinets are crammed

Opposite The leftmost bay of the residence, as with other sections of the façade, have the louvered windows painted in a contrasting color.

Above Surrounded with classical columns and arches, the atrium at the center of the house includes a pond filled with fish and live plants. In the semi-open areas behind, the furnishings are a mix of Chinese and European styles.

Right This side parlor provides wall space and flat surfaces to display family photos and memorabilia.

Above The Chyn Pracha ancestral altar is dominated by portraits of the progenitor as well as other more recent relatives.

Right This area of the side parlor juxtaposes objects brought from China with those from Europe.

with porcelain Chinese plates and figurines along with objects imported from Europe and America. A steep stairway, richly carved and fitted with turned balusters, leads to the upstairs area, which is not accessible to the public and thus its details are not known.

In the sixty years after the death of Tan Ma Siang, succeeding generations maintained the house well in homage to their forebears. Khun Pracha Tandavanitj, Tan Ma Siang's grandson and the son of Tan Joo Ee, was a staunch heritage conservationist who opened the home to small numbers of visitors as early as 1985. Over the years, moreover, the house and garden compound have been used as a location for television productions, along with Thai and Hollywood movies. Glimpses of the home can be seen in the well-known international films *The Killing Fields* and *The Young Indiana Jones Chronicles*. Thai authorities granted the family a Conservation Award for their efforts in the 1990s. After the passing of Khun Pracha Tandavanitj in 2007, his widow, Jaroonrat "Daeng" Tandavanitj, began operating the house as a private museum, the only such Sino-Colonial residence in Phuket open to the public.

Above left This downstairs bedroom includes a brass four-poster bed with coverings and window dressings made of white lace.

Above right A painted portrait of the progenitor of the Chyn Pracha lineage, here wearing a Chinese gown from the imperial Qing period.

Right This angled stairway, with its richly ornamented underside, leads to the family's private quarters, which are not open to the public.

Below left A view from the entry hall of the oval glass windows of the doorway.

Below right In order to extract some equity from a valuable piece of inherited property, an eight-unit series of shophouses will be built along the roadside in front of the Chyn Pracha residence. The historic home will remain visible through the gap between the shophouses.

TJONG A FIE MANSION

MEDAN, INDONESIA

1895–1900

Even though Sumatra, one of the six largest islands in the world, has a long history of international trade and migration as a result of its strategic location astride the Strait of Malacca between the Indian Ocean and the South China Sea, the island is usually portrayed as a remote backwater. This is especially true when compared with the northern portions of the mammoth island and the historic cities of Malacca, Penang, and Singapore on the opposite side of the strait. After the Dutch secured central and northern Sumatra in the last half of the nineteenth century, however, an expanding plantation economy began to generate extraordinary wealth in Sumatra. The sleepy outpost called Medan was transformed in a matter of decades into a strikingly cosmopolitan town that by 1905 was dominated by Chinese immigrants who lived among substantial numbers of Arab, Indian, and European residents.

Among the most productive areas of northern Sumatra was the lowland Deli district, where some 30,000 square kilometers of rich soil were planted with lucrative export crops like tobacco, rubber, tea, and oil palm in response to accelerating global demand. The ever-escalating demand for labor to work in the rich tobacco, rubber, and oil palm plantations in the wider region brought an astonishing level of in-migration of both Chinese, first from Penang and Singapore, then later directly from China itself, as well as Javanese. From 1860 to 1920 the region's population grew from less than 100,000 to 1,500,000. By the beginning of the twentieth century, more than half of the population was comprised of immigrant Chinese and Javanese coolies who toiled in a large-scale estate system. Through a system of indenture, a cheap and submissive labor force, exploited by often inhumane recruitment efforts

and maintained by coercion, operated within an international system of capital investment and management that was both adaptive and profitable. Research in recent decades has revealed that these once readily accepted stereotypes of worker exploitation must be leavened by acknowledging both the sometimes successful resistance of indentured laborers against those who controlled them as well as the beneficent efforts of those who became tycoons.

While some 300,000 coolies traveled from China to Sumatra between 1870 and 1930 to work in the plantations, a significant number eventually settled in the towns where they became traders and tradesmen. Among the poorest of the Chinese immigrants were two brothers, Tjong Yong Hian and Tjong A Fie, whose rags-to-riches tale is legendary. Between 1895 and 1900 Tjong A Fie built an opulent mansion, which still stands as a fine example of the cultural eclecticism of a Southeast Asian *belle époque*. The mixing of the latest European-style furnishings, fine arts, and culinary traditions, and the newest inventions with centuries-old styles of Chinese furniture, altars and rituals, food, and costume created a new kind of material modernity. In Medan, the only rival to this avant-garde blending of East and West in terms of spaces and motifs was found in the Sultan of Deli's palace, called Istana Maimoon, which was designed by a Dutch architect and completed in 1888 (Buiskool, 2008: 22).

The Tjong brothers and countless other migrants from China progressively, indeed rather quickly, came to be characterized by new hybrid identities involving both Asian and European elements. Their large new home provided abundant living space for collateral family members, but went well beyond the needs of being merely a residence. The structure also included sweeping rooms suitable for receptions, celebrations, and festivities that could be enjoyed with other important members of the community, whether indigenous royalty or international entrepreneurs and businessmen from the Netherlands, England, the United States, France, Russia, Switzerland, Poland, Germany, and Belgium. The mixing of nationalities of individuals who traveled widely, unparalleled excess wealth, and the spirit of the time—the age of progress—contributed to the flourishing of an international material culture in Medan. While some of the tales told of the Tjong brothers strain credulity, extant photographs from the time provide glimpses of a life of luxury far beyond what one might expect in a distant colony in the Dutch East Indies. Reliable written information is elusive.

Chinese sources, for example, that focus on the lives and contributions of successful Overseas Chinese, usually embroider narratives in an attempt to underscore patriotic fervor and heighten personal beneficence (*Kejia wenhua shujuku*). Although much information about the Tjong brothers is not verifiable and must be used with caution, an indisputable fact is that a remarkable building was bequeathed to us that whispers of the grandeur of times past and a striking openness to accepting new cultural norms.

Both Tjong Yong Hian and Tjong A Fie were born in a village in Songnan township (later combined with two other townships and renamed Songkou) in Meixian county, in the northeastern corner of Guangdong province, an area dominated by a Chinese subgroup known as Hakka (Kejia). Life for Hakka throughout this rugged and resource-poor region traditionally was quite difficult, with most people living a subsistence existence in small villages. Migration from place to place is a prominent part of the narrative of Hakka life, whether internally by land within China or by junk to the Nanyang, the Southern Seas. While the earliest Hakka to migrate to what is now Indonesia went as laborers in the tin mines of Banka and Belitung islands off the southeast coast of Sumatra or traveled to West Kalimantan on the island of Borneo, the Tjong brothers made their fortunes in the more distant frontiers of Java and Sumatra.

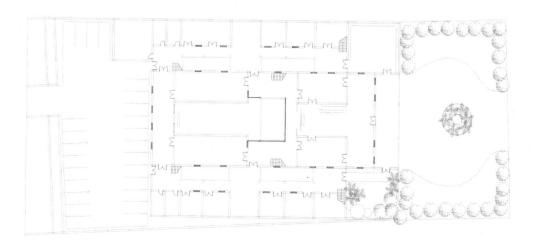

Opposite This bird's-eye view of the Tjong A Fie mansion shows the two-part core structure as well as the flanking wing buildings.

Above With a pair of lions, the triple-bay main gate of the mansion leads to a circular driveway.

Left Floor plan of the residence.

The Tjong brothers were born ten years apart—Tjong Yong Hian (alias Tjong Jong Hian, Zhang Rongxuan; Chang Yü-nan, Zhang Yunan) in 1851 and Tjong A Fie (also known as Tjong A. Fee, Tjong Yiauw Hian; Zhang Yaoxuan, Cheng Lu Hin, Chang Hung-nan, Zhang Hongnan) in 1861 (some records say 1859 or 1860). Both lived to the age of sixty, dying ten years apart, in 1911 and 1921. They were two of seven sons and a daughter of a small-scale shopkeeper who sold rice and sundry goods with an income said to have been insufficient to support a family of ten. As with similar families in that region who lived in distress, Tjong Yong Hian, at an age that is not clear, sailed to

Southeast Asia in hopes of providing some resources to support his family back in their Meixian village. He had the good fortune of making contact with Cheong Fatt Tze (Zhang Bishi), who had been born in the neighboring county of Dabu in Guangdong, then migrated to Southeast Asia in 1856, before becoming an internationally recognized tycoon. Cheong Fatt Tze, whose Blue Mansion is featured on pages 128–39, amassed extraordinary wealth through trade in commodities, tin mining, shipping, and banking, among other interests. Born eleven years before the elder Tjong brother, Cheong Fatt Tze served as mentor, protector, and friend to both brothers, eventually being called "great-uncle" by their children, but they were not related by blood (Chang, 1931: 51). In 1894 Cheong Fatt Tze, who had served as the first Chinese Vice-Consul in Penang for only a year, selected Tjong Yong Hian as his replacement in Penang when he departed on an official trip to Beijing. Besides Cheong Fatt Tze, the brothers also developed close relations with the Sultan of Deli. Since the wealthy in Medan maintained cordial relations with residents and professionals in Penang across the Strait

Left A view of the intersecting gables of the higher main building on the right and the lower flanking wing structure on the left.

Below The Tjong A Fie mansion is a three-bay structure with a mixture of Chinese and Western influences.

Tiled roofs with upturned eaves, calligraphic panels around the doorway, and gables of the adjacent wing units are Chinese while the louvered shutters and fanlights are inspired by Western architectural treatments.

of Malacca, modern ideas and commodities flowed easily as business interests based on personal loyalty increased.

After Tjong A Fie took over the small rice and sundry shop following the death of his father, he begged his mother to let him join his elder brother, Yong Hian, abroad. Family lore, according to Queeny Chang, recalls that "Early one morning, a spirited youth of 18 with only ten silver dollars sewn into his cotton waistband took the *sampan* down the river to Swatow and then embarked on a big wooden junk sailing between the Southern Seas and the homeland" in order to seek his fortune (1981: 17). A Fie arrived at the marshy port of Labuhan in Medan in 1880, joining his elder brother who had already been given the Dutch title Luitenant der Chinezen, and then worked in a shop owned by a friend of his brother. By 1886, when the elder brother was promoted to Kapitein der Chinezen, A Fie was granted the title Luitenant, later becoming Kapitein, and, after the death of his elder brother in 1911, he assumed his title of Majoor der Chinezen.

Early on, he and his brother became business partners, earning wealth, status, and accessibility by providing goods to the expanding plantation enterprises as well as recruiting coolies from Guangdong who arrived in increasing numbers. At the turn of the twentieth century, it was said that the Tjong brothers owned a majority of the real estate in burgeoning Medan, including hotels, banks, warehouses, and residences, in addition to sugar and palm oil plantations. In 1904–5, the brothers joined with Cheong Fatt Tze and other investors to spur the development of a 26-kilometer narrow-gauge line in Guangdong province from the port of Swatow (Shantou) to Chaochow (Chaozhou) on the way to Meixian. Tjong A Fie also financed the construction of what is known in three languages as the "Virtuous Bridge" in Medan in 1916, naming it in memory of his brother. His fame led to the University of Hong Kong in the British Crown Colony awarding him an Honorary Doctor of Laws degree in 1916. After success with a bank in Medan, he joined forces in 1918 with Khouw Kim An, the Majoor in Batavia, whose home is also featured in this book (pages 172–9), to establish the Batavia Bank. In 1918 Tjong A Fie acquired from Dutch authorities the lucrative opium monopoly (Buiskool, 2004: 8). Throughout the early twentieth century, he spread his wealth through cross-cultural philanthropy, including building temples, mosques, churches, schools, and hospitals that are heralded by the citizens of Medan even today, a century later. While unfortunately there is not yet a serious study of the lives of the Tjong brothers, either in terms of family or business, their Medan mansion yields some clues that they were extraordinary men living during complex times of great change.

Queeny Chang, the eldest daughter of Tjong A Fie, who wrote that her uncle was "more ambitious" than her father, has left the only written record describing life in what she calls "Tjong A Fie's Magnificent Mansion" (1931: 19–23ff, 56). Her memories recall the family dynamics, joys, and tensions that filled the house, some of which resulted from the fact that her father was either a thirty-six or a forty-five year old widower with three children when he married her mother, Lim Koei Yap, a proud and uneducated girl of sixteen who had been born on a tobacco plantation. Moreover, Tjong A Fie had an earlier wife, "Mother Lee," who looked after his aged mother in his Meixian village when he sailed to Sumatra. She—"a tall lady with a fair complexion wearing Chinese clothes," according to young Queeny—came from China to Medan with her three children to visit her husband Tjong A Fie just as the new house was completed. While relations were cordial between the two wives for

a period of time, after an explosive fight Queeny's mother abruptly took her and her young brother and returned to her parent's home at the tobacco plantation. After several months of negotiations, the China wife and her children were put on a boat back to Guangdong, and Queeny, her mother, and young brother returned to the mansion. Mothers, cousins, aunts, uncles, in-laws regularly, and assorted friends of different nationalities joined Tjong A Fie and his wife Lim Koei Yap and their seven children born between 1896 and 1919 to keep the house lively.

The Tjong A Fie Mansion

"Everything was magnificent beyond words," is how Queeny described the new home she entered on a propitious date in 1900. An imported generator delivered electricity to brilliantly lit chandeliers that dazzled young and old alike. As the first residence in Medan to have electricity, not only was there no need to contend with oil or kerosene lamps, there was abundant illumination during the nighttime when circumstances demanded that it shine brilliantly through the front windows on both levels. Set back from the road behind an imposing gate that led to a garden and a broad porch, the mansion was unique. While the exterior of the house had an overall modern appearance because of its large windows, square columns, and covered veranda, on closer inspection the structure followed a symmetrical triple-bay plan with carved brackets lifting the roof. Moreover, a pair of flanking side buildings with an unmistakable Chinese gable, mirroring that found on the main building's gables, is found on both sides of the main structure. As early photographs show, the entry porch was arrayed with hanging couplets, lanterns, and signboards of many types. It was on this terrace, which has a much more subdued appearance amidst the trappings of China, that family commemorative photographs over many years were taken. At the rear of the house was an entryway leading to an open area as well as

sheds for parking vehicles. This rear entry was used on a day-to-day basis by the family while the front door was preserved for formal occasions.

Photographs of the interior of the house when it was first occupied reveal spacious rooms composed of both Chinese and European elements. The parlor had an inverted T shape that was covered with encaustic floor tiles said to be the same as those in the Sultan's palace in Jogjakarta. Arranged in alternating clusters of blue and ochre colors in fleur-de-lis and ivy patterns, the encaustic floor tiles may have been imported from one of the famous tileries in Stoke-on-Trent in England. The dado or lower portion of the walls was stenciled with a linear pattern of repeating images of clumps of lotus flowers and a single lotus bud, which together symbolize to Chinese the union of marriage and

fertility. Stenciled ornamentation was also found on the ceilings. While wallpapering had replaced extensive stenciling in much of Europe and America by the end of the nineteenth century, it may be that using wallpaper in humid Sumatra was not practical. Long embroidered panels in vivid colors, replete with traditional Chinese narrative tales, were hung from the cove molding along the edge of several walls. As a formal reception room, the central portion was uncluttered, while furniture was placed in the other areas. Each of the large side alcoves was furnished with Western-style furnishings, including tables, chairs, stands, and paintings. Visitors, of course, were drawn immediately to what was in front of them, a long room filled with a set of eight polished blackwood chairs along the walls and a round table with stools, all

inlaid with mother-of-pearl and marble. The magnificence of the room was enhanced by the exquisite carved filigreed screen that separated this public room from the open courtyard, ancestral hall, and private quarters beyond. Access was through two side openings, which lay adjacent to doors leading to the side rooms. The four panels at the center can be removed, as they were in order to carry the casket of Tjong A Fie in and out of the ancestral hall. Sets of four door panels of this sort usually represent the four seasons by showing four different plants in vases—bamboo, orchids, prunus, and chrysanthemum—but this is not the case here.

The open courtyard behind is sunken slightly with surprisingly only a single outlet to drain what must sometimes be quite copious rainfall. Looking from the courtyard towards the front of the house is the back of the hardwood screen with low relief and in-the-round carvings. Cinnabar and gold colors enhance the darkness of the hardwood. Angled stairs ascend on both sides to the second level, which contained not only a second parlor above the first floor parlor but also an altar room where offerings to Chinese deities could be made, along with numerous bedrooms. Pivoting shutters surround the upstairs gallery.

Except for the Victorian molded glass chandelier hanging from the ceiling, the impressive ancestral hall epitomizes the grandeur that connects the living with the dead in the homes of wealthy Chinese. Four lanterns, each with a tassel, hang symmetrically from the ceiling, which has been stenciled with large floral sprays and birds. In addition, a dramatic painting of a red bat with a hanging basket of flowers and fruits suspended from it decorates the ceiling. A red bat, called *hong fu* in Chinese, symbolizes abundant good fortune because of a homophonous relationship. All of the wooden components, including the alcove-like cabinet, shelves, panels, tables, chairs, and screens, were made in and shipped from China. Queeny recalled a "somber ceremony" that included the lighting of two enormous red candles as well as joss sticks

inserted in an open container on the altar as part of the "house warming ceremony" (Chang, 1931: 20).

The interior of the altar was painted red and included shelves for the tablets of ancestors, the parents of Tjong A Fie who died in China. While Queeny only recalled three tablets, there are today nearly a dozen newer ones. On a carved marble plinth supporting the carved hardwood altar is a modest, but necessary, shrine to Tudishen, also known as Tudi Gong, the Earth God. All around the altar table are carved panels of many shapes and types, each with auspicious narrative meanings. In front of the altar is a square table covered with a red satin cloth embroidered with a pair of dragons and images of Fu, Lu, and Shou, the Three Stellar Gods representing Good Fortune, Emolument, and Longevity. The four Chinese characters *jinyu mantang* have the auspicious meaning "Gold and Jade Fill the Hall." Ancestral portraits of Tjong A Fie's mother and father face each other on opposite walls in the hall.

Above the room to venerate the ancestors is a similar sized room with a simpler altar where offerings to Chinese deities can be made. Just as Queeny recalled, even today the principal image is of Guan Gong, also known as Guan Yu and Guan Di, the Daoist God of War, who, as a martial figure, sits astride a horse and brandishes a sword. Behind him on the altar is a colorful print of Guan Gong accompanied by Zhou Cang and Guan Ping, who were loyal to him. A pair of wooden deer, pronounced *lu* and thus with homophonous association with wealth, serve as candle holders. On the sides of the deer is a circular *shou* or longevity medallion, which with the four surrounding images of bats represent the "Five Good Fortunes"—Longevity, Wealth, Health, Love of Virtue, and a Natural Death in Old Age. The embroidered cloth laid across the table includes images of the fabled Eight Immortals as well as five images of the mythical *qilin*, an animal with a lion's head, a scaled body, and a serpent's tail. The *qilin* is a symbol of rank and privilege, and also represents longevity.

Above the first floor parlor in the front of the house was Tjong A Fie's upstairs parlor, which was entered through openings in the carved and gilded Chinese lattice screen like the one in the room below. With its six pyramidal chandeliers and large shuttered windows, which could be thrown open, the upstairs room must have been light and airy. Stenciled on the ceiling are delicate dragonflies, which have many symbolic associations, including esteem and reverence. This formal parlor was filled only with Western furniture, including rectangular and circular settees, curio cabinets, chairs, and wall stands, as well as paintings, carpets, mirrors, and other decorative trappings. Complementing the grand piano in the downstairs parlor was a tall cabinet pipe organ, a type that gained fame in the late nineteenth century because of its beautiful tones that could be sustained indefinitely,

Framing the two parlors and two altar rooms to complete the rectangular shape of the core building are large rooms. The four deeper rooms in the rear—two upstairs and two downstairs—were used as the bedrooms for senior members of the family. Tjong A Fie and his wife initially used the rooms upstairs, but Tjong A Fie's widow moved downstairs as she became more infirm. The two long wing structures on each side of the core building, which provided living space for the family units living in the house, are set back from the projecting terrace at the front of the house to make space for private gardens, accessible both from the covered terrace and the residential quarters. Between the residential quarters and the core building are four rectangular courtyards that help ventilate the house and provide space for indoor/outdoor plantings. The residential quarters overall include some twenty rooms to serve as bedrooms and for storage, in addition to multiple toilets, and four spaces open to the adjacent courtyards that served as locations for family dining and relaxation.

In spite of living in a large house, Queeny says, "I never realized how wealthy my father was until he told my mother one day that he had bought a rubber estate" and planned to take them to see it in his new Fiat convertible (Chang, 1931: 45–6). Yet, when she went to visit Penang, she became conscious of those who were even wealthier, such as her "great-uncle" Cheong Fatt Tze, whom she refers to as Tio Tiauw-set, and Chung Thye-phin, the son of Chung Keng Quee, whose boyhood home was discussed earlier (pages 102–13).

This expansive mansion, with its large family, provided the stage for domestic celebrations relating to births, birthdays, and weddings, as well as gaiety and solemnity at the coming of the Chinese New Year that was shared with foreign guests. In 1916 the Medan community joined together in a jubilee to honor Tjong A Fie's thirty years as a Dutch-Chinese officer. In 1920 the family celebrated Tjong A Fie's sixtieth birthday, a number that represents the completion of a full cycle of life, and a few months later his and his wife's silver anniversary. Tjong A Fie died just a year later, on February 8, 1921. On the following morning, his mahogany casket, which had been lacquered seven times with *tung* oil as a preservative, was placed in the ancestral hall before the altar, and closed at an auspicious hour, according to Queeny. That morning, a notary read his will to the family that provided for his widow and children, with the remainder placed into a foundation controlled by his male heirs. Following a forty-nine day Chinese-style funeral at the Tianhou Temple, a solemn funeral procession carried his body for burial in an imposing gravesite outside the city. When Tjong A Fie died, he left behind a forty-two year old widow and five children between the ages of two and fifteen in addition to two married children, his eldest daughter Queeny and twenty-one year old son Fa-liong. For a while, his widow and the children lived in Switzerland but returned to Medan before the Second World War. By then, except for the family home, much of the family's wealth was gone. Several of her children and their families continued to live with her in the mansion. Tjong A Fei's widow lived in the house until 1972, when she died at the age of ninety-three, fifty-one years after her husband.

As the twenty-first century began, news reports claimed that Tjong A Fie's mansion "suffers from poor maintenance" (Gunawan, 2001: 1), just as was the case with other fine buildings in what was once the bustling Kesawan commercial and residential area of Medan. By the end of the first decade, however, the investment of time, resources, and energy by the surviving sons and daughters of Tjong A Fie had begun to show significant results in terms of the revitalization of their heritage home. These efforts paralleled the efforts of the Sumatra Heritage Trust that recommended following a step-by-step approach of the need to awaken an understanding of the city's heritage, before then inspiring the public's appreciation of it, followed by achieving a stage where revitalization— actual conservation—of heritage could take place.

The successful launching of The Tjong A Fie Memorial Institute for Chinese-Indonesian Heritage in 2008 was followed by the home being opened to the public in June 2009. With Fon Prawira as Director and other family members playing key roles, this venerable and historic mansion has been brought back to life as a locus for refreshing public memory not only of Tjong A Fie as a man celebrated because of his sensitive multiculturalism and wealth, but also as a vehicle for promoting knowledge of the contributions of Chinese-Indonesians to the country. Increasing visits of school children, members of the broader community, political leaders, and tourists are all discovering new exhibits of photographs and objects that express these legacies in what is arguably Sumatra's finest old mansion.

Opposite above This is an oblique view looking across the skywell towards the back side of the carved screen wall at the head of the front reception room.

Above left One of the painted capitals of the four cast-iron columns that support the galleries around the skywell.

Above right This decoration in the shape of a flower vase is carved and painted on the wooden ceiling adjacent to the skywell.

Below With apartments for family members around it, this is one of a pair of side skywells on both sides of the main structure.

Above The ancestral altar for the Tjong lineage is placed in a room beyond the skywell on the first floor.

Below A detail of a tableaux on the front of the ancestral altar table.

Bottom This small shrine to the Earth God or Tudi Gong is located under the ancestral altar.

Above A close-up of a carved candle in front of the ancestral altar.

Left, top to bottom On the second floor, just above the ancestral hall, is a deity altar used to worship Guan Gong. Viewed from near the altar to Guan Gong, the room is dominated by a table and a richly ornamented ceiling. Stenciled on the walls surrounding the deity altar room is a series of clustered peony flowers. Adjacent to the skywell, with its louvered windows, is a subsidiary altar used for regular offerings to Guan Gong.

Right A European-style side console and mirror in the upstairs parlor.

Above right Surrounding the imported chandeliers of the upstairs parlor are ceiling stencils of dragonflies.

Below right A detail of the fluted granite columns with tenoned brackets that lift the heavy wooden beams.

Below On the second floor is a vast room whose span is supported by granite columns that lift massive wooden beams. This room was used for entertaining large parties. Both the furnishings and the ornamentation mix Western and Chinese forms.

LOKE YEW MANSION

KUALA LUMPUR, MALAYSIA
1892–1904

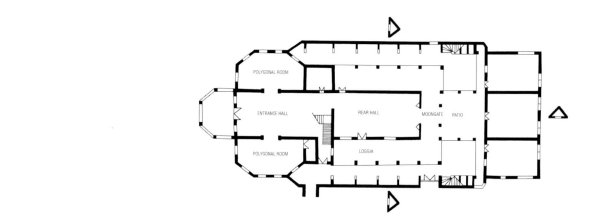

Above and left The floor plan of the Loke Yew mansion shows the balanced distribution of rooms and passageways while the section view reveals the fact that the second structure is higher and broader than the preceding one, both being characteristic of Chinese buildings. The sketch of the portico represents a later addition, while the one seen in the photograph is said to be closer to the original.

Right Photographed at dusk, the restored Loke Yew mansion is a two-storey elongated structure with a symmetrical façade capped by a triangular pediment and portico with an extended canopy.

Loke Yew (1845–1917), Yap Ah Loy (1837–1885), and Chung Keng Kwee (1827–1901) formed an overlapping triumvirate of immigrants of Hakka origin from Guangdong province who amassed fortunes by exploiting the tin ore resources of the Malay Peninsula in addition to other endeavors. While Chung Keng Kwee is associated with Penang, Loke Yew and Yap Ah Loy were key figures in the development of Kuala Lumpur. Chung Keng Kwee's grand residence, which was started in 1893 and described in an earlier chapter (pages 102–13), is still standing, as is Loke Yew's mansion, which was begun in 1892. Both Loke Yew and Chung Keng Kwee lived into their seventies and thus in many ways were able to realize their dreams. Yap Ah Loy, on the other hand, who arrived in Selangor at the age of nineteen after stints in Malacca, died less than thirty years after, in 1885. He had had a rich life, involving communal fighting and peacemaking as well as financial success and near bankruptcy, but died young.

In the 1870s, when Loke Yew was Kapitan China of Kuala Lumpur, which was still a developing frontier town, he lived in "a fairly good loose-board house" that "was surrounded by *attap* houses occupied by his coolies." Located overlooking the market square, it was described in contemporaneous reports as appalling—"the filth of the market is indescribable, everything that rots or becomes putrid, all offal and refuse is thrown on to the ground or into the ditches.... A visitor to Ah Loy's house in the 1870s said it took a strong stomach to get food down in the midst of that stench" (Middlebrook and Gullick, 1983: 93). A fire in January 1881, which is believed to have been started by an overturned

oil-lamp in an opium den, brought about the indiscriminate destruction of the *attap* and timber homes in Kuala Lumpur. In December 1881 a major flood led to further devastation, including Yap Ah Loy's new home. In the ensuing years, with prodigious energy and unflagging enterprise, he not only financed the rebuilding of the growing town using bricks and tile, especially for rows of shophouses, but also built his family another new home. In 1884 his thoughts turned to visiting China, but by the end of the year he fell seriously ill and then died in March 1885. Much of his life's ambitions were unfulfilled because of his early death. Forty years later, in 1924, his widow, Kok Kang Keow, and two of his surviving sons, who had "been reduced to a state of penury," submitted an unsuccessful petition to the British Resident Selangor with claims for an overdue payment for Yap Ah Loy's service a half century before (Middlebrook and Gullick, 1983: 122–3). It has not been possible to locate a photograph of his family's residence home or information about when it was razed. Today, HSBC, formerly called Hong Kong and Shanghai Bank Corporation, occupies the site on Jalan Medan Tuanku.

In 1892, only seven years after his friend Yap Ah Loy's death, Loke Yew, at the age of forty-seven, began to build his own mansion in Kuala Lumpur, an attenuated process that took twelve years to bring to completion. Like Yap Ah Loy and Chung Keng Kwee, the rise of Loke Yew was a rags-to-riches tale. He was born into an impoverished family in 1845 in a small village in Heshan county, part of what is today the sprawling city of Jiangmen in the Pearl River delta area of Guangdong province. While this area is best known as a source region for emigration

Above Classical elements and proportions as well as architectural embellishments along one side of the residence are so dominant that the original Chinese-style entry in the lower right is not very obvious.

Far left Each of the rectangular windows on both levels is shaded with an overhanging Western-style awning.

Center left A bonsai, literally "planted-in-a-tray" after the original Chinese term *penzai*, is used as an ornament on the front porch.

Near left The mixed architectural vocabulary of this element on the upper side of the residence includes a bat or dragon motif, both of which are quintessentially Chinese motifs.

to North America and Australia, many Hakka also left the area for Southeast Asia.

Loke Yew's original name was Wong Loke Yew (Huang Ruyou), that is, his surname was Wong/Huang. It is said that after his mother died when he was very young, he was sent to a distant village to work for a prosperous family surnamed Loke, Lu in standard Chinese. Sometime after, he adopted the name Loke Yew, in part because of the auspicious homophonic associations with *lokeyew/luyou*, "having good fortune." As a young teenager, he signed on as a coolie, known also at that time as "piglets" or *zhuzi* because of the pen they were restricted to on the ship that took them to Singapore where his first job was in a provision shop on Market Street. Within four years he had accumulated sufficient capital to open his own shop with the chop or trademark Hing Loong. In time, he struck out, seeking opportunities in the open-cast tin mining business that was then thriving in the Larut Matang region of Perak in northern Malaysia. In the ensuing years, however, the speculative nature of the tin mining enterprises was driven home as he lost considerable amounts of money as the world price of tin plummeted before market conditions turned again to generate great profits. Furthermore, Loke Yew saw early

the value of diversification of his assets as he moved into real estate, transportation, and revenue farming.

Loke Yew, like other rising capitalists who were born in China but lived among European colonialists, sought to attain the social graces and even lifestyles of those he admired and depended upon. When it appeared that wealthy Chinese might not be able to ride as first-class passengers on a new rail line through the Malay States, Loke Yew, in 1904, created a handbook titled *Etiquette to be Observed by All Chinese First Class Passengers*, including the following admonitions as reported in the *Straits Times* (adapted from Godley, 1981: 5):

You are requested to be polite and courteous to ladies and relinquish your seats to ladies if the carriage is crowded. Never allow a lady to stand.

Staring at people (especially at ladies), expectorating, talking in a loud tone of voice, laughing loudly—all are considered ungentlemanly and bad manners.

Your hat should be removed when you enter a carriage in which there are ladies.

We know little of Loke Yew's family life except for the fact that he married at least three times, had eleven children, and traveled abroad, including perhaps twice to Europe with his family, once in 1902 and then again in 1904–5, during which time it is likely they selected furnishings for their new home in Kuala Lumpur. His first and perhaps his second wife were probably of humble origins and died young (Smith, 1920: 110–11). Upon the death of his wife, Lim Shuk Kwei, in 1914, her relatives introduced Loke Yew to her cousin, Lim Cheng Kim, a well-educated nineteen-year-old whose Peranakan family also was in the tin mining business. He married Lim Cheng Kim that same year, when he was sixty-nine or seventy, and fathered three children, a son and two daughters, over the next three years before dying of malaria in 1917. His final will expressed his intentions (Wisma Loke, 1970: 9):

I BEQUEATH free of duty all my plate and plated articles, books, pictures, prints, glass, china, furniture and other household effects, motor cars, horses, carriages and other vehicles whatsoever, horses and harness unto MY TRUSTEES UPON TRUST … the house standing on land in Kuala Lumpur aforesaid comprised in Certificates of Title numbered respectively 1122, 1134 and 1135 herinafter referred to for the use and enjoyment of all my issue and their wives until twenty-one years from the death of my said wife or myself whichever be the later.

While raising her young children and especially concerned about the health of her eldest son, Loke Lim Cheng Kim decided to move the family to Switzerland in 1919 where the children thrived and gained a lifelong appreciation for nature. After returning to Kuala Lumpur, perhaps a decade later when her son Wan Tho entered Cambridge University, she managed her deceased husband's business interests. At the same time, she began a new career for herself and Wan Tho in 1935 as the principals in a company that became the entertainment conglomerate Cathay Organisation. Loke Wan Tho, who had been born in the Loke Mansion in 1915, just two years before the death of his father, subsequently became well known and wealthy in his own right as a cinema magnate with avocational interests in ornithology, photography, poetry, English literature, antiques, golf, and, like his father, philanthropy. Loke Wan Tho tragically died in a sightseeing airplane crash in 1964 in Taiwan at the age of forty-nine. His mother lived to the age of eighty-six. After her passing in 1981, the Loke Cheng Kim Foundation was established in Singapore to assist needy students there to pursue further education in foreign universities.

From the 1930s on, and with family members living in Singapore, Kuala Lumpur, and elsewhere, the ageing Loke Yew Mansion was occupied only by caretakers and its future was uncertain. Its use as a family residence was impractical, its structure was derelict, its integrity had been neglected, and its glory had faded. When Kuala Lumpur was occupied by the Japanese in January 1942, the residence was appropriated by the invaders who refashioned the home to meet their requirements as the headquarters of the Kuala Selangor Division of the Japanese Army, occupying it until the end of the war in August 1945.

Over the next thirteen years, the once proud mansion served variously as a school, a headquarters for the criminal investigation department of the police, and a special branch training center (Wisma Loke, 1971: 11). In addition, the spacious grounds, once covered with coconut palms, rubber trees, even an experimental paddy field, lawns where elephants and other larger animals roamed, as well as an extensive pond and outbuildings like stables and coach houses, were sold to developers.

Today, the once verdant and sprawling gardens are occupied by tall buildings, streets, and vacant lots. Over the years, only a fenced half-hectare came to be retained surrounding Loke Yew's mansion, with most of the space used for parking and storage. This reduction of the extensive estate grounds and the spacious areal context within which the residence was placed substantially diminished the overall grandeur of the building. Moreover, the structure was effectively unoccupied from 1958 until the 1970s, with the result that its dignity continued to fade because a series of additions and renovations had marred its integrity while continuing weathering from the elements led to obvious levels of deterioration (Clague, 1972: 107–9). Few doubted that there was a likelihood of the demolition of a once proud but now anachronistic structure at some future time.

Yet, in 1970, with the approval of the Trustees of the Loke Yew Estate, Peter Clague, a proprietor of a firm called Asia Antiques, set out to make the historic residence a showplace for the arts of Malaysia specifically and Southeast Asia generally. Significant restoration work was done over a six-month period to remove walls that had been put into place dividing once spacious rooms into smaller offices, to bring back to life some of the applied ornamentation, and to remove decades of accumulated additions, detritus, and grime. Renamed Wisma Loke (Loke House), the building was reborn late in 1970 with gallery space for Asia Antiques and the Samat Art Gallery as well as rooms of the Malaysia College of Music. Throughout the 1980s, the building became the home of an art gallery and antiques showroom called the Artiquarium and subsequently, until about 2000, space was occupied by the Lim Kok Wing Art School, a facility of the Limkokwing University of Creative Technology. As recently as January 2006, the building was being described as in a "sad state" with the original iron balustrades and vertical window bars missing, extensive water damage, and deteriorated mural paintings (Hwang, 2006–7: 2).

Fortunately, because of the subsequent confluence of interests and circumstances, Loke Yew's nearly derelict mansion was given a reprieve when Dato' Loh Siew Cheang of the law firm Cheang & Ariff committed the resources necessary to rescue this historic structure, which not only straddles three centuries but also is now the oldest surviving residence in Kuala Lumpur. Subsequent to the Badan Warisan Malaysia's nomination of the Loke Mansion as a National Heritage site, and while renovation work was still incomplete, the Cheang & Ariff law firm began to occupy the building in November 2007. In 2008 a newspaper article declared that the "dilapidated building has been given back its soul" (Kam, 2008).

Loke Yew's penchant for diversification and his extraordinary ability to make money was matched by the range of his philanthropy. His fame is memorialized in Kuala Lumpur with a prominent street, Jalan Loke Yew, bearing his name. He is well known also as a co-founder with his Tamil Indian friend K. Thamboosamy Pillay and the city's last Kapitan China, Yap Kwan Seng, of the Victoria Institution, an English-stream boys' school, in 1893. In Singapore, he not only also has a street named after him, Loke Yew Street, but five wards of the venerable Tan

Tock Seng Chinese Hospital bear his name. In Hong Kong, Loke Yew was instrumental in establishing an endowment fund for Hong Kong University in 1912 as well as providing a twenty-one year interest-free loan when the university was facing bankruptcy in 1915. Hong Kong University granted him an honorary Doctor of Laws degree in 1917, just a month before he died. In 1956 the university named the Great Hall in the Main Building after him, and, with the support of Loke Yew's grandchildren, created the Loke Yew Professorship in Pathology in 2008. Loke Yew himself was well noted for his myriad gifts to many deserving organizations. "A hundred dollars here and a thousand Straits dollars there helped innumerable projects for the public good to make ends meet" (Godley, 1981: 14). He is said to have contributed fighter planes for the Great War. In 1920 he was compared by the British author C. A. Middleton Smith to Andrew Carnegie, a shrewd immigrant to America from Scotland, who built great wealth in steel manufacturing as a Captain of Industry before giving it away to public libraries, universities, and other endeavors both in the United States and

his homeland Scotland. One gained wealth in tin, the other in steel, but both "commenced their careers with almost every possible handicap. They lacked friends, connections, education, and money. They possessed industry, shrewdness, financial genius, and good health. After they had succeeded, they used a portion of their wealth for the endowment of learning" (Smith, 1920: 107–8).

The initial construction, subsequent decay, and now extensive restoration of the Loke Yew mansion in Kuala Lumpur have returned the spotlight to one of Southeast Asia's most energetic, entrepreneurial, and public-spirited capitalists. In a hagiographic chapter titled "A Chinese Captain of Industry," C. A. Middleton Smith in 1920 declared, "Towkay Loke Yew, if he had possessed the advantage of the education which thousands of young Chinese of to-day obtain, would, in all probability, have figured as one of the great men of history. As it is he has won the fame of the pioneer. In the Straits Settlements and the Dutch East Indies the men of the oldest race on earth have shown their amazing industry and adaptability to the new conditions of life, which science has ushered in to almost every land but China.... It is because Towkay Loke Yew devoted his astonishing ability and ceaseless industry to the cause of progress that his life of industry should be made known outside his own circle of acquaintances" (Smith, 1920: 111–12).

The Loke Yew Mansion

What is known today as Loke Yew's Mansion actually emerged as an expansion of an earlier home constructed at the beginning of the 1860s by Cheow (also Chow) Ah Yeok, a Cantonese ally of Kapitan China Yap Ah Loy and close friend of Loke Yew. When Cheow Ah Yeok died in 1892, Loke Yew purchased the dwelling and land, spacious grounds of approximately 4.5 hectares that sloped down towards a tributary of the Klang River. With the assistance of an architect, Loke Yew designed

Above Framed with slender blocks of granite, the main entry includes a *tanglong*, also called a *muzha men*, an ingenious sliding cage-like structure comprising rounded horizontal bars of *chengai*, a durable and dense hardwood that is common in southern China.

Right Each of the side rooms is pentagonal in shape with access through an imposing arched doorway framed with a pair of fluted Doric pilasters that project slightly from the wall

a large, somewhat eccentric mansion in an eclectic style that was to be grafted on to Cheow's earlier, more modest Chinese-style home. Portions of Cheow's original structure were retained as single-storey buildings at the rear of the new mansion. When Cheow's home was built, it was said to have been the earliest brick home in Kuala Lumpur, a time when others were timber and thatch. By the time Loke Yew's mansion was under construction some thirty years later, and more than a decade after the 1881 conflagration, skilled masons in Kuala Lumpur were numerous and building materials from the extensive brickfields and kilns originally established by Yap Ah Loy in the suburban area known today as Brickfields were readily available by rail.

In 1902 Loke Yew and his family traveled with Mr Robson, the editor of the *Malay Mail*, to Europe, where Loke Yew had the good fortune to attend the coronation of King Edward VII in London. Besides collecting objets d'art and furniture for his new home in which he emulated the lavish style then in vogue in Europe, he purchased a steam yacht and his first automobile. Loke Yew's wife was "credited with being the very first Straits Chinese lady to ride in an auto having taken her maiden trip in the spring of 1903" (Godley, 1981: 13). A garage was added as an outbuilding near the new residence. Loke Yew and his family held a grand house warming party when their residence was completed. Afterwards, he and his wife were enthusiastic in welcoming overseas friends and acquaintances to many types of affairs inside their home and in the adjacent gardens.

The Loke Yew mansion clearly reflects an international mixture of architectural and ornamental styles with clear classical proportions: Chinese door and window treatments accompanied by a dash of European influences; flamboyant Dutch-style gables set atop a colonnaded veranda; imposing classical columns, semicircular arches, and pediments; a Chinese moon gate; floor tiles from several countries; Scottish cast-iron balusters; half-round Chinese-style roof tiles; corrugated metal roof panels; a spacious balcony terrace—all components of an evolved Palladian style that emphasized symmetry. Loke Yew's new home was the first private residence in Kuala Lumpur with electricity for interior lighting.

The Loke Mansion is a two-storey structure with a symmetrical front elevation, ground and second floor plans, as well as side elevations of the extended rear section. A variety of modifications over the years to the front altered the nature of both the front terrace as well as the extended portico over the entryway. Originally, the driveway at the front of the residence was much lower than it is now, so that the main doorway was reached by ascending a series of stepped terraces, but gradually this front area was filled in. The recent renovation of the entry portico, while at the higher grade level, brought back a façade that is in harmony with what existed during Loke Yew's time. The pair of lions seen today at the entry, however, will surprise many when they realize that they are not of Chinese origin but are from Czechoslovakia, a whimsically appropriate addition by Dato' Loh Siew Cheang to a building that is intrinsically eclectic and a bit eccentric. The arrangement of interior spaces is essentially symmetrical.

The pair of clear glass door panels of the current entryway, which is approximately 3 meters high and 1.5 meters wide, has behind them a quintessential set of southern Chinese door elements framed by four blocks of granite. First is a *tanglong*, also called a *muzha men*, an ingenious cage-like structure comprising rounded horizontal bars of *chengai*, a durable and dense hardwood, set into a frame that can be easily slid open or closed. *Tanglong* are still common features of rural and urban dwellings throughout Guangdong, Loke Yew's home province, where there has always been a need to keep door panels open in order to facilitate cross-ventilation due to high temperatures and sometimes oppressive humidities. Behind the *tanglong* are heavy wooden doors that can be closed and secured at night. To increase ventilation, there is also a pair of rectangular windows alongside the *tanglong*, with lozenge-shaped ventilation ports above the windows, each of which has vertical metal bars. A horizontal board once hung above the entryway with the characters *Dong Xing Yuan*, "Garden of Eastern Prosperity," but today the sign reads "CHEANGARIFF."

The elongated main hall inside the door is nearly seven meters in height with decorative floor tiles in a blue floral pattern set in a russet and off-white field similar to those found in Victorian catalogs at the

Right At the rear of the main building is a moon gate room. Here, the view of this room is from the covered terrace.

Below This view is from inside the moon gate room looking towards the covered terrace outside.

time. On each side of the main hall is a side room with a pentagonal outer wall, with each surface punctured by a rectangular window, also with metal bars. On the exterior, each of these windows, as well as those above on the second floor, is shaded with an overhanging Western-style canopy. Each side room is entered through an imposing arched doorway framed with a pair of fluted Doric pilasters that project slightly from the wall and reach from floor to ceiling.

On the left wall immediately inside the doorway is an empty niche with three characters, *Wang Xiang Tang*, across the top and two four-character phrases along the sides. Some have speculated that this niche was an ancestral shrine while others have called it a coat of arms. Neither is correct. The niche is for the placement of an image of the God of Wealth or Caishen, a common figure found in Chinese shops and homes

to "attract" wealth and prosperity. The three characters on top recall the story of Lin Zhaotang, a Zhuangyuan or Number One scholar in the Qing Imperial Examinations, who during the nineteenth century in Guangdong province is said to have guaranteed prosperity in several days to the poor owners of a congee shop whom he had befriended by writing these characters above the niche for their God of Wealth.

At the end of the main hall is a wooden staircase leading to the second floor, with an archway leading to a long room beyond. At the rear of this long room is a moon gate, a complete circle over two meters in diameter, which can be shuttered by a heavy set of folding doors made of *chengai* wood reinforced with four iron segments. Until the 1970s the moon gate had been "lost," having been bricked up many years before, perhaps during the Japanese occupation period. The area outside the moon gate is an expansive covered patio area framed by multiple arches separated by massive columns that support the roof terrace above. This area is connected as well with verandas that run on both sides of the core building. With wooden louvers or glass panels on the upper portions of the outer arches, the open areas are sheltered from rain and direct sunlight while admitting breezes. Thus, this expansive area, which is approximately the same size as the interior spaces, provided pleasant and protected places for the family and their guests to eat meals, pass time, and entertain. To the left of the moon gate is a large wooden cabinet recessed into the outer wall with double doors composed of four folding panels covered with glass. Here the family kept tea sets and other service items for visitors. Three rooms, which may have been part of the original 1860s house, are directly opposite the moon gate. It is not clear what the original purpose of these rooms was, but there is speculation that the middle room was a family dining room with the other ones serving as a kitchen and pantry, while an elongated series of adjacent rooms that jut out in an L shape were used by the family's servants. As a result of the recent renovation, lattice doors made of elm from China and cut glass panels of European origin have been installed on the outside of these rooms. On one side of the covered patio is a pond filled with gold fish that is frequented by a pair of resident tortoises. On the other side is a lush rock garden.

The moon gate, when viewed from outside, is framed within a red square and has a medallion-like configuration with two pairs of Chinese characters and a number of raised plaster ornaments, each with a symbolic meaning. The small characters, *langui*, and the two larger characters, *tengfang*, together form a four-character proverb with the meaning "May Your Progeny Be Prosperous and Your Family Illustrious." This is a well-known phrase found in the children's reader *Youxue Qionglin* (Exquisite compendium for children to study), which was published in the eighteenth century and was used in private academies in China and in Southeast Asia. The gold fish recollects the homophonous association between the Chinese characters for "gold fish," *jinyu*, and those for gold and jade, also *jinyu*, which together have the meaning "riches." The eagle *ying* symbolizes a "hero" or "heroism," the bat, pronounced *fu*, is homophonous with *fu* meaning "good fortune" or "blessings," among others. There is a protective amulet beneath the medallion in the shape of an animal.

Stairs lead up from the patio to a formal outside terrace, which is framed on one side by columns and arches of a veranda that rings the upstairs rooms above the main building. It is not clear how most of the rooms on the second level were used by the Loke family except

Below Said to be the original entry to the old Chinese-style residence constructed in the 1860s by Cheow Ah Yeok, this colorful gate includes a painting depicting the literary proverb "There are sometimes people who 'add flowers to brocade,' but how many people 'send coal in snowy weather'."

Above right A recent addition to Loke Yew's mansion is a copy of a Sichuan-style teahouse, which is patterned after a photograph taken by Chester Ong in the author's book *Chinese Houses*.

for the pentagonal rooms at the front which were perhaps separate bedrooms for the husband and wife. The extent of the space on the second level suggests that there were ample bedrooms for family members and guests as well as sitting rooms, all of which had access to both the covered veranda ringed with dramatic arches and columns and the outside terrace.

Looking out from the covered patio on the ground floor is a simple Chinese-style gateway with double leaves painted red and a sliding *tanglong*. When viewed from the inside, this side gate is simple and unadorned, but when viewed from the outside, it is clear why the structure is called "The Painted Gate." Believed to be one of the entryways to the 1860s home built by Cheow Ah Yeok, this adorned entryway has a vivid central painting above it with calligraphic texts within panels on both sides as well as a pair of landscape paintings on the sides. Molded plaster sculptures in low relief, one a pair of magpies and the other a mythical *qilin*, are found along the outer frames of the gatehouse. The scene depicts two men seated at a table being approached by a third man with three attendants nearby. The pictorial composition includes a moon gate, a walled enclosure, and a gnarled tree, and is labeled *jinshang tianhua tu*, which has the direct meaning of "adding flowers onto brocade," usually translated as "making a good thing even better." Yet, this colorful tableau actually has a broader meaning based on the literary proverb *jinshang tianhua changshi you, xuezhong songtan neng ji ren*, "There are sometimes people who 'add flowers to brocade,' but how many people 'send coal in snowy weather'." This is an admonition that there are usually many fair-weather friends—always individuals who are ready to flatter you when you are successful, but unwilling to reach out to you during a time of need.

Just outside "The Painted Gate" is an area paved with blocks of stone with an L-shaped timber-framed open structure extending out from the wall of the older back section of the Loke Yew residence. When we encountered this building, we were puzzled not only by its familiarity—we were certain we had seen it somewhere else—but also because it seemed to "fit" well even though it appeared alien to the overall architectural style of the Loke mansion. Before long, we realized that many aspects of the building looked quite similar to those found in Deng Xiaoping's residence in Sichuan province, which had been featured in our *Chinese Houses: The Architectural Heritage of a Nation*. Further probing revealed that Dato' Loh Siew Cheang, who led the restoration of the Loke mansion, had seen the photographs in our 2005 book and decided to replicate it as an addition to the mansion as an informal place for staff and clients to relax and discuss matters. Although it is certain that Loke Yew never traveled into interior China to visit places like Sichuan, where the vernacular architectural forms differ stylistically from those found in his home region in Guangdong, we suspect that he would have approved of this fanciful addition.

TAN BOON CHIA RESIDENCE

RASA, MALAYSIA

1918

Some old residences age gracefully, maintaining their original form while outwardly taking on the patina of age. Muted colors and obscured ornamentation, the inevitable products of high temperature and humidity as the years pass, barely suggest what was once obvious to all. Few passersby give old residences more than a glance, remaining clueless to the circumstances that gave rise to the buildings.

Occasionally an aged structure is restored to its past grandeur. Such is the case of the mansion built some 50 kilometers east of Kuala Lumpur in 1918 by Tan Boon Chia, one of Malaysia's pioneering tin mining magnates during the first quarter of the twentieth century. The Tan Boon Chia residence was among the earliest mansions built by an Overseas Chinese who made his mark and fortune in the then Federated Malaysia States. Rasa was an early trading and mining center that gained fame in the tin rich state of Selangor, in an area where the first tin-fields were

Right A projecting portico-like structure at the front of a mansion, called a *porte-cochère*, enabled those arriving in a vehicle to alight without experiencing the vicissitudes of nature. It was a common architectural feature throughout the nineteenth century. Today, a pair of large buckets, which are artifactual vestiges of the tin mining in Selangor, have been added.

Below The Chinese-style entryway with couplets and a horizontal board proclaiming the home region of the Tan lineage.

discovered and the mineral tin mined. Malaya was later to become the world's leading producer.

After standing rather quietly along a country road in Rasa for more than six decades, the mansion was restored to its original glory in 2008. Now, all notice the presence of this architectural jewel. The restoration of the mansion was led by Tan Siew Lay, and was financed wholly by the Estate of Tan Seng Kee, a son of Tan Boon Chia.

What is known of Tan Boon Chia's life is fragmentary, gleaned more from newspapers than academic treatises. Yet, if the completion and furnishing of his magnificent home can be used as evidence, he indeed prospered as a young man. The Chinese language website of Anxi county in Fujian province proudly lists Tan Boon Chia (Chen Wensheng) as well as two of his sons, Tan Chin Siong (Chen Zhenxiang) and Tan Seng Kee (Chen Shengqi), as three of its most distinguished emigrants.

Tan Boon Chia, a migrant from Anxi's Penglai township where he was born in 1868, came with little to Malaya and rose through diligence and sacrifice to become a successful tin miner and planter. Arriving "as a penniless youth, Tan began to earn his living by transporting goods and supplies on a cart for the tin mines around the area. Pulling the cart himself, he carried out this back-breaking job until he

saved enough to buy his first tin mine. In time, Tan invested in a tin dredger, and as his business prospered he bought a few more mines and went into other business ventures, such as the purchase of rubber plantations" (Ramli 2002).

Called "One of Selangor's Leading Residents," he died in 1931 after being "prominent in the commercial and social life of this State for many years" (*New Straits Times*, October 29, 1931, p. 14). In the years that followed, Tan Boon Chia's sons continued to prosper, as they owned seventeen tin mines, several marble quarries, as well as rubber plantations in Selangor and in neighboring areas. The Tan family apparently embraced the technological revolution that was transforming tin mining in Malaya as modern Western machinery—especially dredging and hydraulic methods in open cast mines—increasingly came to replace more traditional labor-intensive methods that had served Chinese entrepreneurs so well in the past. In fact, in the two decades before World War I, the tin mining industry in Malaya overall more than doubled its output. The Tan family's good fortune was abruptly disrupted however with the Japanese invasion of Malaya in 1941. According to news reports, they hurriedly left their home, choosing to raise their families in other places like Kuala Lumpur and Singapore.

   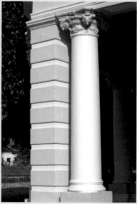

Above left to right A canopied window with colored glass and a festooned plasterwork trim above. Plasterwork with point-and-dart ornamentation atop one of the balconies. A balcony with elaborate Western-style ornamentation. Spiral scrolls give character to the capital atop this decorative column alongside the *porte-cochère*.

Below The extension on the left is the alcove off the reception hall, while the balcony is off the upstairs sitting room. Adjacent are extensions for the dining room and upstairs parlor.

Tan Boon Chia's Residence

The date "1918" and the name "Tan Boon Chia" are emblazoned on the façade of the *porte-cochère*, the extended portico-like structure that extends out from the core structure of the residence. Today, one also sees on the ground in front a pair of large buckets, representative vestiges of the heyday of tin mining in Selangor. Linked with more than a hundred other buckets on a chain-like assemblage that operated as a dredge atop a floating vessel, each bucket scooped out ore from alluvial deposits at the bottom of ponds.

In spite of the external flourishes, which are clearly Western in style and characteristic of the times when the house was built, the interior floor plan echoes Chinese patterns: a sequence of halls and courtyards. After mounting shallow steps, which are framed by a pair of columns with Corinthian-style capitals, a visitor encounters both a double-leaved hardwood door as well as a sliding *tanglong*, which is comprised of strong wooden cross bars that secures the opening while allowing air to enter. On the leaves of the door are two pairs of characters 壽山福海 that literally read "Longevity Mountain, Good Fortune Sea" but which expresses the blessing "Longevity as enduring as the mountains, Good fortune as boundless as the sea." Above the door are the two characters 穎川 Yingchuan, referring to the original homeland in Henan province of the principal branch of those with the surname Tan, which in *pinyin* romanization is spelled Chen. On the inside, the door is "locked" by sliding two wooden bolts.

Polished marble floors are found throughout the home with a mixture of Chinese and Western furniture and ornamentation. On the first floor are two rectangular halls, which are joined to each other by an elaborate wooden openwork gilded screen with four lattice panels and two side door openings. An alcove, which projects out from the main walls, forms a bay that extends the room on both ends with the result that natural lighting is enhanced. The second room includes a stairway that leads to the second level. While Chinese-style hardwood furniture of different periods dominates these two rooms, the windows and ceiling treatment are Western.

Just beyond the second hall is a perpendicular space that serves as a dining room. With patterned floor tiles, colored glass panels, hanging lights, and four columns along each side, this room is strikingly informal. Beyond the columns are a pair of open courtyards, one of which has a well. Following the dining area is the family's altar room with a shrine inset into the wall. This is a unique altar in that it is surfaced with colored mosaic tiles that have painted characters and images on them. Above the altar are the characters 颖川堂 "Yingchuan Hall." Offerings are presented daily to the Tan forbears who are represented by three ancestral tablets. Tan Boon Chia's descendants continue to participate in periodic rituals to demonstrate the honor and respect they have for their ancestors.

Off to the side via a narrow corridor is a formal dining room set with Western dishes for ten people. On the wall is a long horizontal painting of the Drunken Eight Immortals, each with his own attribute, at leisure and inebriated. A small kitchen is adjacent to the dining room. Just beyond the altar room is an elongated wing with a perpendicular courtyard at the center with multiple bedrooms facing it on the ground and second floor. Two stairways lead from this area to the second floor.

The rooms on the second floor of the core building duplicate those on the ground floor in extent, but each has polished wooden floors rather than the marble or tile found on the ground level. It is likely that at least one of the rooms in the front of the house was a master bedroom.

Today, however, instead of beds, the rooms on the second floor are furnished with chairs and tables in various formal groupings.

Above Jutting out from the side of the reception hall is a bright alcove with Chinese furniture.

Below With its marble floor, plasterwork, and wooden ceilings, the reception hall expresses Western aesthetic notions that are matched by Chinese treatments, including a richly ornamented screen wall, vertical paintings, palace-style lanterns, and Chinese furniture.

Top Just beyond the formal dining area, with its multiple tables, is this informal eating area. Rectangular skywells on both sides provide abundant light and air in this heavily used area. In the distance is the Tan ancestral altar.

Above left A well is located in a small skywell adjacent to the kitchen.

Above right A view from one rectangular skywell through the informal dining area to the opposite skywell.

Above On the left is an opening in the screen wall that leads to the reception hall. In this room, the Western-style furniture is set up to accommodate multiple groups. The wooden stairs in the background, with Chinese-style interlocked lozenge ornamentation underneath, lead to the second level.

Left These two light fixtures, which hang from similar medallions, are a contrast in styles.

Right A close-up view of the sliding *tanglong* at the front entry.

Left This ornamented panel on a cabinet depicts San Yang Kai Tai, whose meaning is wordplay in which *yang* refers to the three *yang* or goats that bring prosperity.

Right On the second floor, one room opens to another because of the placement of many doors and interior windows.

Below left In the rear of the residence is an elongated skywell with flanking bedrooms on both the first and second floors.

Below right The kitchen, which is furnished with Chinese cabinets and pottery items, is located in a back corner of the residence.

Above A second floor bedroom staged with a couch bed, tables and chairs, a variety of framed textile pieces, and an antlered stag.

Right The magnitude of the mansion is evident when all of the building comes into view along the south elevation.

KHOUW FAMILY MANOR

JAKARTA, INDONESIA

1807 or 1867

Built by prominent members of Indonesia's Peranakan Chinese community during the nineteenth century, the Khouw family manor once was one of the most elegant residences in colonial Batavia. Today, what is left has been sadly truncated—some say "amputated"—from its original magnificent extent and is dwarfed—some say "suffocated"—by high-rise buildings. Like many other families in Southeast Asia whose ancestors migrated from China in the distant past, there are few facts about the early Khouw forebears. Even with more recent successful descendants, who in the middle of the twentieth century bequeathed this stunning residence to posterity, recollections of facts relating to earlier generations remain obscure. Neither the particulars of when the first member of the family reached Indonesia are known nor is it certain where in Tong'an county in Fujian they hailed from. In a city that in the past had a large number of fine Chinese-style buildings, what remains today of the Khouw family manor provides not only a window on the changing fortunes of ethnic Chinese over the past century and a half but also reveals the vagaries of historic preservation in contemporary Indonesia.

There is even uncertainty as to whether the Khouw manor was constructed in 1807 or 1867, two dates fully sixty years apart. This is because a painted panel above a door along the outside veranda of the middle structure indicates simply the traditional calendrical designation *dingmao*, "fire rabbit," which only appears in the sexagenary cycle combining the ten "Heavenly Stems" and the twelve "Earthly Branches" once every sixty years. Unfortunately, there is no specific reference to the reign periods of either the Jiaqing Emperor (r. 1796–1820) or the Tongzhi Emperor (r. 1861–75) that would help fix the exact year, either 1807 or 1867. In any case, whether the complex was constructed by the rich patriarch Khouw Tian Sek in 1807 or later, in 1867, by his son Khouw Tjeng Tjoan, the residence itself was one of three mansions built in close proximity along the fashionable Molenvliet West (now Jalan Gajah Mada), which were occupied by Khouw Tjeng Tjoan and his two brothers, Khouw Tjeng Po and Khouw Tjeng Kee. Unfortunately, there is a near absence of information about the patriarch or his sons except the fact that they were wealthy. Furthermore, extant old photographs of sumptuous Chinese-style dwellings, which were mixed among older Dutch mansions and hotels along Molenvliet West, are sometimes erroneously identified as the home of Khouw Tjeng Tjoan, but may have been a home of one or another of his brothers. While it is said that Khouw Tjeng Tjoan moved into the sprawling residence of 100 rooms with as many as fourteen wives and twenty-four children, nothing is known of the exact date when he actually occupied the home or indeed the life of his sprawling family.

The residence of Khouw Tjeng Tjoan, who died perhaps in 1880, in fact stands less as a testament to himself than to his successful son, Khouw Kim An, who was born in 1879, most probably in the house. Khouw Kim An received a Dutch education before rising to prominence in banking and business circles in Batavia. Aware that the colonial authorities were indifferent to the education of both Peranakan Chinese and new immigrant Chinese, called *totok*, he worked with his distinguished father-in-law, Phoa Keng Kek, and several other prominent members of the Peranakan Chinese community to establish the Tiong Hoa Hwee Koan (THHK) or Chinese Association. This organization not only promoted Confucianism and Chinese culture, in general, including Chinese language study, but also worked to force the colonial authorities to permit Peranakan children to attend Dutch-medium schools. Khouw Kim An's own importance in the Chinese community was underscored by his appointment by the Dutch to the rank of Luitenant der Chinezen in 1905, Kapitein der Chinezen in 1908, and then promotion to Majoor der Chinezen from 1910 to 1918. After an unexplained hiatus, he was reappointed Majoor der Chinezen and served from 1927 until 1942. As with other eclectic homes built at the time, extant photographs provide glimpses of what must have been a life of luxury and ease that involved modern, generally Western, elements as well as Chinese accents. The significance of Khouw Kim An's residence led to it being designated a heritage site in 1931 under the Monumenten Ordonantie, the first effort by the Dutch to recognize historic structures in their colony.

Majoor Khouw Kim An died in 1945 while interned by the Japanese during their wartime occupation of Indonesia, and the family dwelling was subsequently abandoned by his sons in the waning years of Dutch rule after the defeat of the Japanese invaders. In 1946 the old residence was either sold or donated so that it could be transformed into the headquarters of the Sin Ming Hui (New Light Foundation), a Peranakan-dominated association whose purpose was to provide education, health, and general social services to the Chinese community, as they were to eventually become citizens of the new Republic of Indonesia. In the first half of the1960s, during the reign of Soekarno, as discriminatory laws against Chinese Indonesians proliferated, Sin Ming Hui changed its name to Perhimpunan Sosial Tjandra Naja, now simply Candra Naya,

Left The side elevation of the two remaining halls. On the right is the front hall and on the left the broader middle hall. Above the residence can be seen the formed reinforced concrete structure that is part of the commercial/residential complex being built over and around the Khouw family manor.

Opposite below From just inside the front door, one sees first a simple screen wall that blocks the more private area beyond, which includes a skywell. It is likely that this outer area, with two adjacent rooms, served some commercial purpose.

Above A detail of the gable ornamentation on the second hall, which has a swallowtail ridgeline.

Above A view of the front veranda, with a wooden framework lifting the extended eaves, which has been extended with corrugated materials.

the term used to designate the remnants of the Khouw manor complex standing in 2009. While the nearby residences of his two brothers were bulldozed, with no visible trace of them remaining, there are plans to reconstruct those portions of the Khouw manor that had been demolished in order to restore at least the shell of its once grand extent.

The Khouw Kim An Manor

In plan, elevation, and section profile, the Khouw Kim An manor is quintessentially Chinese. In terms of its width, depth, and height, the manor was an imposing structure that occupied a 2250-square meter footprint on a 1.5 hectare plot. The truncated version photographed in 2008 occupied only a fraction of this. The quadrangular shape of its ground plan comprises structures and courtyards—closed and open spaces—in archetypical patterns similar to those found in China. While buildings and associated courtyards are axiomatic elements of Chinese architecture, those found in the Khouw manor are deployed in a manner that both mimics models common in Fujian and Guangdong and reveals elements that are in tune with the requirements of an equatorial location on the Indonesian island of Java.

As with many larger dwellings in China, the fully developed quadrangular manor was essentially symmetrical, defined by three parallel buildings aligned horizontally, which were framed by a complementary pair of elongated wing structures arranged perpendicularly along the side of the three parallel structures. Along the south side of one wing, the symmetry was broken with the addition of a walled area entered through a gate for the use of servants and tradesmen. While each of the buildings was separated from the others by courtyards of various sizes, each was also interlinked so that one could pass from side to side and front to back within the large complex completely under the cover of a roof. The near symmetry of the front elevation is made dramatic by the fact that the three horizontal structures, placed one behind the other, increase in height from front to back, from 8.2 meters in the front to 13 meters in the rear. While the first two structures were single storey—these are the only two original buildings still standing—the double-storey rear structure not only had an overall height of 13 meters but also spread 46.95 meters, which is the full extent of the building's overall width. The rear building and elongated wing structures were demolished sometime after 1995. At one time, passageways led from the main structures into the perpendicular side wings with passage through narrow courtyards of various shapes and sizes.

The organization of space along an internal longitudinal axis through ever-heightening structures from front to back speaks of a conscious design with an implicit hierarchy. The front hall served as a space to welcome guests or conduct business while the extensive rear area provided private apartments on two levels for many collateral family members. It is not clear from the evidence we have where the ancestral altar was placed, although it seems likely that it was located in the expansive middle hall. The day-to-day attention required by the multitude of deities suggests that another altar was probably in the central bay of the rear hall, probably on the upper floor but conceivably also on the lower floor or indeed in the front hall.

Subdued red clay tiles, called Javanese *daun* or "leaf" tiles, cover the roofs, which are double pitched at an approximate angle of 45 degrees. The lower front hall has less depth than either the rear hall or the generously broad middle hall. Found on each building are the upturned ends of the ridgeline, each with a prominent pointed tip that are called swallowtail or *yanwei* style ridges throughout southern China. Wooden columns and beams connected by carved supports and simple *dougong* brackets were used to create a veranda along the front of the main structure and to span the spaces surrounding the first courtyard. Each of the columns supports a purlin along which the roof rafters are laid.

There are three striking aspects of the Khouw manor that differ from patterns normally seen in southeastern China and a smaller number of minor elements: the overall structure was oriented so that it faced due east; windows were numerous and large, especially along the back wall of the two-storey structure; and corrugated metal roofs were attached to tile roofs. Throughout most areas of China, where dwellings often face south or southeast, windows are rarely found on the back wall of such dwellings. For the most part, this is because cold winter winds in those areas blow from north or northwest, with the result that a solid back wall acts to protect the home from the intrusion of cold air. Since the Khouw manor faces east and thus the back faces west *and* there are no dramatic seasonal differences in prevailing winds or temperature, there was little need to consider blocking cold airflow. On the other hand, in this location near the equator and not too distant from the coast, maximizing the flow of air into and through a dwelling was of critical importance in order to help alleviate high temperatures and high humidities. Because the open and closed spaces promoted varying patterns of temperature differences, this then led to differences in pressure and resulted in movements of air that were brought into the residence by the abundant and large nature of exterior fenestration as well as sculpted ventilation

ports through some of the interior walls. Orienting a dwelling complex east to west in the equatorial region, instead of having the façade facing a southerly direction as is so common in China, meant that the intense midday rays of the sun struck the dwelling from the side rather than from the front or back.

Builders of Chinese-style houses in the equatorial regions, where rainfall was not only copious but also intense, learned early that the slope of traditional roofs as well as the breadth of the area under the eaves was insufficient to move falling rainwater away from the columns. Until the middle of the nineteenth century, extensions along the eaves were made possible using *attap* thatch as a lightweight roof covering that only required slim rafters to hold it. In time, new materials such as corrugated galvanized iron panels, which had been invented in Europe in the 1820s, began to be employed throughout the colonies because of their versatility, especially in terms of bending strength and relatively low cost. Subsequently, by the end of the nineteenth century, corrugated steel sheets began to be used, and then later fiberglass became common. The roofline extensions on the front of the Khouw family manor extend 2.75 meters beyond the front columns, a generous distance, to throw rainwater away from the building. Photos from 1995 also show the use of corrugated sheets as shades above doors and windows on the outside of the house. All in all, innovations in orientation, fenestration, and extension provided improved levels of human comfort for those living in the residence. Some authorities see window shutters, window bars, marble floors, glass skylights, and ironwork ornamentation in Candra Naya as "obvious Indisch-style elements," but it should be pointed out that all of these were also found in residences in southeastern China at the time. Still, it is useful to view the Khouw manor as a "melting pot" structure incorporating a variety of eclectic elements.

Today, one cannot see any of the original furnishings within the home and the overall ornamentation is quite sparse except for that which is integral to the remaining parts of the house—doors, ridgelines, and wooden framework. On both ends of the sloping eaves at the front of the house are found large red roosters, the pronunciation of which, *da ji*, is homophonous with the two characters *daji*, meaning "good

luck," emblazoned on their puffed breasts. On each of the two leaves of the entry doors is a pair of common Chinese characters, *fuhai*, "Good Fortune Sea," and *shoushan*, "Longevity Mountain," which are shorthand for the antithetical eight-character couplet *fu ru donghai, shou bi nanshan*, "May One's Fortune Be as Vast as the Eastern Sea, One's Longevity as Long as the Southern Mountain." With a ring pull at the center, each of the pair of brass doorknockers is carved to represent the *baqua*, the powerful Eight Trigrams amulet with its combinations of broken and unbroken lines.

The first hall, a building with less depth than the second hall, is empty today, with only its wooden framework to suggest that it once was an important space to receive visitors. The sawn wooden panel, with doorways to the left and right, effectively blocks viewers from looking into the house from the outside. This screen wall also separates this public space from the courtyard and altar room beyond. There may have been an altar with deities here. Above the doorways are pairs of two characters, *jiyang* and *antai*, meaning "Auspicious *Yang*" and "Peaceful and Safe," with the first two written from right to left and the other two from left to right, an odd convention that is used throughout the house in the characters above doorways. It is likely that the central wooden panel served simply as a screen to block anyone looking into the more private areas of the house. It is doubtful that an altar of any type was located in front of it; indeed, neither furniture nor ornamentation was placed in front of this bare wall. The adjacent rooms may have been used for business purposes. Through the doorways one can glimpse the double-hung sash windows of the rooms adjacent to the second hall, which may have served many purposes, from storage of ritual paraphernalia to use as bedrooms. The rooms themselves had large windows along their sides. In the open spaces above the wooden panel and doors are carved decorative blocks of wood, spaced so that air will pass through the room. The dropped ceiling is Western in style, with a rosette from which a lighting fixture once was attached. After moving through the passageways and looking back, one sees another four-character phrase, *jun ye hong tu*, with the meaning "A Lofty Enterprise [and a] Grand Plan."

After crossing a courtyard with covered side areas spanned by exquisitely carved timber framing that lifts the adjacent peaked roofs in traditional style is the second, broader hall, a semi-private space, with a wooden wall punctured by a pair of doorways, one on each side about two-thirds across this important space. The middle panel between the doors was once the location of a large altar, probably venerating the Khouw ancestors. What has happened to this altar and the associated tablets is a mystery. The characters written above the doors here read *gui zi lan sun*, again from right to left with the other pair oddly left to right. These four characters represent an idiom meaning "[May You Have] Famous and Talented Posterity [Sons and Grandsons]." No doubt this middle hall once contained sumptuous furniture arranged in a formal fashion and its walls were brightened with portraits of ancestors, paintings, and calligraphic scrolls filled with auspicious meanings. It was in this room in front of the altar that ritual was carried out according to a regular calendar, in addition to periodic commemorative functions relating to birthdays, weddings, and funerals.

Once one passes through either doorway and glances back to look at the characters above the doorways, one sees four very simple characters with complex meanings, *san duo jiu ru*, with the first two written from right to left and the other two written from left to right. These four characters together recall the "Three Abundances," *duo fu duo shou*

duo zi —good fortune, longevity, and male offspring—and the "Nine Similitudes (*Likes*)" from the "Blessing" section of the *Book of Songs* expressing the following felicitous notions (Waley, 1960: 175–6):

> May heaven guard and keep you,
> Cause there to be nothing in which you do not rise higher,
> *Like* the mountains, *like* the uplands,
> *Like* the ridges, [*like*] the great ranges,
> *Like* a stream coming down in floods;
> In nothing not increased.
> …
> To be *like* the moon advancing to its full,
> *Like* the Sun climbing the sky,
> *Like* the everlastingness of the southern hills,
> Without failing or falling,
> *Like* the pine tree, the cypress in their verdure—
> All these blessings may you receive!

A central door then led into an open courtyard or garden that was positioned before the two-storey private family quarter.

With its striking roofline accentuated by a series of six symmetrically placed upturned ridge ends, the tall two-storey structure in the rear was the everyday domain for the Khouw family, an intimate area comprising rows of bedrooms, sitting rooms, and an altar room. Facing eastward over the broad courtyard below, a long narrow veranda ran the full length of the building on the second level. In the central portion, along the second level in the back of this third structure, a shorter recessed area overlooked a garden. As in traditional Chinese families, it is likely that women and children spent most of their time in this quiet rear sanctuary of open and closed spaces. Each of the rooms in the building had large windows that allowed air to pass into and through the rooms. Even as recently as 1995, when the manor was last thoroughly photographed by Naniek Widayati and before several of the main structures were razed, the property had already become neglected in appearance and limited in use.

Opposite above A view looking across the skywell, which now is covered over, to another screen wall, before which once was probably an altar, that begins access to the middle hall. On both sides are rooms, possibly bedrooms, with large double-hung windows opening to the skywell area.

Above A close-up view of the carved wooden supports for the "corridor" surrounding the skywell in front of the middle hall.

Right A view of the elaborate wooden framework adjacent to the skywell, which now has a temporary screen covering it.

Destruction or Preservation

In 1988 and again in 1993, government authorities heralded the relict building as a significant heritage site, declaring that it should be preserved even as its use as a home and institution had passed. The heirs of the Khouw family sold the manor and surrounding open land to the Modern Group, a property developer, in 1992. Construction began in 1995 in the immediate environs of the old manor on a thirty-storey hotel, apartment, and retail complex, even in the face of some public criticism about erasing one of the last vestiges of Jakarta's history. Sadly, to facilitate this extensive development, the side wings and associated buildings in the rear were summarily demolished, leaving only the principal pair of structures that framed a courtyard clutched within the towers of the new buildings rising on the site. Although the property developer signaled a willingness to reconstruct some parts of the manor that had been demolished, the overall development was halted in 1997 due to Indonesia's economic crisis. This left the status of the Khouw manor unresolved while even minimal conservation work was aborted.

Tragically, a year later, in May 1998, widespread rioting, arson, looting, murder, and rape, much of which was directed at Chinese Indonesians, erupted in Jakarta's Glodok Chinatown, not far from the Khouw manor, in addition to about fifty other locations throughout Jakarta. The subsequent trauma, outrage, and shame relating to these events forced introspection about the nature of ethnicity in Indonesia as well as reflection about ways to express cultural diversity. In the Glodok area, large new commercial buildings, especially the hulking Glodok Plaza and Pasar Glodok, were constructed to erase the destruction caused during the rioting and to jump-start the commercial revitalization of the community.

The unfinished commercial development which enshrouded the relict Khouw manor, now almost universally referred to as Candra Naya, began to garner attention again in 2001. This was, in part, because the economy was improving but also because Candra Naya had become a symbol of the ethnic Chinese, whose material presence was likely to be substantially obliterated with the demise of Jakarta's last surviving, even if incomplete, Chinese mansion. In mid-2001 the *Jakarta Post* reported that the building "remains in limbo" even as suggestions came from many quarters about what to do with it ("Conservation," 2001). Most recognized that the developer had already illegally destroyed major portions of what was an historic, protected building, one which by then had assumed greater significance because of the May 1998 riots. Meetings of government leaders, business people, and developers sought ways to move beyond the frustrating impasse. The developer postured that the remnants of the old structure in the midst of the new building made it impossible for them to maximize profit from their enterprise. Others spoke of the need to restore the magnificence of the manor even in the face of being seemingly overwhelmed by new construction around it. Moreover, it was divulged that *fengshui* experts, together with spirit mediums, were employed in a quest for impartial guidance.

In June 2001 the *Jakarta Post* reported that a suggestion had been made that the mansion be moved in order to preserve it since the owner could not properly maintain it nor was the government willing to contribute to the building's proper conservation. This proposal generated controversy, with one observer stating, "We shouldn't see the building as a mere object because it also has a soul" ("Conservation," 2001). Soon, some people began to focus on dismantling the mansion and rebuilding it as part of a Chinese Cultural Park, which would be attached to Taman Mini Indonesia Indah (Beautiful Indonesia in Miniature Park) in the suburbs of eastern Jakarta, six kilometers away from its original location. Conceived three decades earlier by President Soeharto's wife, the Taman Mini Indonesia Indah project had grown substantially over the years as a "museum of museums," all splayed around a grand lake filled with islands that replicate the Indonesian archipelago. Some saw the creation of a Chinese-Indonesian Cultural Park as part of that complex as an opportunity to express and highlight the role of ethnic Chinese in the evolution of Indonesia as a multicultural country. Much controversy swirled around the proposal to dismantle and relocate the Khouw family mansion, especially in reaction to the formal petition by the property developer who was eager to clear the site in order to complete the modern complex surrounding it.

Far left The eaves framework in front of the middle hall. The doorway once led to the side or wing structures, which have been demolished.

Left A view of the area adjacent to the skywell showing the carved hardwood framework.

Left This linking passageway at the back of the middle structure once led to the side or wing structures.

Above left A scroll painting on the outside wall above one of the entrances to the middle hall from the now-demolished side building.

Above right A vignette placed at the end of an eaves line in the front hall.

By 2003 many had come to see that not only was Candra Naya "rare, unique, and special" but that a line needed to be drawn between development and conservation, putting pressure on the government to make a commitment towards the preservation of the residence (Yuliandini, 2003). In the face of lobbying from preservationists, community activists, and government agencies, some of whom highlighted the historic significance of the building beyond its ownership by the Khouw family, the Governor of Jakarta in July 2003 rejected the proposal to relocate Candra Naya to the Taman Mini Indonesia Indah cultural park, taking a strong position about maintaining the building in situ as a rare component of Jakarta's vanishing cultural heritage (Nurbianto, 2003).

While Candra Naya will not be demolished and moved, a decision was made to create a replica as part of the newly designed 4.5 hectare Chinese-Indonesian Cultural Park at Taman Mini Indonesia Indah. Yet, even here there is controversy since the design incorporates a monumental entryway, a colossal hall said to represent the Forbidden City, a seven-tier pagoda, and rows of shophouses, in addition to a reproduction of the Khouw family manor, a collection which some say represents more about imperial China than the southeastern provinces that were the homelands of Indonesia's early Chinese. Others say that all these iconic buildings will eventually house exhibits about Chinese-Indonesians. According to a May 2008 news report, the project "is currently creeping along because of lack of funding. So far, only a gate has been built" (Winarti, 2008). While I have not seen the detailed plans of the Chinese-Indonesian Cultural Park, a concept drawing reproduced in a 2003 publication shows only a truncated Candra Naya. Neither the official Taman Mini website nor high-resolution Google maps offer any glimpses of the new Chinese portions that have been described in news reports as finished or under construction.

In the middle of 2009, the historic Khouw family manor or Candra Naya existed in a "cave," given shape by the surrounding soaring futuristic structure made of unfinished concrete and glass panels. Surmounted by a temporary pitched cover to protect it from the elements, the two halls await the rebuilding of all of those portions that were demolished. PT Wismatama Propertindo, a Hong Kong–based property company, which acquired the site and unfinished buildings in May 2007, plans to complete the two 24-floor apartment towers, a

21-storey hotel, a 16-floor shopping mall, and an 8-floor podium. This revitalized development will be called StarCity, whose promotional tagline is "Experience Living Next Door to the Celebrity You Adore." The developers promise that the historic home will be brought to life as an integral part of the property when the entire project is completed. The model of the finished mixed-use development, which rests in the sales room, shows a fully restored Candra Naya surrounded by mature trees, all of which is covered by a spanning arch of translucent panels. While the saved nineteenth-century building with its re-created sections will likely become a café within the StarCity mega complex, only time will tell the degree to which visitors will recall not only the building's important history as the home of a prominent Peranakan family but also the ethnic controversy that led to its escaping the wrecker's ball. The publication of a book, *Rumah Mayor China Di Jakarta/Mansion of The Chinese Major In Jakarta*, in mid-2008 by Naniek W. Priyomarsono, who has studied the building in detail for two decades, provides a tangible but incomplete record of and an argument for the preservation of a site important to all Indonesians who value their multicultural heritage. According to Abidin Kusno, "the importance of Candra Naya lies not only in … [its] architectural attributes as signs of a disappearing history; the home also has a symbolic value for both the present and the future of the ethnic Chinese in Indonesia" (2003: 164). In 2009 news reports again called attention to the challenges of maintaining a historical property that "can hardly breathe. But, it is not willing to die yet" (Winarti, 2009).

Right StarCity has been built over and around the Khouw family manor, which is "buried" deep within its soaring structure.

EXPERIENCE
LIVING NEXT DOOR
TO THE CELEBRITY
YOU ADORE

starcity

OEY DJIE SAN PLANTATION HOME

TANGERANG, INDONESIA

Late 19th Century

A century ago, Tangerang, located some 20 kilometers to the west of Jakarta and now the second largest urban area on the outskirts of the capital, was heavily populated by Chinese immigrants who served as farmers in the plantations as well as shopkeepers and laborers of many types. It is said the area had attracted Chinese traders as early as the fifteenth century, who married local women and became a distinct community known as Cina Benteng, abbreviated as Cibeng. The community is well known for maintaining old Chinese customs, some of which can be observed in the vicinity of the Boen Tek Bio Temple, even as few of the mixed race or pure Chinese still speak the Chinese language. While today the area has been absorbed into greater Jakarta and is a hub of manufacturing, there were until recently a few areas with buildings and grounds that evoked plantation agriculture during the nineteenth century.

In early June 2008, not far from the Cisadne River, was the spacious house of Oey Djie San, who early in the twentieth century had been appointed by the Dutch to serve as either Luitenant or Kapitein der Chinezen for the large Chinese community in the area. Very little is known of him except that he was a founder of the Tangerang branch of the Tiong Hoa Hwee Koan, an organization that fostered pride in Chinese culture and rallied as an anti-Manchu force against dynastic rule in the waning years of the Qing dynasty. Although it is not clear when he or his ancestors arrived from China, or when this residence was built, the Oey family constructed an expansive country house with a mixture of Dutch, Chinese, and Javanese features. The complex is a fine example of hybridization in which the building forms brought by immigrants were modified by integrating indigenous building forms that were more suited to local climatic and social conditions.

Although the overall elements of his extensive domestic structure were still intact when we visited it in the middle of 2008, most of its magnificence had been diminished over time because of neglect. By late 2008 the property on which the home was sited was sold and the dismantling of the residence began. Taken apart brick by brick and timber by timber, the house was quickly reduced to its component parts. Laborers cleaned the bricks and floor tiles while they stacked the disassembled teakwood timbers, many carved with Chinese motifs. There was a plan, it was said, to sell all of these old building parts, recycling them in new buildings as ornamental pieces.

The pending destruction stirred outrage among those concerned with historical preservation. Mounting a public campaign and putting pressure on political leaders concerning the scope of the likely loss raised awareness in ways that paralleled earlier efforts concerning Candra Naya in Jakarta (see pages 178–9). In mid-December 2008, it was reported that demolition had halted and that a buyer had surfaced who promised to reconstruct the residence on another site. The text that follows is written in the present tense in anticipation of the continuing existence of this historically significant residence.

What is particularly distinctive about the Oey Djie San plantation home is that it is a quintessentially *sanheyuan*-style Chinese dwelling, with additions to its overall composition inspired by Javanese and Dutch colonial architecture. When viewed from a distance at ground level, the dwelling is unmistakably in the style of some rural dwellings in southern China, although the width of the open courtyard is more expansive. The upturned swallowtail ridgeline of the series of horizontal structures and the multisided shape of the gable end profiles also mimic those found in China.

On closer inspection, the first rectangular structure, which is lifted by an impressive Chinese-style wooden framework, and which has a

Opposite above One of a pair of lions, here the female protecting her cub.

Opposite below When viewed from a distance, the dwelling is unmistakably in the style of rural dwellings in southern China, although the width of the open courtyard is more expansive.

Above On closer inspection, the first rectangular structure, which is lifted by an impressive Chinese-style

wooden framework, and which has a swallowtail ridgeline on its exterior and a rolled ceiling inside, is out of character with Chinese domestic architecture. It is a Javanese *pendopo*, a well-shaded and airy open pavilion, placed at the front of the residence as a place to receive guests.

Right The male lion playing with a ball and ring.

Below Lattice doors on one of the side buildings.

Top A view from the *pendopo* of the front door of the first structure.

Above A view of the Chinese-style eaves brackets of the *pendopo*.

Above The architectural link between the *pendopo* and the structure of the front hall.

swallowtail ridgeline on its exterior and a rolled ceiling inside, is out of character with Chinese domestic architecture principles in terms of its location. Indeed, while the structural framework, with its many carved components and swallowtail roofline, are clearly Chinese, the absence of walls reveals that the building functions as a *pendopo*, an elementary element of Javanese domestic and palace architecture. A *pendopo* is a well-shaded and airy open pavilion, often referred to as a "gazebo" by those speaking English in Java, placed at the front of a residence as a place to receive guests and for household members to carry out some of their domestic work.

In front of the *pendopo* is a pair of Chinese lions. The *pendopo* is attached to the brick walls of the first enclosed building, which has a large pair of double-hung windows and two sets of ventilation ports in the outer wall set about 2.5 meters above the floor. The black door is emblazoned with four Chinese characters, *gui ling he suan*, invoking the imagery of both the tortoise and the crane as a felicitous wish for a long life. The characters once were bright because of the gold leaf applied to them, but today they are nearly invisible. Atop the door is a pair of octagonal wooden *menzan*, which may be translated as decorative "door pins" or "door clasps," with additional longevity imagery, including a deer, which is said to be able to locate the fungus of immortality, stylized evergreen *lingzhi*, which is the fungus of immortality itself, along with a clump of bamboo.

Inside the front door of the triple-bay structure, one moves from enclosed spaces to open courtyards that are quite similar to those found in ordinary Chinese houses. Pitched ceilings with open-carved wooden frameworks and lattice doorways are found in each building. Courtyards of various sizes, each filled with tropical vegetation, are located adjacent to the structures. From the side courtyards it is possible to see the elaborate motifs found at the apex of each of the gable walls as well as the intricacy of the upturned pointed tips of the swallowtail ridgeline.

Left A detail of a lattice-topped door.

Below left A view from one of the side skywells of the ornamented gable wall with the swallowtail ridge.

Below A view from front entry hall to the first skywell. The lattice doors beyond open to an altar room.

Above A view of the curved components linked in a mortise-and-tenon system to lift the purlins and roof.

Above One of two octagonal wooden *menzan*, decorative "door pins" or "door clasps." Each is ornamented with longevity imagery, including a deer, which is said to be able to locate the fungus of immortality, stylized evergreen *lingzhi*, the fungus of immortality, and a clump of bamboo.

Right A view of an ornamental gable wall and uplifted swallowtail ridgeline from one of the side skywells.

Below The area in front of the lattice doors showing the eaves supports and passageway to the adjacent wing structures.

From any of these vantage points, an observer feels that he is indeed inside a traditional Chinese home.

Beyond the Chinese structures at the rear of the residence is an Indonesian-Dutch style structure, a hybrid form generally called Indische. Reminiscent of eighteenth- and nineteenth-century colonial country houses, this seven-bay-wide rectangular building is capped with a steeply pitched hipped roof with two triangular sides and two trapezoidal ones, the surfaces of which are covered with the same red tiles covering the other buildings. As with other Indische estate buildings, this one is ringed with a broad veranda some 4.5 meters wide with an overhang that extends out an additional 2.4 meters. Large louvered windows and doorways complement the shading overhangs to make the structure quite airy.

When the photography for this book was completed in June 2008, the rooms and courtyards were in a somewhat dilapidated state, with obvious lack of attention to maintenance over a long period of time. The structures were inhabited by a significant number of unrelated households. By the end of the year, the residence was being demolished in spite of the outcry raised by preservationists. Set on a valuable piece of property 2.5 hectares in size, the real estate value of the empty building lot far surpassed the monetary value of the old residence. Selling the land for development of yet another multistoried air-conditioned shopping center complex to many appears as the highest value and best use for the property. Whether the residence itself will be reconstructed and adaptively used for a purpose that will repay those who have rescued it at the time of writing is still unknown. The fate of the residence was still in limbo when this manuscript was completed in mid-2009. Even as most of the structure had been dismantled by the beginning of 2009, there were some mixed, but hopeful, signals that this gracious old home might be reconstructed at some other location.

Top An oblique view of the linked Indische-style residence at the rear of the Chinese-style residence.

Left Sturdy columns along the veranda of the Indische-style residence.

Above Wooden shutters along the deep veranda of the Indische-style residence.

Top The front elevation of the Tjioe family residence, now the St Maria de Fatima Catholic Church.

Above left This bird's eye view shows that the central courtyard between the two halls, as well as the side skywells, have been covered. The eaves overhangs also have been extended.

Below left Rooms in the rear hall, with Chinese-style lattice panels.

Above A view of the nave, where the congregation sits, which once was the open courtyard, and the sanctuary that includes the altar.

Right The filigreed screen wall that blocks the view of the front hall, which is now the sanctuary of the church.

TJIOE FAMILY RESIDENCE (ST MARIA DE FATIMA CATHOLIC CHURCH)

JAKARTA, INDONESIA

Early 19th Century

Roman Catholicism in Indonesia dates to the sixteenth century when its dogma and practices arrived with Portuguese traders. From the nineteenth century onwards, under Dutch colonial rule through Independence to the present, Catholicism has thrived throughout the archipelago. Catholic parish churches and cathedrals in Indonesia, like those of Protestant denominations, generally have an architectural style that is similar to religious buildings found anywhere else in the world. The architecture of Christian churches includes common external elements, such as spires and stained-glass windows, as well as an interior cruciform ground plan of nave, crossing, transepts, apse, and sacristy that are almost universal elements with powerful symbolic meanings for Christians all over the world.

Thus, it comes as a surprise to many that there is a Catholic Church in Jakarta that occupies an early nineteenth-century residence of a prosperous Chinese immigrant, a transformation of a secular to a religious form in the last quarter of the twentieth century. The search for a location in Chinatown for a site to establish the St Maria de Fatima Catholic Church, which commemorates the appearance of the Virgin Mary to three children in Fatima, Portugal, in 1917, began in the 1950s to meet the needs of Chinese Indonesian Catholics who were flooding into the capital city. After outgrowing several small chapels and surpassing 1,000 parishioners, the old residence, which had been owned by the Tjioe family for four generations, was acquired in 1970 for use by the church and for a parochial school.

With its red and gold colors, low-slung tiled roof, wooden framework, bracket sets, open and closed spaces, carved ornamentation, calligraphic inscriptions, and stone lions, the structure is undeniably Chinese in origin. As renovation occurred, many of these traditional elements were preserved and can still be seen around and about the church. When viewed from above, the main components of the original building are clear: a single-storey building in front, a two-storey building in the rear, both flanked by a pair of wing structures. A third building, located behind the two-storey structure, was purchased by the church in 2000 to serve as a residence for the priests. The sanctuary of the church occupies the first two parallel structures and the courtyard between them, which was roofed over to both open and connect the interior space needed for worship. Other infillings of former courtyards also took place. Extended corrugated panel overhangs along the eaves at the front of the complex not only provide a shaded corridor but also throw rainwater a greater distance from the walls than was the case with the original drip line of the tiled roof.

Except for the prominent placement of a cross at a central position along the ridgeline and a horizontal board above the central doorway, the exterior retains much of its original secular flavor in terms of roofline, bracket sets, and fenestration. A gilded screen framed in red sits before the entry at the front of the church. Two majestic lions, a male playing with a ball and a female protecting her cub, are placed along the front of the church, just as they would be found outside any fine Chinese residence or temple. Along the ridgeline from right to left are four characters, *fu shou kang ning*, meaning "Good Fortune, Longevity, Health, Peace." Six other characters, *Nan'an xian* and *Quanzhou fu*, on the ridgelines of the narrow buildings linking the main structure with the side buildings represent the origin of the Tjioe family in Fujian province. Along the ridge of the two-storey back building are the characters *fushou*, meaning "Good Fortune and Longevity," as well as four interlocked round coins with a square hole in the center, which together represent a wish for wealth. On a wall outside the church, a Maria de Fatima Hill was created that in some sense evokes the type of religious iconography found outside Buddhist and Daoist temples, an example of which can be seen in the See Hin Kiong temple in Padang.

The expanded spaces that comprise the two parallel buildings and the roofed-over courtyard have created a broad and well-lighted hall for worship. The red and gold colored columns, beams, and bracket sets all evoke Chinese norms and were part of the original structure of the Tjioe residence. Similarly, the altar table and two lecterns are carved and painted in familiar vibrant colors and patterns, more typical of Chinese temples than homes. The three-dimensional carvings that are part of the wooden framework supporting the original roof appear to be traditional Chinese narrative stories, but it is not possible to verify which ones. Indeed, some parishioners state that the stories are Christian narratives, but this, too, cannot be corroborated. Christian iconography in terms of images and words is, of course, abundant throughout the church. The room behind the altar serves as a sacristy, a place for keeping the priest's vestments and the sacred paraphernalia used during various masses. There is consensus that the modification and transformation of this historical secular residential Chinese building into a contemporary holy place for Roman Catholic services has been successful.

TAN TIONG IE HOME

SEMARANG, INDONESIA

1850s

The Peranakan Chinese population in Semarang is large and generally has lived in neighborhoods of people with a variety of ethnicities, all of whom, of course, should be considered Indonesians. A residence built in the middle of the nineteenth century and lived in for more than a century and a half by Peranakan Chinese reveals the accommodations that have occurred over time. Known as the Tan Tiong Ie residence, the two-storey structure was built in 1850, but the family's forebears in Indonesia go back to the late eighteenth century. The residence was bought sometime in the late nineteenth century from relatives by the great-grandparents of the family now living in it, who have long been in the coffee business with a product line that is still being processed today. Three generations of Tans have been born in this eclectic home since it was purchased.

Set among a garden with mature trees and bushes, the roomy structure is high and sits solidly on the ground. Entered from the gable end, which is not the norm for Chinese homes, but is common with Western-style dwellings, the original façade had a covered porch on the first level with a veranda above it that had broad eaves extending beyond the balustrade. A veranda is also found in the rear on the second level. Using the design of a Chinese architect in 1929, renovation brought about the extension of the first floor porch as a practical remedy to reduce the intrusion of sun and rain. The result is a comfortable and airy space to sit outside in a sheltered environment. Complementing the second storey metal balusters are overhanging wooden fascia and verge boards whose simple carved ornamentation is usually described as being in Javanese style. Leaded glass windowpanes on each of the panels of the three sets of doorways allow light into the large parlor. During the Japanese occupation, in 1942, wooden door panels were added in front of the glass-paned doors for added security.

The rectangular front parlor is furnished with a variety of styles that include Chinese antiques. Given pride of place is an elaborately carved wooden shrine, which was designed by a Dutchman before 1930. The altar houses the ancestral tablet of Tan Tjien Gwan, the great-grandfather who was born in 1842 and died in 1914. Above the altar is the four-character phrase *kesheng zuwu*, meaning "Able to Follow in the Footsteps of the Ancestors," a phrase from the *Youxue qionglin* (Exquisite Compendium for Children to Study). This pithy yet useful reader dates from the Qing dynasty and was widely used in Chinese schools abroad during the early twentieth century.

Top Two automobiles and a carriage parked in front of the Dutch-style Tan Tiong Ie home in 1929.

Above An angled view of the façade of the home. Built in 1850, a porch extension was added to the front in 1929.

Above The front elevation of the residence. Unlike a purely Chinese home, this one is entered through the gable end.

Left A disassembled ancestral tablet.

Right One of a pair of European-style lions on the porch.

Below left The front parlor of the Tan Tjong Ie home contains a mixture of Chinese and European-style furniture. The ancestral altar is to the right.

Below right Given pride of place in the parlor is a wooden shrine, which was designed by a Dutchman before 1930. The altar houses the ancestral tablet of Tan Tjien Gwan, the great-grandfather of the current residents, who was born in 1842 and died in 1914.

SIEK FAMILY HOME (PRASADA MANDALA DHARMA)

PARAKAN, INDONESIA

1905

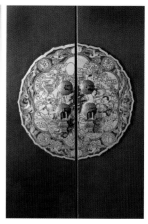

Above left A view through the front door with the screen wall in place.

Above right A close-up of a door medallion showing calligraphic and pictorial symbolic imagery.

Houses are rarely static. Even when a household supervises the building of a new residence in order to create what spaces they feel they require, alterations are frequently made after a family moves in. With an old house resided in over many generations, the dynamic nature of housing reveals itself in adjustments made for changing needs: an added wing as a family grows; renovated rooms for a newlywed couple; separate quarters for multiple wives in a polygamous marriage; doors nailed shut and separate kitchens established when daughters-in-law no longer get along; rooms let to strangers to help with added income; renovations made that reflect changing tastes, available resources, and cultural influences; among many other reasons. In some cases, a stately residence might even be effectively "abandoned" when family members move away without a responsible successor to take over the maintenance of the ancestral home. As can be seen in several chapters of this book, old Chinese homes have even been reborn as churches, schools, museums, boutique hotels, or, even in recent times, used as facilities to earn income by transforming human dwellings into homes for swiftlets whose nests are coveted as an ingredient necessary to impart a distinctive texture to birds' nest soup.

The coastal towns settled by Chinese immigrants in Indonesia are all relatively well known, especially when compared with the inland towns of the archipelago's main islands, where fertile soils and a salubrious climate enticed some Chinese to settle down and trade with Javanese for high quality rice, tobacco, and opium. Some of these inland towns are in the upland hinterland of the port city of Semarang on the Java Sea. Here, in sight of the Merapi and Merbabu volcanoes in the east and the Sumbing and Sindoro volcanoes in the west, are less-known cities such as Salatiga, Temanggung, Magelang, and Wonosobo, and small towns like Parakan. Little research has been done on when Chinese first came to many of these inland places.

Among the earliest traces of Chinese settlement in the western part of Parakan is a tombstone, dated 1821, of a lady with the married name Sie who had been born a Tan. Although extant Chinese houses seen today in Parakan were built much later, there is evidence that families who built houses in the town at the end of the nineteenth and beginning of the twentieth century had actually been residents for many decades. One such family is the once wealthy Siek family, whose progenitor, Siek Hwie Soe, is said to have arrived in Parakan in 1821. His descendants built a grand Chinese-style residence in 1905 attached to an Indische-style residence. The 1905 home fell into disrepair a half-century later when the family moved to Batavia, leaving the building to a relative as caretaker. In 2006 the century-old Chinese residence was acquired by a Buddhist monk named Aryamaitri, whose father had grown up in Parakan, and who is now an abbot in the Ekayana Buddhist Center in Jakarta. With guidance from Abbot Aryamaitri, the glory of the original Chinese residence was restored as the building was transformed into Prasada Mandala Dharma, a retreat for Buddhist meditation. The renovation was completed at the end of 2007 with a celebration during the Chinese New Year in February 2008.

It is said that Siek Hwie Soe was an energetic young man who came under the wing of a rich man already in the area named Loe Tjiat Djie. Young Siek had the good fortune of marrying the boss's daughter. On one of his return visits to China in the 1840s, Siek Hwie Soe convinced his nephew, Siek Hwie Kie, to join him in the booming business venture in Perakan. Siek Hwei Soe eventually succeeded his father-in-law, Loe Tjiat Djie, in the business of importing gambier. While gambier is not a

Opposite below An evening view of the façade of the Chinese-style section of the Siek ancestral home, which was built in 1905 and renovated a century later to become the Prasada Mandala Dharma. Two steps lead up to the veranda of the three-bay house, which has parallel wings.

Above A view along the front veranda showing the exposed wooden framework and a rolled iron roof.

commodity well known in the twentieth century, in the mid-nineteenth century gambier and pepper were two important plantation crops in Indonesia. Until the 1830s, most of the gambier produced in Southeast Asia was sent to China, but afterwards, as plantations expanded in Malaya and the Netherlands Indies, today's Indonesia, increasing amounts were exported to Britain where the resin from the gambier plant was used in the tanning and dyeing industries. The color known as "khaki," a Persian or Hindi word meaning "dust-colored," was first derived from an extract from leaves of the gambier shrub. The traditional processing of gambier involved the picking of young leaves, which is a natural source for tannin, then boiling the leaves in a shallow cast-iron pan, before pressing them to extract concentrated syrup, which was then dried in cake form for shipping. By the end of the eighteenth century in the Netherlands Indies, gambier, which is an astringent, also was being

added as a paste and wrapped around an areca nut as a betel quid to be chewed by those wanting a mild narcotic. By late in the nineteenth century, betel chewing was being replaced by tobacco smoking, employing another lucrative plantation crop promoted by Chinese businessmen (Reid, 1985: 538–9).

Chinese firms in Singapore and Johor, at the tip of the Malay Peninsula, dominated the gambier markets in the nineteenth century, with Chinese traders in both Sumatra and Java also playing roles. The Parakan Siek family's firm was called Hoo Tong Kiem Kie, which also established a cube sugar factory in Semarang at a time when the sugar industry was undergoing a boom in Java. Hoo Tong was a "brand" name for the Siek family, referring to a location in Shanxi province, today called Wanrong, which is reputed to have been the origin of this branch of the Siek lineage. After Siek Hwie Soe died in 1882, the company was divided into two parts, Hoo Tong Kiem Kie in Parakan and Hoo Tong Seng Kie in Semarang. The Parakan enterprise was controlled by Siek Tiauw Kie, who most probably was brought to Parakan in early 1840 at the age of nineteen to help his uncle, while the Semarang operation was handled by Siek Tjing Liong, Siek Hwie Soe's son. It appears that the family owned an extensive series of contiguous building lots on Gambiran Street.

Siek Tiauw Kie had several wives of Chinese descent in Parakan, with three sons between them born in the 1860s—Kiem Tan, Oen Soei, and Kiem Ing. Some say he also had a wife or two in China. His Parakan sons are said to have all studied in China and spoke Hokkien better than the Malay language common in Parakan. Siek Tiauw Kie, the father, died at sea in the 1890s while returning from China to Parakan. By then, his family had become quite prosperous, expanding their business to trading in rice and tobacco. It is likely that the Indisch-style house, which one can see to the rear of the 1905 Chinese-style house, was already constructed in order to meet the needs of an expanding family when the father died. When the new Chinese-style house, facing north, was built, it was connected to the Indisch-style house, which faced

south. Initially, the expanding estate was the joint property of the three brothers, but the 1905 house and the older connected house behind it eventually became the residence only of Siek Oen Soei and his four wives and many children, then later his grandchildren. Siek Oen Soei's two brothers built their own homes, one across the street and the other a distance away on Sebokarang Street. In like fashion, his older sons built homes of their own away from the home they grew up in. Other remaining family members, including secondary wives, moved from room to room to meet various needs and preferences. Siek Oen Soei moved with Soen Hae Yong, his favorite and youngest wife, as well as one of his granddaughters to the pleasant west wing with rooms facing the front courtyard. It may be that this was done following the Javanese tradition that a retired person should move to the west part of the house, nearing the sunset.

In time, the main house was left empty, quieted because of the dispersal of relatives as new families were established. After Siek Oen Soei's death in 1948, the residence was given to his youngest son, Siek Bian Bie, whose family then moved en masse to Batavia during the tumult accompanying the birth of the new republic. Elderly people in Parakan still sometimes refer to the house as the "SBB House" because of the link with the initials for Siek Bian Bie, as well as "Huis Gambiran," the "The House on Gambiran Street." For more than a half-century afterward, the residences were only looked after by a caretaker, except for occasional family gatherings, until the Chinese-style residence was acquired by Monk Aryamaitri, who restored it to its former state. The older Indische-style residence has remained in the Siek family and is lived in by Siek Bian Bie's son when he returns during the tobacco harvest season.

While these two different buildings functioned together as a single home for the Siek family for much of the first half of the twentieth century, there is insufficient information to discuss them as a unit. The sections below will look at each in terms of spatial form, architectural detail, and ornamentation.

Below The central door is on the left and the altar on the right. Ahead is one of two alcoves off the main hall on both sides. The portable screen placed in front of the door effectively blocks any view of the altar by passersby.

The Indische-style Residence

Indische-style dwellings, which were neither Javanese nor Dutch but included elements of both as well as subtle Chinese influences, were built throughout the towns, cities, and even rural areas of Indonesia in the nineteenth century. Houses of this type in Parakan and elsewhere in Indonesia were usually termed *landhuis*, which can be translated into English as "villa" or "country house." While there is no universal consensus on what were the basic elements of such houses, they all show clear adaptation to local climatic conditions in Indonesia, which is hot and humid year round, with heavy seasonal rains. Attention was especially paid to providing shade, encouraging air movement, and having cool floors made of marble or other stone. Most such structures had spacious verandas, high ceilings, prominent ventilation ports, and broad eaves overhangs. Architectural details reflected Dutch and Javanese traditions. Carved fascia boards, the horizontal band projecting below the edge of the eaves, were copied from the practice of European

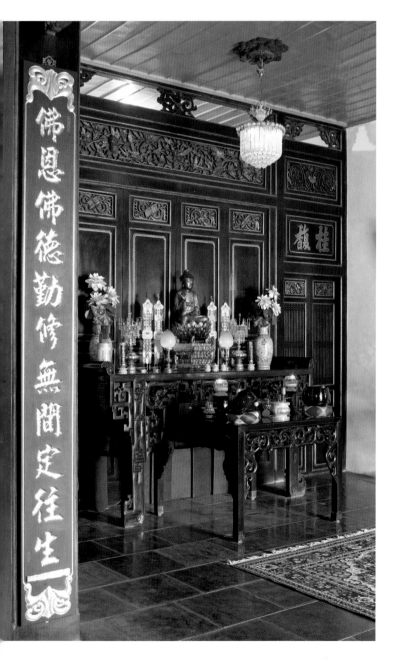

houses in big cities like Jakarta and Semarang, as were the colonnades of cast-iron columns and balustrades and fanlights above doorways and windows. Low and wide verandas, in addition to building materials, followed local Javanese traditions. But it was the life within the walls that was truly Indische.

Pauline Milone says that "Indische culture became largely the pace-of-life, graces, aristocratic attitudes and arrogated priviliges [*sic*] of Indonesian civilization mixed with some of the material uses, technology, élite fashions, and Christianity of European society" (1967: 411). Milone was writing, of course, about influential people in the major cities and their suburbs where Eurasians, especially, built spacious Indische mansions with gardens called *heerenhuizen* and *landhuizen*. On pages 180–5, the expansive Oey family home in Tangerang is discussed as a true Peranakan version of a hybrid residence with an amalgamation of not only an Indische-style structure and a Chinese-style one but also the incorporation of a full *pendopo*, an elementary feature of Javanese domestic architecture in the layout. It thus seems reasonable to assume that similar variant forms were built even in small towns where intermarriage took place between Chinese and Javanese, who, at the same time, were aware of the Dutch cultural elements in their milieu. In the areas of cuisine, dress, and residence, the hybridity of modes of living was clear and can be called Peranakan. The Indische-style house belonging to the Siek family was their attempt to pattern a lifestyle after that of a Dutch or Eurasian family in one of the larger cities. It is a curiosity that the house directly faces south towards the Sumbing volcano, a direction that would have been avoided by those knowledgeable about Chinese *fengshui*. It is likely that *fengshui* did not play much of a role before the twentieth century in Indonesia since early immigrants from China were possibly not conversant with the precepts generally known back in their home villages. On the other hand, the Chinese-style dwelling attached to it faces north towards the Java Sea and has the volcanoes to its back, a siting most Chinese would consider less troubling.

Built on a stone podium, which is accessed from the courtyard by climbing five steps to a front veranda, this building is a single-storey three-bay structure with a hipped roof. The symmetrical floor plan incorporates a middle hall running from front to back with two adjacent rooms on each side. The furnishings seen today are a mix of antiques, perhaps original pieces, and more contemporary furniture. Some old Chinese paintings still hang on the walls. The courtyard in front accommodates a well, several trees, and many potted plants. Along the outer walls on both sides are side rooms. There once was an altar in this residence, but it was moved to the Chinese-style house once that structure was completed.

The Chinese-style Residence

Completed in 1905, the residence of the Siek brothers eventually became the home of Siek Oen Soei. The decision to build a Chinese-style dwelling attached to the pre-existing Indisch-style home no doubt reflects the resurgence of Chinese identity at that time. Throughout the nineteenth century some immigrants saw themselves as mere sojourners, ready to return to their home village in China once they had saved sufficient resources. Others, like the Siek family, had established their extensive enterprises in Semarang and Parakan

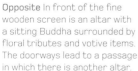

Opposite In front of the fine wooden screen is an altar with a sitting Buddha surrounded by floral tributes and votive items. The doorways lead to a passage in which there is another altar.

Above Behind the main altar is another altar with the Maitreya Buddha (the future Buddha) facing the open courtyard. A main altar facing the door and a Maitreya Buddha behind facing backward is a pattern common in Buddhist temples.

Left A corner nook adjacent to the courtyard, which is on the left, with the Maitreya Buddha on the right (out of view).

Above A view of the passageway behind the main altar, which passes the altar to the Maitraya Buddha, who faces the courtyard.

even as they made periodic return visits to China. Nonetheless, their identity as Chinese remained strong.

At the time, one way of demonstrating success, declaring class distinctions, and expressing wealth conspicuously was by building an exemplary residence. Other ways included clothing styles, the carriages used, and a general lifestyle that included entertaining as well as participation in periodic celebrations such as at the New Year in addition to marriages and funerals. As can be seen throughout this book, successful businessmen constructed substantial dwellings throughout Southeast Asia, each reflecting in one degree or other their attachment to China and knowledge of Chinese culture, including building practices. While it is certain that Peranakan Chinese in major towns and cities like Singapore, Batavia, and Penang lived more lavish lifestyles in larger homes than those in smaller places such as Medan, Parakan, and Semarang, those who were wealthy in smaller or more remote towns lived comparatively better than their neighbors. Less fulsome written records exist for successful small town Chinese, which contributes to the clouds of uncertainty about their lives.

Extant old houses, of course, whisper of life in the past. The 1905 house of the Siek brothers, which subsequently came to be the principal residence of Siek Oen Soei and his son Siek Bian Be over the course of five decades, clearly demonstrates a desire to express their Chineseness.

Their Chinese-style residence, sited so that it faced north towards the sea, perhaps purposefully looked beyond towards distant China. The mountains, actually volcanoes, mentioned earlier, were as they should have been in the back. Facing Gambiran Street and near the homes of other family members, this house was separated from the street only by a low wall with a metal picket-like fence. In China at the time, because of turmoil and the general tendency to live a more private life, high walls would have been the norm. By comparison, Chinese-style dwellings throughout Southeast Asia were usually more open, reflecting not only generally more secure and peaceful circumstances but also the need to facilitate breezes that would cool the residence. Inside the demarcating fence was an elongated courtyard with two steps leading up to a veranda for the three-bay house with its parallel wings. Flanking the central bay of the veranda, the outer edges of the other two bays are marked by cast-iron balustrades, replaced in the recent restoration by wooden ones. Today, one also sees a pair of carved stone lions, like those found outside palaces and temples, which were added by the abbot after restoration work was completed.

The overall plan of the inverted U-shaped dwelling includes a core structure with a pair of wing buildings that extend to the front, a common pattern known as *sanheyuan* in China. Three integrated courtyards—one in the rear and two narrow ones tucked between the main building and the wings—open up the interior of the large complex to both air and light. The rolled roof of the front veranda is extended with a prominent eaves overhang. The square columns resting on stone bases, which rise to support the roof, are chamfered and highlighted with gold paint. Mortise-and-tenoned joinery connects short posts that lift the purlins. Elongated wooden supports, which are not common in domestic architecture in China, spread the load of the purlins and are supplemented by beautifully carved brackets in each of the four directions where columns and beams meet.

At both ends of the veranda are arched doorways leading into the narrow perpendicular courtyards. The doorways themselves, by comparison with those seen in China, are smaller in dimension and more lavish in the surrounding ornamentation, which is quite colorful, with linked floral motifs. A scroll-like narrative tale is set above each doorway. The central doorway is grand, with the horizontal board seen today above it with the four characters *Yuanfa Chanyuan*, the first two of which, *Yuanfa*, refers to the name of Abbot Aryamaitri's teacher, while *chanyuan* means "Hall for Meditation." It is likely that the Siek family had a horizontal board at this same location, but there is no record of what characters it carried. From the street, passersby can see a grand three-tiered chandelier hanging in the main hall. Just inside the doorway is a pair of portable wooden screens, the top part of which has a simple pattern of vertical lattice and the lower part carved panels. The screen, which is new, effectively masks the altar beyond from being visible to those passing along the street outside. Surrounding the door pulls is an

exceptionally handsome brass disk filled with auspicious ornamentation and the four-character wish, *shou bi nanshan*, "May You Live as Long as the Southern Mountains."

The main hall inside the door has an inverted T shape with a pair of side alcoves flanking the main central space holding the altar. Each of the facing alcoves on both ends of the room is furnished with a set of chairs and table as well as a mirror and objets d'art. Two framed paintings in each alcove collectively show the images of the Eighteen Luohan or Arhat, Buddhist monks who postponed achieving nirvana, *niepan* in Chinese, in order to continue living so as to help others. Depicted as elderly monks with shaved heads, each is identifiable because of associated symbols. Images of Arhat are more commonly seen in temples, monasteries, and other religious sites, usually in small niches along the walls, than in homes. Facing the front door of the residence and leading to the intimate space behind is an elaborate wooden screen wall of carved panels, calligraphy, and ventilation apertures, with a pair of passageways. This important feature was original to the residence of Siek Oen Soei.

Just in front of the imposing ornamented wooden wall is a high carved altar table with a gilded statue of a seated Shakyamuni Buddha, said to be new and made in China. Around the Buddha image and on a lower table is a variety of votive offerings and ritual paraphernalia. Together, the tables and wooden wall screen dominate the main hall. Offerings of tea and sugar are made on the first and fifteenth of each lunar month. At other times of the year, fresh fruit as well as cooked

Opposite below An Indische-style house is attached in the rear to the Chinese houses, each of which faces in an opposite direction.

Left The broad veranda of the Indische-style dwelling.

Below The family's well is in the courtyard in front of the veranda.

dishes are offered. Today, a recording of Buddhist chants that plays non-stop provides a serene atmosphere for prayer.

The doorways alongside the altar each have two characters above them, *guifu* and *fanglan*, which is reversed, a combination that is usually expressed as *lanfu guifang*, in addition to a variety of other orderings, but always with the same meaning, "Fragrant Cassia, Fragrant Orchids." These doorways flanking the main altar lead to a narrow passageway with another altar with access also to a pair of side rooms. On this altar, the Thousand-armed and Thousand-eyed Bodhisattva Guanyin, whose many arms represent her limitless capacity to help others, faces an elongated semi-open room with a cast-iron balustrade and steps that lead down to a back courtyard. Located in the interior of the dwelling, this semi-open room nonetheless is a critical space that provides access to most areas of the house. While two of the larger bedrooms are adjacent to this living space, other bedrooms, toilets, and the kitchen are found within the flanking wing structures.

Throughout Indonesia countless old houses stand as derelict relicts with only hints of the vitality of the families that once occupied them. In some cases, a family may have died out without familial heirs so that the residence is like an abandoned orphan with no one to care for it, indeed even to claim it. Over time, there will be deterioration of its structural integrity, leading perhaps to eventual collapse. Sometimes old homes are effectively abandoned by far-flung heirs who are unable to agree on a course of action for the property that will both benefit themselves as stewards of their family patrimony *and* breathe new life into an old building. Examples of these courses of action, indeed inaction, are evident throughout this book. In some cases, as with the rebirth of the Siek family house as the Prasada Mandala Dharma, a threshold has already been crossed leading to both preservation and adaptive reuse. Sensitive restoration work of a Chinese-style dwelling has preserved the layout and ornamentation of a building constructed at the beginning of the twentieth century, in the process modernizing it to meet the needs of the twenty-first century with the adaptive reuse of the old spaces, some of which are clearly in accord with old practices while others are new.

KWIK DJOEN ENG MANSION (INSTITUT RONCALLI)

SALATIGA, INDONESIA

1920s

Salatiga, which is located less than 50 kilometers south of Semarang, is spread out at the foot of Mount Telomoyo, a conical volcano on the west side of the road on the way to Solo (Surakarta). From Solo northward to Semarang and eastward to Surabaya are some of Java's most productive sugarcane fields. It was here during the first three decades of the twentieth century that great wealth was amassed and lost by Kwik Djoen Eng, who had arrived in the late 1870s in search of opportunity from Taiwan, which itself had been settled by individuals from Fujian and had once been controlled by the Dutch in the seventeenth century. After amassing a fortune and power, he "retired" to Shanghai at the same time his commercial empire and vast fortune were disintegrating in Java.

In 1894 Kwik Djoen Eng and four of his brothers joined together in Solo to create a trading entity called NV Kwik Hoo Tong Handelmaatschappij, abbreviated as Kwik Hoo Tong and KHT, that came to rival the empire built by "sugar king" Oey Tiong Ham. In the early years, KHT imported tea from Taiwan before turning to opium farms and opium trade, but increasingly its commercial empire expanded internationally in ways that were uncommon for Chinese entrepreneurs in the Netherlands Indies. Kwik Hoo Tong, whose principal commodity was sugar, was not merely a regional commercial firm that operated within the norms of traditional Chinese family business practices. Rather, it was a multifaceted enterprise that utilized modern financial mechanisms embedded in international banking and capital raised from the sale of stock, with a far-flung network of branches throughout East and Southeast Asia. Many factors contributed to the eventual unraveling of its commercial empire: deteriorating relationships among the brothers; consolidation of wealth and power in the hands of one family member, Kwik Djoen Eng, and his four sons; surging indebtedness to banks;

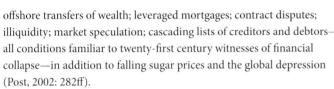

offshore transfers of wealth; leveraged mortgages; contract disputes; illiquidity; market speculation; cascading lists of creditors and debtors—all conditions familiar to twenty-first century witnesses of financial collapse—in addition to falling sugar prices and the global depression (Post, 2002: 282ff).

As Kwik Djoen Eng was reaching the pinnacle of his wealth and power in the late 1910s, he turned his attention to the creation of a veritable palace for his family on a 12-hectare site, with half around the residential complex inside a wall and half beyond. Kwik Djoen Eng abruptly left Salatiga in 1920, first for Hong Kong and then Shanghai, just as construction was about to begin on his glorious mansion. There are no contemporaneous accounts of the design of the complex or of the building activity that involved artisans from China who labored over a four-year period to complete the grand residence. Designed by a team of architects and fitted with imported polished stone and tile, the walls and windows as well as the courtyards and passageways were all ornamented and fitted with a plethora of Chinese and European motifs. How the home was furnished, if at all under the circumstances, is still not known.

Several photographs taken when the building was completed and before the gardens matured attest to both its grandiosity and the eclectic nature of its architectural style. Set on an elevated site above the road, with a middle gate, there was also entry through a Chinese-style gate that looped around a landscaped pond with a Chinese *jiashan*, a rockery of piled stones on an island in the middle, a common feature of traditional Chinese gardens. It may have been that the off-center Chinese gate was positioned to satisfy the requirements of *fengshui*. In overall scale and the disposition of its elements, Kwik Djoen Eng's residence was built as a veritable palace, an ostentatious statement of his achievements. The plan is symmetrical in layout with a core building, a set of parallel wing buildings, and a back building, all of which were interconnected by covered passageways. Hardly whimsical, the four pagoda-like structures and the central domed cupola were purposely designed to represent himself, the father, and his four sons. One can only speculate whether the apparent heightened elevation of the four pagodas was an implicit expectation that his sons would surpass him in wealth and power. Or is this just an illusion? Within the walled property, gardens, ponds, walkways, pavilions, and pergolas, even a small zoo, were installed for the hoped for enjoyment of succeeding generations of his family. Changing financial conditions and wartime exigencies, however, aborted his intentions of living in extravagant circumstances.

Opposite above When completed in the early 1920s, the Kwik Djoen Eng mansion was a veritable palace, with five pagoda-like spires. Although the vegetation had not yet reached maturity, the garden, which was entered through a Chinese-style gate on the right, was designed to be grand.

Opposite below With its rooftop pagodas and the central cupola removed, the expansive home was transformed into a retreat and educational center for the Roman Catholic Fathers of Immaculate Conception.

Top left Utilizing marble, glazed tile, etched windows, and stained glass, this grand entry hall opens into even more expansive interior rooms.

Top right The etched glass mirror panes along the side of the entry hall all bear Chinese motifs.

Above From today's dining area looking towards what once was probably built to be the location for the Kwik family ancestral shrine. In addition to an intricately carved cornice that spans the entryway, the room is elevated above what is now the dining area.

By 1932–3 a concatenation of deteriorating circumstances led to the bankruptcy of Kwik Hoo Tong. Kwik Djoen Eng himself, who was ensconced in Shanghai, was by then half-blind and no longer in control of either his fortune or his family. Members of his family left Java in late 1933 for China amidst allegations of illegal transfer of resources, effectively abandoning their grand home in Salatiga, as the family's assets were liquidated. Kwik Djoen Eng died in 1934 in China, without having ever had the opportunity to live peacefully in the grandeur and quietude of Salatiga. After his death, family members, who by then were scattered outside Java, returned from time to time in an attempt to reclaim family property, but ultimately failed.

During the Japanese occupation of Java during the Second World War (1942–5), it is said that the property was used to confine Dutch internees. After the war, both the police and the army used the building before it was sold. The property was subsequently acquired by Fathers of Immaculate Conception (FIC) di Indonesia Brothers, who removed the ostentatious exterior components of the residence when extensive renovation was carried out in 1969–70. The rooftop pagodas and the central cupola were razed, and in their place trapezoidal hipped roofs covered with Javanese red tiles were installed. Some of the covered passageways also were eliminated as the residence was converted to meet the needs of those coming for religious retreats and educational pursuits. The spacious surrounding gardens were tidied up, with spaces set aside for those seeking solitude. While the interior no longer appears like a home, with space now reorganized with furnishings to meet the needs of groups for meals, meetings, instruction, and leisure, the installed ornamentation along the walls, windows, and doors is as it was designed for the Kwik family.

For the most part, the motifs throughout the mansion are Chinese in origin but are framed in modern compositions of glass and wood. The entry hall is lined with etched and painted glass panels depicting the Baxian, the Eight Immortals, with adjacent calligraphic inscriptions

and Chinese landscape scenes. Beyond the entry hall is a large rectangular room with high ceilings that opens to a room surrounded by Chinese figure paintings on glass. Separating these two spaces is an arched decorative frieze, called a *feizhao* in Chinese, with auspicious imagery carved in wood. It would have been in an area like this that a family's ancestral altar was placed. Stained and painted glass panels throughout the residence direct changing patterns and hues of light into the rooms. Beyond the large public rooms in the core building, most of the other rooms have been broken up into small bedrooms and offices. The Institut Roncalli, maintained by Brothers FIC and named to memorialize Pope John XXIII, celebrated its fortieth anniversary in this once grand mansion in 2008.

Opposite above Looking towards the front of the mansion—the entry hall is just beyond the doors— is a partial view of an elongated dining room, which once may have been a parlor.

Opposite below A close-up of an alcove with marble, tile, and stained glass.

Top left A side skywell in the rear of the building.

Top right The Chinese pavilion in the garden to the rear of the mansion.

Above A fountain with masks of Bacchus in the garden adjacent to the home.

Left An interior corridor running from front to back, with porous brickwork on the right, that leads to a skywell.

LIEM COMPOUND

LASEM, INDONESIA
19th Century

Below left Situated in a walled compound, the nineteenth-century Liem house is essentially Chinese in style although it has a broad Indische-style veranda in front.

Below right The front veranda of the residence was extended by the addition of a shed roof.

Lasem, which is located some 110 kilometers to the east of Semarang, was one of the river-mouth settlements that developed in significant numbers along the Pasisir or northern coast of Central Java. Facing the sea, with teakwood forests to its south, Lasem served as a provisioning center for coastal maritime trade as well as an import and export-oriented roadstead for seaborne trade beyond the archipelago. For much of its history, Lasem was noted for its shipbuilding. Teak logs were floated down the stream to yards where boats were fashioned from the timbers. With shallow waters along the coast and shifting sandbars at the mouths of the streams, the fortunes of Lasem and other riverine settlements varied as environmental conditions shifted. Over time, the small town also gained fame for the craft shops set up by Chinese owners to produce wax-resist dyeing, known as batik, either using the stamp or *cap* method along with the method called *tulis* that utilizes a wax-filled pen. Although the art of batik textile production is generally considered of Southeast Asian origin, the technique has a long and continuing history within China as well.

The earlier Majapahit-era buildings, which predate the Chinese settlement, were located farther inland and included the sultan's *alun-alun*, a place for official discussions with commoners and periodic ceremonies. Along one side was the *kraton* or palace and, after the local population was converted to Islam in the sixteenth century, a mosque was built on another side that faced towards Mecca. Local lore tells of the arrival of a Muslim Chinese named Bi Nang Un, a crew member on one of Zheng He's ships, who stayed behind in the early fifteenth century to help spread Islam, a subject that remains controversial.

While there is some evidence that Chinese seafarers visited Lasem as early as the thirteenth century, it was not until the fifteenth century that Chinese first created a permanent settlement on the east bank of

the river. Today, the closest Chinese house is about 50 meters from the stream, but local residents claim that the stream was once closer to the houses, diverted by the Dutch to reduce opportunities for smuggling by the Chinese. The Chinese continued to increase in numbers so that by 1815 Lasem was a Chinese town with a greater proportion of Chinese residents than any other town along the north coast of Java. Periodic anti-Chinese riots erupted that impacted the population in the town over the next century. However, it was only from late 1959 that Lasem began to empty. First, the introduction of regulations to outlaw retailing in small shops in rural areas by "aliens" drastically impacted those of Chinese heritage. Many moved to cities elsewhere in Java, while others sought refuge in China, Hong Kong, Singapore, and Malaysia. As a result, the Chinese settlement in the northern part of Lasem was emptied out, becoming a forlorn shell of its past prominence.

The configuration of this early settlement is still evident in the layout of Lasem's lanes as well as its residential and other structures, some of which are said to date to the late 1700s. The oldest Chinese houses in Lasem are hidden in compounds behind high brick walls, while local lore says that originally the walls were made of short wooden batten boards. One of the expansive surviving dwellings, which dates to the nineteenth century, is inside the walled Liem compound. Now essentially abandoned and derelict, it is maintained by a caretaker. Like many early Chinese houses in Indonesia, the structure includes three parallel buildings with open courtyards in between. The first and third buildings are single storied while the middle one has two storeys and is elevated on a slightly higher podium with walls constructed of red bricks. Each building is divided into three *jian* or bays, with a set of

Above The second of three buildings is a two-storey structure with bedrooms for the family.

Far left An oblique view of the two-storey structure and a side building.

Left Beyond these two buildings is a third, lower structure with a brick courtyard in front of it, which is said to have provided living space for servants and a place for them to wash and dry clothing.

perpendicular buildings set off from the core structures. In response to copious rainfall, there are broad overhangs on the front and rear of all of the buildings, with that on the front building elongated as a shed roof. Baked terracotta roof tiles and square floor tiles are used throughout. Windows and columns are all made of local hardwoods. Behind the first structure is a veranda with a double-sloped roof supported by masonry columns. Except for simple bracket arms that lift the narrow eaves overhang, the inverted V shape of the adjacent open area is supported by an uncomplicated post-and-beam construction. Viewed from the end of the structure, the gable is ornamented with a hanging fish beneath an upswept swallowtail ridgeline. An expansive kitchen, today filled with old clay pots, is adjacent to the front building.

Viewed from the back of the first structure, the second two-storey one was clearly the locus of domestic life. Here were the bedrooms and altar room. With front, back, and side windows and a broad veranda, the spaces in this structure are all well ventilated. Hardwoods were used for the columns and the brackets, some of which are carved in Chinese style. Beyond these two buildings is a third, lower structure with a brick courtyard in front of it, which is said to have provided living space for servants and a place for them to wash and dry clothing. In a back corner of the property are old horseshoe-shaped graves. Tall trees found throughout the compound provide shade.

Above left The Liem ancestral altar is located in the front building.

Above right The gate to the neighboring Chinese compound.

HAN FAMILY
ANCESTRAL HALL

SURABAYA, INDONESIA

Late 1870s

Among the oldest and best-known Chinese lineages in Indonesia is that of the Han family, whose roots in the archipelago go back to the beginning of the eighteenth century. The remarkable scholarship of Claudine Salmon, using genealogical records and other documents in Malay, Chinese, English, Dutch, French, and Indonesian, as well as field work in China and Indonesia, together with comments by a living Han descendant, trace in considerable detail the Han family history from their native village in China to their life as new immigrants in Central Java before achieving prosperity in East Java in the nineteenth century (Han, 2001; Salmon, 1991, 2001a, 2001b). This chapter will only make limited use of this historical information while focusing on an important piece of architectural evidence of their past status, which is a prominent marker of the present Han family's Chinese heritage and their posterity: the Lofty Ancestral Hall of the Han on Jalan Karet in Surabaya.

Han Siong Kong, the progenitor of this Han lineage in Indonesia, was born in Tianbao village, Zhangzhou prefecture in Fujian, in 1673. It is not certain when he left his village to voyage south, but family history records that he settled in Lasem, a riverside port along the north coast of Central Java midway between Semarang and Surabaya. Subsequently, his five sons and four daughters, who were likely to have been born of a local mother, eventually abandoned Lasem, some converting to Islam, with sons taking young Javanese girls as their wives, while others maintained their Chinese identity and practices after marrying Peranakan girls. Salmon has mapped the dispersal of Han Siong Kong's children and grandchildren, revealing also the family lore as to why they all fled Lasem: "... a thunderstorm broke during Han Siong Kong's funeral and his children abandoned the coffin in the forest in order to take shelter. The story goes that the coffin was buried by a mysterious power. The deceased is believed to have taken revenge for the lack of filial piety of his children by calling down curses on them and descendants; consequently none of his descendants has so far dared to pass through Lasem" (1991: 61). A member of the ninth generation told us that it was only in the seventh generation that any member of the Han family dared to visit Lasem.

One of Han Siong Kong's sons, Han Bwee Kong, otherwise known as Han Boeij Ko, was appointed as Kapitein der Chinezen, prospered materially in East Java, and had more than a dozen sons and daughters. On Han Bwee Kong's death, in 1778, he was succeeded as Kapitein der Chinezen by his third son, Han Chan Piet, who was only nineteen at the time; in 1810 Han Chan Piet attained the title of Majoor der Chinezen. Successive generations expanded their estates "on which they grew paddy, sugarcane, indigo, maize, coconut palms and similar crops; they also relied on tracts of land rented on long lease contracts instigated by the Government, which wanted to promote the production of sugar and, to a lesser extent, that of coffee and indigo" (Salmon, 1991: 74). With these and other diversified economic enterprises, the family multiplied and flourished as some members fully assimilated with the Javanese. In 1876, nearly a century after the death of Han Bwee Kong, his descendants in Surabaya founded the Han Sie Lok Hian Tjo Biauw, the Lofty Ancestral Hall of the Han, in his honor. The ancestral tablet of Han Siong Kong, his father and the progenitor of the Hans, is kept on the altar in this ancestral hall.

The Han Family Ancestral Hall

The principal purpose of a freestanding ancestral hall, sometimes called a lineage hall, is to provide a formal structure to house ancestral tablets. Throughout history, such halls have varied in size, but generally by the Qing dynasty they were built large enough to be sufficiently commodious for descendants to assemble and collectively carry out scheduled rituals honoring their forebears. Moreover, any ancestral hall is also a symbolic structure, which by its scale and ornamentation proclaims the accumulated status of a lineage while declaring the relationships of male members to a known or reputed progenitor. The placement of ancestral tablets in tiers on the altar within a hall for as many generations as possible, as well as the display of a genealogical chart of essentially all generations, manifests publicly the links among members of a lineage. In the past in China, the decision to build an ancestral hall usually came

Opposite above One of two window-like ventilation ports on the exterior wall, with symbolism of dragons and a longevity emblem.

Above The veranda of the Han family ancestral hall has an especially high roof supported by solid columns.

Right A *pintu pagar* half-door with dragons and a stylized longevity emblem.

Below right A carved amulet of a head above the hinge of the *pintu pagar* panel.

at a time of a family's efflorescence, often many generations after the death of the progenitor of the lineage.

In Indonesia, not only did financial capacity and social status play a role in the decision to build an ancestral hall, doing so was also itself a declarative statement of Chinese identity in communities in which Chinese were often a minority. From time to time, nostalgia as well as the periodic revivalism of interest in Chinese heritage, especially Confucianism, stoked the desire of a family to express their Chineseness publicly. In Bahasa Melayu, the Malay language spoken by Peranakans, Chinese ancestral halls are usually referred to as *rumah abu* or "house of ashes," which sometimes indeed are places maintained by temples where the cremated remains of the deceased are respectfully housed in cinerary urns in facilities that in English are usually called columbaria. In a Chinese ancestral hall, on the other hand, usually the only ashes found are those cradled in an incense censer. The table in the hall, with an ancestral altar on it, is called *meja abu* or "table of ashes"; keeping the ancestral altar at home is known as *piara abu* or "keeping the ashes"; performing rituals at the ancestral altar is *sembayang abu* or "paying respect to the ashes."

Chinese ancestral halls often provide rooms to accommodate family members visiting from other towns as well as those family members in need of a place to stay because of financial or other difficulties. Thus, it should not be surprising that multiple bedrooms and a kitchen are common spaces in the Han ancestral hall. In addition to observances that follow an annual calendrical cycle requiring obeisance to the ancestors, the occasion of funerals and weddings also provide obligatory opportunities for family members to assemble at the ancestral hall. Well into the twentieth century, such Chinese observances were common throughout Southeast Asia for even those who were many generations removed from their immigrant ancestor. Since ancestral halls are essentially surname-based lineage associations, there traditionally were no religious proscriptions in terms of who in the lineage could pay respects to the ancestors. Thus, even Christian or Muslim family members have generally been welcome.

Top left A view looking towards the front entry—note the inside view of the open ventilation port on the right—with skywells on both sides of the elongated reception hall.

Center left A view from the reception hall towards the ancestral altar in the distance.

Bottom left The veranda alongside the reception hall is supported by cast-iron columns.

Above right A series of cast-iron columns alongside the skywell of the reception hall.

Below right Looking into the side room, one can glimpse the rare circular ancestral chart.

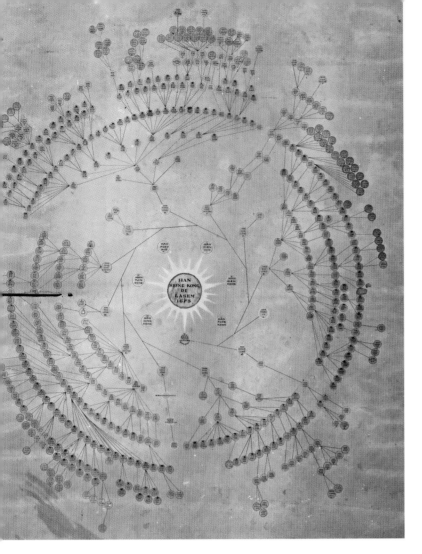

Above The circular ancestral chart of the Han family shows descend-ants arranged along concentric circles around the pivotal ancestor, Han Siong Kong.

Right top and bottom Formal ancestral portraits line the ancestral hall.

The overall form, extent, and materials used in ancestral halls in China vary in the same degree as other vernacular buildings. This is true also in Southeast Asia. The front elevation of the Han family ancestral hall presents an amalgamation of Chinese with other influences. The swallowtail ridgeline, red clay tiles on the roof, recessed entryway on the front wall, and pair of carved circular ventilation ports are all distinctively Chinese. Salmon's photograph of the ancestral hall of the lineage branch to which Han Siong Kong belonged in his home village in China reveals a similar three-part swallowtail profile even as the shape of the roof tiles and the fenestration differ. Unlike vernacular buildings in Fujian, which are usually not tall, the roof of the Han family ancestral hall is indeed lifted to a great height by a pair of Western-style columns, clearly a Dutch architectural influence. Ho Puay-peng, in his study of ancestral halls, shows that similar columns were used in halls in both Hong Kong and Guangdong, but there the heights were much less than that seen in the Han ancestral hall (2005: 299). The additional height no doubt derives from an attempt to adapt to the higher temperatures and higher relative humidities in Surabaya.

The organization of interior space follows Chinese hierarchical patterns in which the more public space is towards the front and the

private space is deeper into the structure, a pattern that some recognize as following Javanese norms (Indrani and Prasodjo, 2005: 44–65). On the other hand, it is possible that the Javanese followed Chinese practices. In this case, there is a linear dimension to the ancestral hall, with it being divided into two sections along an axis, which culminates in the ritual hall with the ancestral altar. Upon entering the heavy wooden doors at the front, there is a rectangular reception hall aligned in the middle of a pair of courtyards on each side, mimicking the openness experienced in a Javanese home. With chairs arrayed along the sides, this open hall provides a pleasant and airy space for assembling. Open spaces—skywells—are generally found as well within ancestral halls in southern China, but they are placed directly along the central axis of the structure and not in pairs along the sides of spaces as in the Han family ancestral hall (Ho, 2005: 310). A similar pattern can be seen

in the Kioe Seng Tong, the Thung family ancestral hall, in Bogor, West Java, which shows both Chinese and Dutch architectural influences. Here, the open skywells are situated in pairs along the sides of the central hall or *ting* instead of along the central axis.

Through the double doorway on the far end of this reception hall, visitors are able to glimpse in the distance the lights of the ancestral altar, which is the climax of a long spatial sequence marked by closed, open, and then closed spaces: a pair of side rooms followed by a pair of flanking courtyards, and then the side rooms adjacent to the altar itself. On one wall in the first side room on the right is a dramatic large-scale genealogical chart with descendants arranged along concentric circles around the pivotal ancestor Han Siong Kong. Portraits of deceased Han family members and past family celebrations held within the ancestral hall also are memorialized in old photographs hung on the walls. The

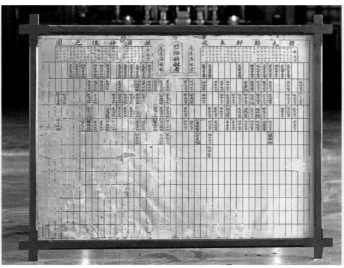

Above The ancestral altar is centered in a room framed with carved hardwoods.

Far left With a red banner showing the Eight Immortals, the votive table in front of the altar holds incense, candles, and a censer.

Left This is a traditional-style genealogical chart of the Han family.

open sequence is a combination of a transitional room with no walls, which is separated only by three European cast-iron columns from the adjacent courtyards that bring substantial natural light throughout the day into the sacred space. The marble floor, the ceiling with geometric patterns, the elaborately carved teakwood wall panels, and the furniture all highlight the significance of this elongated space, which culminates in the elaborate altar chamber. These are in striking contrast to the terrazzo-like floor, plain ceiling and walls, and basic chairs of the area at the front of the building.

The altar itself includes a carved open box set on a table to hold the elevated rows of ancestral tablets. A long table in front is accompanied by two smaller square tables with lighted candles, which are today electrified, incense burners, statues, and recent offerings of fruit and tea on them. The lowest table is draped with a bright red cloth covering that depicts the Eight Immortals, the Baxian, as well as the Three Stellar Gods, Fu, Lu, and Shou.

Large portraits of Han Bwee Kong and his wife, both dressed in formal Qing-dynasty finery, face each other on opposite walls in front of the altar, with a two-character phrase and a pair of couplets placed around them. The two characters, *chuangye*, above Han Bwee Kong, the son of the immigrant Han Siong Kong, acknowledge him as "Founder of the Enterprise," while the characters *chuifan* above his consort read "Setting an Example from the Past." Auspicious patterns are carved on all of the woodwork associated with the altar. Above the doorways leading to the back portion of the hall is a pair of double-character phrases, *guangqian* and *houyu*, meaning "Glorious Beginnings" and "Later Abundance"; these four characters sometimes appear in ancestral halls as *guangqian yuhou* with the meaning "Honor the Ancestors, Benefit Future Generations." The four-character phrase above the altar, *chunqiu feixie*, is a reminder to posterity to "Never Slacken Throughout the Year."

The rear section of the building serves more utilitarian purposes, including four bedrooms, storage rooms, and space for a kitchen. According to a current trustee, there were Han family members living in the ancestral hall until the late 1980s, but today the rear space is only occupied by a caretaker.

Confucian codes of propriety mandated a hierarchically ordered society with its most fundamental expression being the family. *Xiao* or filial piety, according to neo-Confucianism, is not only an obligation when parents are alive but also a duty to recently deceased parents and their parents and grandparents for as many generations as can be recalled. Rituals evolved not only to sustain these practices but also to remind those living of the necessity of family solidarity. The busiest times at the Han family ancestral hall are at the New Year in January/ February, at Qingming in April, the days before the Hungry Ghost Festival on the fifteenth day of the seventh lunar month, and on the eve of the lunar New Year in January/February. In preparation for these festivities, the hall is swept clean, lanterns are hung, and the altar is draped with red cloth. Offerings to the ancestors are abundant during these times. A photograph taken early in the twentieth century in the Han family ancestral hall shows the tables laden with offerings. Today, the observances in Surabaya are muted in comparison with those of the past. Still, in spite of social changes in families—intermarriage, religious conversion, and limited knowledge of the Chinese language—some senior members of the Han family actively promote the maintenance of their inherited ancestral hall as well as an awareness by the younger generation of their Chinese cultural heritage.

Above This faded and deteriorating photograph shows the bountifully laden tables in front of the ancestral altar.

Below This ancestral portrait of Han Bwee Kong, the son of the immigrant Han Siong Kong, faces one of this wife on opposite walls in front of the altar. Both are dressed in formal Qing-dynasty finery. The two-character phrase reads *chuangye*, which acknowledges him as "Founder of the Enterprise."

HAN AND THALIB RESIDENCE

PASURUAN, INDONESIA

Early 20th Century

Pasuruan, located some 60 kilometers south of Surabaya at the eastern end of Java, is washed by the Strait of Madura. As a port, it welcomed Chinese and Arab settlers, many of whom married local women, from the sixteenth century onward. The area has had a mixed history of development involving not only Javanese and Madurese peasants and Dutch colonialists but also Peranakan Chinese and Hadhrami Muslims from the Arabian Peninsula. While the earliest homes of immigrants can no longer be seen in Pasuruan, it is still possible to see how the changing fortunes of families is reflected in their old homes.

After nearly a century of turmoil in the 1700s, the Pasuruan region became depopulated and unproductive, with only a subsistence peasant economy based upon rice. Yet, in the last decades of the eighteenth and early nineteenth century, descendants of Han Siong Kong, a Chinese immigrant from Fujian who first settled in Lasem around 1700 and who had subsequently moved to Surabaya where the family gained prominence, began to seek opportunities along the Madura coast. Especially notable in this regard were the sons of Han Bwee Kong, who had been appointed Kapitein der Chinezen in Surabaya (page 204). The Han family was clearly Peranakan, with some members even converting to Islam and becoming local élites, while others clung firmly, though incompletely, to their Chinese heritage as they lived their entrepreneurial lives in East Java in areas both to the west and south of Surabaya. There is evidence that not all the Han in the Pasuruan area were directly related to Han Bwee Kong, and thus they are not represented in the Han family ancestral hall in Surabaya (pages 204–9). Indeed, there once was an ancestral hall in Pasuruan for a different Han family branch (Han, 2001: 44, 46).

In the early part of the nineteenth century, when Pasuruan was still considered a frontier area, the Dutch East Indies Company (VOC) set out to transform East Java through the cultivation and processing of sugarcane as part of its efforts to gain wealth from an area they called Oosthoek, the "Eastern Salient," that projected towards the Hinduized island of Bali. The impact on Javanese peasants, whose lives up until then had centered round the small-scale production of rice, was substantial as a paternalistic system of sugar cultivation and manufacturing was initially coercive before becoming ostensibly voluntary wage labor a half century later. Descendants of Chinese immigrants during this time gained substantial wealth and power from management of both the sugarcane fields and the processing mills. Han Kik Ko, one of the sons of Han Bwee Kong, gained rights to land for sugarcane estates that

Opposite above An early oil painting of the Han/Thalib residence.

Opposite below A view of the façade and side showing two separate halls with Chinese roofs.

Top and above Two views along the broad veranda at the front of the home.

Left Inside and outside views of the side veranda of the residence.

Above The capacious living and dining room with the ancestral altar in the room behind.

Left A modern-style bedroom just off the living room.

Left This elaborate carved stone ancestral altar is unique. Ancestral tablets no longer are seen on the tiers since the home has been occupied for decades by a Yemeni Arab family.

stretched from Pasuruan southward to Probolinggo. His three sons, together with cousins, further extended the family's entrepreneurial interests and community power throughout the receding frontier.

With the laying of the railroad from the larger port of Surabaya to Malang in 1879, Pasuruan's importance was diminished and over the next several decades its prosperity waned. Prosperous Europeans preferred Malang to Pasuruan because of its elevation and cool weather, effectively forsaking the declining city. Early in the twentieth century, an observer noted that "the fine homes built by the Europeans have been abandoned for a song to the Chinese, for which reason the Chinese quarter in this city has an appearance of wealth and comfort which one looks for elsewhere in vain" (Cabaton, 1911: 92). Cabaton's observation reveals that he was unaware that some prosperous Chinese in Pasuruan indeed had already built grand homes, evoking both Chinese elements as well as the modernized Indische style that was in fashion. After a century of exploitative sugar production, a prolonged period of economic turbulence, and social upheaval, the Eastern Salient was threatened by volatility in world sugar prices. Once the global Great Depression reached the Netherlands Indies throughout the decade after 1929, export prices dropped, immediately impacting peasant farmers and workers as well as those Chinese and Europeans who earlier had gained wealth from it.

Well-built Indische-style homes, which had been modified to meet the needs of Chinese in Pasuaruan, once again changed hands as real estate passed from one owner to another. One grand residence, which is still standing and is well maintained, was bought by Mohammad Thalib, a Yemeni Arab, in 1938 from a wealthy Chinese who is said to have been a descendant of the fabled Han Kik Ko, one of the early sugar barons in East Java in the early part of the nineteenth century. Expressing a sense of "modernity" in a style that can be labeled Indische, the layout contains elements that echo Chinese domestic architectural forms. Constructed with an awareness of the hot and rainy environment characteristic of Indonesia, the residence has many tropical features: steeply pitched roofs with projecting overhangs; a grand veranda supported by columns across the front, which is broadened with a vine-covered pergola; galleries along the side, which are framed by arches; large shuttered doors and windows; cool marble and tile floors; embossed metal ceilings; and spacious interior rooms that flow together. Above the overhang of the front veranda is Arabic script with the Malay word DAROESSALAM— "Abode of Grace"—written beneath it.

Indische-style buildings in the Netherlands Indies generally have variants of hipped roofs without gables, with triangular and trapezoidal surfaces slopping downwards to the walls. When the Pasuruan residence is viewed from an angle, however, it is quite clear that the sequence of the structures, one behind the other, reveals double-pitched roofs and gable walls that are decidedly Chinese. Examples like this can be seen not only in Souw Tian Pie's nineteenth-century Batavia residence (page 30) but also countless homes in Fujian and Guangdong provinces.

NA SONGKHLA RESIDENCE

SONGKHLA, THAILAND
1878

The elongated Myanmar–Thai–Malay Peninsula that connects the heartland of contemporary Thailand in the north with Malaysia and Singapore in the south was a crossroads for the old Maritime Silk Route before the fourteenth century, and continued being prominent in the six centuries afterwards. Chinese traders from southern China superseded Arab merchants in this region well before the thirteenth century in search of "the strange and the precious" (Jacq-Hergoualc'h, 2002: 32, 64–5, 342). From the eighteenth century onwards, Chinese merchants came to dominate the Sino-Siamese trade, sailing in ocean-going junks in quest of commodities—rare woods, birds' nests, spices, ivory, rhinoceros horn, decorative birds, resins, fruits, hides, rice—that were marketable in China. Exports from China to Siam at the time were principally manufactured goods such as textiles, preserved foods, medicines, crockery, porcelain, tiles, umbrellas, fans, paper, brass and copperware, and furniture. The need for these products increased as Chinese settled throughout Thailand in the nineteenth century. While the significance of this trade is acknowledged by historians, details are sketchy about the cultural interaction of Chinese sojourners and settlers with the indigenous populations, especially in that portion of the peninsula known today as Southern Thailand.

As other chapters in this book reveal, not only are descendants of Chinese immigrants numerous in Malaysia, Singapore, and Indonesia today, but there remains in these places many fine old homes, temples, and other community buildings that attest to the hard work, affluence, power, and influence of individual immigrant Chinese as well as the communities within which they lived. Those of Chinese background in what was once Siam are also numerous, yet the surviving residences of early Chinese immigrants are far fewer, but not completely absent in Thailand. Communities of Chinese were not only found in the imperial capitals at Ayutthaya and Bangkok, but were established all along the eastern coast of the narrow isthmus at sites adjacent to shallow estuaries and protected bays where coastal and seagoing boats could be afforded protection and access to interior markets.

In what is today Southern Thailand, historians assert that the essential evidence of past Chinese presence in the region rests principally on archaeological finds, such as old coins, pottery, statues, and votive objects, and only rarely with architectural artifacts, either still standing or destroyed. While this is certainly true of the remote past, we scoured the four Southern Thai provinces—Pattani, Narathiwat, Yala, and Songkhla—along the coast of the Gulf of Thailand in search of old Chinese houses in order to document their presence. Alas, we could only locate one, the Na Songkhla residence in the town of Songkhla, which

Above left The exterior gate to the compound viewed from inside the courtyard.

Left A panoramic sweep from the exterior gate, including the stream and bridge that lead to the gate of the residential compound.

Above A view from the broad bridge looking towards the gate of the symmetrical residential compound.

Right The sweeping stairway from the courtyard to the main building.

once was the seat of an old Malay Kingdom with heavy Srivijayan influences, at a site favored by Chinese traders and settlers between the seventeenth and nineteenth centuries.

It is not clear why the Chinese heritage in Songkhla has been essentially erased in this region even as people of Chinese descent continue to live there. It may be that very few Chinese actually amassed sufficient resources to build a fine home in Chinese style, or that they may have built a sumptuous home elsewhere in a more cosmopolitan area of Siam, adjacent Malaya, or even back in China. Another reason may be that the Chinese never attained the critical mass that they did in other Muslim areas, such as Malaysia and Indonesia, which would have emboldened them to assert their Chinese identity. Muslims in Thailand only represent 3 percent of the total population, while in this region—except for Songkhla—they exceed 70 percent, with the number reaching nearly 90 percent in Pattani. Today, the neighboring town of Hat Yai, the largest metropolitan center in Southern Thailand, is dominated by Chinese Thai while Songkhla has far fewer. It may be that it was only a rare Chinese, like Na Songkhla, who had both the power and the financial resources to assert his Chineseness via the construction of a Chinese-style residence. Whatever the reason, the Na Songkhla residence is an exceptional building deserving of recognition.

Wu Rang and Na Songkhla

There is little information about the Chinese immigrant progenitor of the Na Songkla family and the generations that succeeded him. Nonetheless, the historical record points to an individual and his descendants who flourished in the port town of Songkhla, secured the support of Thai royalty, established a veritable dynasty of local governors that lasted many generations, and even today are notable citizens of Thailand. G. William Skinner notes that "King Taksin was instrumental in embarking one of the most remarkable Chinese families in Thai history on a long record of governmental service in southern Siam" (1953: 21).

Wu Rang, also known as Wu Yang and sometimes called Chin Yiang Sae Hao, like other impoverished villagers in the Zhangzhou area of Fujian province, left his village of Xinxing in the middle of the eighteenth century at the age of thirty-four. In Fujian at the time, officials as well as commoners understood well the dire economic situation. Both advocated maritime trade and trade-related sojourner migration as safety valves in order to escape Fujian's unbalanced man–land ratio. The *Amoy Gazetteer* stated this dilemma as "The fields are few but the sea is vast; so men have made fields from the sea" (Cushman, 1993: iii). Perhaps leaving from the thriving port of Yuegang in 1750, Wu Rang

Left Looking back towards the entry to the compound from a position under the stairway. The lions at the foot of the stairway are visible.

Right A glimpse of the lion pair.

Below Within the residence itself, there is a modest courtyard with a stairway leading to the second floor.

sailed by junk across the South China Sea to Songkhla where he worked as a vegetable gardener and fisherman before taking up tobacco farming. In 1758 he married a local woman from nearby Phatthalung along the shores of Lake Songkhla, who bore him five sons over the following ten years (Xia, 1953: 40ff).

In time, Wu Rang's potential was recognized by the royal family in Siam. The revered King Taksin, who himself had a Chinese father, granted Wu Rang monopoly rights as a tax farmer in 1769 to harvest birds' nests from two offshore islands for the export market with the obligation of paying the royal treasury 50 catties of silver for that right. King Taksin took Wu Rang's eldest son, Wu Wenhui, with him back to Bangkok to serve as a royal aide. Described as "an honest, efficient, and successful tax farmer, who regularly sent the annual proceeds to the capital," Wu Rang was rewarded by King Taksin with the governorship of Songkhla, a role he continued even after the demise of King Taksin in 1782 until his own death in 1784 (Skinner, 1953: 22).

When Wu Wenhui sought an audience with King Taksin's successor, King Rama I, after his father's death, he was granted the same administrative title as his father, Governor of Songkhla. After serving in military campaigns, he was accorded greater honors. When Wu Wenhui died in 1812 without heirs, the Songkhla governorship passed to his brother and then to succeeding generations. Astonishingly, the Songkhla governorship remained in the Wu family for nine generations, only ending in 1904 during the reforms of King Chulalongkorn (Rama V). Family patriarchs of the Wu family thus served as the "Chinese rajah" of Songkhla, dominating the political and economic life of the region for 135 years from the latter quarter of the eighteenth century onwards.

In towns such as Songkhla, "Chinese functioned as monopolists ... [and] also served as middlemen in the interior to supply the Bangkok market with goods required for the China junk trade," according to Jennifer Cushman, and thus Wu Rang likely had a lucrative concession (1993: 110). He clearly enjoyed a cordial relationship with the royal family, which itself was a major player in the Siamese junk trade with China. From Songkhla, small packet boats plied the coastal waters not only to Thonburi and Bangkok, which had successively become the imperial capitals after the destruction of Ayutthaya in 1767, but also to regional towns. Trading patterns changed commerce after the conclusion of the Opium War in 1842, establishing a system that favored foreign steamships in carrying goods to and from Chinese ports. It is not clear what specific impact there was on the type of monopolistic trade practices enjoyed up to that time by Na Songkla and his descendants.

According to Skinner, "It is interesting to note the progressive Thai-ification of Wu Yang's [Rang] descendants. His sons all spoke Chinese and were buried in the Chinese style. His grandson T'ien-chung [Tianchong] was cremated (1817) but his ashes were buried in an imitation Chinese grave. T'ien-sheng, also a grandson, was a Theravada Buddhist by faith, learned Chinese only as a second language, and was cremated two years after his death in full Thai style. The great-grandchildren spoke no Chinese, did not even have Chinese names, and intermarried within the family and across generations in a fashion that would have appalled their grandfather. In 1916 the family adopted the Thai name of Na Songkhla ('Na' in surnames is the Thai counterpart of the German 'von' or the French 'de')" (1953: 150–1). In spite of the deterioration of the lucrative junk trade between Siam and China in the nineteenth century, the family descended from Wu Rang continued to flourish because of royal patronage and assimilation.

Above left Antique cabinets on display in an upstairs room.

Above right A carved screen, which probably once stood inside an entry to block the view of an altar.

Left A detail of the gilded carving on a panel of the antique cabinet above left.

The Na Songkhla Residence

The Na Songkhla residence was constructed in 1878 by Phraya Sundranuraksa, also known as Net Na Songkhla, who at the time was deputy governor of the region. He served during the reign of young King Rama V, revered widely as Chulalongkorn, as Thailand entered a transformative period of modernization, reform, innovation, and openness. Net Na Songkhla occupied the residence with his family only for sixteen years, after which the family's home became for two years the official residence of Phraya Yomarat (Pan Sukhum), the state governor of the expanded administrative area of Nakhon Si Thammarat. Subsequently, from 1896 to 1917, the residence began its transformation into an administrative center, first for local needs, then from 1917 to

1953 as the governmental hall for Songkhla province, before being neglected and effectively abandoned for the next twenty years. Over a period of nearly eighty years, much of the majesty of the old home was ruined as spaces came to serve mere utilitarian requirements. In 1973 the Thai government acknowledged the historical significance of the Na Songkhla residence by registering the relict building as a National Monument before beginning the restoration work necessary to overcome decades of neglect. In 1982 the expansive building was designated as the Songkhla National Museum, with the public function of housing not only artifacts relating to the Na Songkhla family but also objects about the region's varied history: Dvaravati and Srivijaya art, local arts and crafts, as well as Thai and Chinese ceramics, and woodcarvings (*Songkhla National Museum*, 2008: 4–5).

The Na Songkhla residence is a magisterial structure, outstanding for its expansive scale, the assemblage of its exterior and interior components, and its glistening white walls and vivid crimson trim. These elements are suggestive of its one-time grandeur even as the building today is a rather stodgy museum bereft of the life that once filled its spaces when it was a home. While the building is clearly a Chinese-style structure with some striking Western elements, there also appears to have been some conscious, while minor, adaptations derived from traditional Thai dwellings called Ban Thai or Ruen Thai (Askew, 2003: 259ff; Ramasoot, 2008: 78ff). Traditional Thai dwellings, of course, differ fundamentally from traditional Chinese dwellings, especially in terms of their using an elevated skeletal frame with light external walls instead of solid walls built directly on the ground. While both Thai homes and traditional Chinese houses found in the southern portions of the country employ terraces and verandas as common spatial units, those found in traditional Thai dwellings are typically larger, longer, and deeper. Terraces and verandas are the most significant Thai spatial elements grafted on to what is fundamentally a Chinese structural type.

The overall ground plan of the Na Songkhla complex was situated to face west towards Songkhla Lake, the largest lake in Thailand, while its rear areas were framed by the mountainous spine of the narrow peninsula in the south of the country. With high ridges to its rear and a body of water to its front, this pattern followed traditional Chinese *fengshui* norms. A low outer perimeter wall encompassing a grassy expanse separates the world outside from the walled residential compound inside. Whether this perimeter wall was an original feature of the dwelling complex is not clear.

As a visitor today passes through the tall, tiered entry gate along the western outer walls towards the less formal gate of the residential compound itself, it is necessary to first cross a broad, tile-surfaced bridge over a languid stream passing in front of the dwelling. The symmetrical façade includes not only a traditional Chinese-style entry gate reached by a splayed staircase with five treads, but also walls that extend to the gable ends of a pair of perpendicular single-storey side buildings. Stepping inside the entry gate, one enters an inverted U-shaped composition: a seven-bay two-storey building dominated by a symmetrical pair of grand stairways in Beaux Arts style and a pair of facing side buildings. These together envelop an extensive grassy courtyard. It is doubtful that the central area was originally covered with grass, but might have been surfaced with crushed shells or sand. The side buildings, with their deep overhangs, perhaps once served as utilitarian spaces where servants gathered foodstuffs brought from nearby villages, processed grains and other agricultural products, used looms to weave cloth, and stored implements and conveyances. The depth of the eaves overhang assured shady and cool workspaces even during times of heavy rainfall, functioning much like a *palai* or semi-outdoor terrace in a traditional Thai house.

Sweeping upward, the grand stairway leads to a long balcony with a shed roof set just below the main roof with its uplifted swallowtail profile. A pair of lion statues today rest at the base of the stairway. Couched between the pair of staircases is a rounded archway leading through a passage into the dwelling's inner courtyard. After passing from the broad outer courtyard through the passageway, one enters a much narrower, somewhat constricted quadrangular courtyard surrounded by buildings on four sides: two separate horizontal buildings linked by a pair of parallel structures. At the head of the courtyard, which is paved

Above The entry to a principal side room on the second level is entered through an imposing classical Western-style architectural form that contrasts with the traditional Chinese wooden framework. As is characteristic of Thai dwellings, the floors of the second level are laid with polished wood.

Above The uplifted swallowtail ridge tip of the main building has poly-chromatic gable ornamentation with an unknown theme.

Above Ornamentation on the upper gable showing a plaster representation of the God of Wealth, Cai shen.

Above Large-scale door panels with a carving of a pair of dragons chasing or holding a flaming disk or orb—some say a pearl—usually described as a sun, a Buddhist symbol representing wisdom.

Above A carved plaster frieze at the corner of a wall.

with tiles, is a Y-shaped stairway leading upstairs to the family's private quarters. In traditional Thai dwellings, and to some degree in traditional multistoried Chinese residences, there was a pronounced verticality in how space was used: downstairs was informal public space while upstairs was formal and private. The function of the rooms surrounding the inner courtyard on the ground floor is not clear.

Each of the surrounding buildings on the second floor includes several commodious rooms, the specific uses of which are no longer clear. It is likely that the rearmost room was a formal space that served ceremonial purposes, including perhaps for the placement of an ancestral altar. The other large rooms most likely were bedrooms and sitting rooms for use by family members, especially women. As the images clearly reveal, each of the rooms is set back approximately four meters from the open courtyard to form a covered veranda. Sturdy timber columns form the vertical supports for a wooden *chuandou*-style framework of threaded beams mortised into short posts that directly lift the roof purlins, quite similar to structures found throughout southern China. The placement of lesser columns serves to extend the depth of the covered veranda. Contrasting with the piled Chinese-style wooden framework is a pair of classical Greek Revival entryways, each with a pair of pilasters, a formal arch, and an impressive triangular pediment with a recessed tympanum set atop a rectangular entablature.

The floors inside the rooms and on the surface of the covered veranda are made of polished teakwood, quite unlike those found in homes anywhere in China. Following Thai custom, family members and visitors would remove their shoes either upon reaching the second floor or

before entering any of the rooms. Antique furniture is displayed along the walls of several of the rooms, but it is not possible to determine how the bedrooms were furnished when the residence was occupied by a family. Following Thai custom, it is possible that some of the rooms provided shared sleeping space, called *ruan*, and that other rooms were used by family members who sat together on the wooden floor in a circle when sharing meals. While the doors currently seen in the museum are simple and functional, carved wooden doors once were placed at the entry of each of the rooms on the second floor. Some examples of the elaborately carved doors are on display and are the equal of any seen in surviving houses in China.

Unlike homes in southern China, exterior shuttered windows are abundant on all of the walls of the Na Songkhla residence in order to enhance cross-ventilation. As the rear elevation shows, there are seven doorways along the back of the house that open to a broad terrace. This level of opening in the rear would have been very uncommon in China for climatic reasons. The rear upper storey also is remarkably open, with its wooden doors and balustrades. Side walls also have shuttered windows that can be opened. As with expansive houses in China, servants no doubt circulated through the dwelling throughout the day opening and closing the shutters to capture wind and avoid sunlight in order to maintain cool ambient temperatures in the interior. All of the principal buildings have flush gable walls with upturned swallowtail ridgelines with clay figures embedded beneath them. In the triangular space in the upper walls of each gable are ornamental elements, only some of which have been restored. Some are readily

recognizable images of Chinese origin, with auspicious meanings, while others are of indeterminate meaning.

The Na Songkhla residence was built more than 100 years after the arrival of Wu Rang, whose family had by then changed through intermarriage and the adoption of many Thai customs. There is no information available concerning the nature of the Na Songkhla families in the nineteenth century in terms of marriages and children. Among Thais and Chinese at the time, it was common for successful men to have multiple families, and it is likely that this commodious home sustained an extended family characteristic of the times. Because of the nature of maritime trade, moreover, it is likely that family members involved in Sino-Thai commerce maintained their Fujian dialect as a means of communication. While there is no way to establish this with certainty, it is possible that some of them even returned periodically to the home region of their forebears in China, where they saw fine examples of Chinese domestic architecture that they tried to replicate in Songkhla. On the other hand, it was not uncommon to bring master carpenters and masons from China to build grand Chinese-style residences in a distant town far from China itself. With a sizable purse to draw funds from, knowledge of traditional Chinese domestic architectural forms as well as inspiration from the currents of architectural innovation sweeping the Victorian era, including Classical Revivalism, the Na Songkhla family and their employed craftsmen fashioned a distinctive residence that represents well the Chinese diasporic heritage in Thailand.

Above A view from the northwest showing the side elevation of the dwelling, with the rear section to the left and the front low wing structures on the right, adjacent to the courtyard.

Right A moon gate along one side of the residence.

Below This view of the rear building and partial view of one side shows the abundance of doors and windows that insure the flow-through movement of air from front to back as well as side to side. The solid shutters are opened and closed throughout the day to control the intrusion of the sun and control ventilation.

POSAYACHINDA RESIDENCE

BANGKOK, THAILAND

Mid-nineteenth Century

Chinese traders established homes and shops along the banks of the lower Chao Phraya River before the Bangkok area became the Siamese capital after the destruction of Ayutthaya by the Burmese. The first Chinese village was called Ban Kok, but Chinese were forced to move from this site in 1782 when King Rama I decided to occupy it for the construction of the Royal Grand Palace. Chinese settlers then moved approximately two kilometers downstream to an area that was called Soi Sampheng, which continues to this day as the heart of Chinatown. As Bangkok's population grew to 401,300 in 1828, the town was dominated by 360,000 Chinese immigrants and their descendants who created a veritable Chinese settlement inhabited by men capable of meeting all their needs. "The earliest nineteenth-century visitors to Bangkok remarked specifically that Chinese were dominant among boatbuilders, blacksmiths, tinsmiths, tailors, leatherworkers, and shoemakers" in addition to merchants, skilled tradesman, unskilled laborers, fisherman, and farmers. By the 1860s "practically the entire industry of Siam had passed into Chinese hands," comprising "almost every craft known to man" (Skinner, 1953: 117–18). Indeed, Bangkok at the time was a Chinese town in a Siamese kingdom.

Into the early twentieth century, Bangkok was an overwhelmingly Chinese city with large numbers of recent immigrants. It is said that the city's population gradually shifted to a Thai majority, but a high percentage of those claiming to be Thai actually had some Chinese ancestry. It is against this background that one can appreciate that Bangkok's Chinatown at the beginning of the twenty-first century is much more than the type of exotic ethnic enclave found in Vancouver, New York, San Francisco, or Sydney. The nucleus of that early settlement on the east side of the river today has become a famous attraction. This is not only because of the plethora of restaurants—many specializing in expensive sharks' fin and birds' nest dishes—fresh produce stands, herbal medicine shops, souvenir stalls, gold shops, and pawnshops

along the major roads, but also for the vitality of its residential, commercial, manufacturing, and warehousing activity that can only be experienced within the cramped labyrinth of Chinatown's small lanes and narrow alleys.

Contrasting with the city's grand palaces and revered temples, which are not too far away, the extensive Chinatown neighborhood includes some striking shophouses, residences, and temples built by nineteenth-century Chinese settlers. While many deteriorating shophouses can be glimpsed by anyone strolling the constricted lanes, several old Chinese homes are essentially unknown except to those who still maintain them as part of their family heritage or the small fraternity of historical preservation cognoscenti who learn of them and guard that knowledge. Preserving sprawling old residences in an area where land values are high, indeed where demolition all too often comes easily in order to raise a profitable high-rise building, is a paradoxical aspect in the identity of Bangkok's Chinatown.

Difficult to find because of the need to pass from one narrow lane to another and then on to still another as bustling veins branch off from major commercial arteries, the Posayachinda residence is an outstanding example of a Chinatown home said to be some 150 years old. While relatively hidden deep in Chinatown's maze not too far from the Royal Orchid Sheraton Hotel and the upscale River City shopping complex, this very old house is still standing and accessible because of the conscious efforts of devoted descendants of Soa Hengtai, who wish to honor their family's history by preserving the building. In addition, the creative entrepreneurial spirit of an eighth-generation descendant, Poosak Posayachinda, has brought about adaptive reuses of the noteworthy dwelling in order to make its preservation economically sustainable. Even after having undergone some dramatic renovation, this very old Chinese home still retains its essential historical integrity while serving new functions.

Opposite above A detail of one of the panels on the entryway above showing a variety of symbols relating to longevity, including Shou Xing, the Stellar God of Longevity, an evergreen tree, a deer, a crane, and a peach of immortality.

Above A full view of the entryway, which at one time led directly to the edge of the river.

Above left The name Heng Tai and a protective amulet above the door.

Above center A close-up of the protective amulet with a *bagua* and a scowling animal, said to be a lion, holding a sword in his mouth.

Above right One of the pair of painted paper lanterns hanging at the entryway.

Right Even the inside of the entryway has wall paintings.

The Posayachinda Residence

Little is known of Soa Hengtai, the progenitor of the Posayachinda family, except that he arrived in Siam sometime between 1824 and 1851 during the reign of King Rama III. Family lore recalls that Soa Hengtai received a royal concession for the lucrative trade in birds' nests in what is today southern Thailand soon after arriving in Bangkok. In the ensuing years, Soa also played a key role in the informal private remittance system utilized by Chinese sojourners and settlers to send money back to family in their home villages, in the process earning for himself a substantial income.

Karl Gützlaff, a Christian missionary among the Chinese in Siam for three years in the early 1830s, described how the remittance system functioned (1834: 167).

A part of their hard earnings is annually remitted to their kindred who are left in their native land; and it is astonishing to see what hardships they will suffer, to procure and send home this pittance. A man of tried honesty is appointed to collect the individual subscriptions of the emigrants, who also engages to go home with them, and there make an equitable distribution to the donees. The subscriptions are regularly noted down, and certain per centage [sic] paid to this commissioner. Before he goes on board, a banquet is given by the subscribers, and then he embarks with all the wishes which human voices can utter, for his prosperous passage. On arriving at his native shores, he is welcomed by all those who are anxiously waiting for this supply.... Good faith is surely not a virtue of which the Chinese can generally boast, though there are honourable individual exceptions; at the same time, it must be admitted that their affection towards their kindred is very strong; neither time nor distance can withdraw their attention from the beloved objects they left behind in their native land. If an emigrant can send but a dollar he will send it; he will himself fast in order to save it. Indeed, he will never send home a letter unless accompanied with some present; he will rather cease writing than send nothing more substantial than paper.

Gützlaff acknowledged the miserable existence of swindlers who took advantage of the illiterate whose filiality was unyielding and admirable, but it was the needs of the greater number that interested him and he praised reputable agents such as Soa Hengtai.

According to an observation by Gützlaff's wife, most Chinese in the early 1830s lived in houses in Bangkok that were "nothing more than a miserable pile of either wood, or bamboo and attap, so that a spark sets them on fire in a moment" (Gützlaff, 1834: xxxviii). While it is not known how many other large Chinese-style residences like that of Soa Hengtai were constructed in the nineteenth-century remaking of Bangkok, in aggregate they represented significant elements in the transformation of the town as sojourners became settlers.

There are no records of Soa Hengtai's children, grandchildren, great-grandchildren, or great-great-grandchildren. However, in the following generation—the grandfather of Poosak Posayachinda—one was a court photographer for King Rama V, also known as Chulalongkorn, who

reigned from 1868 to 1910. With the Thai name Luang Navakaenikorn, the court photographer was also a poet and sent his children to Assumption College, a highly regarded Catholic institution with French connections, which enjoyed royal patronage and was also attended by some of the crown princes.

The Posayachinda residence is an inverted U-shaped structure with a wall and gate along the front, a pattern commonly found in Fujian. At one time, the building had twenty-one separate rooms, but over time some were consolidated. While today the residence is surrounded by multistoried homes that make it difficult to appreciate its external extent, the building originally stood in a relatively open area only 20 meters away from the river. During those early days, visitors were likely to have been impressed as they approached the brilliant entryway of the home. In addition to the fanciful ornamentation made of glazed tile shards along the ridgeline, a *daojing* or "inverting mirror" is located at a central position and raised above the ridgeline on a protruding disk. Mirrors of this type, which are described in manuals used by *fengshui* practitioners, traditionally were considered neutralizing objects said to be capable of overturning any antagonistic element reflected in them, including presumably the contemporary tall building now facing the mirror here.

In addition to the upturned ridgeline, the recessed entryway has a crimson doorway with two pairs of Chinese characters proclaiming *heng yuan tai lai*, "Persevering from Afar, Arriving in Thailand," as well as eight "framed" paintings with raised figures along its walls. The characters *heng* and *tai* are a play on the brand name used by the Soa family in their business ventures. The characters are repeated on a horizontal board above the door, where there also is a *bagua* plaque, and at several locations throughout the home. Two painted hanging lanterns complete the ornamentation of the entryway, one of which has an incorrect set of characters for Soa Hengtai's name in Chinese while the other has Nanchuan, presumably the name of Soa's ancestral home in Fujian. I have not been able to locate such a place. The paintings include auspicious symbols, pithy sayings, and floral arrangements. Four unconventional Chinese characters also appear painted above the door. If one disaggregates the eight characters embedded in the contrived

Opposite above and below Between the main building (above) and the entryway (below), the current owner has installed a dive pool in the courtyard.

Top With its polished hardwood floors, the second floor veranda looks out over the courtyard. On the left are openings leading into the ancestral hall. A doublestepped set of timber columns and beams extends the overhang substantially to protect the area from both sun and rain.

Above An ornamented window with vertical bars pierces the wooden panel wall separating the ancestral hall from the veranda.

Above A view through a passageway on the second floor leading to a series of side rooms used as bedrooms.

characters, an eight-character phrase emerges that should be read *qingqi nanyuan caizhu fangbian* with the common meaning *Tianguan cifu*, "May the Heavenly Official (Deity of Heaven) Bestow Blessings." This auspicious phrase is seen widely in southern China and in Southeast Asia on a poster displaying Tian Guan, the Deity of Heaven, dressed in formal attire and holding a scroll with the well-known four characters *Tianguan cifu*, with, of course, the general meaning "May You Be Prosperous." One of the panels on the right, in fact, shows Tian Guan, minus his head, holding such a scroll, as well as a *ruyi*—"May You Have Whatever You Want"—scepter. On the reverse side of the entryway, there is also a series of framed paintings, including a rectangular one above the doorway featuring the fabled Baxian or Eight Immortals.

The rear building, a wide, two-storied structure, faces the river to its west. A pair of lower perpendicular side buildings, which once served as kitchens and places for storage, flanks what was once a broad, open courtyard. The ground floor rooms are set back with the veranda on the second floor overhanging them. Today, these ground floor rooms have been modernized for occupancy by Posayachinda family members without disturbing their external appearance. The shaded terraces provide pleasant places to relax, eat, and work, much as they would have in the past.

A pair of brick stairs leads to the second level, which, following Thai domestic style, has wooden floors made of teak planks. Wooden columns and an elaborate wooden framework, similar to that found in fine homes in southern China, lift the purlins supporting what was once a tile roof. In the upper spaces between beams, posts, and struts, woodcarvings and painted panels are an added embellishment. According to family members, the original old roof tiles were given to a temple in Phuket that was undergoing restoration about thirty-five years ago. In their place, corrugated cement roofing sheets, which were molded to look like roof tiles, were placed over the purlins instead of common roof tiles.

Above and opposite below
A glimpse of the sequence
of five sets of crimson swivel
door panels that lead into
the ancestral hall just off
the veranda.

Opposite top left A detail
of a carving set among the
wooden framework that
supports the roof of the
veranda.

Opposite top right A framed
triptych of Chinese images
above the ancestral altar.

Opposite center Carved and
painted components of the
wooden framework that
supports the veranda on
the second floor.

Unfortunately, many of these panels have cracked, allowing rainwater
to seep into the upper storey. The verandas and rooms found on the
upper floor are readily cooled by breezes and shaded by deep overhangs,
providing comfortable spaces for family life.

No room is more significant than the broad, three-bay-wide hall that
is entered through five sets of swinging door panels painted crimson
with gold lattice panels and gold trim. Just outside the door, as one might
find in any home in Thailand, is a low table with an image of the Buddha.
The large room is divided into three areas, with two side rooms separated
from the main hall by painted sets of nine door panels. Like those found
in other Chinese residences, the carved wooden altar, which is set on a
high rectangular table, has a lower square table in front of it. Ancestral
tablets are found in the rear portion of the altar, with photographs of
three revered and more recently deceased members of the Posayachinda
family in front. On the square table are accouterments used in paying
respect to the ancestors. Today, all of the rooms on the upper floor,
which once would have been considered prime spaces for living, are used
for storage. The reason can be easily explained in that the upper storey is
difficult to air-condition, a necessary amenity in contemporary Thailand,
because of the porosity of the wooden walls, while air-conditioning the
rooms on the lower level is significantly easier and less costly.

Aside from the modernization of facilities in the old house, such
as bathrooms, kitchens, sound systems, and air-conditioning, which
contribute to comfortable living, there is a major alteration unlike
anything we have seen in other Chinese homes. In 2003 Poosak
Posayachinda constructed a four-meter-deep diving pool that essentially fills the once open courtyard. According to the *Bangkok Post*, he
expended two million baht, approximately US$56,000, on the project
to meet the needs of his thriving, heretofore internet-based recreational
sport business. Called Dumnam.com, it is a full-service firm selling
scuba diving equipment and offering diving courses and tours to famous
seaside sites in Thailand. The decision to build a diving pool within his
home, made possible by the availability of the large, open courtyard,
offered a means to generate substantial income to maintain the old
residence, and provides a way to overcome "the difficulty of securing
prime-time slots on weekends for his diving classes at commercial
pools." In 2004 he made an even greater investment of four million baht,
over US$112,000, to refurbish portions of the old house. In addition,
he extended his enterprise to include another of his ventures by adding
an air-conditioned kennel, an effort he calls an avocation rather than a
business since it has not yet been profitable. Dubbed by the *Bangkok Post*
as a five-star "dog hotel," the facility opened in December 2004 "just in
time to serve his main target market, expatriates with family pets, as they
leave Thailand for the Christmas holidays" (Hemtasilpa, 2004). Poosak
is well known around the world as a breeder of Beagle dogs. According
to his X-Plorers website, he began breeding dogs, first Collies, in 1987
and Beagles in 1997, crediting American breeders for mentoring him.
It is certain that Soa Hengtai, himself an entrepreneur with substantial
talent and much success, would appreciate the spirit and enterprise of
his descendants who not only are prospering but also maintaining the
family's ancestral home as well as honoring their ancestors.

WANGLEE MANSION

BANGKOK, THAILAND

Late 19th Century

The consciousness and power of *guxiang*—"ancestral home" or "native place"—is a recurring theme in the life histories of Chinese sojourners and settlers throughout Southeast Asia, indeed the world over. Attachment to *guxiang* traditionally ranged from sentimental nostalgia of times gone by to levels of activity involving regular visits, substantial investment, a preference for working with kinsmen from that area to the exclusion of others, and eventual return. Regional based institutions such as clan associations and temples, like guildhalls in China, not only provided aid and support to those sharing surnames and common origin but also served to promote traditional values and provide opportunities to participate in China's modernization. Deep-seated

place-based solidarity based on *tongxiang*—the bonds of common origin even when there were no direct bonds of kinship—provided a vehicle for maintaining traditional religious, economic, and social activities. The continuation of regional identity was reinforced as those from a *guxiang* spoke a common dialect, enjoyed home-style delicacies, participated in periodic rituals such as those attending to graves at the Qingming festival, enjoyed cultural performances, contributed collectively to disaster relief, and raised funds as a group to build schools, hospitals, roads, and bridges. In addition, those living far from home were comforted that death would be attended by proper attention to ritual and burial, including even returning bodies or bones to a home village. Because new arrivals from the *guxiang* was a continuing condition, replenishing those who died or moved on, memory of the ancestral home was kept fresh and sentiments remained lively for long periods of time. Yet, for countless Chinese living abroad, *huigui guxiang*, "returning to one's native place," whether gloriously or even quietly, was a dream that never went away.

Of course, as examples throughout this book reveal, countless descendants of Chinese immigrants throughout Southeast Asia severed contacts with their *guxiang* even as they continued to value their Chinese heritage. Whenever family members sank new roots in their adopted homeland, varying levels of awareness of their cultural heritage continued, a condition made complicated by intermarriage and politics. While losing the ability to speak Chinese, they frequently maintained customs, traditions, and names that declared their "Chineseness." After family members returned to their home village, usually little came to light about how they passed the rest of their days. Yet, in some cases, old residences still stand in both a home village and in the adopted homeland that are reminders, physical markers, in the past lives of sojourners and settlers.

A good example of venturing abroad in search of economic opportunities over several generations while maintaining roots in a home village in eastern Guangdong province is that of the descendants of Chen Huanrong (1825–90). The tale is not a simple one with a common conclusion, but is a narrative of varying trajectories and contrasting visions of what constitutes "Chineseness." Some Chen family members, after long periods abroad, did return to their home village to live out their days as Chinese in a glorious manor, leaving behind fine residences that still stand. While other descendants eventually chose to adopt a new nationality with some acknowledgment of their "Chineseness," they continued to honor their ancestors by maintaining the "old" residence of their overseas forebears. They, too, support the ancestral residence back in their progenitor's home village; indeed, the overseas descendants have contributed substantial sums of money in recent years for its restoration after decades of neglect. Thousands of miles apart, the grand Wanglee Mansion in Bangkok, Thailand, and the expansive Chen Cihong manor in Chaozhou, Guangdong (pages 262–7), have become lasting material emblems of the identities forged by Chinese migrants over a century ago.

Above After having undergone extensive restoration in 2008–9, the front gables of the Wanglee mansion reveal an extraordinary polychromatic assemblage of paintings, calligraphy, and three-dimensional figures.

Right Beyond these carved lattice door panels is the ancestral hall of the Wanglee lineage. The characters above the door express Wong Li (Wanglee), the "chop" for the family's firm, and the Chinese characters for their Thai name.

From Kintyelung to Wanglee

Family lore points to Chen Huanrong, also called Chen Xuanyi, as the destitute villager without either land or a house whose entrepreneurial spirit led him to leave Qianxi village in Chaozhou prefecture to begin a journey towards acquiring a fortune beyond China. Born in 1825, he was one of only twenty-three family members of four generations living in the village at the time, and was himself an eighth-generation descendant of Chen Huanxian (1646–1709), one of whose sons founded the village. Signing on as a young crew member on a junk plying the coastal waters, Chen Huanrong saved sufficient money to join with his brothers and some cousins to buy their own vessel while they continued to look for still other opportunities to multiply their wealth. Judging that Hong Kong, established less than a decade before as a British colony, was "a portal to the increasingly lively economy over much of the Pacific," Chen Huanrong established a small import–export firm there in 1851. Called Kintyelung (Qiantailong), this family enterprise, which imported rice from Southeast Asia to China and exported local Chinese products to the Nanyang, over time was to gain great prominence in Hong Kong. Indeed, "Hong Kong was an ideal site for thousands of Chinese business establishments specializing in the movement of goods, information, people, and money. Most of these businesses maintained exclusive connections with stores and financial institutions in China and abroad, sometimes as administratively integrated branches, but usually on the basis of less formalized connections through kinship and village ties" (McKeown, 1999: 314–15, 319).

Above Below the ancestral hall on the second floor is this large parlor for formal entertaining. The extensive use of Thai teak for columns, wall surrounds, window frames, as well as the beams and joists that support the wooden floors above is apparent.

Far left In front of the parlor and adjacent to the courtyard is this broad veranda.

Left Details of the painted ornamentation on the exterior wall of the entry gate to the mansion.

As the firm prospered in Hong Kong, Chen Huanrong's sons, Chen Cihong, Chen Cixiang, and Chen Ciyun, played increasing roles as he contemplated expanding his growing empire to areas of Southeast Asia where Chinese emigrants were found in great numbers. Bangkok in Siam, later called Thailand, beckoned because for at least a half century more than half the population of the royal capital was Chinese. Even towns some distance away from the capital throughout the kingdom attracted increasing numbers of Chinese.

Born in 1843, Chen Cihong, also known as Tan Tsu Wong, Tan Siew-Wang, and Tan Chue Huang, was Chen Huanrong's eldest son. In 1871 Chen Cihong was dispatched by his father to Bangkok to establish a permanent presence with two firms, each of which used the old-style romanization Hong or "trading company" to describe them. In Bangkok,

Chen Cihong's rice firms competed well with others that emerged as merchant contenders along the banks of Bangkok's Chao Phraya River, at that time called the Menam.

A river location was chosen in order to facilitate the arrival of unhusked paddy rice grown by Siamese farmers in areas beyond the city but transported by small boats owned by itinerant Chinese paddy dealers to the mill. Once processed, the rice was then shipped out by junks and steamers to markets in Singapore and China. Chen Cihong introduced modern steam-powered mechanized milling that proved more efficient than old-style hand milling, a transition that had begun before his arrival by Western companies. In 1877 the British consul in Siam noted, "Up until very recently foreigners were the sole owners of rice-cleaning mills, which also until very lately have been highly remunerative. Now however, the indefatigable Chinese were setting up mills, and they are not only the principal owners of rice milled at the European mills, but likewise enter into arrangements in regard to freight, insurance and other matters with their owners, and change in such transactions must be a loss to the Europeans" (quoted in Skinner, 1957: 103–4). At first the Chinese employed Scottish engineers to run the mills, but these men were soon replaced by well-trained Chinese engineers from the Guangzhou region of Guangdong province. The exasperated British consul lamented, "It is impossible under the conditions of trade prevailing in the East for the European to compete with the astute Chinaman in this particular [the rice] business." Within a short period, Sino-Thai firms commanded the European markets, especially as rice mills now ran day and night in order to maximize profit on their investments and to meet burgeoning demand. Chen Cihong's brothers established associated branch firms of Kintyelung—Tan Seng Lee, later called Tan Guan Lee, in Singapore and Saigon; Kien Guan Lee in Annam, today's south Vietnam; and Tan Wan Lee in Shantou, China—as components in a diversified business network that came to involve insurance, banking, remittances, tobacco, hotels, and other real estate (Choi, 1998: 30).

With milling rice and the importing and exporting of a range of commodities and products at the core of their business, each of the firms had both an English name and a name using Chinese characters. The most famous of the two firms was called in English Chop Wong Li, a name derived from Chen Hong Li Hong, "Chen [Ci]hong's prosperous (*li*) Hong (*hang*)." Over time, this name was transformed into Wanglee, which was the "account name" used for business purposes by Chen Cihong in his early business dealings in Bangkok, eventually supplanting Kintyelung, the original name for the firm used by his father in Hong Kong. Wanglee is used today as both the surname for the Thai family as well as the name of the family's holding company in Bangkok.

The Wanglee Mansion

What is known today as the Wanglee mansion was built by Chen Cihong in 1881 based on a design similar to that of the family of his sixteen-year-old wife from the genteel Posayanont family. While the ancestry of the Posayanonts was Chinese and they maintained a two-storey riverside home that evoked Chinese architectural styles, they considered themselves Siamese and maintained close relations with the court. Chen Cihong, who at the time still sported a queue and had a wife and family back in China, established relationships because of his marriage to Miss Nu that helped the family business to thrive. In 1908, when Arnold Wright's *Twentieth Century Impressions of Siam* was published, the home was noted as "the residence of Tan Lip Buoy," one of Chen Cihong's four sons since his father by then had returned to his native village and family in China, where he built an even more extensive residence, which is shown on pages 262–7. In the first decades of the twentieth century, the descendants of Chen Cihong played key pioneering roles in many of Siam's nascent but vitally important businesses—rice trading, shipping, banking, insurance, and later real estate—emerging over time as one of the country's most prominent élite business dynasties. Today, in its fifth generation, the Wanglee family enjoys a reputation in Thailand similar to that of the Rockefellers in America less than a century ago.

The Wanglee Mansion is a two-storey *sanheyuan*-style U-shaped structure along the west bank of the river. As with other mansions

Above Although this back corner room has not yet been restored, the spiral wooden staircase leading to the second floor is clearly the room's visual and utilitarian focus.

Below Located at the end of the veranda outside the ancestral hall, this entryway leads to one of the family's apartments on the second floor. On the left is a recessed cabinet in the wall with the entry centered within a wooden divide with glassed shelves and storage space behind carved wooden doors.

built at the time facing the river, it sat amidst commercial/industrial buildings needed to process unhusked grain and transport milled rice. At the center of the outer wall is an impressive recessed gate with polychromatic ornamentation along the roofline and walls. The high gables that rise atop the pair of end walls are ornamented in a fashion reminiscent of the Wang Derm palace residences. The central courtyard is ringed by rooms on the first level and a gallery on the second floor that open into bedrooms and other family spaces. In the rear of the second level, behind a beautiful set of door panels, is the Wanglee ancestral shrine. As is the custom in other Thai homes, the floors are made of polished teak. Throughout 2008–9 the mansion underwent extensive renovation, not only to restore the magnificence of the exterior ornamentation but also to grapple with solutions to the recurring problem of flooding that had destabilized the walls.

TRAN FAMILY HOME

HOI AN, VIETNAM

1802

Eighteenth- and early nineteenth-century visitors to the port of Faifo, the name commonly used then for Hoi An, regularly commented on the views from the granite hills of the town with its temples, grottos, and sturdy homes. While John Crawfurd described Faifo as having a single street with some 600 Chinese families that swelled to a Chinese population of "not less than ten thousand ... during the season of the junks," the town was actually larger than this (1828: 286ff). At the time, there were two long lanes parallel to the river and several cross streets, each of which was lined with narrow, elongated shophouses, merchant houses, and godowns. Even today, the façades, rooflines, and building plots of this area at the historic core of Hoi An are much as they were two centuries ago. The Phung Hung residence, described next, is an example of the type noted by Crawfurd as being "built of stone and lime, and very neatly and substantially roofed with tile."

Crawfurd and his party strangely seem to have missed noticing more expansive homes some 150 meters away from the river that were built behind walled enclosures. One such home, which had been built in 1802 and still stands, was the residence of Tran Tu Nhuc. Tran, whose surname in Chinese is rendered as Chen, had served as an emissary to China, appointed by the southern Nguyen emperor Gia Long, who himself was noted for his acceptance of Confucian orthodoxy and who built a grand Chinese-style palace in Hue. Nothing specific is known of the ancestors of Tran Tu Nhuc, except that they migrated from China a hundred years before.

Had Crawfurd visited Tran's residence, he would have noted both the grandeur of its overall scale as well as the simplicity of its layout, especially in comparison with the architecture of buildings near the river. The succession of its rooms and the elegance of its furnishings mark the residence as that of a cultured man. Tran Tu Nhuc's residence includes both family living rooms as well as a formal space to honor the ancestors of the Tran lineage. Descriptive literature prepared for visitors today usually describes the building as the Tran family "chapel"

or "shrine," somewhat downplaying the residential function of the structure without recognizing that the ancestral altar room—"chapel" or "shrine"—is a common component of Chinese residences.

The residence sits behind an ochre-colored wall on the corner of Le Loi and Phan Chu Trinh Streets where a gate leads to a large paved courtyard studded with areas of mature trees and other plantings. Structurally, the building has a triple-bay frame with post-and-beam construction that lifts the roof structure of purlins, rafters, and roof tiles between the masonry walls on both ends. The timber columns are unadorned and only minimal carvings embellish the upper portions of the wooden framework.

No section of the building is given more prominence than the reception hall, whose full wall of lattice door panels spatially links it with the entry courtyard. While access to the building today is through a narrow alcove painted blue to the right of the lattice panels, the triple set of lattice panels once served as "doorways": those on the left traditionally were used by men, the right by women, and the central section only opened during the lunar New Year called Tet and during other festivals when ancestors were invited to return home. Today, this reception room is furnished with blackwood chairs and tables with one set in a Western fashion and another in a Chinese formal order. Engraved horizontal boards, calligraphy, porcelain vases, and assorted objects collected by the family are displayed on the walls and tables. The recessed Tran (Chen) ancestral hall is rather modest in size yet includes the full range of ritual paraphernalia commonly associated with them: censer, candles, offerings, and ancestral tablets. Beyond the altar area is a shed-like roof supported by Western-style columns that leads to the back or inner garden with potted plants, much of which is raised and framed by a stone retaining wall. Approximately half of what was once the residence is used today as a shop selling Vietnamese handicrafts and souvenirs, and thus it is not possible to understand well how the structure functioned once as a family home.

Above left On the left back wall is a series of lattice panels that open out to the front garden.

Above right Just opposite the previous image, this is a formal sitting area in the reception hall.

Right Here, in an alcove off the reception hall, is the Tran (Chen) ancestral altar.

PHUNG HUNG
RESIDENCE

HOI AN, VIETNAM

Late 18th or Early 19th Century

Located on Nguyen Thi Minh Khai Street a few steps from the Japanese covered bridge, which is said to date from the 1600s, the Phun Hung residence is a two-storey, triple-bay wooden structure with masonry sidewalls. A carved veranda or balcony overhangs the recessed entryway, a characteristic feature of shophouses/terrace houses where wooden panels can be removed so that goods inside can be displayed for sale.

After entering the front doorway, it is possible to see deep into the building. While the height of the ceilings is relatively low on both levels, at the center of the house is a double-height covered atrium with light streaming in from several directions, as well as a balustrade passageway around the upper storey. Steep stairs in the rear of the building lead to the second floor, an area of relatively unadorned woodwork—columns, beams, door panels, transoms, soffits, and shutters. Much of the second floor is an open area that functions not only as a family sitting area but also as the site for family ritual. Two altars are located here in association with this large room; one, which functions as an ancestral altar, is to the side, while the other is a deity altar that is mounted high below the rafters. On one edge of one room is a perforated trapdoor-like panel inserted in the floor, which can be removed to hoist large pieces of furniture and other large items from below. Openings of this sort also are used during periods of flooding, including in September 2009 when the river overflowed due to the ravages of a typhoon that poured three meters of water into the historic homes, in order to quickly move furniture and other goods to a dry area.

Above Profusely ornamented with carved calligraphic boards, paintings, and lanterns, the ground floor of the Phung Hong house is set to welcome visitors.

Below left The two-storey, triple-bay Phung Hong house is a typical pre-modern shophouse-cum-residence.

Below center Adjacent to the atrium, with its streaming shafts of sunlight, the upper storey is relatively bright.

Below right The view along the upstairs veranda, with its over-hanging roofline, looks toward the portal of the Japanese covered bridge.

Above It is not clear whether the mother-of-pearl inlaid furniture was made locally or imported from China.

Right Running from front to back, the upstairs area is open, serving not only as a sitting area but also as a place for regular ritual.

DIEP DONG NGUYEN HOUSE

HOI AN, VIETNAM

Late 19th Century

Built in the late nineteenth century by Diep Dong Nguyen, a Chinese merchant about whom little is known, the front ground floor room of this residence once served as a dispensary for Chinese medicines, called *thuoc bac* in Vietnamese. Glass-enclosed cases lining the walls were used to store the covered jars and boxes filled with a cornucopia of dried herbs, woody plants, and animal parts. Today, the shelves hold the owner's collection of blue-and-white porcelain and other objects and the space is organized as a sitting room rather than as a shop. An altar at the front pays homage to the Three Stellar Gods, Fu, Lu, and Shou, while wall hangings and calligraphy are all Chinese.

The upstairs rooms, which were the private space for the family, include Western elements, such as colonial-era lamp fixtures and windows, in addition to a display of the collection of Chinese antiques of the current owner. Two altars are also found upstairs, one focusing on the early immigrant forebears of the lineage and the other recently deceased family members who are commemorated with photographs. Nearby also is a commodious study with bookcases and a desk accompanied by art objects and photographs.

Above This room, just inside the entry, was once the dispensary for a Chinese medicine shop but now serves as a space to display the owner's antiques.

Left Painted in a blue pastel color and embellished with two pairs of intersecting lozenges and paper ornaments, the façade is clearly in Chinese style.

Right With colonial-era light fixtures and paneling, the living room is outfitted with Chinese furniture and ornamentation.

Above With photographs of deceased family members and other remembrances on the walls, this is the family's library.

Below Two adjacent altars are found in this upstairs room. The one on the left commemorates those early forebears who came from China, while the one on the right recalls more recently deceased relatives.

AN HIEN GARDEN HOME

HUE, VIETNAM

Circa 1880

Hue, the former imperial capital of Vietnam, is well known for its palaces and tombs as well as its well-preserved homes, many of which are set within extensive gardens that date at least to the nineteenth century. As with house–garden compounds in China, the buildings, vegetation, and rockeries are designed as integrated components of a complex. Based upon principles of Chinese *fengshui*, called *Phong thuy* in Vietnamese, there is an interplay between the buildings and their environs with both geometric and asymmetric aspects.

One of the best known garden homes in Hue is called An Hien or "Cloud Pavilion," the translation of the Chinese characters that are inscribed on the imposing gate leading to the house that announces its location near Hue's Perfume River (Huong Giang). Covering over 4600 square meters, the garden includes plantings of flowers and herbs as well as trees in addition to ponds, walkways, and walls. The single-storey residence in the garden was built around 1880 for the eighteenth daughter of Emperor Duc Duc and thus is generally viewed as having a royal provenance, but ownership and occupancy over the past hundred years have been in many hands. Solid columns set on stone bases lift the extended eaves and the wooden framework. Within the home, the central area is reserved for an ancestral altar, but beyond this area on both sides the furnishings are sparse and space is used flexibly.

Above Near the center of the garden is this single-storey structure, which includes not only the family's ancestral altar but also bedrooms and sitting rooms.

Right A corner of the An Hien garden house.

Opposite Dominating the principal building in the An Hien garden house is the ancestral altar for the lineage of the current occupant.

SYQUIA MANSION

VIGAN, PHILIPPINES

1830

Below Viewed from two angles along the street, it is clear that the overhang on the second floor, which is supported in part by braces and is called a "flying gallery," is lined from end to end with sliding *kapis* shell panels that are opaque on the outside but translucent from the inside.

Right The *sala* or drawing room, with a large portrait of Gregorio Syquia hanging at one end of the room above a Chinese chest. A portrait of his great-granddaughter Victoria is set on an easel.

The Ilocos region along the northwestern coast of Luzon in the northern Philippines is only 700 kilometers from the coastal ports of Fujian and 400 kilometers from Manila. While Hispanic antiquarianism has helped shape the contemporary public perception of Vigan, the region's most important town, as a veritable museum of Spanish colonial culture, the area actually has a rich precolonial history with extensive links to China. According to a thirteenth-century Chinese chronicle, seafaring traders and pirates from coastal China crossed the South China Sea to the Philippines in their flat-bottomed junks to barter manufactured goods such as porcelain, iron censers, colored glass beads, and iron needles for commodities such as pearls, beeswax, betel nuts, and animal skins (Chau, 1911: 160).

It is not certain when Chinese actually settled in Vigan. While local authors today claim that this occurred well before the arrival of the Spanish, there is insufficient historical evidence to confirm such assertions. What is certain is that when Chinese actually settled in Vigan during the Spanish period, they married local women and raised children who were physically and culturally mestizo. The mixing of Chinese and Ilocano cultures pervades Vigan. One example can be cited here: clay jars for storing water and foodstuffs that are still made today resemble traditional indigenous vessels but are fashioned as they have been for several centuries using potters' wheels, a clear Chinese influence. Prior to the arrival of Chinese settlers and craftsmen, locals used the simpler paddle-and-anvil method of pottery making.

In 1572 the Spanish conquistador Juan de Salcedo was sent to northern Luzon to establish a base at Ciudad Fernandina before occupying the strategically sited trading settlement at Vigan, then an island detached from the mainland with easy access to the mountainous hinterland by three rivers. Following the *Leyes de Indias* (Laws of the Indies) promulgated by King Philip of Spain in 1573, Vigan was laid out in a rectilinear checkerboard pattern of parallel streets focusing on a Plaza Mayor, a central open space, with a church, an archbishop's residence, a school, and public offices ranged around it. Houses were to be built with courtyards, attention to airflow, and sufficient space to stable horses and other animals. A succession of increasingly substantial churches attests to the growing importance of the town. The imposing St Paul Vigan Cathedral seen today was built between 1790 and 1800. In addition to ornamentation, such as Fu dogs carved above its doorway, that suggests Chinese influences, the cathedral is graced with a pagoda-like bell tower adjacent to it.

Sangleys and Family Life

While the tourism industry and mass media writers refer to sections of Vigan as "colonial" and "Hispanic" neighborhoods, earlier in the twentieth century the same areas were referred to as Kasanglayan—"Where the Sangley live"—or Kamestizoan—"Where the Chinese mestizos live." *Sangley*, a Spanish term used to describe those of pure Chinese ancestry, was derived from a Chinese term variously accepted as *changlai* ("frequent visitor"), *shanglü* ("traveling merchant"), or *shengyi* ("trade" or "business"). For much of the Spanish colonial period, the *sangley*, who were also called *chino* by the Spanish, were thought to be immune to conversion to Catholicism and other aspects of Hispanic culture, unlike the more receptive indigenous people. While this led initially to cultural pluralism as an element of colonial policy in which there were distinct communities of Spaniards, Chinese *sangley*, and native *indio*, over time the differences became less distinct. During the Spanish colonial period, this tiered system of legal classification of different "races" was used for purposes of administration and taxation. *Sangley* artisans and merchants, in particular, "filled occupations which the Spanish scorned and for which the *indios* were believed unsuited" (Wickberg, 1965: 8). *Sangley*, as well as travelling merchants from China, also played increasing roles in the lucrative China–Manila–Mexico galleon trading system, which was inaugurated in 1565 and continued into the early nineteenth century. Luxury goods like porcelain, ivory, silk, precious stones, copper cash, mercury, and lacquerware from China, as well as spices from the Nanyang, the Southern Seas, were aggregated at Manila and then carried in galleons across the Pacific to Acapulco on

Mexico's west coast. The sailing routes depended upon favorable winds for voyages that spanned a four-month period. From Mexico the goods were carried overland to Vera Cruz for transshipment by sea, first to Cuba, and then across the Atlantic Ocean to Spain in annual treasure ships. In exchange, vast quantities of Mexican and Peruvian silver were transported via the Philippines to China. To facilitate this trade, the number of Chinese living in the Philippines, not counting transient merchants and traders, increased from forty to more than 15,000 by the beginning of the seventeenth century (Schurz, 1939: 27). By the end of the eighteenth century, Vigan was a thriving port as part of a trading network involving China, Nanyang, and Manila with a reach to both the Old and New Worlds.

Throughout the eighteenth and nineteenth centuries, the boundaries separating Spaniards, some of whom were actually of Mexican descent, Chinese *sangley*, and native *indio* increasingly became blurred because of intermarriage and conversion. Accompanying these transformations was the rise of both pure Chinese and hispanized Chinese mestizos to economic and social prominence. Assimilation was an ongoing process in which Chinese, Spanish, and indigenous elements created a Philippine culture quite unlike the process elsewhere in Southeast Asia where Chinese migrated. According to Edgar Wickberg, a principal scholar of Chinese life during the colonial period, "Culturally, the mestizo was unique. Unlike the *baba* of Malaya or the *peranakan* of Java, the Chinese mestizo in the Philippines was not a special kind of local Chinese. He was a special kind of Filipino. The law identified him as such and so did he. The legal identification with the Philippines was automatic upon birth; he was not required to disassociate himself with China upon reaching majority; indeed, the reverse was the case. It took a special effort for a mestizo to identify himself with China, an effort the majority did not wish to make, given the mestizo cultural outlook" (1965: 31). Indeed, by the beginning of the twentieth century, a distinct form of Filipino culture emerged as a declaration of national identification.

Spanish Catholicism was the catalyst for restructuring cultural patterns, with baptism and marriage together being the principal steps towards assimilation. Mestizo children of mixed parentage were usually raised by their devout Catholic mothers as hispanized Catholics, with less and less identification with China. It was common for a *mestiza*, a

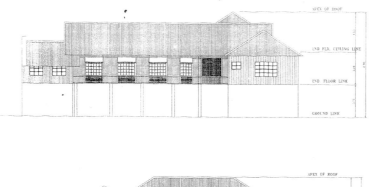

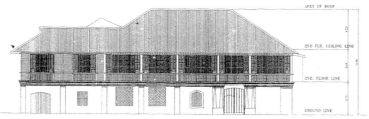

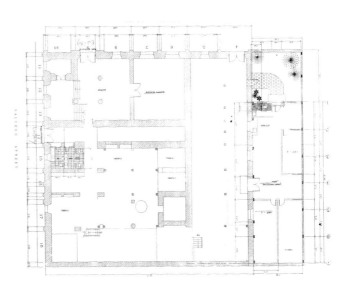

daughter of a mixed marriage, to marry a *sangley* just as her mother had done. Once Chinese *sangley* had converted to Catholicism—conversions that were often nominal in intent but quite practical—they moved freely throughout the archipelago. Moreover, as the Spanish spurred the development of agriculture, manufacturing, and commerce, Chinese immigration continued to grow substantially. By the middle of the nineteenth century, exports to China from all over the archipelago included mother-of-pearl, tortoiseshell, ebony, rice, birds' nests, salted fish, and black pepper, in addition to sugar, tobacco, coffee, and the fiber plant abacá.

It was in this context that the Syquia family and their residence took shape in Vigan in the nineteenth century, with the blending of cultures evidenced not only in the name Syquia itself but also in the form and furnishings of their large home. To some in the Philippines and beyond, the name Syquia, along with surnames such as Singson, Crislogos, Tanjuatco, Ongpin, Limjap, and Yangco, is loosely Spanish sounding, but each underwent transformation from an actual Chinese name to one that is vaguely Hispanic. Many such families thus were able to transform their identities and blur their heritage via the recasting of their names, conversion to Catholicism, and marriage.

Thus, it is not surprising that there it is usually difficult to trace back clearly the family history of a *sangley*. It is a historical curiosity of great significance that what we know of the life of Vicente Romero Syquia, the progenitor of the Syquia family in Vigan, is provided only through sketchy evidence found after his death in a case argued before the United States Supreme Court in 1913, which was on appeal from the Supreme Court of the Philippine Islands, then an American colony.

Born in 1822 in an unknown place called Am Thau in the environs of Xiamen, the port city then generally called by foreigners Amoy, Sy Qui Ah, as he was initially known, left home for the Philippines in 1812. At first he lived with relatives in the Binondo area of Manila where he worked as a salesman and clerk. Sometime before 1852, he moved to Vigan, where, according to the official court record, he "entered the service of a merchant at an annual salary of 200 pesos." During that year, he was converted to the Catholic faith and was baptized in the parish church as a condition of marriage to Petronila. His full Chinese name, Sy Qui Ah, was transformed into Vicente Romero Sy Quia, with a concomitant makeover of his identity. The next year, he married Petronila, "the banns being regularly published and the marriage public-ly solemnized according to the rites of the church, as a preliminary to which he affirmed under oath, and the civil and ecclesiastical authorities certified, after inquiry, that he was then unmarried. Shortly after the marriage, he and Petronila took up their permanent home in Manila. They were then without any particular property other than 5,000 pesos which she received from her mother and brought into the conjugal society. He became a merchant, and, through their united efforts, they

accumulated real and personal property amounting at the time of his death to upwards of 600,000 pesos" (US Supreme Court, 1913: 228/337).

The middle name of Petronila Singson Encarnacion, said to have been a member of one of Vigan's aristocratic families, suggests that she also had Chinese blood, but even less is known of her than of her husband. They had three sons and two daughters. After Vicente died intestate in Manila in 1894, his property was distributed in 1900 to his widow, sons, and grandsons.

The possibility of an overlapping life for Vicente Romero Sy Quia, otherwise known as Sy Qui Ah, the poor Chinese immigrant who achieved financial and social success, was revealed in a 1905 lawsuit brought by individuals who claimed to be his Chinese grandsons, granddaughter, and great-grandson. They asserted that Sy Qui Ah had married their mother, Yap Puan Niu, who had died in 1891, in 1847 when he returned for a visit to his home village near Xiamen. They alleged that Sy Qui Ah, in fact, had stayed with their mother in China for three or four years, which was sufficient time to father two sons. Witnesses from the home village in China testified to the marriage and the children. However, others offered conflicting testimony that Sy Qui Ah had been in the Philippines during this time. A peculiar aspect of the case was that "Yap Puan Niu, the alleged Chinese wife, visited in Manila at the home of a brother of Sy Qui Ah twice during the life of the latter, and second, because two of the plaintiffs were adults living in Manila at the time of Sy Quia's death and during the eleven years intervening before the suit was brought" (US Supreme Court, 1913: 228/337–8). Ultimately, the US Supreme Court affirmed the Philippine decision, which went against the case presented by the plaintiffs. As the court decreed, "the lips of Sy Quia and Yap Puan Niu had been sealed by death" and thus there was no way to clarify the possible ambiguities in the life of a Chinese immigrant who indeed may have maintained links, perhaps even marital ties, with his home village while subsequently accommodating himself to the precepts of the Roman Catholic Church and the life of a man of wealth in his adopted country. In fact, similar tales of the complex family relationships with multiple wives, questions of paternity by children spread over vast territories, and contestation by reputed heirs are recurrent themes in the

narratives of Chinese migrants throughout Southeast Asia. However, it is a rare case that is disclosed and adjudicated before the US Supreme Court with American notions of familial practices dominating.

The home or homes occupied by Vicente and Petronila Sy Quia remain undiscovered, but that of their son Gregorio and his family is well known now as the Syquia mansion in Vigan. Built in 1830 by Justo Angco, whose surname also suggests Chinese ancestry, this magnificent residence was given as a dowry gift to his daughter Estefania when she wed Gregorio Syquia in 1875. Considered a cultured family, the Syquias fitted the old home with refined furnishings that reflected their affluence at the time from landholdings and businesses. As an astute businessman, Gregorio was able to increase his family fortune significantly. No longer considered a *mestizo de sangley*, he did not speak Chinese but only Spanish and the local Ilocano language. It is said that he was such a "loyal Spanish subject that he received the Isabela la Catolica medal, an honor awarded to subjects who have contributed greatly to the honor and grandeur of Spain" (Pacis, 206: 119). At the end of the nineteenth century, the family apparently still practiced some Chinese rituals even as they were observant Catholics. When Vicente Syquia, who had been born in China, died in 1894, his grandson Tomas "donned the nine silk suits that were later placed on the corpse of his grandfather, in accordance with Chinese funeral custom" (Chu, 2005: 75–6).

The home passed eventually to Tomas Syquia, whose daughter Alicia Syquia married Elpidio Quirino, son of an impoverished jailkeeper in 1921. Elpidio Quirino, a lawyer who rose from positions in local politics in Ilocus Sur to national politics as Secretary of Finance, Secretary of the Interior, and Secretary of Foreign Affairs, became Vice-President of the Philippines in 1946. He was catapulted to the presidency in 1948 upon the unexpected death of the incumbent president and served as the sixth President of the Philippines from 1948 to 1953. Because he and his wife used the Syquia mansion as their home during their marriage, the residence is often mistakenly referred to as President Quirino's ancestral home. While the serial occupation by related families suggests that the appellation Angco–Syquia–Quirino is more precise, the Syquia mansion is accepted as its name today. The residence is still occupied by descendants who have preserved it as a family heritage site, with furnishings and memorabilia that include items related to Vicente Syquia, who never lived in the house; Gregoria Syquia, who gained it as a residence through marriage; and Elpidio Quirino, who occupied it with his wife well before he became president.

The Syquia Mansion

The Syquia mansion, a 180-year-old home that has been continuously occupied by related families, is layered with a multiplicity of architectural and ornamental influences—indigenous, Chinese, Spanish, Filipino, and even American—of sufficient complexity that they must be treated together. Prior to the arrival of Chinese and Spanish settlement, archetypical dwellings throughout the archipelago, whether along the rivers or in the cordillera, were built of wooden poles and bamboo strips with thatched roofs. Usually rather box-like in shape and comprising a square frame tied to posts, this indigenous form, and its variants, was quite small. While Chinese and Spanish settlers preferred solid structures built of mortared brick or stone, they found merit in the form of lighter and airier indigenous homes that were elevated above the ground. This is not only because such houses were built in settlements near streams where flooding occurred or where water tables were high, but also to reduce potential damage during earthquakes. Augusto Villalón points out that the simpler older form and the apparently more complex newer form, called *bahay no bato* or "house of stone," were "in essence ... the same structure enlarged and dressed in different clothing" (2003: 210). Both

Far left An alcove with a sitting area adjacent to the *sala*. A bedroom is seen in the rear.

Left A sideboard cabinet.

included a lower storey and an upper storey, with the elevated space used for daily living while the space beneath was employed for storage, the stabling of animals, and sometimes business.

Smaller *bahay no bato*, such as those found in Vigan, sometimes use freestanding tree trunks within the walls to lift a second floor. Between the wooden posts, curtain wall infilling utilizes stone or bricks. Because of the substantial mass of the Syquia mansion, in addition to outer lower walls some 94 cm thick, brick and cement posts coated with lime plaster are employed to support the great expanses in the rooms above. The second-storey structure, with 76-cm-thick walls, overhangs the heavy mortared walls beneath, with a series of 14-cm posts spaced along the length of the walls.

The ground floor area is cool throughout the day, not only because of the thick walls but also the stone flooring of roughly cut granite blocks. Transported to Vigan as ballast on Chinese junks arriving from Fujian, granite of this type is still referred to as *piedra china* or "Chinese stone" in the Philippines. This entry-level area provides suitable utilitarian spaces for a stone well, stable for horses, and garage for carriages and automobiles, as well as storage for all kinds of bulky items. The exterior walls at ground level are pierced with four large windows secured with ornamental metal grilles and wooden shutters, in addition to three street-level doorways. The main entry is through an arched opening in a pair of heavy wooden doors into an area usually referred to with the Spanish word *zaguan*, an open vestibule that leads to formal stairs to the second floor. In some residences, the generous ground floor space was used for a shop or an office in addition to domestic utility, but this does not seem to have been the case at any time with the Syquia home. One large room on the ground floor of the mansion today serves as a museum of artifacts owned once by President Quirino. Here are found a massive bookcase, a gaming table covered with green felt that seats seven, framed news clippings, photographs, and other memorabilia from his career. The *zaguan* opens in the rear to a rectangular courtyard with the overhanging second floor rooms supported by timbers. While today uncluttered and with a bit of greenery, this open area was originally used as a spot to store fodder for horses, collect manure, and accumulate rainwater in a cistern. Overall, the ground floor, including enclosed and open spaces, covers approximately 2000 square meters.

The J-shaped stairway to the main residential floor above rises with two flights: first, one of three steps entered through a lobate arch to a landing covered with glazed tile, after which one turns to make a steep climb. The landing area is especially bright because of the presence of a pair of windows opening to the street. Casual visitors usually were received on this landing and did not have an invitation to actually enter the residence beyond. The second, longer, and broader staircase ascends from the landing, slowly revealing to visitors the grandeur of the home it leads towards. Flanked by balusters made of hardwood, the wooden stairway is a grand accent whether one is entering or leaving the home. At the head of the stairs is a pair of solid newel posts with a tracery pattern of overlapping circles in the register above the encircling balusters. The successive use of stone, tile, and then wood from the streetside entry to the home above creates a welcoming sequence for visitors as they move from public space to the family's private quarters.

Wood is the dominant material used on the second level. Flooring throughout is deep rose-colored narra wood that has been polished to a beautiful sheen. The partitions between the rooms are constructed of sawn timber arranged vertically and supported by horizontal chair rails. Each of the doorways linking adjacent rooms is set off as a wooden unit with a hinged door; some have a hemispheric light at the top. Carved open wooden fretwork with floral and geometric patterns forms the upper register of all of the interior walls in order to facilitate the circulation of air within the house. The abundance of high-quality wooden furniture and the earth tones of the draperies combine to accentuate the naturalistic feel of the residence.

The space at the top of the stairs is, in effect, a sizeable parlor that functions as an *antesala*, a prologue not only to the larger formal *sala* or drawing room but also to other adjacent rooms entered through broad doorways: drawing room, dining room, five bedrooms, bathrooms, kitchen, pantry, informal eating area, as well as a second floor courtyard and a chapel. Given the number of chairs and their grouping in the *antesala*, this room at the core of the residence functioned well to accommodate large gatherings who then could spread into the adjoining areas. Because the elaborately carved straight-back, rocking, and reclining chairs in this room are made of narra hardwood with woven cane (*solihiya*) surfaces, they are quite cool to sit on.

Dominating one wall of the room is a very large, but not full-scale, reproduction of *Spolarium*, a vivid allegorical painting by Juan Luna y Novicio (1857–99), which national hero José Rizal used to reference the maltreatment of Filipinos during the colonial period through the gruesome spectacle of mortally wounded or dead gladiators in the Roman coliseum. The original, which is seven by four meters in size,

Top This chest, with carved images of junks and pagodas as well as a floral frame, was made in Fujian.

Above left This statue of a saint, which is found in the chapel, has a painted porcelain head with a Chinese face and is said to have been made by a Chinese artisan.

Above right A brass vase with a curling dragon motif brought from China.

Below The master bedroom containing this ornate double bed plus an *aparador* (armoire) on the left and a dressing table on the right.

won a gold medal at Madrid's Exposición Nacional de Bellas Artes in 1884. Today, the original painting occupies an entire wall in the National Museum of the Philippines. This shocking and emotional painting is considered an iconic expression of late nineteenth-century colonial suffering in the Philippines, and is a call to express outrage at injustices.

Double doors with sag draperies connect the *antesala* with the *sala*. Furnishings in the drawing room include nineteenth-century Filipino pieces as well as more modern furniture in European style from the early twentieth century. The pegged floorboards in this room are especially wide. Along the front walls is a pair of large Venetian mirrors hung between the three windows facing the street, similar to those seen in Malacca and Singapore Peranakan homes. Marble-topped side tables called *consolas* and wall sconces hold a variety of molded statues. Along one wall is a large camphorwood chest, a type typically produced in Fujian, the province where Vicente Syquia was born. The chest is ringed with a floral pattern that highlights a scene of a tiered pagoda and a pair of seagoing junks, each with a flared bow, high stern, double masts, and "dragon eyes" along the sides, a style which is typical of Fujian province. A large portrait of Gregorio Syquia hangs at one end of the room above the Chinese chest, while a portrait of his wife Estefano faces him on the opposite wall. A portrait of their great-granddaughter Victoria is set on an easel nearby. After the death of her mother by the Japanese, Victoria assisted her father as the Philippine First Lady at the age of sixteen when he became President of the country.

Beyond this room is a smaller one that is replete with images of family members, including the progenitor of the family, Vicente Syquia. With his black cap and blue robe, he is dressed as he might have been when he arrived in the Philippines from China. It is not clear from the image whether he still had a queue, the braided hanging hairstyle at the back of the head worn by Chinese during the Manchu dynasty. Nor is it known whether he cut his queue when he was baptized a Catholic and was embraced by a genteel Vigan family.

One of the most elegant rooms in the residence is the brightly lit dining room, a long room with a rectangular table called a *comedor* that seats eighteen. Matching side chairs along the walls suggest that several more guests could be accommodated comfortably at the table when necessary. With a highly polished wooden floor, brown accents on the walls, earth tone draperies, and sumptuously carved hardwood furnishings, the room is stylish and welcoming. The dining room is well ventilated from the outside with windows along opposite walls as well. Five wooden display cabinets with dishes, glassware, silverware, and bric-a-brac are aligned along one wall, with three others along the opposite wall. At some point, and still seen today, two *punkah* cloth fans were suspended above the table. Known to the Arabs as early as the eighth century, *punkah* fans were common in the tropical areas of the British Empire. In the nineteenth century, their popularity spread to East Asia and even the southern sections of the United States. The nearby kitchen in the Syquia mansion was clearly suitable for preparing food for a large dinner party.

An *oratorio*, a private chapel for use by family members, focuses on three assemblages of figures encased in elaborate wooden cases. The central assemblage depicts the Holy Family, Virgin Mary, St Joseph, and Jesus as a child, the one on the left the stoning of St Stephen, who was the first martyr, and the single woman on the right is the Virgin Mary. In front of these objects of devotion are three kneeling chairs, called *reclinatorios*, which are used for private prayer, along with candlestick holders, lanterns, flowers, and other devotional items are arrayed around the room.

Adjacent to both an informal dining area and the *sala* is an *azotea*, a terrace covered with terracotta tiles, which was built atop the roof of the ground floor *zaguan*. Surrounded by an abundance of potted plants aligned along the walls, with a white water fountain at its center, this area maintains a visual connection with the adjoining rooms through trellised openings, and is especially welcoming as a place to enjoy when shade arrives at different times during the day. Here also laundry could be dried and children could play. In the evening, guests could gather here to cool off before dinner and then return afterwards to enjoy the view of the stars in the nighttime sky.

When *bahay na bato*, such as the Syquia residence, were constructed during the first half of the nineteenth century, influences were essentially limited to those from China and derived from Spanish colonial inter-actions in Latin America in addition to underlying indigenous vernacular traditions in this Ilocos region of the Philippines. However, by the late nineteenth century and continuing into the initial decades of the twentieth century, fashions and innovations from throughout the world found their way into the homes of the affluent, even in small towns such as Vigan. During the last thirty years of the nineteenth century, indeed, there was a veritable "carnival of Neo-styles" being adopted by wealthy families, with revivalist notions making it possible for "Renaissance lilies and scrolls [to] curl on the spandrels of Gothic arches in a room lit by Chinese-inspired panels" (Zialcita and Tinio, 1980: 157). These additions brought about curious juxtapositions, especially in terms of furniture, objets d'art, and curios, but also in how ventilation panels were carved,

window grilles were fashioned, electric fixtures were hung, and modern plumbing was installed. In the early twentieth century, window glass sometimes replaced *kapis* shells, and sheets of tin and iron with ornate patterns pressed into them, which were the rage in America and Europe, found their way into renovated old homes in Vigan.

As elsewhere in the Philippines, the Syquia mansion makes use of a modified double-wall system that overhangs both sides of the house that face the streets. Called a *galería volada* or "flying gallery," this cantilevered feature not only shades the interior from the sun but its openings help regulate the flow of air into and out of the house. Thus, the *galería volada* provides both insulation from the outside heat and ventilation between inside and outside. When viewed from streetside, the panels and openings of the façade appear opaque, but from inside they are fundamentally transformed to a bright, light, and airy appearance. This is because the structure and form of the outer wall comprises balusters or metal grillwork as well as sliding solid panels and lattice windows called *ventanas* fitted with flat *kapis*, also spelled *capis*, shells that create a translucent screen of shimmering light-filtering squares. *Kapis* shells are obtained from the *Placuna placenta*, a bivalve with remarkably flattened, paper-like outer surfaces, that are collected from the shallow bays and coves along the coastal waters surrounding the Philippines. Although there are references in the literature to the fact that translucent shells have a long history of use in China, I have not found them in any of the homes I have visited there. Below the sliding *kapis* window panels of many old homes are *ventanilla*, sliding panels that are opened for ventilation purposes. In the Syquia home, either a row of balusters or open metalwork and solid panels secured these floor level openings.

During the Spanish colonial era in the Philippines, many of the towns in the Philippines were redesigned and rebuilt with elements that expressed an imported European heritage that comingled with Chinese and indigenous influences. Vigan, the third largest town after Manila and Cebu during these centuries, however, is the only such settlement that has retained its traditional morphology and atmosphere. Here, in the Ilocano region, is found the greatest concentration of *bahay na bato* residences, a majority of which were built by Chinese mestizo families who gained wealth through marriage and enterprise. Many of these houses, including the Syquia mansion, are imposing structures that proclaim not only affluence but also the fusing of global and local influences.

Above With its highly polished wooden floor, brown accents on the walls, earth tone draperies, and sumptuously carved hardwood furnishings, the brightly lit and well-ventilated dining room was undoubtedly a center for entertaining. The room is dominated by a rectangular table called a *comedor* that seats eighteen. Wooden display cabinets for dishes, glassware, silverware, and bric-a-brac are arrayed at both ends.

Right The second floor courtyard, called an *azotia*, is adjacent to an informal dining area.

YAP–SANDIEGO ANCESTRAL HOUSE

CEBU CITY, PHILIPPINES

Mid-18th Century

Situated along a narrow alluvial plain, the elongated mountainous island of Cebu is blessed with a sheltered harbor that was entered in 1521 by the Portuguese explorer Ferdinand Magellan and his armada. These explorers, who were sailing under the Spanish flag and had been traveling westward in hopes of reaching the Moluccas, the fabled Spice Islands, were the first Europeans to reach the Philippines. Chinese, Arabs, Malays, Indians, and Japanese traders, of course, had preceded them, centuries before. It was here, on Mactan Island, only a few kilometers from Cebu, that Magellan was killed, unable to complete the circumnavigation of the globe that his sailors subsequently accomplished in his name. Spanish settlement in Cebu began decades later, in 1565, after which priests spread Catholicism, crops were introduced from the New World, and both a Chinese and Spanish mestizo culture emerged. Even with limited level land, a rugged cordillera, water shortages, and poor soils, Cebu's central location favored its rise as a regional entrepôt with ties that reached great distances abroad. Archaeological evidence has uncovered abundant Chinese ceramics, which affirms the presence of Chinese traders at least a century before Europeans arrived. Europeans, moreover, regularly commented in their diaries on the presence of numerous Chinese merchants who came to obtain gold, precious stones, and cotton, even hogs, in exchange for Chinese manufactured goods. Trade also flowed to and from Siam via Cebu as evidenced by the fact that about one-third of excavated porcelains on the island are of non-Chinese origin (Fenner, 1985: 15–20).

Cebu initially was considered as the center of this new empire, but once Manila was conquered it became the capital of the Spanish Philippines instead. By 1596 some 200 Chinese lived in the Parian or "Chinese Quarter" of Cebu, a sprawling ghetto or ethnic enclave for Chinese settlers adjacent to the geometric Hispanic town and originally connected to the sea via a narrow estuary. Nearby was a separate peripheral settlement of native Cebuanos. As Manila increased in population, size, and importance, Cebu languished throughout the seventeenth century that followed. This was principally because Spanish interest turned to the tripartite galleon trade, which spanned the Pacific and Atlantic oceans, exchanging New World American silver for Chinese luxury goods, especially silks that were then forwarded to Spain. Chinese traders found greater commercial opportunities in closer Manila than in the more distant Cebu, which overall lost population even as the number of Chinese mestizos increased. It is well known that the Spanish introduced New World crops—corn, tobacco, and cacao—from Mexico to Cebu and other areas in the Philippines. Beginning with Ping-ti Ho in the 1950s, China scholars have focused on the significance of American food crops, including also potatoes and peanuts, as critical elements in

the subsequent dietary-demographic revolution that occurred in China, but the full path from Mexico to China remains unclear. Moreover, the role of Chinese mestizos and Chinese traders in Cebu as critical links in the chain of transmission of these transformative crops to the villages of coastal China is still not well understood.

In the late eighteenth century, however, as the colonial economy became more integrated, Chinese mestizos, who lived in provincial towns and had also become landowners, came to play key roles in the still sluggish interisland trade. Yet, as late as 1800, Cebu was still an "embryonic city" that had not yet begun to thrive (Mojares, 1983: 13ff). During the ensuing period of economic growth, the once separate residential areas became more fluid, with migration from China increasing quite rapidly, especially in the middle of the nineteenth century, as the Philippines became more open. In 1834, responding to colonial economic reforms, Manila became an open port to world markets for Philippine raw materials, such as coconut oil, coffee, tobacco, beeswax, sugar, and abaca that could be sourced in Cebu. A contemporaneous account in the late 1840s stated: "These mestizos are very rich, industrious and active; one may say that all the commerce that takes place, not only with Manila but also with the other islands of the archipelago, is maintained by them and a very few Chinese. The City of Cebu owes the fortune and richness it enjoys to their activity, for without them it (the City) would lack many necessary articles provided for the sustenance of its inhabitants" (quoted in Fenner, 1985: 83). The arrival of new Chinese immigrants was in such numbers that Chinese mestizos petitioned the Spanish colonial authorities complaining about competition. In 1860 Cebu City itself became an open port for international trade, with links especially to the United States and England. No more than twenty Chinese merchants and artisans resided in the port area of Cebu City prior to 1860, but by the census of 1894 the number had reached 1,416 in the city and on the island (Fenner, 1985: 112–13). Most were from Fujian, with which they maintained contact, and were unskilled, but significant numbers operated shops and workshops of infinite variety.

Although probably not representative, Domingo Gandiongco was one Chinese immigrant who rose quickly in one generation from shopkeeper to property owner. After marrying a Cebuana from an élite family, his children became leading citizens in Cebu, bequeathing a heritage that is recognized even today. Chinese not only acquired wealth from fixed real estate, they also played key roles in the newly thriving abaca industry.

Top left A corner of the *zaguan*, with a Catholic votive altar piece as well as a display of dishes.

Top center Antique pots and old paintings on display.

Top right With angels on display at its foot, these steep stairs lead from the ground floor *zaguan* up to the *antesala*.

Above The top of the stairs in the main room.

Opposite A view of the great room on the second floor.

Once abaca, a, strong plantain fiber used in the making of rope, string, fishing nets, and textiles, had begun to emerge as a profitable export commodity in the 1820s, enterprising Chinese immigrants and mestizos became both producers and traders of this commercially significant agricultural product.

Converting to Catholicism was one way for Chinese to ease into relationships with Spanish élites since a baptismal sponsor "could be counted upon as a creditor, bondsman, and protector." It was common for the newly *Chino Cristiano* to take the surname of his baptismal *padrino* or patron. Yet, only 50 percent of the wealthier Chinese in Cebu were Catholics in the 1890s. Moreover, unlike earlier, when Chinese were obliged to cut off their long braided queues before baptism, they were now permitted to keep them, a condition that facilitated their periodic return visits back to Fujian where Qing authorities considered the queue mandatory. Well-to-do Chinese also sent their sons back to Fujian for formal education and to be influenced by kinsmen. Merging Chinese deities with the Catholic pantheon led

inexorably to distinctively idiosyncratic religious behavior at home and in worship outside in churches and shrines, hallmarks of Philippine syncretism still observable today (Wickberg, 1965: 188–94).

While it was during this century and a half that Chinese immigrants and Chinese mestizos built substantial homes in Cebu, there is a paucity of reliable source materials to write definitively about individual circumstances. Luxurious lifestyles of wealthy Cebuano, Spanish, Chinese mestizo, and Chinese entrepreneurs shared common features after 1860 as the inventories found in wills attest. "Large, well-constructed houses, lavishly decorated with locally-made furniture and European luxury goods, became a measure of financial achievement," providing not only comfort but also venues for entertainment (Fenner, 1985: 159). Their capacious two-storey homes provided ample room for storing carriages and stabling the horses required to draw them. But, in spite of some well-built, even grand, residences, they were clearly in the minority since most were houses constructed of bamboo, wood, and nipa palm (Mojares, 1983: 53).

Surviving residences from the eighteenth and nineteenth centuries are rare in most urban areas of the world where economic development and increasing population have led to their destruction. In Cebu and other areas of the Philippines, this dearth is compounded because of earthquakes and massive destruction during the Second World War. Major portions of the Cebu Parian and nearby sections of the port city were leveled during bombing by American airplanes in an effort to slow the Japanese invasion in April 1942. Not only were fragile old heritage structures razed but also irreplaceable documents and photographs were lost that would have been keys to establishing the nature of forebears of any family (Briones, 1983: 1–2).

Rare photographs of streetscapes in the Parian district taken at the beginning of the twentieth century, as seen on page 36, show abutting residences and shops that include a tile-roofed arcade several meters wide. Supported by sturdy logs and providing shade from both rain and sun, these residences began to be demolished in the 1920s, first due to changing tastes and then as streets were widened. Small shops selling goods for daily needs sometimes were located on the ground floors for the convenience of those living in the neighborhood.

Records, drawings, and photographs presented by Resil B. Mojares in a book detailing the Casa Gorordo, which was built in the middle of the nineteenth century, underscore the key role played by Chinese carpenters and masons in building local houses. Laborers from southern Fujian, unlike Chinese from other parts of the country, were quite familiar with stone and stonecutting since granite was a common material throughout the region from Quanzhou to Xiamen. Cutting blocks of coral stone, which was harvested from dormant reefs and has the textures of its origins, did not provide much of a challenge to them. The prominent Gorordo family, which had as its progenitors a Spaniard who married the daughter of a Chinese mestizo family named Garces, built a grand home, which is reminiscent of the Syquia mansion in Vigan (pages 240–7) (1983: 81ff).

Two other Cebu houses in the Parian date to the middle Spanish colonial period. One, built in 1730, which served as the residence of the Jesuit Superior in Cebu, is comprised of two interconnected structures joined by a covered walkway. A second, which was described in 1950 as "the oldest house in Cebu, and possibly in the Philippines," has a less certain provenance. In the well-regarded book about Casa Gordordo, it was claimed that the house had been built "in 1738 by a Garces and then bequeathed to Garces family members" (Mojares, 1983: 82). In recent years, this history has been disputed. The structure has been renamed the Yap–Sandiego ancestral home and is now dated to the middle of the eighteenth century.

The Yap–Sandiego Residence

Much smaller and older than Casa Gorordo, the Yap–Sandiego residence nonetheless shares many characteristics with it. While Casa Gorordo dates to the mid-nineteenth century, there is firm speculation that the Yap–Sandiego residence was built a hundred years earlier. It is not possible to establish with any assurance the family circumstances that led to its initial construction or trace its transfer from family to family until 1859. Around that time, Juan Yap, an ancestor of the present owner, Val Sandiego, and from a place outside Cebu, married a Chinese mestiza named Maria Florido who was from the Cebu Parian, and had three daughters. Their eldest daughter Maria married Mariano San Diego, hence the linking of the Yap–Sandiego name. Mariano San Diego became the Cebeza de Barangay, head of the Cebu Parian community. The residence thus has been in the Sandiego family for more than 150 years.

As a two-storey structure with a rectangular ground plan, the base of the building is walled with cut coral stone blocks, with an upper wooden structure resting on the stonewalls, supported on the inside by roughly hewn tree trunks. The roof profile is hipped with four sloping surfaces covered with locally made red clay tiles. The building today has two openings along its side, but it is said that originally the main door was on the shorter wall along a narrow lane, which was blocked in the 1930s when a warehouse for the Lim Bon Fing y Hijos firm was built on the adjacent property. Yet, it may well have been that the doorway on the shorter wall led to a garden or orchard. In any case, this former passageway today has a shrine placed before it. It is likely in the past that the lower level was used to stable horses and carriages or used for storage. Today, it is furnished with secular and religious antiques.

Steep wooden stairs rise from the lower level to a large room above. While today there are no partitions to divide its spaces, originally there were four rooms: a *caida* or foyer; a large *sala* or parlor, which overlooked the back garden and well; a *comedor* or dining room; and a single bedroom called a *cuarto*. When this house was built, window openings were wide and covered with planks, unlike the more elaborate *kapiz* shells and *ventanillas* employed in the Syquia residence in Vigan, as shown in the previous chapter. From the inside of the room, one can see the supporting timbers for the roof as well as the clay tiles laid atop them. There is no ceiling, so it is possible to see the accumulation of soot on the inside of the roof tiles as a result of the oil-lamps used during the eighteenth and nineteenth centuries.

While some of the antiques seen in the house today were handed down by the Yap–Sandiego family, others more broadly represent those

Opposite above Once divided into several rooms, the upstairs area today is completely open and set up to display period antiques.

Above A view of the corner of the upstairs room.

Left A small table with an abacus and books. The box on the right, with the characters 麻雀, meaning "sparrow" in ancient China, holds the game known today as Mahjong 麻將.

that would have been found in the past in a Cebuano mestizo household. Many of the statues of saints have Chinese features. In presenting this old house to the public, Val Sandiego, the current owner, views the structure as a "House for All Seasons" and as a center for re-creating the traditions and cultural activities of his family in the past. Throughout the year, the façade and interior are decorated according to festivals and occasions representative of the varied history of Cebuanos: Santo Niño (Holy Child Jesus) festival in January, Chinese New Year in January/February, the Passion during Lent, the Flores de Mayo to honor the Virgin Mary in May, Philippine Independence from Spain Day in June, the feast of St John the Baptist in June, the Founding of the Parian Parish in October, and Christmas in December. The fluidity of mestizo culture in the Philippines is one of its hallmarks. While, for generations, mestizo families gradually distanced themselves from links with China and their Chineseness—sometimes even expunging it altogether—today more are resurrecting whatever vague associations there once were in order to declare their pride in the rise of China and the seeming endurance of its civilization. For many families who are looking back to their roots, there are gray areas and incomplete synapses. Old houses and inherited familial objects, which echo distant and incomplete memories, serve as quintessential touchstones that help establish links with an elusive past.

QIU FAMILY RESIDENCES

MEIXIAN, GUANGDONG, CHINA

1921 and 1934

The dream of amassing wealth in a distant land through hard work and luck, and then returning to one's native place in China to live a comfortable life, "a glorious homecoming in splendid clothes," *yijin huanxiang* (also *yijin ronggui*), was unfilled for most poor Chinese who sojourned abroad. Yet, in villages throughout Fujian and Guangdong, one can still see conspicuous examples of ostentatious residences that reveal that there indeed was material success and the realization of dreams, at least for some. Two contrasting residences stand side by side in Liangmei village, Baigong township, Meixian county, in eastern Guangdong province, that reveal the investment in new homes, the hope of a large family living together, and the evolution of aesthetic preferences among returning migrants.

Meixian, known historically as China's Hakka homeland, is the source region for countless out-migrants, not only to Southeast Asia but throughout the world. Unlike in adjacent Fujian where many Hakka constructed the unique multistoried fortresses known as *tulou*, structures that are best known in their circular forms and as Five Phoenix Mansions, Hakka in eastern Guangdong built a distinctive style of building known as *weilongwu* or "encircling dragon dwellings." De Xing Tang, an example featured in the author's *Chinese Houses: The Architectural Heritage of a Nation*, was built between 1905 and 1917 by a Hakka who returned from Southeast Asia (Knapp, 2005: 176–201). Even those who lived in humble dwellings in small villages aspired to live harmoniously as an extended multigenerational family in a large traditional *weilongwu*.

Discussed below are two residences in Meixian county that were constructed by members of the Qiu family who sojourned and amassed wealth in Batavia, which the Chinese called Bacheng. Those who migrated to Java had followed in the footsteps of other Hakka villagers who had been in earlier waves of Hakka migration to the island of Banka where they mined tin, or Kalimantan on the island of Borneo where they prospected for gold. Newly arriving Hakka immigrants to Batavia at the beginning of the twentieth century typically turned

their hand to trading and various other enterprises, which linked them into Chinese networks that sometimes made it possible to attain wealth rather quickly. Family members arrived at a time when the Dutch had relaxed their restrictions on where Chinese could live and how they could earn their living. Incomplete records show that Qiu family members prospered as rice merchants, sourcing rice for international export markets.

Considered *Cina totok*, literally "Chinese of pure blood," whose connections remained with their ancestral homeland, they were distinguishable from the local-born Peranakan Chinese, who by intermarriage and accommodation had created a distinctive hybrid Chinese-Javanese identity and culture. While the *totok* community grew significantly in the early decades of the twentieth century as new immigrants from China settled down in Indonesia, some even bringing wives to live with them, many remained attached to their home village, working hard towards the day when they could return home. The completion of two homes, one in 1921 and the other in 1934, provides concrete evidence of the realization of the Confucian aspiration of returning well-off and retiring in comfortable surroundings in the company of an extended family, perhaps even the ultimate, "five generations living under one roof."

Opposite above The outer gate of Di Hua Ju, which is located to the right of the building complex.

Above The main entry, with the three characters Di Hua Ju—"Residence of Brothers"—above the doorway.

Below The full façade view looking across the pond to the five-bay main structure, with its pair of side wing structures. Vermilion Cultural Revolution graffiti is still visible on the walls.

Di Hua Ju

While the two residences appear dissimilar in form and ornamentation when viewed from a distance, closer inspection reveals that they both share common Hakka architectural features. The impressive scale, the structural complexity, and the presence of their names written above the main entryway all express the hope that an extended, content, and prosperous family would occupy the new homes. The older residence, Di Hua Ju or "Residence of Brothers," was constructed between 1914 and 1921, while Lian Fang Lou, which means "Hall of Amalgamated Fragrances," was built between 1931 and 1934. Completed just twelve

years apart during the early twentieth century, they represent the fulfillment of hopes and ambitions of living family members and a statement of aspirations and expectations for future generations. Given that both residences are adjacent to each other, with a low ridge behind them and coursing water in front, and that they share a common southeast orientation, it is certain that the overall site was selected with careful attention to *fengshui*. With family prosperity increasing in the years between their construction, it is not coincidental that Lian Fang Lou, the second, more modern residence, was sited essentially the same way as the first one, the more traditional Di Hua Ju.

The overall plan of Di Hua Ju is oval in shape, with a rectangular

building between two hemispheres, the one in the rear being matched in the front with a half-moon shaped pond, which altogether creates a distinctive building form. Abutting up against a hillslope where the gradient changes, the curved rear portion of the residence is elevated higher than the core rectangular unit and the pond. Like other *weilongwu* with encircling arcuate back walls, Di Hua Ju appears like an enormous omega Ω, a symbolic armchair, securely set on a hill slope in order to protect the family from danger while providing them with the comfort of prevailing breezes and effective drainage. The arching upslope part of the house is like an open fan, with an arc comprising rooms assigned to each family as well as a shared open bay, wider than the adjacent rooms, which serves ritual purposes. The floor plan of the core building is both symmetrical and hierarchical. It is made up of a five-bay-wide horizontal structure, flanked by a pair of perpendicularly oriented buildings. The middle bay is the most ornate and ritually important portion of the dwelling: a lower hall inside the entry, an upper hall just beyond a small courtyard, and a main hall behind. Today, these spaces sadly lack the kinds of ornate furniture, altars, and uplifting ornamentation that most certainly characterized them in the past. This central sequence of three halls and two skywells was considered communal space, that is, joint property belonging to the lineage. The co-residence function of this large dwelling was realized in the separate "apartments" with bedrooms, skywells, and corridors for each of the brothers and their families. Enclosed within exterior walls without windows, there was a clear sense of family cohesion. Whatever breeze and light enters the dwelling comes from the front, which faces southeasterly, drawn into the doorways or entering via the open skywells that punctuate it. Throughout the building, wooden columns, beams, and door panels are abundant, just as in any fine traditional dwelling.

One can see architectural elements in *weilongwu* that are found also in traditional *siheyuan* courtyard-style residences—bilateral symmetry, axiality, hierarchy, and enclosure—with some distinctive features: the presence of upper, middle, and lower halls, multiple skywells throughout, a change in elevation from high in the rear to low in the front, and a large pond. Combining the upper hemisphere with the lower hemisphere, some say, created a powerful *taiji* diagram, the composition that includes the complementary *yin* and *yang* pair, which represents stability, interdependence, and mutuality. No one doubts that this residence has good *fengshui*. Yet, with the vermilion slogans of the Great Proletarian Cultural Revolution still visible throughout the residence, it is clear that the Qiu family and their home suffered considerably during that tumultuous period. The residence is now quite tidy, with the accumulated debris and grime of decades all swept away.

An attempt has been made in the main hall to create a simple ancestral altar with an urn to burn incense and a vase of flowers placed on two forlorn tables. Four old portraits and a few more recent photographs are all that is left as a reminder of those who died. Whatever ancestral tablets once existed must have been destroyed during the Cultural Revolution. The central image is of Qiu Yiliao, credited with building the residence for his sons. Dressed in a Western suit and sporting a mustache, he appears to have the shaved forehead characteristic of those who still wore the queue before the fall of the Qing dynasty. The text above his portrait indicates that he was of the nineteenth generation of the Qiu lineage and his image depicts him when he was sixty-one upon his return to Batavia in 1900. Today, there is a sense of melancholy in the empty rooms of Di Hua Ju that stems from the lack of evidence of the vigorous family life of brothers who once lived there together.

The idiomatic name "Residence of Brothers," Di Hua Ju, is derived from the cryptic phrase *ditang bingmao, hua'e xianghui*, which states a botanical reference: "When the petals of the Japanese yellow rose (*kerria japonica*) are luxuriant, the calyx [the whorl below the colored petals] is similarly glorious." This is said to have the implicit meaning that "the harmonious relations among brothers leads to sons who flourish." It is not known how many sons and their families resided together in Di Hua Ju when it was completed, but it is said that at one time more than seventy related people lived there. While today only a single Qiu descendant and his family, totaling five people, live in the "Residence of Brothers," the family proudly counts among the living descendants more than thirty individuals who are highly educated professionals, some with doctoral degrees as college professors ("Fuyu tese," 2006). None, of course, continues to live in the village, a sign itself of success. Di Hua Ju has now been registered as a provincial-level heritage site.

Above A view of the second skywell with another screenwall.

Left In addition to traditional-style paintings, this sidewall of the back hall includes the admonition that Marxist–Leninist principals guide thinking.

Above A view through a sequence of passageways, with abundant Cultural Revolution slogans still visible.

Left A close-up of a New Year's papercut above a simple altar. The papercut includes an inverted *fu* character for Good Fortune and four characters meaning "Celebrate the New Year."

Right One of the residential areas in the wing buildings that is lined by skywells.

Lian Fang Lou

Planned in 1928 as a joint project by four brothers who had become wealthy as rice merchants in Indonesia, Lian Fang Lou or "The Home of Amalgamated Fragrances" took three years to build between 1931 and 1934. Deteriorating photographs of the half-completed building as well as one celebrating its completion hang in the ancestral hall. Very little is known of the Qiu brothers, Qiu Xingxiang, Qiu Qingxiang, Qiu Qixiang, and Qiu Linxiang, or their relationship with their relative Qiu Yiqing who built the adjacent Di Hua Ju. It is said that they have descendants in Indonesia and Hong Kong as well as elsewhere in China, but only several family members continue to live as caretakers in this once grand home. In November 2006, descendants from near and far joined some 700 others in the commemoration of Qiu Xingxiang seventy-two years after his death.

With its broad façade and ostentatious trappings, the two-storey Lian Fang Lou appears out of place in a rural setting, where it rises from the surrounding rice fields adjacent to the traditional single-storey Di Hua Ju *weilongwu*. Even a casual observer sees this structure as an unusual fusion of architecture with a diverse assortment of ornamental elements, which Chinese architects call *Zhong-Xi hebishi*, implying a harmonious assemblage of Chinese and Western styles. The building was designed by an architect from neighboring Chaozhou, who was likely familiar with the Western architecture that was being built in Hong Kong and Shantou (Swatow). Eclectic architectural forms were in fashion in urban as well as rural areas of East Asia between the First and Second World Wars.

From a distance, there is little in the façade that is obviously Chinese, but closer inspection reveals that the Western architectural elements incorporate Chinese and Western components. The main two-storey building extends some 38 meters in width, with a pair of connected wing buildings augmenting the façade another 19 meters. The symmetrical façade includes a grandiose three-level central feature, which includes an entry portico, a second floor balcony, and a rooftop aerie topped by a lofty dome. Less pronounced but no less ornate are the entry porticos surmounted by an ornamental arch located symmetrically on each side. Between the two-storey main structure and the lower side wings are recessed doorways that lead to a long corridor with a rectangular courtyard within it. Between the doorways along the façade on each level are rectangular ornamented windows.

The entryways and windows incorporate a profusion of detail using both Chinese and Western motifs and symbolism. Chinese architects describe the building as being *baluoke* (Baroque) and *luokeke* (Rococo) in style because of the dramatic, multistoried projection at the center of a rigidly symmetrical plane and the sumptuousness of the ornamental elements. Referencing the building to a European style of the seventeenth and eighteenth centuries, however, ignores the influences of the later Beaux Arts and Classical Revival architectural styles that

Opposite above The sweeping arc of the rooms in the rear of the Di Hua Ju residence.

Opposite below The broad façade of Lian Fang Lou, "The Home of Amalgamated Fragrances," has a paddy field in front.

Right A close-up view of the three protruding tower structures that provide entry into Lian Fang Lou.

were in fashion in the world early in the twentieth century. One phase of the Beaux Arts style is characterized by "an abhorrence of undecorated surfaces," a *horror vacui*, as some have termed it (Poppeliers, et al., 1977: 30). Certainly, every surface and niche of the façade of Lian Fang Lou is saturated with images and forms in two distinct idioms, Chinese and Western, together in excess of those found in abundance on traditional Chinese buildings. There is a dynamic rhythm to the columns and pilasters, the protruding entrance terraces, the variety of shapes, and the profuse ornamentation.

Behind, that is, inside, what is essentially a Western façade is a traditional Hakka floor plan, a spatial layout described by architects as *san tang si heng*, "Three Halls with Four Transverses," just as was found in the smaller Di Hua Ju nearby. Accessed through the central entryway are the three halls aligned one behind the other: lower hall, middle hall, and upper hall, with a pair of skywells separating them. Traditionally, it was along this axis that the most prolific and meaningful Chinese-style ornamentation was found. The glorious screen walls, called *luodi zhao*, that are more than a mere *pingfeng* or screen, which mark the edge of halls adjacent to skywells, and the mismatched pieces of antique furniture placed together in some of the rooms, are all that remain today of the magnificent furnishings that once must have graced the Qiu residence. A low table, assorted old photographs, small incense holders, candlesticks, and small cups in the upper hall only hint at what once must have been the location of a splendid ancestral altar that celebrated Qiu forebears back many generations.

The two decoratively carved partition-like screens along the main axis between the three halls, with open passageways to the right and left, each have four swinging panels in their body. Normally kept closed, these panels could be swung open, when needed, for celebrations and funerals.

Below A close-up of an ornamented window, with carved stone pieces and a painting of a pastoral scene.

The lower and middle sections of these folding doors are solid while the upper register is carved openwork, which has been gilded. The paintings are no longer visible but the doors, including the gilded portions, have been cleaned. The narrow panels across the top as well as the upper portions of the doorways include auspicious patterns. A matching pair of screens located on both sides of the first skywell, just in front of the middle hall, makes this area one of great beauty, especially as sunlight courses across the open spaces.

There are altogether fifty-two rooms for family use in the residence, fourteen reception rooms and halls used communally, and more than thirty utility spaces, collectively an abundant number of spaces to accommodate an extended multigenerational family comfortably. As the floor plan reveals, on each side of the central grouping of three halls there is a complete residential unit with its own entryway. Comprising thirteen rooms, two halls, two large rectangular skywells, covered corridors, and separate stairways to the second floor bedrooms and storage rooms, each of these units easily could accommodate the four brothers and their families. The rooms in the outer wings provided

space for the work of servants, with an ancillary building for livestock. Upstairs, in addition to bedrooms and storage rooms, there was another upper hall, which may have been used for worshipping Buddhist and Daoist deities or, indeed, the Qiu ancestors. Unfortunately, no one living in the residence today has a clear memory of its use.

Six of the eight skywells are rectangular in shape, each one opening up space to light and air on both the first and second floors. The two outer skywells lay between the two-storey core structure and the single-storey utility wings. Each of these outer skywells has an entryway from the front, which, while not as grand as the three main entrances, is clearly an imposing formal architectural form, with columns, carved panels, and an elevated pediment. When the panels of the full door are not closed, a swinging half-door is used to keep children in and roving animals out.

One particularly unusual characteristic of the Qiu home, a feature we had not seen before in a Chinese residence, is the presence of a large roof garden covered with grass. From a distance outside the building, an observer notices only the line of the low parapet with bottle-shaped

Near right Showing one of the entry towers and the balustraded surround, the sodded roof, with its magnificent views of the countryside, would have been a pleasant place in the evening.

Second right A view from roof level looking down through one of the slender rectangular skywells.

Third right A corridor around one of the skywells on the second floor.

Far right Each of the protruding towers has a balcony, with stucco detail work and pendulous ornamentation.

Far left A side room, which is separated from the first skywell inside the entry hall.

Center left A slender skywell that separates the core building from the residential portion of the residence.

Left A make-shift shrine to deceased family members in a back room of the residence.

balusters that rims what appears to be a flat roof, punctuated by the three towering entryways. There is no suggestion whatsoever of a profile reminiscent of a Chinese-style roof. After climbing the steps to the roof garden, the ostentatious ornamentation on the façade can be seen easily.

The roof space is not a formal garden with trees and shrubs. There is, strangely, even an absence of the potted plants and rock features commonly found within open courtyards of Chinese houses. Given the placement of the balustrades, the finish work on the ornaments, and the focus on the cupola, the roof garden was clearly designed as a place to view the sinuous mountain scenery in the distance at all points of the compass and the lush green rice fields nearby during the day, as well as a place to view the moon and stars on a clear night. The use of reinforced concrete as the medium for the construction of the building made it possible to support a lawn on the roof. A by-product of a roof of this type is that it reduces the absorption of solar radiation, thus keeping the rooms inside cooler than they would be otherwise. At the beginning of the twenty-first century, this type of roof is indeed a "green roof," one that is considered eco-friendly and enjoyable.

Unlike a monumental Chinese building in which the horizontal and vertical dimensions are proportional and the roof perhaps its most conspicuous feature, here only the multifaceted façade commands attention. The Western façade of Lian Fang Lou, moreover, was the public face of the Qiu family, which declared that they were not only wealthy but also modern and Western. Yet, as we have seen, the façade in some ways is actually only a decorative "mask" that barely hints at the Chinese life lived behind it. A residence of this sort is a statement of conspicuous consumption by nouveau riche who had witnessed a world beyond village China that they wished to import home.

CHEN CIHONG MANOR

CHAOZHOU, GUANGDONG, CHINA

1910s to 1930s

While many successful businessmen in Southeast Asia returned to spend only the last years of their lives in the comfort of their birthplace, some returned earlier. Chen Cihong, who had been at the center of the region-wide family business network based in Thailand known as Wanglee (pages 228–31), chose to retire and return to his *guxiang* in Guangdong province when he was in his forties, sometime between 1883 and 1891 (Choi, 1998: 31). Although records are not clear, it appears that he continued to revisit Bangkok from time to time, until around 1900 when he returned permanently to Chaozhou.

By the late 1880s, Chen Cihong had already started to build a mansion in Bangkok along the Chao Phraya River, and was preparing to turn over the management of the Siam enterprises to his son. In

the meantime, Chen Cihong and members of his extended family purchased extensive land holdings in their home village some 25 kilometers inland from the port of Shantou. Here they built homes and ancestral halls, established a small textile factory and a market to sell oxen, and contributed to worthy causes such as relief for the poor and building schools for those living around Qianxi. Chen Cihong's sons, grandsons, and other relatives continued to purchase village lands well into the twentieth century, especially in the 1920s when other landowners with fewer resources found themselves in financial difficulties after the area was ravaged by a typhoon in 1922 (Choi, 2006: 13–18).

Many of the early Chen houses were specially built for those family members who remained in China, such as women, children,

Opposite above The entryway to Chen Cihong, with a *tanglong*, a sliding bar gate, and details of the fenestration.

Opposite below After passing through the entryway, one arrives in a long courtyard, with the core of the symmetrical residence to the left and subsidiary rooms aligned along the outside walls.

Above A side skywell and its associated rooms behind a wall adjacent to the courtyard.

Left The linking entry between a pair of skywells.

Below left Stuccoed ornamentation above one of the barred windows in the outer wall.

Below right A close-up of a brass door pull, with the *shuangxi* or "doubled happiness" emblem on it.

Bottom Rooftop ornamentation, with unique Western-style floral ornamentation on the ends of the drip tiles.

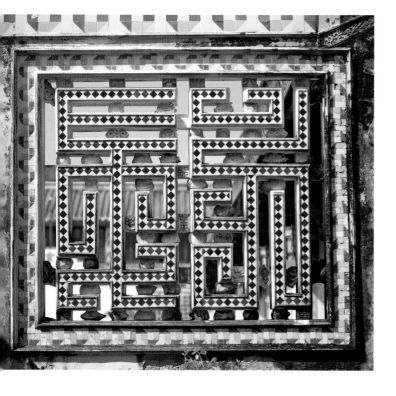

and the elderly, while their menfolk resided in Bangkok or elsewhere, returning only periodically. Housekeepers sometimes were employed to maintain large, near empty residences. The grand manor of Chen Cihong, portions of which can be visited today, began to be developed in 1910, the second year of the reign of China's last emperor, Puyi. Even after Chen Cihong's death in 1921, work continued on the expansive complex of four major walled compounds, and was not completed until the late 1930s. Using a vast area of level land that had been acquired over several previous decades, the Chen manor took shape behind high walls that created a veritable hidden village within the fortified walls. In fact, a remote relationship had already developed between common villagers and the Chen family "not only as a result of the tension between landlord and tenants, but also because of the distance the family kept from the remaining villages. For instance, during festivals, instead of going to the temple or to worship in front of the entrance of the house like other villagers did, the family had the deities brought into the houses for family members to worship. When [Chen] Cihong died in 1921, his body was kept in a purpose-built stone house, locally called 'coffin house.' The corpse was kept in the house for some 15 years until the family finally found an auspicious gravesite" (Choi, 2006: 15).

Although few details are known, the Chen family also acquired imperial honors and degrees granting them titles that were emblazoned on their new residences, serving as reminders to other villagers of their exalted status.

Visitors to the manor of Chen Cihong today enter a large walled compound of such generous size that they assume that it *alone* is the manor. Called Shan Ju Shi, this single-walled complex, however, is actually the newest of the four contiguous complexes that constitute the larger Chen manor, which were constructed adjacent to each other in order to accommodate the families of Chen Cihong's three sons in the hopes that they also would return to their ancestral village. Adjacent to the pond to the west of today's parking lot, the other three complexes, Langzhong Di, Shoukang Li, and Sanlu Shuzhai, remain unrestored and are occupied by countless families as well as workshops of many types employing villagers. It is impossible now to appreciate that these badly deteriorated buildings once were grand like Shanju Shi. They not only demonstrate a lack of maintenance over a long period of time but also reveal the conditions under which they have been utilized for so long by people who have not appreciated them. All the buildings retain scars of the Great Proletarian Cultural Revolution in terms of political graffiti.

The name Shan Ju Shi, which means "Managing the Household Well," is a phrase borrowed from the *Analects of Confucius* that refers to Confucius's appraisal of Jing, a scion of the ducal family of Wei. While rather abstruse in terms of its original meaning, the three characters are viewed by contemporary villagers as simply meaning "Good Residence." Although Shan Ju Shi is today interpreted as if it were Chen Cihong's residence when he was alive, the complex actually was not begun until a year after his death. As the last complex to be built, it was to house the family of his youngest son, Chen Litong, who died before the construction was completed in 1939, a delay exacerbated by the Japanese invasion. Chen Litong's estate was left to his widow to manage.

Occupying more than a quarter of the total ground plan of the larger manor, Shan Ju Shi has within it some 200 *jian* or bays of many sizes, some of which are individual rooms while others are linked together to form a room. The building complex sits to the north of the other buildings and is adjacent to a rectangular lotus pond on its south. The ground plan of the complex is colloquially referred to as *si ma tuoche*,

Above An upstairs passageway that links areas of the residence.

Left An interior skywell showing adjacent rooms and the overhanging balcony on the second floor.

Below A wall covered with tiles in a diamond pattern. Here also is a *tanglong* gate.

Above A view of the full courtyard from the balcony. The main entrance to the complex is at the far end of this image, while the residence is on the right.

Below A series of rooms surrounding a skywell. One wall is adorned with a mosaic tile pattern with the character *ji* for "Good Luck."

"four horses pulling a cart," a configuration referring to a series of courtyards in a core building flanked on each side by narrow lanes, actually slim courtyards, running from front to back. "Four horses pulling a cart" is a variant of a common layout for residences found throughout Guangdong province called *si dian jin*, "four points of gold," which involves four structures with double-pitched roofs, each with a gable end, that mimics the Chinese character for gold, with the four structures enclosing an interior courtyard. The overall layout represents a large cart, while the four horses are metaphorically used to suggest the overall magnitude of a cart that would require many horses to pull it.

Because the southern wall is two storeys high, the complex appears from a distance to be a veritable fortified compound, somewhat similar to the type of walled villages lived in by Hakka in neighboring areas of Guangdong province and in the Gannan area of southern Jiangxi province, as well as in Hong Kong. On the other hand, once one gets closer, the presence of abundant windows on both levels along the exterior walls opens the complex up to air and light to a degree not found with traditional Hakka walled villages constructed during times of turmoil. While the window openings are framed in granite panels in traditional fashion, each is surmounted by decorative designs molded in plaster. The sinuous lines and flowery embellishments of these window treatments have both Victorian and Art Nouveau characteristics. Small ceramic tiles were fitted into sets of frames surrounding the windows and into shapes on the wall that are quite different from traditional fenestration in China. For protection, each of the windows is secured with iron rods and can be shuttered on the inside if need be. The main entryway includes an ingenious "gate," called a *tonglong*, which is formed from horizontal wooden bars that slide as a unit into granite sockets hewn into the door frame. The opposing northern wall, which also has a gateway, is also two storeys high, while the walls on the east and west are only a single storey.

Passage through the *tonglong* gate leads to a large rectangular courtyard. On the right of the courtyard are shallow service rooms and on the left a classical series of halls and associated courtyards, which are oriented due east. Such an orientation helps reduce the penetration of the most intense rays of the sun into the dwelling during the afternoon. The elevation view of the halls complex has a broad three-bay structure at its center with a recessed bay in the front. A pair of parallel wing buildings is separated from the central building by recessed entryways leading to rectangular lanes that serve also as courtyards running towards the rear. The three halls—entry hall, middle hall, and rear hall—recede towards the most private part of the residence. Separated from each other by two open courtyards, both the podiums on which the halls sit and their rooflines increase in height from front to back. The front-to-back courtyards and the pair of narrower parallel courtyards are connected with each other by doorways. As in traditional Chaozhou dwellings, there are abundant wood and stone carvings throughout. A unique feature, however, is the proliferation of ceramic tiles on the surfaces of both the halls and courtyards. While exhaustive research has not been done yet on the source of the ceramic tiles, they are interpreted as having been imported from England, Spain, and Italy. Along the northern and southern outer walls, the rooms and corridors are covered with ceramic floor and wall tiles, with each of the connecting doorways along the passageways topped with colorful plaster treatments.

Left One section of the unrestored Lang Zhong Di is still used as a factory.

Below Another section of Lang Zhong Di, with a richly ornamented entryway, serves as a clothing factory.

Bottom left Magnificent carved wood, stone, and brick, which have been painted, are common in the unrestored section of Lang Zhong Di that is still used as a factory.

Bottom right A view through doorways in an unrestored section of Lang Zhong Di.

DEE C. CHUAN VILLA

GULANGYU, XIAMEN, FUJIAN, CHINA

1926

Gulangyu, an idyllic islet with a salubrious climate some 700 meters across the bay from the port city of Xiamen, is known in modern Chinese history as one of the International Settlements set up during the Treaty Port era, as an area governed by a council of foreigners and exempt from Chinese jurisdiction. Occupied first by British troops at the end of the Opium War in 1842, it was not until 1859 that a foreigner, an American, built a villa on Gulangyu, unleashing a seventy-five year frenzy of construction of disparate architectural styles that generously can be called eclectic. In addition to grand homes for foreign residents, imposing Christian churches, impressive schools, a Masonic Lodge, a club with a library and billiard room, and more than a dozen foreign consulates, several hundred villas were constructed on the island by Overseas Chinese who had amassed great wealth throughout Southeast Asia, yet yearned to return to a comfortable life in China. William Brown, an American teaching at Xiamen University, assesses the buildings as a "madcap marriage of Western and Chinese architecture, ... [a] hodgepodge of houses ... born of foreigners schizophrenically grasping at the East while clinging to the West, and of Chinese clinging to their roots while grasping all things 'modern'..." (Brown and Pan, 2005: 178). While his comments may be considered a bit intemperate if pointed only at Gulangyu, what can be witnessed there actually was characteristic of the early decades of the twentieth century throughout coastal China. Indeed, during those times "the lure of the foreign," as it has been

Opposite With evergreen trees planted within concentric circles that form walkways around the fountain, the three-storey Dee C. Chuan villa expresses the grandiose neoclassical architectural style in vogue throughout the world in the 1920s.

Left An arched window on the upper portion of the façade.

Right The streetside gate bearing the characters "Ronggu" leads up a path to the residence.

termed by Frank Dikötter, swept the world. "Foreign, in Europe and out of Europe, was no longer merely exotic: to buy foreign was to be modern" (2006: 2).

Available maps of the island portray what appears to be a maze of irregularly shaped lanes with oddly angular intersections and unusual configurations for the various blocks. This asymmetry arises from the fact that the granitic island is quite rugged, with limited level land. Covering an area of only 1.77 square kilometers, the jagged topography of Gulangyu, which was said to be "barren and impracticable for productive purposes," afforded countless building sites to meet the idiosyncratic *fengshui* demands of those intent on preserving their fortunes. Indeed, the island had long been viewed by Chinese in the region as auspicious since its zoomorphic configuration was said to be that of dragon: at the wharf is Longtou, the "dragon's head," and across the island is a rocky spit said to be its tail (Giles, 1878: 8, 25). Accessing the scattered building lots at high locations necessitated the creation of myriad serpentine lanes that wind up and down the hillocks, standing in for the undulating back of the dragon.

Among the best preserved of Gulangyu's well-sited hybrid villas is one built in 1926 by Dee C. Chuan, who by then had become renowned as a timber baron, banker, shipping magnate, and real estate tycoon in the Philippines. Architecturally designed, his residence, as with others on Gulangyu, is a unique blend of Western and Chinese forms in terms of mass and spatial organization, features such as façade, fenestration, floor plan, room types, and ornamental elements, and methods of construction. The fact that Dee C. Chuan built such a mansion in the International Settlement reveals not only his international outlook, adventurous spirit, and aesthetic taste but also the global mobility, entre-preneurial character, and transnational activity of many generations of his family. Wealth and talent clearly flowed both ways from Fujian to the Philippines and back, with side roads leading to other international entrepôt in Asia. In the decade after the American occupation, which began in 1895, fully 80 percent of the Chinese in the Philippines had active kinship relationships with the migratory networks servicing four counties—Jinjiang, Tong'an, Nan'an, and Longqi—in Fujian. In 1896, the fact that there were only 194 Chinese women in a population of about 66,000 Chinese males in the Philippines, an astounding unbalanced sex ratio, is a clear indication that the males who had migrated maintained wives and families in China (Wickberg, 1965: 174).

Dee C. Chuan was born with the name Li Qingquan in 1888 in Shizhen village in the Jinjiang area of Fujian (Dee and Dy are common ways to romanize the surname Li in the Hokkien dialect). Although born in China, his father and grandfather, along with many others in his family, had been settled in the Philippines for generations, thus

his being China-born was a statement of the ties that his family continued to maintain with their ancestral village. Both his grand-father and subsequently his father built up a timber and building materials business in the Philippines that he later inherited and further developed. As a young boy, he was educated in Xiamen at the bilingual Anglo-Chinese Tongwen Institute, then, at the age of thirteen, joined his father, Calixto Dyyco, in Manila soon after the ouster of the Spanish from the Philippines and its becoming a colony of the United States. Three years later, he was sent to St Joseph's College in Hong Kong to master English. When he returned to the Philippines at the age of eighteen, he succeeded as head of the lumber business with the early retirement of his father. In time, Dee C. Chuan & Sons became the preeminent integrated hardwood manufacturing and trading company in the Philippines.

It is not possible to determine when Dee C. Chuan began to think of building a grand home in Fujian, but it is certain that he and other family members regularly passed through Xiamen as they journeyed between Manila and Jinjiang. Over many decades at the turn of the century, they witnessed the dramatic architectural transformation of Xiamen, with much of the effort guided and funded by Hokkien Overseas Chinese from Indonesia, the Philippines, and Vietnam, among others. Road were realigned, modern shophouses and public buildings were constructed, public parks were opened, and fine residences were built in Xiamen (Mei, 2003: 95–124). In addition to contributing to the modernization of their "hometown" city, they also welcomed the opportunity to make money through property development.

The decision by Dee C. Chuan to built his own lavish residence on Gulangyu was but part of a greater plan to house his large family nearby. In the early 1920s on Gulangyu, he built a villa complex called Dee/Li Family Manor, with individual residences for both his father and his uncle, and then another villa for other family members. In 1926, when he was only thirty-eight years old, he completed his own mansion. Called "Ronggu," his estate was constructed on a promontory along Qishan or Flag Hill overlooking Xiamen's harbor. At the time this up-hill residence was built, family members arrived by ferry from Xiamen, disembarking at Longtou (Dragon's Head) wharf before mounting a sedan chair, which was carried on the shoulders of two bearers uphill on the steep path to their residence. After traversing a series of interlinked lanes that climb up from the ferry station, the home was reached via a short, narrow lane with steps leading to a gate. Beyond the gate was a pathway that continued through the extensive garden, actually two gardens, in front of the house. At the beginning of the pebble-stone pathway can still be seen the date "1926" embedded into it using darker colored stones. The first garden was built in Chinese style with rockeries,

Top right A sofa and display cabinets behind the entry screenwall in the dining room.

Center right A view from an upstairs balcony of the garden and fountain in front of the villa.

Bottom right Stairs leading from the second to the third floor.

Bottom left The floor plan and section view of the Dee C. Chuan villa.

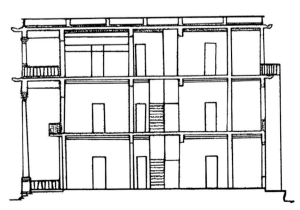

winding steps, pebbled paths, and pavilions that have expansive views of the harbor. At the apex of the ceiling of one of the pavilions is a brightly colored orange pumpkin with two geckos crawling across it. Between this Chinese-style natural landscape composition and the residence is a formal Western-style garden composed of symmetrical plantings of barrel cacti and inlaid pebble walkways arranged in concentric circles, with a fountain at the center.

The Dee C. Chuan Mansion

Framed by four lofty, spire-like evergreen trees planted within the concentric circles that form a walkway around the fountain, the three-storey mansion exemplifies the grandiose neoclassical architectural style that was in vogue throughout the world at the time. Neoclassical architecture, which emerged late in the eighteenth century, subsequently evolved throughout the nineteenth and early twentieth centuries in forms that differed from country to country. With its tall, fluted columns, open ground floor veranda, arched entryway, minor second storey balcony, larger third storey balcony, parapet, and cast cement balustraded stairways, Dee C. Chuan's mansion evokes to some degree an American antebellum plantation house. Extravagant, oversized mansions with sumptuous furnishings and ornamentation like this were being built in many Chinese cities at that time, yet there has not yet been a comprehensive study of this architectural phenomenon in China. Like a modern skyscraper, the building has a load-bearing structural frame made of cement, a skeleton that was infilled with red brick exterior curtain walls.

In the interior, the floor plan was not only generous in extent, it included clearly defined functional rooms: a rectangular entry hall, side rooms, dining room, staircase hall, sitting rooms, bedrooms, storage rooms, kitchen, laundry, and basement, as well as rooms for servants of many types. The first floor plan, which is shaped like an inverted T with a narrow service outlier in the rear, served as the center for the family to entertain guests. An interesting feature separating the entry hall and the dining room behind is an elaborate wooden screen. While considered

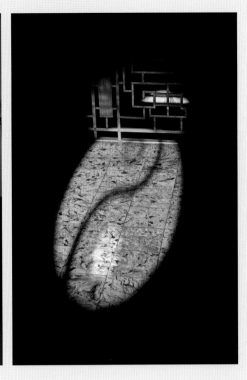

modern in style at the time in terms of its simple lines, the function is
similar to that found in traditional Chinese residences where the central
portion is a screen with a pair of openings on each side. Many of the
traditional-style residences seen in this book provide examples of this
form and function. A wide set of stairs rises to the second and third
floors where suites of rooms provided space for sleeping and family
leisure. Throughout the house, high ceilings, large windows, louvered
shutters, and transoms facilitate the movement of air, keeping it quite
cool even at the hottest time of year. Tile and marble floors are cool to
bare feet. Hardwoods from the Philippines were brought to Gulangyu
where they were fashioned into door panels and frames, wall paneling,
screens, and louvered doors and windows. Many of the wooden tables
and chairs are composite designs with both European and Chinese
elements, fashioned out of Philippine wood rather than Chinese blackwood. Pressed glass, some colored, and floor tiles of European style
are found throughout the house. Craftsmen—carpenters, masons,
blacksmiths, and painters—were brought from Jinjiang to carry out the
work on the residence under the supervision of a Western architect.

Dee C. Chuan died of tuberculosis in California in 1940 at the age
of sixty-two, and his body was returned to the Philippines for burial.
His sons, George Dee Se Kiat and Robert Dee Se Wee, who had begun
to play roles in the family business during the preceding decade,
succeeded him as family entrepreneurs. Dee C. Chuan's final resting
place is in Manila's Chinese Cemetery, a unique place some call the
"town of the dead" because of its residence-like mausoleums, many
with running water, wooden furniture, and air-conditioning. His
mausoleum is truly a grand structure, which, like his mansion in
Gulangyu, is multistoried with stairways winding to the second level.
A permanent caretaker lives in a small home adjacent to the mausoleum
to keep it tidy and prepare periodic offerings. Descendants continue to
visit and honor their illustrious forebear. The legacy of the Dee family
is well known throughout the Philippines.

Opposite above This master
bedroom, which has a mixture
of Western and Chinese-style
furnishings, has doors that lead
out to the veranda overlooking
the garden.

Opposite center A sitting area
within the bedroom.

Opposite below On the third floor
is a broad hallway with tables and
a seating area.

Above left Dee C. Chuan's three-
storey Chinese-style mausoleum
in the Manila Chinese Cemetery.

Above center Within a Chinese
frame that is reminiscent of an
ancestral altar is a portrait of
Dee C. Chuan and his wife.

Above right Because of sunlight
streaming in through a window, an
image of the *yinyang* symbol shines
on the floor of the mausoleum.

Right A cast concrete Chinese-
style pavilion in Dee C. Chuan's
garden in Gulangyu.

Below This pumpkin with a gecko
is placed as an ornament on the
ceiling of the garden pavilion.

ZHANG BISHI MANOR

DABU, GUANGDONG, CHINA

Early 20th Century

The intense emotional attachment to the native soil of an ancestral homeland, a birthplace, is universal, yet the notion has mythic qualities within the Chinese tradition. Such melancholic nostalgia is rooted in idealized notions of family and village life in the *guxiang* (native place). Such notions are subjects that have been celebrated in poetry and prose throughout Chinese history, from Sima Qian and Li Bai to Lu Xun and Shen Congwen. As the preceding chapters show, the homes built by returning Chinese on Chinese soil were sometimes a grand pastiche of styles and elements, a veritable scrapbook of their complicated and cumulating lives. In some cases, however, the inclusion of both modern Western elements and exuberant traditional Chinese ornamentation is absent in such planned retirement residences. Such is the case with the retreat built by Zhang Bishi (Cheong Fatt Tze), whose sumptuously ornamented Blue Mansion in Penang is shown on pages 128–39.

Zhang (Cheong), as will be recalled, was an extraordinary multi-national entrepreneur, a tycoon whose rags-to-riches story is one of the best known in Southeast Asia. While building his venerable Blue Mansion as he neared the age of sixty at the peak of his international fame and in the twilight of his eventful life, he began to construct a large traditional residence to retire to in Celong village, his birth-place in Dabu county, Guangdong. Received at the imperial court by the Empress Cixi, celebrated in San Francisco, New York City, and Washington for his wealth and worldliness, and the recipient of count-less honors, Zhang nonetheless yearned for end-of-life "happiness" in the quietude and order of his *guxiang*.

It is not clear how often he visited his home village as an adult, but local historians point out that he did come from time to time to supervise construction of his retirement home. It is said that he stayed in a large residence across the rice fields from the grand manor that he was building, not too far from his birthplace, which was reorganized as the Zhang ancestral hall, and the home of Zhang Chengqing, the family

Opposite above The offset entryway leads to an elongated courtyard.

Opposite below Held in the embrace of a ridge behind it, which is studded with family graves, Zhang Bishi's retirement manor looks out across fields of ripening rice.

Above The same three characters *Guang Lu Di* ("Residence of Glorious Emolument") that appear above the doorway into his Penang mansion reappear with his Dabu manor.

Left The horizontal board above the ancestral altar, here with the door panels closed, proclaims the "Hall of Five Awarenesses," which are rendered in various forms. *The First Awareness*: We are aware that all generations of our ancestors and all future generations are present within us; *The Second Awareness*: We are aware of the expectations that our ancestors, our children, and their children have of us; *The Third Awareness*: We are aware that our joy, peace, freedom, and harmony are the joy, peace, freedom, and harmony of our ancestors, our children, and their children; *The Fourth Awareness*: We are aware that understanding is the very foundation of love; *The Fifth Awareness*: We are aware that blaming and arguing can never help us but only create a wider gap between us.

manager of Zhang Bishi's wine company, which peculiarly mimics in plan and decoration the sumptuous Penang mansion. Behind the new home is the bend in a stream, with a designated wharf, that connected easily to other waterways that eventually reached the coast at Shantou and then the Nanyang beyond. Shallow-draft riverine vessels, which could be poled or swept along using sails, provided a comfortable and leisurely mode of transport for Zhang and other villagers through an area of tortuously rugged terrain. Tragically, in 1916, just a little more than a year after Zhang Bishi's extraordinary fifty-day trip to America, he was struck with pneumonia at the age of seventy-six while visiting one of his wives in Batavia (Jakarta). As with other sojourners, his wish was to have his body, his bones, transshipped back to the soil of his

guxiang for burial. Unlike others, however, his coffin traveled first to Penang and then on to Singapore and Hong Kong to receive the eulogies of other overseas Chinese as well as foreigners before reaching his remote village for entombment.

The expansive retirement residence he built reflects an enduring, but unfulfilled, dream of multigenerational residency, a large family living together. The residence, which faces north and has an entryway facing northwest, has an overall area of 4180 square meters. It is embraced from behind by an undulating ridge studded with family graves and faces other topographic features essential for harmonious *fengshui*. Reflecting the fact that Zhang judged Dabu to be a safe rural redoubt, only a low wall and substantial exterior fenestration mark its periphery, a marked variation from the veritable redoubts characteristic of other Hakka buildings in nearby areas. Except for the offset entry gate, the manor is symmetrical in ground plan, with three main halls, which rise in height from front to back at the center, a set of four flanking wings whose rooflines also rise, and a somewhat arcuate back wall that mimics a feature of classic Hakka *weilongwu*. Inside, there are thirteen skywells and scores of rooms of various dimensions. While the timber framework and the wall paintings throughout his residence are well executed, they are rather plain, especially in comparison with the adornment of the Blue Mansion. Moreover, unlike the Blue Mansion, whose cut-and-paste porcelain mosaics are truly extraordinary, none are found in his Dabu home. It is not possible to say whether this was by design to live somewhat simply or whether it reflects the fact that Zhang did not live long enough to take up residence and turn his attention to adding layers of opulence to his surroundings.

In the tranquility and fraternity of an idealized village life, Zhang clearly expected to return both to a time and place where traditional

moral codes remained vital, where human relations remained harmonious, and where the simplicity of life would contribute to the revitalization of his fundamental spirituality. In spite of—or perhaps because of—vast wealth and a life with at least eight wives and families, his dream did not materialize. Today, Zhang Bishi is celebrated as a "famous patriotic overseas Chinese" but during the Great Proletarian Cultural Revolution his descendants were exiled from his Dabu properties, which became the homes of poor peasants. His Penang and Dabu homes provide tangible evidence of an astonishing life lived, as the imperial system was declining and coming to an end in a transitional period as China began to embark on a difficult road to social, economic, and political modernization.

In a village epitomized by the sublime beauty of its mountains, streams, rice fields, and old houses, which only recently have been blemished in a limited way by modern transformations, plans are afoot for the development of a multi-use tourist area to be called "Dabu Cultural Village of Hakka Customs," with Zhang Bishi's retirement home as its centerpiece. The surrounding hillsides, fields, and streams are planned to showcase not only Hakka culture but also Chinese "wine culture," which is related to one of Zhang's major achievements, the founding of the Chang Yü Pioneer Wine Company in 1892 at Chefoo, the treaty port known today as Yantai, in Shandong province. As a Mandarin-capitalist straddling two worlds, even Zhang Bishi's once secluded *guxiang* is slated for linkage with the broader world via both new roads, technology, and streams of international visitors.

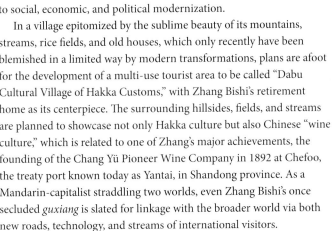

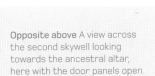

Opposite above A view across the second skywell looking towards the ancestral altar, here with the door panels open.

Left A view from the second hall looking across the first skywell towards the entry.

Top right Wooden framework within the second hall.

Second right A view across the pond towards Zhang Bishi's birthplace, which subsequently became the Zhang lineage ancestral hall.

Third right Reminiscent of Zhang's Penang Blue Mansion, as seen on page 128, this Dabu home was constructed by Zhang Chengqing, who was the manager of Zhang Bishi's Chang Yü Pioneer Wine Company.

Bottom right While following the general idea as employed in the Penang mansion, this balustrade around the first skywell was made of wrought iron in a local workshop in China rather than ordered as cast iron from Scotland, as seen on page 136.

Aasen, Clarence T., *Architecture of Siam: A Cultural History Interpretation*, Kuala Lumpur: Oxford University Press, 1998.

Abidin Kusno, "Remembering/Forgetting the May Riots: Architecture, Violence, and the Making of 'Chinese Cultures' in Post-1998 Jakarta," *Public Culture*, 15(1), 2003, pp. 149–77.

Andaya, Barbara Watson and Leonard Y. Andaya, *A History of Malaysia*, New York: St Martin's Press, 1982.

Andrade, Tonio, *How Taiwan Became Chinese: Dutch, Spanish, and Han Colonization in the Seventeenth Century*, New York: Columbia University Press, 2008.

Askew, Marc, "'Ban Thai': House and Culture in a Transforming Society," in Ronald G. Knapp (ed.), *Asia's Old Dwellings: Tradition, Resilience, and Change*, New York: Oxford University Press, 2003, pp. 259–82.

Azlan Ramli, "Waiting for a New Lease of Life," *Sunday Mail*, Malaysia, July 14, 2002.

Bagares, Gavin Sanson, "Old Parian House Soon to Showcase Local Heritage," *Sun-Star*, Cebu, June 12, 2005. http://www.sunstar.com.ph/static/ceb/2005/06/12/life/old.parian.house.soon.to.showcase.local.heritage.html

Berliner, Nancy Zeng, *Yin Yu Tang: The Architecture and Daily Life of a Chinese House*, Boston: Tuttle Publishing, 2003.

Bird, Isabella L. [Mrs J. F. Bishop], *The Golden Chersonese and the Way Thither*, New York: G. P. Putnam's Sons, 1883.

Blussé, Leonard, "Batavia, 1619–1740: The Rise and Fall of a Chinese Colonial Town," *Journal of Southeast Asian Studies*, 12, 1981, pp. 159–78.

_____, *Strange Company: Chinese Settlers, Mestizo Women and the Dutch in VOC Batavia*, Dordrecht-Holland: Foris Publications, 1986.

Briones, Concepcion G., *Life in Old Parian*, Cebu City: C. G. Briones, 1983.

Brown, William N. and Pan Weilian 潘维廉, *Discover Gulangyu* [*Meili Gulangyu* 魅力鼓浪屿], bilingual edition, Xiamen: Xiamen daxue chubanshe 厦门大学出版社, 2005.

Buckley, Charles Burton, *An Anecdotal History of Old Times in Singapore, from the Foundation of the Settlement Under the Honourable the East India Company, on Feb. 6th, 1819, to the Transfer to the Colonial Office As Part of the Colonial Possessions of the Crown on April 1st, 1867*, Singapore: Fraser & Neave, 1902.

Buiskool, Dirk A., "Medan: A Plantation City on the East Coast of Sumatra 1870–1942—Planters, the Sultans, Chinese and the Indian," paper presented at the 1st International Urban Conference, Surabaya, 2004.

_____, "Tours Through Historical Medan and Its Surroundings," Medan: n.p., 2008.

Cabaton, Antoine (trans. Bernard Miall), *Java, Sumatra and the Other Islands of the Dutch East Indies*, London: T. Fisher Unwin, 1911.

Campbell, John Gordon Drummond, *Siam in the Twentieth Century, Being the Experiences and Impressions of a British Official*, London: E. Arnold, 1902.

Campo, Joseph Norbert Frans Marie à, *Engines of Empire: Steamshipping and State Formation in Colonial Indonesia*, Hilversum, The Netherlands: Uitgeverij Verloren, 2002.

Cao Chunping 曹春平, *Minnan chuantong jianzhu* 闽南传统建筑 [Traditional architecture of Fujian and Guangdong], Xiamen: Xiamen daxue chubanshe 厦门大学出版社, 2006.

Carstens, Sharon A., *Histories, Cultures, Identities: Studies in Malaysian Chinese Worlds*, Singapore: Singapore University Press, 2005.

Chan Yeh Lih, "Conservation of the House of Tan Yeok Nee," in Chan Yeh Lih, Heng Chye Kiang, and Gretchen Liu (eds.), *The House of Tan Yeok Nee: The Conservation of a National Monument*, Singapore: Winpeak Investment & Wingem Investment, 2003, pp. 40–93.

"Chang Had $200,000 for Pocket Money; China's Rockefeller Spent Many Thousands Here in Buying Gifts for Friends," *New York Times*, June 13, 1915, p. 10.

Chang, Queeny, *Memories of a Nonya*, Singapore: Eastern Universities Press, 1981.

Chau Ju-Kua [Zhao Rukuo] (trans. Friedrich Hirth and William Woodville Rockhill), *Chau Ju-Kua: His Work on the Chinese and Arab Trade in the Twelfth and Thirteenth Centuries, Entitled Chu-fanchï*, St Petersburg: Printing Office of the Imperial Academy of Sciences, 1911.

Chen Ta, *Emigrant Communities in South China: A Study of Overseas Migration and Its Influence on Standards of Living and Social Change*, New York: China Institute of Pacific Relations, 1940.

Chinprasert, Silpchai (photographer Jamnong Srinuan), *Wat Matchimawat, Mural Paintings of Thailand Series*, Bangkok: Muang Boran Publishing House, 1983.

Choi Chi-cheung, "Hometown Connection and the Chaozhou Business Networks: A Case Study of the Chens of Kintyelung, 1850–1950," paper presented at the XI International Economic History Congress, Helsinki, August 21–5, 2006. http://www.helsinki.fi/iehc2006/papers2/Chicheung.pdf

_____, "Kinship and Business: Paternal and Maternal Kin in Chaozhou Chinese Family Firms," *Business History*, 1, 1998, pp. 26–49.

Chu, Richard T., "The Chinese Mestizos of the Philippines," in Teresita Ang See (ed.), *Tsinoy: The Story of the Chinese in Philippine Life*, Manila: Kaisa Para sa Kaunlaran, 2005, pp. 75–83.

Clague, Peter, "Wisma Loke," *The Straits Times Annual*, Kuala Lumpur: Straits Times Press, 1972, pp. 107–9.

"Conservation of Historic Building Remains in Limbo," *The Jakarta Post*, June 2, 2001. http://www.thejakartapost.com/news/2001/06/01/conservation-historic-building-remains-limbo.html

Crawfurd, John, *Journal of an Embassy from the Governor-General of India to the Courts of Siam and Conchin-China: Exhibiting a View of the Actual State of Those Kingdoms*, London: H. Colburn, 1828.

Cullinane, Michael, "The Changing Nature of the Cebu Urban Elite in the 19th Century," in Alfred W. McCoy and Ed. C. De Jesus (eds.), *Philippine Social History: Global Trade and Local Transformations*, Honolulu: University of Hawai'i Press, 1982, pp. 251–96.

Cushman, Jennifer Wayne, *Fields From the Sea: Chinese Junk Trade with Siam During the Late Eighteenth and Early Nineteenth Centuries*, Ithaca: Cornell University Press, 1993.

Cushman, Jennifer Wayne and Craig J. Reynolds, *Family and State: The Formation of a Sino-Thai Tin-Mining Dynasty, 1797–1932*, Singapore: Oxford University Press, 1991.

Dai Zhijian 戴志坚, *Min Tai minju jianzhu de yuanyuan yu xintai* 闽台民居建筑的渊源与形态 [Origins and Morphology of Vernacular Architecture in Fujian and Taiwan], Fuzhou: Fujian Renmin Chubanshe 福建人民出版社, 2003.

De Viana, Lorelei D. C., *Three Centuries of Binondo Architecture, 1594–1898: A Socio-Historical Perspective*, Manila: University of Santo Tomas Publishing House, 2001.

De Witt, Denis, *History of the Dutch in Malaysia*, Petaling Jaya, Malaysia: Nutmeg Publishing, 2007.

Dikötter, Frank, *Exotic Commodities: Modern Objects and Everyday Life in China*, New York: Columbia University Press, 2006.

Edwards, Norman, *The Singapore House and Residential Life, 1819–1939*, Singapore: Oxford University Press, 1990.

Fenner, Bruce Leonard, *Cebu Under the Spanish Flag, 1521–1896: An Economic–Social History*, Cebu City, Philippines: San Carlos Publications, University of San Carlos, 1985.

Flecker, Michael, "A Ninth-Century AD Arab or Indian Shipwreck in Indonesia: First Evidence for Direct Trade with China," *World Archaeology*, 32(3), February 2001, pp. 335–54.

Frost, Mark Ravinder, "Emporium in Imperio: Nanyang Networks and the Straits Chinese in Singapore, 1819–1914," *Journal of Southeast Asian Studies*, 36(1), 2005, pp. 29–66.

Gao Zhenming 高鈐明, Wang Naixiang 王乃香, and Chen Yu 陈瑜, *Fujian minju* 福建民居 [Vernacular Dwellings of Fujian], Beijing: Zhongguo Jianzhu Gongye Chubanshe 中國建筑工业出版社, 1987.

Gerini, G. E., John Carrington, and Walter Burke, *Old Phuket: Historical Retrospect of Junkceylon Island*, Bangkok: Siam Society, 1986.

Giles, Herbert Allen, *A Short History of Koolangsu*, Amoy: A. A. Marcal, 1878.

Godley, Michael R., "Chang Pi-shih and Nanyang Chinese Involvement in South China's Railroads, 1896–1911," *Journal of Southeast Asian Studies*, 4(1), 1973, pp. 17–30.

_____, "The Late Ch'ing Courtship of the Chinese in Southeast Asia," *The Journal of Asian Studies*, 34(2), 1975, pp. 361–85.

_____, *The Mandarin-capitalists from Nanyang: Overseas Chinese Enterprise in the Modernization of China, 1893–1911*, Cambridge: Cambridge University Press, 1981.

Gottschang, Thomas R. and Diana Lary, *Swallows and Settlers: The Great Migration from North*

China to Manchuria, Michigan monographs in Chinese studies, Vol. 87, Ann Arbor: Center for Chinese Studies, University of Michigan, 2000.

Guangdong sheng zhengxie 广东省政协, "Nanyang jugu Zhang shi Xiongdi" 南洋巨贾张氏兄弟 [Nanyang Businessmen: The Tjong brothers], *Huaqiao cangsang lu* 華僑滄桑錄 [Record of the Boundless Native Places of Overseas Chinese], Guangzhou: Guangdong Renmin Chubanshe, 1984.

Gunawan, Apriadi, "Medan Strives to Save Historical Buildings," *The Jakarta Post*, April 22, 2001, p. 1.

Gützlaff, Karl Friedrich August, *Journal of Three Voyages Along the Coast of China, in 1831, 1832, & 1833: With Notices of Siam, Corea, and the Loo-Choo Islands*, London: F. Westley and A. H. Davis, 1834.

Hamidah Atan, "Opulence of Yam Chuan Mansion," *New Straits Times*, Malaysia, February 23, 2000.

Han Bing Siong, "A Short Note on a Few Uncertain Links in the Han Lineage," *Archipel*, 62, 2001, pp. 43–52.

Hemtasilpa, Sujintana, "Stylish Dive for Dogs," *Bangkok Post*, September 20, 2004.

Heng Chye Kiang, "Traditional Houses in Chaoshan," in Chan Yeh Lih, Heng Chye Kiang, and Gretchen Liu (eds.), *The House of Tan Yeok Nee: The Conservation of a National Monument*, Singapore: Winpeak Investment & Wingem Investment, 2003, pp. 21–39.

Heuken, Adolf, *Historical Sites of Jakarta*, Jakarta: Cipta Loka Caraka, 2007.

Hirth, Friedrich and W. W. Rockhill (trans.), *Chau Ju-kua: His Work on the Chinese and Arab Trade in the Twelfth and Thirteenth Centuries, Entitled Chu-fan-chi*, St Petersburg: Printing Office of the Imperial Academy of Sciences, 1911.

"Historical Discovery of No. 8 Heeren Street, Malacca: A Joint Cultural Preservation Project Under 'Ambassador's Fund for Cultural Preservation' Between U.S. Embassy Malaysia and Badan Warisan (Heritage Trust) Malaysia. http://usembassymalaysia.org.my/malacca/m1.htm

Ho Puay-peng, "Ancestral Halls: Family, Lineages, and Ritual," in Ronald G. Knapp and Kai-Yin Lo (eds.), *House Home Family: Living and Being Chinese*, Honolulu: University of Hawai'i Press, 2005, pp. 295–322.

Hsu Wen-hsiung, "From Aboriginal Island to Chinese Frontier: The Development of Taiwan Before 1683," in Ronald G. Knapp (ed.), *China's Island Frontier: Studies in the Historical Geography of Taiwan*, Honolulu: University of Hawai'i Press, 1980, pp. 3–29.

Huang Weijun 黄为隽, et al., *Min Yue minzhai* 闽粤民宅 [Vernacular Dwellings of Fujian and Guangdong], Tianjin Shi: Tianjin Kexue Jishu Chubanshe 天津科学技术出版社, 1992.

Hwang, Andrew, "The Sad State of Loke Mansion, Medan Tuanku, KL," *Buletin Warisan*, December 2006–January 2007, p. 2.

Indrani, Hedy C. and Maria Ernawati Prasodjo, "Tipologi, Organisasi Ruang, Dan Elemen Interior Rumah Abu Han Di Surabaya" [Typology, Spatial Organization, and Interior Elements of the Han Ancestral Hall, Surabaya], *Dimensi Interior*, 3(1), 2005, pp. 44–65.

Jackson, James C., "Kuala Lumpur in the 1880's: The Contribution of Bloomfield Douglass," *Journal of Southeast Asian History*, 4(2): 1963, pp. 117–27.

Jacq-Hergoualc'h, Michel, The *Malay Peninsula: Crossroads of the Maritime Silk-Road (100 BC–1300 AD)*, Leiden: Brill Academic Publishers, 2002.

Jordan, David K., http://weber.ucsd.edu/~dkjordan/chin/china.html (China Related Sources)

Kam, Patsy, "Restored to Glory: A Dilapidated Building Has Been Given Back Its Soul," *thestar online*, Malaysia, July 21, 2008. http://thestar.com.my/lifestyle/story.asp?file=/2008/7/21/lifeliving/1541934&sec=lifeliving

Khoo Kay Kim, *The Western Malay States, 1850–1873: The Effects of Commercial Development on Malay Politics*, Kuala Lumpur: Oxford University Press, 1972.

King, Phil, "Penang to Songkhla, Penang to Patani: Two Roads, Past and Present," *Malaysian Journal of Tropical Geography*, 33(1/2), 2002, pp. 93–102.

Knapp, Ronald G., *China's Old Dwellings*, Honolulu: University of Hawai'i Press, 2000.

_____, *Chinese Houses: The Architectural Heritage of a Nation*, North Clarendon, Vermont: Tuttle Publishing, 2005.

Knapp, Ronald G. (ed.), *China's Island Frontier: Studies in the Historical Geography of Taiwan*, Honolulu: University of Hawai'i Press, 1980.

Knapp, Ronald G. and Shen Dongqi, "Changing Village Landscapes," in Ronald G. Knapp (ed.), *Chinese Landscapes: The Village as Place*, Honolulu: University of Hawai'i Press, 1992, pp. 47–78.

Kohl, David, *Chinese Architecture in the Straits Settlements and Western Malaya: Temples, Kongsis, and Houses*, Kuala Lumpur: Heinemann Asia, 1984.

Lee Ho Yin, "The Singapore Shophouse: An Anglo-Chinese Vernacular," in Ronald G. Knapp (ed.), *Asia's Old Dwellings: Tradition, Resilience, and Change*, New York: Oxford University Press, 2003, pp. 115–34.

Lee Kip Lin, *Emerald Hill: The Story of a Street in Words and Pictures*, Singapore: National Museum, 1984.

_____, *The Singapore House, 1819–1942*, Singapore: Times Editions and Preservation of Monuments Board, 1953.

Lee, Peter and Jennifer Chen, *The Straits Chinese House: Domestic Life and Traditions*, Singapore: National Museum of Singapore and Editions Didier Millet, 2006.

Lim Huck Chin and Fernando Jorge, *Malacca: Voices from the Street*, Malacca: Lim Huck Chin, 2005.

Lin Lee Loh-Lim, *The Blue Mansion: The Story of Mandarin Splendour Reborn*, Penang: L'Plan, 2002.

Liu, Gretchen, "The House of Tan Yeok Nee," in Chan Yeh Lih, Heng Chye Kiang, and Gretchen Liu (eds.), *The House of Tan Yeok Nee: The Conservation of a National Monument*, Singapore: Winpeak Investment & Wingem Investment, 2003, pp. 13–19.

_____, *Pastel Portraits: Singapore's Architectural Heritage*, Singapore: Singapore Coordinating Committee, 1984.

Lohanda, Mona, *The Kapitan Cina of Batavia, 1837–1942: A History of Chinese Establishment in Colonial Society*, Jakarta: Djambatan, 1996.

Lu Yuanding 陆元鼎 and Yanjun Wei 魏彦钧, *Guangdong min minju* 廣東民居 [Vernacular Architecture of Guangdong], Beijing: Zhongguo Jianzhu Gongye Chubanshe 中国建筑工业出版社, 1990.

Marshall, Edward, "Talk with the Morgan of China: Chang Chen Hsun, Richest of Chinese Financiers, Discusses the Needs of His County in the Present Crisis," *New York Times*, Magazine section, June 6, 1915, pp. SM4–5, 7.

McKeown, Adam, "Conceptualizing Chinese Diasporas, 1842 to 1949," *The Journal of Asian Studies*, 58(2), 1999, pp. 306–37.

Mei Qing, "Houses and Settlements: Returned Overseas Chinese Architecture in Xiamen, 1890s–1930s," Ph.D. thesis, Chinese University of Hong Kong, 2003.

Middlebrook, S. M. and J. M. Gullick, *Yap Ah Loy, 1837–1885*, Kuala Lumpur: Malaysian Branch of the Royal Asiatic Society, Reprint No. 9, 1983.

Milone, Pauline Dublin, "Indische Culture, and Its Relationship to Urban Life," *Comparative Studies in Society and History*, 9(4), 1967, pp. 407–26.

"Model Restoration Project in Malacca" http://www.badanwarisan.org.my/conservation/8heeren.php

Mojares, Resil B., *Casa Gorordo in Cebu: Urban Residence in a Philippine Province, 1860–1920*, Cebu: Ramon Aboitiz Foundation, 1983.

Nasution, Khoo Salma, "Baba Nyonya Culture in Penang and Phuket," *Proceedings of a Symposium on the Phuket-Penang Relationship*, Phuket, Thailand, September 20, 2008, pp. 57–65.

_____, "Heritage of Phuket Town" and "Phuket's Old Town Movement," *Lestari Heritage Network*. http://www.lestariheritage.net/phuket/webpages/mov01.html#History

_____, "Penang and Phuket: Once Siamese Twins," *The Peranakan*, December 2006, pp. 14–15.

_____, *Sun Yat Sen in Penang*, Penang: Areca Books, 2008.

Needham Joseph, Christian Daniels, and Nicholas K. Menzies, *Science and Civilisation in China Volume 6: Biology and Biological Technology, Part 3, Agro-Industries and Forestry*, Cambridge: Cambridge University Press, 1996.

"Notices of Pinang," *Journal of the Indian Archipelago and Eastern Asia*, 8, 1858, pp. 182–203.

Nurbianto, Bambang, "Governor Turns Down Candra Naya Relocation," *The Jakarta Post*, July 8, 2003. http://www.thejakartapost.com/news/2003/07/08/governor-turns-down-candra-naya-relocation.html

Ong Poh Neo, *Brown & Gold: Peranakan Furniture from the Late 19th Century to the Mid 20th Century*, Singapore: Privately published, 1994.

Pacis, Carla Mendoza, "Nostalgia for Bagoong," in Amy Besa and Romy Dorotan, *Memories of Philippine Kitchens*, New York: Stewart, Tabori & Chang, 2006, pp. 118–20.

Pan, Lynn, *The Encyclopedia of the Chinese Overseas*, Singapore: Editions Didier Millet, 2006.

_____, *Sons of the Yellow Emperor: A History of the Chinese Diaspora*, New York: Kodansha, 1994.

Poppeliers, John, S. Allen Chambers, and Nancy B. Schwartz, *What Style Is It?*, Washington, DC: The Preservation Press, 1977.

Posayachinda, Poosak websites: Dunam.com http://www.dumnam.com/; x-Plorers http://www.x-plorersbeagles.com/index.php?p=about

Post, Peter, "The Kwik Hoo Tong Trading Society of Semarang, Java: A Chinese Business Network in Late Colonial Asia," *Journal of Southeast Asian Studies*, 33(2), 2002, pp. 279–96.

Prasodjo, Maria Ernawati, *Studi Interior Pada Rumah Abu Han di Surabaya* [Study of the Interior of the Han Ancestral Hall in Surabaya], Surabaya: Universitas Kristen Petra, 2004.

Priyomarsono, Naniek W., *Rumah Mayor China Di Jakarta/Mansion of The Chinese Major in Jakarta*, Jakarta: SUBUR Jaringan Cetak Terpadu, 2008.

Purcell, Victor, *The Chinese in Southeast Asia*, London: Oxford University Press, 1965.

Ramasoot, Saithiwa, "Dismantle, Reassemble, and Modify: An Adaptive Reuse of the Traditional Thai House," Ph.D. thesis, Department of Architecture, University of Pennsylvania, 2008.

Reid, Anthony, "Betel-Chewing to Tobacco-Smoking in Indonesia," *The Journal of Asian Studies*, 44(3), 1985, pp. 529–47.

_____, "Flows and Seepages in the Long-term Chinese Interaction with Southeast Asia," in Anthony Reid and Kristine Alilunas-Rodgers (eds.), *Sojourners and Settlers: Histories of Southeast Asia and the Chinese*, Honolulu: University of Hawai'i Press, 2001, pp. 15–49.

Reid, Anthony and Kristine Alilunas-Rodgers (eds.), *Sojourners and Settlers: Histories of Southeast Asia and the Chinese*, Honolulu: University of Hawai'i Press, 2001.

Sakulpipatana, Pranee, *Hokkien Chinese in Phuket*, privately printed, 2002.

Salmon, Claudine, "Ancestral Halls, Funeral Associations and Attempts at Resinicization in Nineteenth-Century Netherlands India," in Anthony Reid and Kristine Alilunas-Rodgers (eds.), *Sojourners and Settlers: Histories of Southeast Asia and the Chinese*, Honolulu: University of Hawai'i Press, 2001a, pp. 183–202.

_____, "The Han Family of East Java: Entrepreneurship and Politics (18th–19th Centuries)," *Archipel*, 41, 1991, pp. 53–87.

_____, "Some More Comments on 'Uncertain Links' in the Han Lineage," *Archipel*, 62, 2001b, pp. 43–52.

Schurz, William Lytle, *The Manila Galleon*, New York: E. P. Dutton, 1939.

See, Teresita Ang (ed.), *Tsinoy: The Story of the Chinese in Philippine Life*, Manila: Kaisa Para sa Kaunlaran, 2005.

Shen Binghong 沈冰虹, *Lingnan diyi qiao zhai: Chen Cihong guju ji qi jiazu* 岭南第一侨宅: 陈慈黉故居及其家族 [The #1 Overseas Chinese House in the Lingnan Region: The Residence and Family of Chen Cihong], Shantou: Shantou Daxue Chubanshe, 2001.

Skinner, G. William, *Chinese Society in Thailand: An Analytical History*, Ithaca: Cornell University Press, 1957.

_____, "Mobility Strategies in Late Imperial China: A Regional Systems Analysis," in Carol A. Smith (ed.), *Regional Analysis: Vol. 1, Economic Systems*, New York: Academic Press, 1976, pp. 327–64.

Smith, C. A. Middleton, *The British in China and Far Eastern Trade*, London: Constable & Company, Ltd, 1920.

Song Ong Siang, *One Hundred Years' History of the Chinese in Singapore: Being a Chronological Record of the Contribution by the Chinese Community to the Development, Progress and Prosperity of Singapore … from the Foundation of Singapore … 1819 to Its Centenary … 1919 … With … Portraits and Illustrations*, London: J. Murray, 1923.

Songkhla National Museum, Songkhla: Regional Office of Archaeology and National Museums, 1997; corrected edition 2008.

Stuart, Jan and Evelyn S. Rawski, *Worshipping the Ancestors: Chinese Commemorative Portraits*, Washington, DC: Freer Gallery of Art, 2001.

Sutherland, Heather, "From the Particular to the General: Local Communities and Collective History, *CHC Bulletin, Newsletter of Chinese Heritage Centre*, 1, March 2003a, pp. 4–6.

_____, "Southeast Asian History and the Mediterranean Analogy," *Journal of Southeast Asian Studies*, 34(1), 2003b, pp. 1–20.

Tan, Jessica, "Giving in Kind," *Forbes.com*, March 3, 2008. http://www.forbes.com/global/2008/0310/047.html

Tan Kim Lwi, Agnes, *A Son of Malacca: Tun Dato' Sir Cheng Lock Tan*, 2nd edition, Singapore: n.p., 2006.

Tan Siok Choo, "Heeren Street," *New Straits Times Annual*, Kuala Lumpur: Straits Times Press, 1983, pp. 40–51.

_____, "The Tan Family Saga," *New Straits Times Annual*, Kuala Lumpur: Straits Times Press, 1981, pp. 20–5.

The Story of Loke House: A Man and His Home in the Early Days of Kuala Lumpur, Kuala Lumpur: n.p., 1971.

Tio, Jongkie, *Semarang City: A Glance into the Past*, Semarang: Privately printed, 2007.

Trocki, Carl A., *Opium and Empire: Chinese Society in Colonial Singapore, 1800–1910*, Ithaca: Cornell University Press, 1990.

US Supreme Court, Sy Joc Lieng v. Gregorio Sy Quia, 228 U.S. 335 (1913), Rochester NY: Lawyers Co-operative Publishing Co. http://supreme.justia.com/us/228/335/case.html

Villalón, Augusto F., "The Evolution of the Philippine Traditional House," in Ronald G. Knapp (ed.), *Asia's Old Dwellings: Tradition, Resilience, and Change*, New York: Oxford University Press, 2003.

_____, "The Historic Town of Vigan," *Living Landscapes and Cultural Landmarks: World Heritage Sites in the Philippines*, Manila: ArtPostAsia, 2005, pp. 203–19.

Waley, Arthur (trans.), *The Book of Songs*, New York: Grove Press, 1960.

_____, *The Way and Its Power: A Study of the Tao Tê Ching and Its Place in Chinese Thought*, New York: Grove Press, 1958.

Wang Gungwu, *China and the Overseas Chinese*, Singapore: Times Academic Press, 1991.

_____, *The Chinese Overseas: From Earthbound China to the Quest for Autonomy*, Cambridge: Harvard University Press, 2000.

Wang Ta-Hai (Ong Tae-Hae), *The Chinaman Abroad; An Account of the Malayan Archipelago: Particularly of Java, By Ong-Tae-Hae, Translated from the Original, by W. H. Medhurst*, London: John Snow, 1850.

Warren, James Francis, *Ah Ku and Karayuki-San: Prostitution in Singapore, 1870–1940*, Singapore: Oxford University Press, 1993.

_____, *Pirates, Prostitutes and Pullers: Explorations in the Ethno- and Social History of Southeast Asia*, Crawley, Western Australia: University of Western Australia Press, 2008.

_____, *Rickshaw Coolie: A People's History of Singapore, 1880–1940*, Singapore: Oxford University Press, 1986.

_____, *The Sulu Zone, 1768–1898: The Dynamics of External Trade, Slavery, and Ethnicity in the Transformation of a Southeast Asian Maritime State*, Singapore: Singapore University Press, 1981.

Wee, Bonnie, "Showcase of Straits Legacy," *New Straits Times*, Malaysia, April 12, 1999.

Welch, Patricia Bjaaland, *Chinese Art: A Guide to Motifs and Visual Imagery*, North Clarendon, Vermont: Tuttle Publishing, 2008.

Wheeler, Charles J., "Cross-cultural Trade and Trans-regional Networks in the Port of Hoi An: Maritime Vietnam in the Early Modern Era," Ph.D. dissertation, Yale University, 2001.

Wickberg, Edgar, *The Chinese in Philippine Life: 1850–1898*, New Haven: Yale University Press, 1965.

Widayati, Naniek, "Candra Naya Antara Kejayaan Masa Lalu Dan Kenyataan Sekearang," *Dimensi Teknik Arsitektur*, 31(2), 2003, pp. 88–101.

Widodo, Johannes, "Medan: The Advent of a North Sumatran Modern City," *Medan: Understanding Heritage*. http://medan.m-heritage.org/about_medan/index.html

Winarti, Agnes, "Candranaya Strives to Breathe Beneath Skyscraper," *The Jakarta Post*, February 27, 2009. http://www.thejakartapost.com/news/2009/02/27/candranaya-strives-breathe-beneath-skyscraper.html

Wisma Loke: The Story of Loke House, Kuala Lumpur: n.p., 1970.

ACKNOWLEDGMENTS

Wong Yeetuan, "The Big Five Hokkien Families in Penang, 1830s–1890s," *Chinese Southern Diasporic Studies*, 1, 2007, pp. 106–15.

Wright, Arnold, *Twentieth Century Impressions of Siam: Its History, People, Commerce, Industries, and Resources*, London: Lloyd's Greater Britain Publishing Co., 1908.

Wright, Arnold, and H. A. Cartwright, *Twentieth Century Impressions of British Malaya: Its History, People, Commerce, Industries, and Resources*, London: Lloyd's Greater Britain Publishing Co., 1908.

Wu, Nelson Ikon, *Chinese and Indian Architecture: The City of Man, the Mountain of God, and the Realm of the Immortals*, New York: G. Braziller, 1963.

Wyatt, David K., *Thailand: A Short History*, New Haven: Yale University Press, 2003.

Xia Dingxun 夏鼎勛, "Minqiao Wu Yang ji qi zisun"閩侨吴阳及其子孙 [The Hokkien Overseas Chinese Wu Yang and His Descendants], *Huaqiao Xinyu* 华侨新语, 1953, pp. 11–12, 40–51.

Yen Ching-Hwang, "Chang Yu-Nan and the Chaochow Railway (1904–1908): A Case Study of Overseas Chinese Involvement in China's Modern Enterprise," *Modern Asian Studies*, 18(1), 1984, pp. 119–35.

_____, "Class Structure and Social Mobility in the Chinese Community in Singapore and Malaya 1800–1911," *Modern Asian Studies*, 21(3), 1987, pp. 417–45.

Yuliandini, Tantri, "Candra Naya, Test of Commitment to Preservation," *The Jakarta Post*, May 29, 2003. http://www.thejakartapost.com/news/2003/05/29/candra-naya-test-commitment-preservation.html

Zheng Dehua 鄭德華, *Guangdong qiao xiang jian zhu wen hua* 廣東僑鄉建築文化 [Architectural Culture of Overseas Chinese in Guangdong], Hong Kong: Sanlian Shudian (Xianggang) Youxiangongsi, 2003.

Zhu Diguang 朱迪光 and Mai Juanjuan 麦娟娟, "Zhong-Xi hebi Lian Fang Lou" 中西合璧联芳楼 [Lian Fang Lou: Harmonious Western–Chinese fusion], Kejian Wenhua Shuju ku 客家文化数据库 [Hakka Digital Database]. http://sglyj.meizhou.gov.cn/modules/dept/article.php?storyid=311 November 10, 2008.

Zialcita, Fernando N., *Authentic Though Not Exotic: Essays on Filipino Identity*, Manila: Ateneo de Manila University Press, 2005.

Zialcita, Fernando N. and Martin I. Tinio, *Philippine Ancestral Houses (1810–1930)*, Quezon City, Philippines: GCF Books, 1980.

While reviewing the illustrations and text for *Chinese Houses: The Architectural Heritage of a Nation* (2005), Eric Oey, the Periplus/Tuttle publisher, asked whether I would consider doing field work and research for a book on Chinese houses in Southeast Asia. I was intrigued by the idea, having actually never thought of Chinese houses outside of China, yet my initial reaction was one of skepticism that such a book was possible, questioning first whether indeed there were old Chinese-style homes still standing and, secondly, how I would find and get access to those that could be located.

Forty years of experiences in China and Taiwan had provided me with a range of knowledge and sufficient confidence that made it possible to carry out relatively unfettered rural field work there. Even as I was finishing up *Chinese Bridges: Living Architecture from China's Past* (2008), other research topics in China continued to beckon. Still, the prospect of taking a detour and commencing a fresh China-related research agenda outside the boundaries of China proved quite attractive, even as significant challenges seemed likely.

I had lived in Singapore for more than a year in the early 1970s and traveled throughout Malaysia and Thailand, yet I had no recollection of seeing any Chinese-style residences except for the ubiquitous and often nondescript shophouses. While I recalled reading that some immigrants had built Chinese-style homes in Southeast Asia, in truth I had little sense of what forms they might have taken. Preliminary archival research turned up photographs taken in the early twentieth century of what indeed were residences in Southeast Asia like those traditionally built in southern China. The issue, however, was whether any were still standing at the beginning of the twenty-first century.

After further discussions with Eric Oey in the summer of 2007, who promised to assist in making some initial contacts, I agreed to take on what I knew would be a demanding project with increasing optimism that the effort would not be totally fruitless. Indeed, just contemplating the search for elusive old Chinese homes, whether derelict or renovated, was exhilarating, and I increasingly looked forward to this quest.

Chester Ong, the masterful photographer who collaborated with me on both *Chinese Houses* and *Chinese Bridges*, and I decided to begin the project in fall 2007 by first revisiting Guangdong and Fujian, which had been the home provinces of most Chinese emigrants to Southeast Asia. Not only did we want to better understand the regional characteristics of homes in these two provinces, but we also wanted to visit residences build by Returned Overseas Chinese, those who had been successful in the Nanyang and returned to their home villages. This initial foray was followed by three separate lengthy trips in 2008 to Singapore, Malaysia, Indonesia, Thailand, and the Philippines in search of old Chinese houses. In late Fall 2009, we returned to the remote mountainous areas of Guangdong province to photograph the planned "retirement" homes of Cheong Fatt Tze (Zhang Bishi) of Penang and Tjong A Fie of Medan.

Early on, we projected finding and documenting approximately twenty old residences, but in time we visited and photographed nearly four times as many that were built between the late eighteenth and early twentieth century. Nearly forty of these are featured in this book, with glimpses of most of the others as well. Some of the homes have a distinctive patrimony in that they are linked to historical figures, but the origins of some are only sketchy. It has been enlightening to reconstruct the nature of past social, economic, and geographic conditions, and link them to family histories, which I see as one of the major contributions of this book. Because the materials collected far exceed what can be presented in this book, which is structured around individual residences, a companion volume will be published in 2011. This second book will be structured topically in order to focus on the full range of material objects enjoyed by Peranakan Chinese families within their architectural spaces or settings—the rooms—of their terrace houses, bungalows, and mansions during the late nineteenth and early twentieth centuries. These objects will provide opportunities to discuss the symbolic meaning of recurring motifs and the use of the objects in daily life and periodic life passages, subjects only explored tangentially in *Chinese Houses of Southeast Asia*.

A book of this scope could not have been written without the generous support of countless individuals throughout Southeast Asia. Critical initial contacts were facilitated by the Periplus team: Eric Oey and his wife Christina Ong in Singapore and Malaysia as well as Judo Suwidji and Joko Santoso in Indonesia. Others in the Periplus family were also incredibly helpful: Noor Azlina Yunus who made some key contacts in Malaysia, as well as Tessa Bombong and Yohana Cai who made arrangements throughout Indonesia and quickly did some necessary translations for us. We owe special gratitude to Anton Ong who traveled with us throughout Sumatra and Java, not only seeing to it that travel arrangements were smooth but facilitating contacts with countless home owners. In addition, he measured and sketched floor plans and served as photographic assistant.

As readers below will see, the list of those who provided assistance is quite lengthy and it is not possible to remark on all of the help given, which ranged from opening family homes to us, responding to countless questions in person and via email, providing published and unpublished written materials, suggesting follow-up options, and in some cases critiquing my texts. Without the generosity and kindnesses of individuals in six countries, this project could not have been carried out. While we owe special gratitude to those who willingly opened their treasured family homes to us, thanks are also due to curators and managers who also were so helpful:

Singapore: Johnson Tan, Ong Poh Neo and Dr James Khoo Chee Min, Irene and Tak Min Lim, Peter Wee, and Alvin Yapp provided our first glimpses of Chinese-style terrace houses and helped acquaint us with the rich material culture of times past. Jean Wee Mei-Yin, at the time Curator of Baba House that was once the home of the Wee family, welcomed us during three visits that gave us an opportunity to experience not only ongoing restoration work but also the fascinating details of a "living museum." Peter Lee, the Honorary Curator of the Baba House and intimately involved in decisions regarding its conservation and furnishing, was generous in sharing his knowledge. Finally, although we only corresponded via email, I am grateful to Wee Lin, descendant of Wee Bin whose home became the Baba House, for helping me understand what life once was like within the family's residence. Kelvin Ang Kah Eng, Head (Heritage Studies), Conservation & Urban Design Division of Singapore's Urban Development Authority, not only

shared his knowledge but played a key role in helping identify people we needed to meet in Singapore and beyond. Julian Davison, author of books on Singapore's architecture, maintained a vigorous email exchange with me of pertinent information. Christine Khor Seok Kee, Director, National University of Singapore, Centre for the Arts, was steadfast in her support of the project. Heng Chye Kiang of the Department of Architecture of National University of Singapore offered especially useful advice concerning the Tan Yeok Nee residence. Intan Salam, Director of Conference Center and Business Operations, Executive MBA Program Asia, The University of Chicago Booth School of Business, and See Ying Hwee, Associate Director, Asset Management, ING REIM (Singapore) Pte Ltd, are thanked for facilitating the permission for photographing the restored Tan Yeok Nee residence. We were pleased that Linda Lee gave us permission to photograph her family's *rumah panggung*, an elevated Malay-style residential form favored by some Peranakan Chinese families early in the twentieth century

Malacca: We were indeed fortunate that the gracious Tan Siok Choo, granddaughter of the celebrated Tan Cheng Lock, took an early interest in our project and opened the Tan ancestral home for several days of photography. One highlight was her generous offer for us to spend a night in this historic home. We had the good fortune also to be under the guidance of Josephine Chua, a spirited protector of Malacca's heritage, who seemed to know everyone in town. With her husband Tan Hoon Keong and son Daniel, we were able to gain many insights and meet individuals who opened their homes to us. Two contrasting buildings, one lived in by Chee Gim Chye on Jonker Street and one directed by Chee Swee Hoon on Heeren Street, gave us insights into the differing roles of extended families in maintaining heritage buildings. The fine restoration of an eighteenth-century shophouse on Heeren Street was introduced to us by its very knowledgeable curator, Colin Goh, with the permission of Elizabeth Cardosa, Executive Director of Badan Warisan Malaysia. A short distance down the street, Serge Jardin and Kok Chern Lee, known as KC, have lovingly restored an old terrace house as a B&B. Calling it The Snail House, they are committed to introducing visitors from throughout the world to the wonders of Malacca. Betty Ong

of the Persatuan Peranakan Cina Melaka, which is housed in a rambling terrace house building, helped us understand better the role of Peranakan Chinese social organizations in the past as well as today. Cedric Tan's successful restoration of a terrace house without any outside sources of funding highlights what can be done by a private individual to meet his family's needs.

Kuala Lumpur: During our first visit to Malaysia's capital, we only spent time photographing the 1918 manor of Tan Boon Jia in Rasa on the city's outskirts, with the assistance of Ong Pit Ewe and courtesy of Peter Soon Seng Mah. When we subsequently learned that the residence of the illustrious Loke Yew was not only standing but recently restored to house the Cheang & Ariff law firm, we made plans for a special return visit to Kuala Lumpur because of the generous assistance of Dato' Loh Siew Cheang and Christopher B. W. Wong.

Penang: Like Malacca, the island of Penang is blessed with abundant historical architecture and a coterie of avid citizens interested in historical preservation. A fifth-generation Straits Chinese, Khoo Salma Nasution, a prolific author and resource for understanding Penang, privately undertook the restoration of the home known as the Dr Sun Yat Sen Penang Base. Her interest in our project included linking us to a network of her friends throughout the region, an effort that is very much appreciated. An expansive complex of residences with a magnificent ancestral hall, the ancestral manor of Kee Lai Huat in Sungai Bakap in Province Wellesley on the mainland was introduced to us by the energetic and knowledgeable Dato' Kee Phaik Cheen, with assistance from her brother Kee Yong Chuan, and cousin Kee Yong Hee. Chester's return visit to Penang at her invitation to photograph the Kee family's commemoration of Cheng Beng (Qingming), the day when descendants remember their ancestors at shrines and at cemeteries, will be featured in our next book. Of all the restored residences in Penang, The Blue Mansion, which was restored by a group led by architect Laurence Loh and his preservationist wife Lin Lee Loh-Lim, now has pride of place reborn as a boutique hotel. Although we did not have the pleasure of meeting these principals, Eric Fam Soo Seng, the manager of the property, graciously welcomed us and shared his knowledge of what was once the mansion of the fabled

Cheong Fatt Tze. What was once the magnificent townhouse residence of the wealthy Chinese immigrant Chung Keng Kwee was rescued from dilapidation and restored by Peter Soon Seng Mah as the Pinang Peranakan Mansion as a venue to exhibit his comprehensive collection of antiques of the unique Baba-Nyonya culture. After visiting the mansion, I had the good fortune to learn of the research carried out by Chung Keng Kwee's great-grandson Jeffery Seow. Jeffery and I carried out an extensive email correspondence that gave me the confidence to write a comprehensive essay on his remarkable ancestor. Lim Gaik Siang, an architect, conservation consultant, and council member of the Penang Heritage Trust, introduced us to the vitality of the Teochew community in Penang, especially as it coalesced around the fine restoration of the Han Jiang Ancestral Hall.

Sumatra: Traveling throughout Sumatra and Java in our quest for residences built by Chinese settlers, we nonetheless saw only a fraction of a vast, diverse, and intriguing archipelago that had provided opportunities for Chinese traders centuries before Europeans reached the Indies in the sixteenth century. Although today representing only approximately one percent of the country's population, Chinese remain a highly visible minority. While grand Chinese-style residences in the past declared the commercial success of immigrant entrepreneurship, only a few still stand. Most Chinese of course lived in more modest structures, such as shophouses and single-family dwellings raised above the ground, which are still found in abundance in old river port towns throughout Indonesia. In Padang, in western Sumatra, where gold, coffee, spices, and even the slave trade attracted enterprising Chinese immigrants, we are grateful to the following who opened their family homes for photography: Oey Le Tju, Lim Quanliang, Lucien Angriawan, and Yenni Gunawan. Arguably the most glorious Chinese-style residence still standing in Sumatra is the mansion of Tjong A Fie in Medan, which was constructed at the turn of the twentieth century when trade linkages with Penang were particularly active. Two of Tjong's grandchildren, Fon Prawira Tjong and Mimi Tjong, proudly gave us full access to this historic home. Here, they have established an institute that is open to the public to celebrate the contributions of Chinese immigrants such as Tjong A Fie to Indonesia's economic and cultural development. Although we did not meet Dirk A. Buiskool, local historian and owner of the comfortable Hotel Deli River, we benefitted from his writings and suggestions about places to visit from Padang in the west to Labuan Deli in northern Sumatra.

Java: Jakarta, Indonesia's frenetic capital city, has many beautiful and imposing buildings from the Dutch period, but only a handful of temples and homes built by Chinese. We are grateful for the advice of Adolf Heuken SJ, whose devotion to documenting the architectural history of Jakarta is matched by his passion for preserving not only grand structures but also vernacular ones. In Jakarta, we had the good fortune to meet David Kwa and Sutrisno Murtiyoso, among others, who were generous with their advice as well as willingness to read my developing texts. Their suggestions contributed significantly to the accuracy of my analysis and narrative. From Tangerang on the west end of the island to Pasuruan on the east, as well as towns and cities along the coast of the Java Sea and inland, we encountered wonderful old homes and individuals who were generous in sharing their knowledge: Jongkie Tio, Freddy H. Istanto, Basuki Dharmowijono (Tan Tjoan Pie), Robert Han, Hongky Zein, Br Anjar Trihartono, Fachir Thalib, and Gerardus Adhyanggono. We will long remember Aryamaitri, a Buddhist monk whose father had grown up in Parakan and transformed the Siek residence there into Prasada Mandala Dharma, a retreat for Buddhist meditation where we also spent a peaceful night after a day's hard work. Later correspondence with Widjajanti Dharmowijono, Siok Tjoe Siek, Naniek Widayati Priyomarsono, and Johannes Widodo helped fill some of the gaps in our knowledge.

Thailand: Among the many surprises uncovered during the research was the nature of family and business connections between towns in southern Thailand and places farther south on the Malay Peninsula. Pranee Sakulpipatana, a professor at Phuket Rajabhat University, spent a day guiding us through Phuket and helping us understand that indeed there were Peranakan Chinese in Thailand just as there were in Malacca, Penang, Singapore, and Medan, all linked by trade routes that crisscrossed the Strait of Malacca. We also appreciate the assistance of Patthama Khothong of the Songkhla National Museum.

While I had located photographs of Chinese houses in early twentieth-century books about Siam, finding those still standing proved quite difficult. Yet, through contacts first with the always helpful Kelvin Ang in Singapore as well as Philip Cornwel-Smith, an author and editor, and Richard Engelhardt, retired from UNESCO, in Bangkok, names began to emerge of Thai families that even to this day maintain the nineteenth-century residences of their forebears along the banks of the Chao Phraya. Three wonderful old Chinese-style residences were located and photographed with the enthusiastic permission of family members: Vuttichai Wanglee and Pim Praphai Bisalputra (Oey); Poosak Posayachinda; and Apinan Poshyanonda. The encouragement of Vichit Chinalai, Vichai Chinalai, Lee Chinalai, Pongkwan Lassus, and others was very helpful in solidifying tentative contacts. Throughout the search for these houses, during our field work in Bangkok, and subsequent follow-up, the assistance of Ploynapas Patcharasopachai, a student of Professor Patcharavalai, was essential and is very much appreciated. Terry Miller, an American ethnomusicologist specializing in Thai music, read my texts concerning Chinese homes in Thailand with an eye to catching mistakes of chronology and spelling. Chester is appreciative of the assistance of Mr and Mrs Peter Weldon who facilitated his return visit to the Wanglee Mansion.

Philippines: The inclusion of Chinese-style houses in the Philippines certainly was not an afterthought although locating fine examples proved easier said than done. A. Chester Ong, photographer extraordinaire, grew up in Manila in a family that was well aware of its Chinese heritage, and sensed that such homes did exist but had generally been ignored. Following recommendations offered by the exuberant Ivan ManDy (Li Fayuan), who describes himself as a "passionate, obsessive and saucy 'streetwalker'" and entrepreneurial founder of Old Manila Walks, we were introduced to homes in Vigan, Cebu, and Manila. Carla Pacis and Eduardo Quirino were our hosts as we uncovered the history of the Syquia family in Vigan in northern Luzon, while Val San Diego shared his enthusiasm for documenting the early presence of Chinese traders in Cebu. We appreciate not only their insights but also their willingness, together with Fernando N. Zialcita and Gavin Sanson Bagares, in reviewing the manuscripts describing the two eclectic Chinese-style residences featured in our book. The assistance of Celestino Chan, Ong Pinpin, and Charlie Ngo was critical in choosing one of the oldest houses in the Binondo neighborhood in Manila for photography.

While we began and ended our field work for this book among the villages in Fujian and Guangdong that sent so many émigrés outward to the Nanyang, we decided to complete the book with illustrative essays of homes built between 1910 and 1934 by Returned Overseas Chinese who had become wealthy in Indonesia, the Philippines, and Thailand. In this regard, we wish to thank Louis Ong Han Eng and Chen Ruyi who offered helpful advice about such homes in the Quanzhou region. We are especially grateful for the assistance of Josephine Dee Chung who made the necessary connections to photograph her grandfather Dee C. Chuan's villa on Gulangyu. Following the suggestions of Lee Ho Yin and Lynn DeStefano of the Architectural Conservation Programme, Department of Architecture, at Hong Kong University, and with the cooperation of Selia Jinhua Tan, we spent much of a week among the remarkable *diaolou* (tower residences) in Kaiping, Guangdong province. Although little of that effort appears in this book, more will be forthcoming in another publication. The assistance of Li Xiaoyan in reaching some of the remote Hakka areas of eastern Guangdong was invaluable.

It has been our good fortune that Noor Azlina Yunus was engaged to copyedit our third book for Periplus/Tuttle. Not only does she now have an intuitive sense of how this author and this photographer approach the subject matter, she is an exceptionally skilled editor who has improved our argument by clarifying sometimes cumbersome writing. Much appreciation also is owed to the designer who was given the task of creating a fresh template that would successfully weave images and words into an effective visual narrative that would carry through the introduction and the thirty-seven featured chapters that follow. As the myriad pieces came together, we are fortunate indeed that Eric Oey, the inspiration for the project at the start, committed his time and talents to polishing the book to its refined conclusion. From her desk in Singapore, June Chong skillfully managed this complex enterprise, keeping track of travels,

manuscript revisions, and thousands of images that in lesser capable hands would have led to disarray. We are grateful to Luca Invernizzi Tettoni for granting us permission to use his Vietnam photographs. Finally, we are indebted to the renowned scholar Wang Gungwu for his generous Foreword.

The list below acknowledges the sources of all illustrations not taken by A. Chester Ong. a=above; b=below/bottom; c=center; l=left; r=right; t= top

10–11 Used with the permission of Dato' Kee Phaik Cheen.

12 Anthony Reid, *Southeast Asia in the Age of Commerce*, New Haven: Yale University Press, 1993, Vol. 1, p. 40.

13b Thomas Wallace Knox, *Adventures of Two Youths in a Journey to Siam and Java*, New York: Harper & Brothers, 1881, p. 74.

13r Used with permission of the Kobe City Museum

14 Map drawn by Fajar Wisnu Hardono, PT Java Books Indonesia.

16a Gao Zhenming 高鉁明, Wang Naixiang 王乃香, and Chen Yu 陈 瑜, *Fujian minju* 福建民居 [Vernacular Dwellings of Fujian], Beijing: Zhongguo Jianzhu Gongye Chubanshe 中國建筑工业出版社, 1987, p. 31.

16b Lu Yuanding 陆元鼎 and Yanjun Wei 魏彦钧, *Guangdong min minju* 廣東民居 [Vernacular Architecture of Guangdong], Beijing: Zhongguo Jianzhu Gongye Chubanshe 中国建筑工业出版社, 1990, p. 51.

17 Unknown.

23a Used with the permission of Ho-Yin Lee.

23b Used with the permission of the National Archives of Singapore.

24br Used with the permission of Ronni Pinsler and the National Archives of Singapore.

25t Used with the permission of Malcolm Wade.

25b Used with the permission of KITLV/Royal Netherlands Institute of Southeast Asian and Caribbean Studies.

26a, 26b, 29l, 29r, 31 Used with the permission of KITLV/Royal Netherlands Institute of Southeast Asian and Caribbean Studies.

33 Arnold Wright, *Twentieth Century Impressions of Siam: Its History, People, Commerce, Industries, and Resources,*

London: Lloyd's Greater Britain Publishing Co., 1908, p. 150c.

34b Used with the permission of Luca Invernizzi Tettoni.

36a Teresita Ang See (ed.), *Tsinoy: The Story of the Chinese in Philippine Life*, Manila: Kaisa Para sa Kaunlaran, 2005, p. 47. Used with the permission of The Lilly Library, Indiana University, Bloomington, Indiana.

36c Resil B. Mojares, *Casa Gorordo in Cebu: Urban Residence in a Philippine Province, 1860–1920*, Cebu: Ramon Aboitiz Foundation, 1983, p. 55.

38–39b Used with the permission of Heng Chye Kiang.

70 Used with the permission of the National Archives of Singapore.

71 After *The House of Tan Yeok Nee: The Conservation of a National Monument*, Singapore: Winpeak Investment & Wingem Investment, 2003, pp. 74–5.

80t Used with the permission of Johnson Tan.

80b Used with the permission of the National Archives of Singapore.

90b Courtesy of Baba House Museum.

102t Arnold Wright and H. A. Cartwright, *Twentieth Century Impressions of British Malaya: Its History, People, Commerce, Industries, and Resources*, London: Lloyd's Greater Britain Publishing Co., 1908, p. 576.

120t, 121t Used with the permission of Dato' Kee Phaik Cheen.

128t Wright and Cartwright, *Twentieth Century Impressions of British Malaya*, p. 780.

147b Used with the permission of Fon Prawira Tjong.

151b Used with the permission of KITLV/Royal Netherlands Institute of Southeast Asian and Caribbean Studies.

156t Used with the permission of Dato' Loh Siew Cheang.

188t Used with the permission of Basuki Dharmowijono/Tan Tjoan Pie.

228t Wright, *Twentieth Century Impressions of Siam*, p. 169.

232–9 Photographs used with the permission of Luca Invernizzi Tettoni.

242b Courtesy of Carla Pacis.

271b Courtesy of Mei Qing.

INDEX

INDEX